Golden States

The publisher and the University of California Press
Foundation gratefully acknowledge the generous support
of the Lisa See Endowment Fund in Southern California
History and Culture.

Golden States

How California Religion Went from
Cautionary Tale to Global Brand

Eileen Luhr

UNIVERSITY OF CALIFORNIA PRESS

University of California Press
Oakland, California

© 2024 by Eileen Luhr

Library of Congress Cataloging-in-Publication Data

Names: Luhr, Eileen, author.
Title: Golden states : how California religion went from cautionary
    tale to global brand / Eileen Luhr.
Description: Oakland, California : University of California Press,
    [2024] | Includes bibliographical references and index.
Identifiers: LCCN 2024000458 (print) | LCCN 2024000459 (ebook) |
    ISBN 9780520399723 (cloth) | ISBN 9780520399730 (paperback) |
    ISBN 9780520399747 (ebook)
Subjects: LCSH: Spirituality—California, Southern—History. |
    Alternative lifestyles—California, Southern—History. .
Classification: LCC BL624 .L835 2024 (print) | LCC BL624 (ebook) |
    DDC 204.09794—dc23/eng/20240226
LC record available at https://lccn.loc.gov/2024000458
LC ebook record available at https://lccn.loc.gov/2024000459

Manufactured in the United States of America

33 32 31 30 29 28 27 26 25 24
10 9 8 7 6 5 4 3 2 1

Contents

Figures

Acknowledgments

This book represents a departure from my earlier work on Christian conservatism. I had a lot of help as I made the transition. In the early stages of this project, I visited the Bancroft Library, University of California, Berkeley, where I had access to the Theos Bernard Papers. I also spent a few days at the Graduate Theological Union in Berkeley. I completed much of this project during the pandemic, and I am therefore fortunate that so many archives found a way to make resources available online. I made use of the California Digital Newspaper Collection at the University of California, Riverside. I also had access to the Special Collections at Loma Linda University, the Los Angeles Public Library, the UC San Diego Special Collections and Archives, CSULB Special Collections, and the photo archives at USC and UCLA. Several of these archives granted me permission to use photographs or scans.

Chapter 2 includes a revised version of an article that originally appeared in *Pacific Historical Review* in 2021. Chapter 5 includes an expanded version of a chapter that appeared in *American Quarterly* in 2015. Both chapters benefited from the work of the editors and reviewers who were kind enough to share their expertise. At UC Press, Niels Hooper helped me refine the manuscript so it might have a clearer intervention. Nora Becker helped clarify the production process. At the copyediting stage, Gary Hamel fixed errors in the manuscript and clarified the text. I received an enormous boost from the reviewers for UC Press. David Farber provided specific suggestions, and his enthusiasm buoyed my writing during revisions. A second reviewer offered excellent comments for improving the manuscript by broadening its intervention into Religious Studies. The manuscript is better for having been held to this high standard. Elyse Blankley, Sarah Schrank, and Steven Dean read and provided feedback on chapters. Bob Johnson and Jon Wiener read and commented on every chapter in one form or another. Regan Cameron helped me clear copyright for photographs and to access high-quality scans for publication. My colleague Marie Kelleher served as my informal weekend writing partner. She cheered me up with the history of elf charms, took the author photo, and suggested the book's final title. David Shafer has valued and supported faculty research throughout his time as department chair. Other colleagues in the History Department have helped more informally over the years.

Mike Davis inspired this project in part. When I was still deciding on my next project, Mike took me on a religious and spiritual tour of El Cajon. I know he enjoyed taking visitors on this excursion. Among other things, we toured San Diego Christian College—established by Tim and Beverly LaHaye—and had the distinct impression that the women at the bookstore thought we were on a college visit for me. Mike chatted them up, repeatedly referring to "Tom LaHaye" as he asked questions. Although I never found a way to write about Unarius, another place we visited, the afternoon left me thinking about the ways that religion and spirituality evolved in California and how certain beliefs have become part of a community's civic identity. As the project evolved, Nicole Freitag Gilbertson and Lily Geismer suggested specific examples to explore.

I benefited from comments provided by audiences at the California America Studies Association, the American Studies Association, the Religion in California Symposium held at UC Berkeley, and a joint session of the LA Metro Studies and Autry Museum Western History Group. I presented early work to the CSULB History Department's faculty research seminar. I was fortunate that, as I began this project, Diane Winston and Richard Flory invited me to join the Religion, Politics, and Culture in Southern California working group at the University of Southern California Center for Religion and Civic Life. As a participant in this group, I had the opportunity to learn more broadly about the history of religion in Southern California from scholars at institutions from across the region.

Several friends and family have helped me complete this project by listening to me talk about it, and I'm grateful for their patience and encouragement: Caitlin Murdock, David Sheridan, Adam Wemmer, Jose

Pereyra, Fiona Ngo, Tim and Kathleen Keirn, Jessica and Mihir Pandya, Pamela Roberts, Michael and Katie Militello, Sabrina Fève and Stefan Savage, Clay Marquardt and Betsy Snyder, Ann and Bob Brady, Jeffrey Moll and Margaret Brady, and Brendan Brady and Heather Nelson. My mother, Leah Luhr Snyder, passed away before I had even reached the halfway point of this project, but I'm grateful to her and my stepfather, George Snyder Sr., for encouraging me to pursue my interest in history. I'm also indebted to my siblings—John Paul Luhr, Ann Luhr, Catherine Luhr, Julie Luhr, and Mary Beth Johnson.

I completed most of this project during the worst part of the pandemic. As the world descended into chaos in early 2020, I was privileged to have a sabbatical as well as my health and safety, allowing me to devote time to research and writing.

Introduction

In popular media, Southern California has always had something of a reputation for being a carnival of kooks. In 1938, for example, *Life* magazine surveyed Southern California's collection of "odd and eccentric folk" and concluded that they were responsible for corrupting the region with a "community giddiness" most clearly reflected in its religious fanaticism. Despite the efforts of sober and "hard-headed citizens," the region had become a "great cloud-cuckooland." This feature story relayed a familiar—and Anglo-centric—narrative about the region's history. Seeking a population boost in the late nineteenth century, the Los Angeles Chamber of Commerce aggressively advertised the region's fertile land and agreeable weather to aging and infirm Anglo Midwesterners. Once these migrants assimilated, critics worried they had too fully acclimated to a state of comfortable leisure, which suspended their rationality and cast them into a dangerous vortex of otherworldly inanity. With a climate "ill-suited to settlers from more rigorous lands," the transplants fell victim to mischief perpetrated by "cultists . . . faddists, and politicians," many of whom seemed to hail from foreign lands. According to the article, "undisciplined gullibility" plagued the region. The rare resident who did not follow "day-to-day messiahs" had often established a cult of their own. To convince readers of the "general nonsense" taking place in the region, the magazine packed the feature with snapshots of evangelists, prophets, three hermits (one living in a wooden shack, one in a tree, and one in Laurel Canyon), nudists, graphologists, palmists, seers, fortune-tellers, phrenologists, Rosicrucians, food faddists, a dog funeral, and oranges for sale outside a Chinese pagoda; if readers were unconvinced by this graphic spread, the text assured them that "innumerable" more "addlepates" populated the region.[1]

Life's feature reflected a tendency to identify Southern California as a site where oddballs pursued religious frivolity rather than the more respected orthodox religions.[2] As the story goes, migrants—set adrift from reality by an auspicious climate, the search to cure poor health, and a loosened set of social structures—were susceptible to become immoderate disciples of predatory false prophets lured to the region by the promise of easy spiritual marks. It was as if Southern Californians had left behind the piety and responsibility of the Midwest and East Coast to reconstruct one of the temptations along the traveler's path in John Bunyan's The Pilgrim's Progress (1678)—the Enchanted Ground or the fallen city of Vanity—where profligate people reveled in a perpetual fair of worldly merchandise and titles, base delights, sinners of every stripe, and entertainment that included "juggling cheats, games, plays, fools, apes, knaves, and rogues."[3] Life's modern retelling of this cautionary tale of excess allowed skeptics to dismiss what was, I argue in the chapters to follow, a spiritual yearning many Americans had that was not satisfied through more traditional Protestant churches, Catholic cathedrals, Jewish synagogues, and so on—a longing that generated California's many unorthodox devotional spaces. Like the larger historical record, this Life feature did not take seriously an effort to find a different way of living in America, but simply set it all down to vain superficiality, dilettantism, and naivete if not outright profanity. With a prescriptive sense of religious respectability that was prevalent in the larger national imaginary, the article missed the ways that California became an important site for reconceptualizing communities of belief within the shifting political and cultural contexts of a more globalized American life.

These jeremiads about Southern California religious history persist in the present and, prior to the widespread adoption of, for example, yoga or the national extension of health food stores, were already deeply engrained in the national imaginary.[4] They dismissed the hybrid religious experimentation that was part and parcel of the making of the Southwest and its part in mediating the changing economic and cultural dynamics of the United States. These alternative spiritualities made a long-lasting imprint on Southern California's social and cultural imagination. Over the course of the twentieth century, as the nation moved away from the producerism historically most associated with mainline Protestantism, Southern California became a site for new understandings of self-fulfillment and belief based in an emerging consumer ethic. This book documents and problematizes these transformations, although not in the trivializing manner found in the pages of *Life*. Instead, through a rereading of the region's cultural landscape, the chapters that follow provide an alternative history of California religion and spirituality. They locate the ways that seekers found seemingly more varied paths to achieving golden states of fulfillment than the route followed by the pilgrim Christian. Yet these journeys often remained atomized. *Golden States* argues that, over time, commitment to the emotional and therapeutic needs and desires of individual believers often came at the expense of broader efforts and obligations to achieve collective well-being. In tracing the origins of beliefs and practices from the late nineteenth century into their forms in the more recent past, the case studies that follow therefore highlight the ongoing tensions between pursuing a social good and privileging individual choice. At the same time, the chapters explore the extent to which racial exclusion and economic inequality limited the pursuit of spiritual innovation and health consciousness to a subgroup of affluent white seekers.

Two historical developments, the emergence of consumerism and globalization—both of which promised elements of "progress" or advancement to a higher stage of growth or improvement —help explain the changes to religious encounters and experiences. The cultural transformations that began in the late nineteenth century intensified over the course of the twentieth century as the United States became, in Lizabeth Cohen's framing, "a consumers' republic" in which mass culture mediated how citizens participated in democracy.[5] Affluence, especially among urban white Americans, that appeared in social life in this period also influenced spirituality: self-actualization worked through, not in opposition to, consumer lifestyles. New marketplaces also enabled citizens to participate—in racialized ways—in the abundance created as the United States became an international hegemon with its fingers dipped in all continents. Department stores enhanced aspirational desire by presenting a "world of goods" through immersive retail experiences like shop windows, store displays, and fashion shows.[6] Globalization also influenced the American religious vernacular by offering new expressions of self-understandings introduced to American culture, including non-Western traditions. Processes of exchange and encounter softened the edges of capitalism, but over time they also intermingled with the same economic realities that advanced inequality, both by working against group solidarities and by extending racial and class disparities.

Here it might be useful to draw a contrast between the Calvinist ethic as personified by John Bunyan's Christian in *The Pilgrim's Progress* and the protagonists documented in these pages. Christian walked a "straight and narrow" devotional path, foreswearing worldly temptation, in the hopes of being admitted to the Celestial City, which "shone like the sun" and where streets "were paved with gold," and men walked with "crowns on their heads, palms in their hands, and golden harps to sing praises withal."[7] The central figures in the case studies that follow—whether they were transplanted religious prophets of the early twentieth century or present-day residents of cities mobilizing to protect a civic identity—sought the "good life" celebrated in advertisements for the region, yet the emergence of cosmopolitan tastes allowed them to broaden their journey to deliverance in this world. The promises of restorative leisure, health consciousness, and a deepened personal spirituality were part of the same appeal, a way of improving one's best self by at once attending to interior emotional needs and navigating exterior social relations in a changing economic landscape.[8] Whether they were utopian communitarians, sun-seeking gurus, or Protestant health reformers, Southern California's spiritual seekers drew on America's deepening global encounters and consumer cultures to pair religious (and often personal) reinvention with cultural and spiritual revitalization.

This book turns to three Southern California alternative religious leaders and two communities with deep spiritual social imaginaries to chart the range and historic trajectory of American responses to the nation's transformation from a producer code rooted in religious faith to a consumer-based ethos founded upon personal spiritual growth. In doing so, it surfaces the social and cultural impact of alternative spiritualities on Southern California in the long twentieth century. Each of the first three chapters features a twentieth-century religious figure—Katherine Tingley, the foundress of a utopian commune who drew on historical and religious imaginaries to help establish California's reputation for leisure-based spiritual fulfillment; Paramahansa Yogananda, an Indian yogi who arrived in the United States in 1920, established a network of still-active ashrams in Southern California in the interwar years and early Cold War, and later became celebrated by Silicon Valley executives for his blend of Eastern and Western spiritual and material culture; and Emanuel Bronner, a German-Jewish immigrant soap maker whose product labels became popular within the counterculture for espousing

an "All-One" ethos, an adage his grandsons turned into a call to address the contemporary climate crisis—who might have been labeled as
"addlepates" by *Life* during their careers. The final two chapters each
examine a location—Loma Linda, a Seventh-day Adventist stronghold
whose residents were known for health and longevity due to their abstemious foodways; and Encinitas, a hippie-rich surfing enclave enamored
with spiritual signifiers in civic places—that could have been described
as a "cloud-cuckooland." Each chapter demonstrates how beliefs and
practices drew from existing religious idioms and historical imaginaries
that, over time, became embedded in seemingly nonreligious economic
and social contexts—and, moreover, how those cases all turned on their
own public morality tales that helped to define what "progress" might
mean from an alternative spiritual outlook within contemporary life. As
Southern California emerged as a site for consumer experimentations
in self-fulfillment and belief, personal liberation—whether achieved
through a cultivated lifestyle practice or an ethos of self-improvement—
accrued sacred connotations, often at the expense of social solidarities.
This book contextualizes these stories by expanding the meaning of religious "imagination" to capture the cultural space, beyond doctrines and
institutions, in which normative concepts of religion combined with prevailing ideologies and popular practices to reinvent spiritual belief and
experience. In doing so, it finds how religion as a lived phenomenon was
renegotiated in and through tourist brochures, newspaper articles, public
hearings, court cases, art installations, dietary habits, self-help manifes-
tos, corporate reports, exercise regimes, school curricula, and civic zoning laws.

   In its thematic emphasis on understandings of individual "progress"
toward fulfillment, this work acknowledges the moral and pedagogical
framework that John Bunyan's work provided to American culture and
its desire to inculcate values such as prudence and sobriety in citizens
who were religiously trained in an era before consumer-oriented culture
shifted those values. I argue, however, that even as old lessons persisted,
social changes spawned fresh prophets and generated new parables
sanctioning different values that altered the path for progress defined as
personal meaning and spiritual growth. Most proselytizing involved at
least some kind of entrepreneurship, and modern prophets had ample
opportunity to ply their trade. In seeking personal development, religious seekers did not obey perceived boundaries between secular and
sacred, nor did they observe distinctions between scientific and religious
authority. The paths for achieving "salvation" broadened considerably

in the twentieth century. Southern California provides an exemplar—an advance guard of these changes to a more therapeutic religion in keeping with a cosmopolitan consumerist society.[9] More than that, these practices came to enhance Southern California's "brand" of good living.

The newer path to individual spiritual fulfillment continued to include prescriptive norms. As authors like Barbara Ehrenreich have argued, even as the producerist ethic waned, the moral imperative of personal improvement remained—and, in fact, intensified—alongside a late capitalist economic logic of "perpetual growth."[10] Individuals cultivated a repertoire of techniques for managing and motivating the self as well as interpersonal competencies based in "emotional intelligence" thought to have economic benefits.[11] Rather than spotlighting the beliefs embraced within mainstream religious institutions and practices, the case studies that follow examine how beliefs and practices were represented and advanced within cultural discourses about wellness, fitness, business innovation, multiculturalism, and environmentalism. This work also seeks to surface how exclusionary understandings of race, class, and gender informed understandings of "progress" and "modernity" that were embedded in beliefs and practices throughout the twentieth century. In many instances, affluent Anglos drew on the cultures of racialized (and often non-Western) others while simultaneously excluding these groups from sites of therapeutic leisure or spiritual practice. As religious studies scholar Amanda Lucia has noted, even as white Californians comprised less than 40 percent of the state's population in the recent past, "spiritual seeking" remained a predominantly white enterprise.[12]

This work provides a cultural history of the impact of economic and social changes on the circulation of religious and spiritual ideas at a moment when key aspects of the prevailing social order had weakened. The case studies contextualize shifting beliefs within two broader historical processes of the twentieth century: first, they locate changing understandings of American religious identity within broader socioeconomic transformations, including globalization, the rise of consumerism, deindustrialization, and the rise of the service and technology economies; and, second, they position these changes within transnational and transcultural networks and encounters intensified by globalization.

First, changes in American religious beliefs coincided with socioeconomic transformations that produced new understandings of the liberal subject that had emerged in the nineteenth century during the market revolution and spread with the rise of a consumer society. Catherine Albanese, a scholar of American religion, defines religion as "a system of symbols (creed, code, cultus) by means of which people (a community) orient themselves in the world with reference to both ordinary and extra-ordinary powers, meanings, and values." This understanding of religion centers on the maintenance of social and sacred boundaries such as those between self and society as well as self and a natural or supernatural other.[13] This work interrogates the changes in the religious symbols of Americans as well as broader transformations in how Americans under-stood their relation to society and to broader ideas about, for example, salvation or nature. Scholars see overlapping sites of authority compet-ing for primacy in the twentieth century—including organized religion but also science, nature, and the state—that informed what scholars refer to as the "marketplace of religion" in the United States.[14] The language of the marketplace had real limitations, as—even in religious and spiritual pursuits—it privileged individual choice in the construction of identities while obscuring the power dynamic involved in these transformations.

During this period, understandings of authority shifted from "with-out" to "within" and from external sources of doctrine or creed to personal instinct or intuition. The discursive division between formal religion and spirituality captures the shifting boundaries of authority. Whereas the term *religion* increasingly meant "institutional religious be-lief and practice," the term *spiritual*—which, in American religious life, was often linked with non-Western practices as cosmopolitan seekers ex-plored practices outside British Protestant traditions—came to connote a connection to moral values and mystical religious experiences as well as an understanding of one's place in the world.[15] The recent popularity of the term *spiritual* reflected the increasing desire for a flexible under-standing of belief based on individual preference because of its focus on choices made by the seeker.[16] While empowering the practitioner, the language of "spirituality" diffused into other spheres of American life, including emerging consumer capitalist lifestyles and practices such as surfing and yoga.[17] Along these lines, religious studies scholar Andrea Jain characterizes the emergence of a "neoliberal spirituality" based in an individualistic ethos that "revolves around adherents' ability to dis-cern and certify the merit that leads to the envied lifestyle of balance, wellness, success, freedom, and self-care."[18] The term's association with individual choices aligned it more directly to the proliferating discourses of "self-improvement" in late capitalism: "the freedom to govern oneself, to make individual and privatized choices, and to release oneself from a dependency on the state."[19] *Golden States* therefore questions the extent to which the emerging vocabulary of openness and self-transformation was a somewhat selfish and insulated discourse of individualism that resisted or advanced broader social and racial inequalities.

Second, the global exchanges of the twentieth century, including the rise of American economic and cultural hegemony, meant that the domestic religious imagination expanded like its global markets to become transnational and transcultural.[20] *Golden States* investigates the way that the American religious imagination nurtured global attachments at a moment when the United States was deepening the formal and informal structures of its empire. It is impossible to confine ideas and practices within their "original" or "authentic" cultural location, as syncretic or hybrid practices predate modernity and globalization has occurred in multiple directions.[21] Instead, this work focuses on Southern California to examine how beliefs shifted over time and, further, how such spiritual beliefs and practices that in one era articulated universal concepts of belonging in the longer term became enmeshed in dominant structures that perpetuated unequal domestic and international power relationships. White Americans, in particular, drew upon a range of cultural and consumer practices—including Asian religions but also longstanding vernacular European metaphysical traditions—to identify and critique their modern condition. They possessed the cultural authority to adapt, normalize, and co-opt non-Western religious practices and concepts from traditions like Buddhism and Hinduism and popular "metaphysical" traditions focusing on mind, spirit, and energy that existed outside organized denominations. As a result, a new "global multiculturalism" entered into the American religious imagination—particularly as the United States expanded its imperial power to all parts of the globe in the wake of World War II—to absorb and disarm meaningful difference as advocates drew on a range of traditions made available by consumer society and often reinforced rather than problematized materialism or individualism.[22] These imperial imaginaries advanced notions of world "progress" as modeled by American-style modernization, but this book illuminates the ways that inequality worked through cultural privilege available through Western, national, racial, and class hierarchies.

RELIGION AND IDENTITY

This work seeks to understand the shifting role of religion and spirituality in American cultural identity over the course of the twentieth century. In examining the role of consumerism in religion, American historians have tended to examine the synergistic relationship between consumer capitalism and organized belief systems.[23] Scholars positioned more broadly in religious studies, sociology, anthropology, and American studies have undertaken research that questions the underpinnings of belief itself in late modernity, often choosing to expand notions of belief outside formal creeds and institutional structures. This has led scholars to examine more individualistic spiritual experiences in the context of consumer activities, ritualistic aspects of everyday life, and social patterns.[24] Such studies have moved the location of where religion takes place in the neoliberal era from denominations to the workplaces and marketplaces that have created a "spiritual economy," including problematizing the inequalities that follow market-based logic or models. Religious phenomena—"practices, rituals, beliefs, norms, values, doctrines, objects, institutions"—can, after all, exist in any cultural location.[25]

In the past, research questions tended to characterize these changes as *secularization*, a term that assumed a movement during modernity away from formal religiosity or religious authority toward rational and scientific modes of thought. More recent work, in contrast, has explored "detraditionalization" by connecting, rather than separating, religion from the rest of cultural life and looking for change in thought rather than diminishment in belief. New research reconsidered what might constitute religion in American society, in doing so broadening the terrain of study to include a range of various "religious idioms" available to practitioners as well as an array of locations beyond traditionally "sacred" sites like churches, temples, or shrines. The result has been to see religious belief, like other types of cultural practice, as bricolage, even as scholars like Veronique Altglas have noted that syncretism is not unique to postmodern existence and that these seemingly individualized choices take place within defined social parameters and historical contexts.[26] To be certain, formal religious beliefs, denominations, and congregations remained important to American life, but the turn has allowed scholars to examine cultural meanings that defined individual as well as collective identities within a given social context. Regardless of how and where beliefs exist, their form and practice reveal understandings of both belonging and exclusion.

Rather than setting a definition of what constitutes religion in different settings and time periods, scholars of "lived religion" attempt to understand how religion is "encountered and experienced" in different environments. It allows scholars a mode of inquiry "into what people do that they identify as religious, spiritual or generally as going beyond common-sense understandings of the world."[27] Historians have located a rich tradition of American religiosity that extends beyond the history of revivalism and institutionalized religion organized around denominations to include popular or "vernacular" practices that inform beliefs and lifeways of different groups. In this interpretation, the American religious imagination from the start included new patterns of thought and practice "partially inherited from the past and partially created in the moment."[28] Nineteenth-century liberal progressivism and the religious left—what historian Leigh Eric Schmidt calls the "Spiritual Left"—played an important role in romanticizing and advancing practices like mysticism, solitude, meditation, and individualized spiritual seeking.[29] At the same time, Catherine Albanese argues that polycultural popular religiosity, while often considered to have arrived only in its "New Age" forms in the 1960s, was inherited from classical and medieval European traditions as well as Indigenous, Asian, and African beliefs that solidified into patterns of spiritual seeking by the end of the nineteenth century. Although dating to an earlier moment in history, these "metaphysical" (a term Albanese prefers to "occult" or "esoteric") concepts continued to circulate and become altered over time and, in doing so, reshape the American religious imagination over the course of the twentieth century.[30] Writing about the present, anthropologist Susannah Crockford posits that the term *spirituality* allows for an exploration of the "boundaries of religion and something far more capacious"—including understandings of science—through which scholars can access "the human capacity to imagine other worlds." By creating space for counternarratives to mainstream beliefs to exist, the study of spirituality allows scholars to explore the boundaries "between the occult and science, between stigmatized knowledge and legitimate knowledge, between irrationality and rationality." In studying the recent role of neoliberalism in spirituality, scholars like Crockford take a particular interest in the way an individual's ability to self-locate within these binaries might obscure historical power relations.[31]

Regardless of whether spiritual practices had roots in denominational or vernacular traditions, they became sedimented within broader cultural practices over time. The varied forms of American "lived religion" contributed to citizens' already malleable views of improvement and development, whether as realized by humans or by institutions through advancing technology, civic improvement, or imperialism. The master narrative of United States history has generally assured Americans—at least those in dominant groups—of its national trajectory toward progress.[32] Similarly, the dominant American religious imaginary has viewed "perfectibility"—that is, humans' capacity to progress toward moral, physical, or mental faultlessness—as an achievable goal. Even if they worried about evil, the Calvinists of Massachusetts Bay, like their English counterpart John Bunyan, viewed salvation as an individual journey for members of the "invisible church" who demonstrated their worth through an ascetic' tradition of work and thrift. They formed communities with "visible saints," but their religious path involved relentlessly examining their consciences for evidence of their worthiness for redemption, the status of which they could never fully ascertain.[33] This tendency toward self-interrogation formed a critical piece of the early modern economic ethos—and its overall understandings of subjectivity—most famously hypothesized within Max Weber's concept of the Protestant ethic.[34] By the first half of the nineteenth century, beliefs about predestination softened as more liberal strains of Protestantism, including Universalism and Transcendentalism, emphasized the significant role of free will in receiving grace. Arminian notions of redemption and perfectibility—wherein humans had the free will to accept God's grace—also animated many of the evangelical Protestant reform movements.[35] Befitting a world of strangers, the dominant middle-class ethos that emerged during the Second Great Awakening counseled hard work, thrift, civic responsibility, and self-denial.[36] The reform movements of the antebellum era—including temperance, asylum and prison reform, women's rights, antislavery, and body reforms—which often blended religious, political, and scientific language, provided an interim step toward the expert, state-led movements that began at the turn of the twentieth century.[37]

The growth of the market economy and the anonymous interdependence that undergirded metropolitan life in the late nineteenth century affected notions of selfhood and infiltrated the deep structures of religion. Spiritual progress and perfectibility took on new meanings. The term *corpus*, which once held religious or communal connotations, became attached, for instance, to the more self-invested and temporal modern corporation.[38] The advent of modern Western science, in addition to partitioning "rationality" from belief in some Christian faiths, created a sense that progress might best be achieved by applying systematic observation, measurement, and experimentation to the natural world. From the start, Western notions of growth and development—like those of religious inclusion and exclusion—were also defined by hierarchical and racialized national and civilizational discourses. Industrial technologies and the advent of the factory system likewise symbolized improvement and efficiency of a mechanized world, which in turn altered notions of self.[39] Self-interrogation took on medicalized and clinical tones. Individuals sought answers—or rationalized versions of perfectibility—in religious and scientific understandings of well-being, which often overlapped.

Historians have tried to identify the impact of late nineteenth-century urbanization and industrialization on Americans who lived in urban centers with fewer familial or community ties. A sense of "weightlessness" and unreality characterized the experience of modern life. A new set of disorders—"immobilizing, self-punishing depressions" known as "neurasthenia"—became associated with the emerging white-collar workforce.[40] The self-scrutiny of earlier, salvation-seeking Protestants had provoked guilt; for their nineteenth-century descendants, "for whom salvation became unreal," self-scrutiny created a sense of anxiety. As historian T. J. Jackson Lears explains, white middle- and upper-class Americans addressed uncertainties through therapies that, while often dismissed as fads, "signified a shift toward new secular modes of capitalist cultural hegemony" that emerged in the late nineteenth century.[41] These practices challenged the centrality of the producer ethic to American identity. As mainline Christian traditions struggled to adapt to changing cultural realities, popular metaphysical systems arose to address the spiritual needs of seekers. These practices—developed within mid- and late nineteenth-century liberal Protestantism and amplified in practices of spiritualism, Theosophy, and New Thought—focused on the individual's "experience of 'mind'" through forms that valued reason but also broader training of the human imagination to locate intuition, clairvoyance, revelation, and guidance from higher powers. Ideas of improvement and love remained but within a logic of amelioration and free will; without the fear of damnation, seekers could search for salvation now defined as "solace, comfort, therapy, and healing" in mind and body and often achieved through solitary and mystical means of self-transformation.[42]

The modern marketplace became an important site for individuals seeking to repair their sense of self. Religious truth gravitated toward "subjective religious experience," as leaders shifted their end goal from the "salvation" promised in the next world by Protestant Christianity to "self-realization" in the present day that would revitalize the self through robust activity and emotional force.[43] This was particularly true for white middle- and upper-class Americans who had the time, money, and privilege to remake their identities, although it was possible for racialized "others"—like Paramahansa Yogananda (chapter 2) to draw upon racial assumptions to partake in reinvention. Americans sought experiential consumption that promised recuperation through, for example, strict dietary practices at the Battle Creek Sanitarium, educational programs at the Chautauqua Institution, or the skilled arts and crafts practiced at communities like the Roycroft Colony. Religious institutions and beliefs likewise adapted to the challenges presented by a more scientific and consumer-oriented society by offering a more intense experience. Parachurch organizations like the YMCA and Salvation Army tried to minister a Christian ethos among urban transplants using the new commercial styles of the modern city. Informed by Western scientific discourse, "mind cure" religions like New Thought, Christian Science, and Theosophy promised adherents happiness rather than sin and evil. In 1902, William James referred to these practices, with their optimistic interpretations of evolutionary notions of "progress," as "the gospel of healthy-mindedness." These traditions attempted to reconcile religion and science by providing noninvasive ways to treat modern ailments at a moment when mainstream physicians assumed mental symptoms had physical causes.[44]

The changing realities of late modernity require a further reassessment of the connections between economic systems, expressions of belief, and subjectivity. In the 1970s, the American economy experienced a painful transformation away from the "Fordist" industrial economy of high wages and collective bargaining that had defined the post–World War II era. In its place, historians see the emergence of "neoliberalism," which they associate with the ascendance of market policies favoring free movement of capital, goods, and people, the diminishment of collective action and public institutions that defined liberalism for much of the postwar era, a turn against government regulation in favor of individual choice that was often linked to notions of "freedom," and an intensification of economic inequalities.[45] Ronald Reagan's speeches—where choice became associated with anti-statist "freedom"—exemplified the celebration of markets in political discourse, but historians like Lily Geismer have observed how Democratic technocrats embraced market-based solutions to social problems using public-private partnerships.[46]

Although usually connected to political economy, neoliberalism—with its visions of atomized individuals motivated only by their discrete interests, especially as understood within the "marketplace"—also became a hegemonic discourse within American culture in the late twentieth century. As a cultural concept, classical liberalism had attached its promise of progress—confined to certain privileged populations—to individual potential achieved through rationality and education. Neoliberalism, on the other hand, posited that individual development, and therefore progress, was best achieved through market saturation in all aspects of life.[47] As historian Daniel Rodgers explains, new ideas about human nature that emphasized "choice, agency, performance, and desire" took hold. Historian Gary Gerstle has suggested that the neoliberal era, which stretched from approximately 1970 to 2020, encompassed a combination of free market reforms, the extension of market principles to nonmarket categories of social life, and a maximized understanding of personal freedom.[48] This work takes a particular interest in the impact of the latter two changes on American culture. By tracing the transformation of health and religious reform movements over time, the book contributes to the conversation about the "neoliberalization of culture."[49] The market mentality came to define all entities of American public and private life, simultaneously reifying inequalities and obscuring the basis of these hierarchies by celebrating meritocracy.[50] For privileged consumers empowered by neoliberalism—white, affluent, cosmopolitan—identities became "fluid and elective" as methods of socialization changed and Americans sought out new processes and metaphors for imagining society and self, causing a "thinned out" understanding of society that chipped away at "unifying" beliefs or institutions.[51]

The emancipatory language of individual freedom—a consistent theme of American culture once more surfaced by the New Left in the 1960s—became pervasive within American culture but was still not universally accessible. This ethos helps explain the intensification of individual choice at the expense of collective solidarities. Democratic understandings of civic responsibility and public good contracted; "belonging" became a function of the market. Some populations benefited from and celebrated the movement of ideas and people by embracing new hybrid cultural forms and opportunities for cultural cosmopolitanism. On the other hand, as Gerstle argues, the hard edges of neoliberalism also limited autonomy for marginalized groups. The ideology defined a new kind of "unfreedom" in the rise of the carceral state for minority populations as well as a "neo-Victorianism" aimed at limiting the loosening of social mores, especially for women, by requiring "self-reliance, strong families, and disciplined attitudes toward work, sexuality, and consumption."[52]

The neoliberal order coalesced as the service and knowledge economies pushed American employees away from work at large corporations as well as membership in labor unions, requiring workers to string together multiple jobs. The gig economy that arose after the Great Recession of 2008 forced freelancers to balance a series of "side hustles" and placed an even greater imperative on the continual cycle of skill enhancement and self-care. By 2016, between 20 and 30 percent of workers in the United States and the European Union had participated in freelance work, and at the same time some estimates put part-time workers as high as 40 percent.[53] The knowledge-based economy centered ideas and relationships as the basis of business value. As customer care and enthusiasm became the product itself in the knowledge and service economies, employee engagement became a greater concern of corporate leadership and "emotional capitalism"—the use of (often feminized) emotions rather than "rationalized" management strategies—came to define workplace relations.[54] In place of formal institutional sources of absolute authority (scientific, political, or religious), a new kind of expert arose to measure the fulfillment achieved by "self-anchored striving."[55] The notion of a "growth mindset"—a concept developed by Stanford psychologist Carol Dweck in *Mindset: The New Psychology of Success* that abilities can be developed through hard work—encouraged Americans to hone individual aptitudes.[56] Success derived from passion and persistence ("grit," in the framing of psychologist Angela Duckworth) rather than set talents.[57] Efforts to motivate workers, students, or citizens who were present but disengaged or depressed coalesced around concepts of "well-being."[58]

The market logic of neoliberalism influenced spiritual pursuits by requiring the individual "firm" to focus on self-improvement. Although the "pseudo religion of health"—nominally voluntary but tinged with moral obligation—first emerged during the late nineteenth century, it has become one of the defining attributes of the American economy and its neoliberal cultural ethos.[59] Educational, civic, business, medical, and religious cultures reorganized themselves to instill these attributes, at times through individualized hacks—like the personal "Blue Zones" in chapter 4 or the "Blue Mind" state of chapter 5—rather than cultivated or communal practice. The continuous cycle of self-care and self-improvement, including improved emotional competence, spawned a wellness economy in which the division between skill enhancement and therapeutic leisure—time off from work—became increasingly difficult to distinguish. This focus on flexibility, adaptability, and resilience often came at the cost of efforts to build community solidarities or restore civic capacity. In a system posited to be a meritocracy where the best talents and ideas were thought to flourish, setbacks might therefore be attributed to individual shortcomings, not systemic inequalities of racial and gender discrimination or poverty. The case studies in this work trace efforts at self-actualization achieved through cultural domains such as wellness, fitness, business innovation, multiculturalism, and environmentalism; together, these practices might be called consumer lifestyles that work as self-improvement projects.

California provides an excellent site for examining the changes in American belief and self-fulfillment. In the nineteenth century, Americans viewed their continental empire as a part of the nation's predestined "progress" of "Manifest Destiny." As articulated by Frederick Jackson Turner, the "West" represented energy, individualism, and freedom—the environment where the American character realized its providential potential.[60] This imperial mythology created idealized Anglo uses for western spaces, which were at once imagined as Edenic gardens and untapped landscapes for productive cultivation. Processes of national progress hinged on settler colonialist practices that required the removal and erasure of Indigenous and minoritized peoples. As envisioned by Anglo boosters, California's future was a "white" space distinct from cities in the eastern United States. Elites developed a "regional consciousness" based on a racial progression in which Anglo-Saxon identity had triumphed; this regional identity confined communities of color safely to the past.[61] Progressive-era Anglos complemented these efforts at historical erasure with exclusionary policies intended to create racial homogeneity and contain communities of color within specific spaces.[62] African American migrants, like Anglos, moved to Southern California to pursue economic opportunity and partake of its warm climate. In 1910, there were 7,599 African Americans in Los Angeles. As the African American population doubled in the city over the next decade, Anglo residents limited African Americans' ability to participate in community life by placing race-restrictive covenants on property deeds (a practice affirmed by the California Supreme Court in 1919), segregating accommodations at public parks, pools, and beaches, refusing service at restaurants and on jitneys, and limiting employment opportunities.[63] During the Mexican Revolution (1910–1917), over a million Mexicans fled north to the United States, including Los Angeles, where they were the largest immigrant group in the city; they lived throughout the city (often in subpar housing) but rarely among Anglos who sought to bar people of color from integrating their communities.[64] While smaller in number, the Chinese and Japanese communities were also targeted by policies that left them with little access to city services or housing stock; in 1913, the state's Alien Land Law outright barred Asians from owning land.

The California health economy allowed Anglo seekers to mix spiritual quests with recuperative health practices that became imbued with sacred meaning. Southern California became a space for realizing both national and individual notions of "progress"—a place onto which boosters projected understandings of self-discovery and reinvention. As historian Lawrence Culver has shown, twentieth-century Southern California became a "frontier of leisure" where elective and recuperative consumptive practices became a way of life, quite separate from the laboring spaces of the rest of the country. Anglo migrants drew upon the property and labor of people of color as well as a range of cultural traditions to inform and enhance their recreational experiences.[65] As early as the 1850s, a range of voices—including civic boosters, newspaper editors, railroad tycoons, religious seekers, and wealthy disabled people—lauded California's potential for "wellness" practices, which included therapeutic leisure as well as physical and mental recuperation. Visitors learned to "reconnect" to nature as part of their journey, and this came to have spiritual connotations.[66] Soon a flourishing health resort economy sprung up to promote the state's weather, its proximity to ocean breezes and snow-capped mountains, and its garden-like abundance as keys to healthful living. These early efforts attracted other lifestyle movements that attached cultural and moral value to consumer and leisure activities.[67] Seekers—mostly white, often looking to repair a sense of cultural dislocation—searching for a sense of belonging turned to a range of therapeutic, bohemian, alternative, and exotic belief systems available via California's cultural marketplace.[68] The practices and spaces of leisure became associated with whiteness, often through exclusionary and expropriative practices. Communities of color found separate spaces for leisure, like Sleepy Lagoon (frequented by Mexican Americans), the African American–owned Bruce's Beach, and Val Verde (known as "Black Palm Springs").[69] When Black spaces impinged upon Anglo leisure, however, they met their demise, as when, in 1924, city managers in Manhattan Beach used eminent domain to seize an African American–owned beachfront hotel—one of the few accessible spaces where African Americans could comfortably enjoy the seaside—or when, in 1965 and 1966, the affluent tourist destination of Palm Springs razed Section 14, a downtown residential area owned by the Agua Caliente Band of Cahuilla Indians and populated by African American families, with the intention of redeveloping the area in what a California attorney general report subsequently called "a city-engineered holocaust."[70] These examples demonstrate how Anglos excluded marginalized groups from sites of therapeutic leisure and spiritual practice.

GLOBAL EXCHANGE AND EMPIRE

Over the course of the twentieth century, global exchanges informed the development of an American transnational religious and spiritual imagination. The global circulation of goods and ideas affected the world, but globalization was not "Americanization." Instead, the history of religion in the United States suggests that the emergence of multiculturalism among liberals included the borrowing of religious wisdom from a multitude of traditions.[71] In the late nineteenth century, expanded nation states constructed boundaries capable of disrupting connections. Historians have sought to "open up" these political constructions to the interventions of new world historians by undertaking analyses that place the state in imperial or transnational approaches, allowing for an improved understanding of encounter and exchange. They have also noted the continued relevance of formal empire—defined as "a political unit that encompasses an extensive sweep of territory containing various peoples or politics" with varying levels of autonomy and rights and disparities in power. Historians of empire and global capitalism have found instances of "interimperial" or "transimperial" collaborations evident through the interchange of "individuals, goods, capital," and ideas.[72]

Historians use transnational and transimperial frameworks to trace the social and cultural histories of global networks. Social historians note the formal and informal networks that promoted cross-cultural cooperation through organizations created along affinities of class, religion, gender, and race. While creating new boundaries of inclusion by formulating universalistic goals or beliefs, these groups—ranging from the International Olympic Committee to the League of Nations to transnational religious groups like the Salvation Army—also at times reified the unequal power-based particularistic imperial or national relations. Political and economic organizations often excluded non-Western entities, but religious and cultural symposia in particular allowed colonized participants to articulate their vision of "civilization" to the international community and, at times, create "global solidarity among anticolonial movements."[73] The World's Parliament of Religion in Chicago in 1893, for example, celebrated the universality of religious truths by featuring the ten "world religions" (excluding Native American religions), but its organizers implicitly saw Protestantism as the belief system against which all other truths might be compared. Nevertheless, Swami Vivekananda, one of the first Indian-born gurus to come to the United States and the founder of the Vedanta Society, used his speech to characterize his religion as one that offered "both tolerance and universal acceptance" and to offer a critique of Western materialism and Christian missions.[74]

Historians have also deployed transimperial and transcultural frameworks to create cultural histories that document the multidirectional flow of goods, ideas, and power. As historian Kristin Hoganson explains, Americans were fascinated with American and European imperial culture, which ranged across household goods, fashion, cooking style, travel, and entertainment. The "consumers' imperium" that emerged as the United States expanded its commercial and political power around the world allowed Americans to create new identities and ways of belonging using an ever-expanding menu of globalized goods.[75] The "American Way" of mass consumption—started even before Henry Luce coined the term the "American Century" in 1941—involved "a mass production and mass marketing system that imagined an ever-widening abundance of goods within a culture that emphasized buying and selling, desire, glamour, and flexible, purchase-driven identities."[76] These economic and cultural resources traversed national boundaries and created new ways of belonging based on shared practices or values even through indirect contact; at the same time, however, the "globalized culture of consumption" by which Americans engaged in the "exchange, appropriation, and reframing" of consumer and cultural products also obfuscated unequal power relationships.[77]

This book fits within narratives of global exchange because the burgeoning sense of "domestic cosmopolitanism" available to Americans included health advice and religious ideas.[78] The same transimperial circuits that delivered goods like tea, Oriental rugs, and fabrics via imperial routes in the late nineteenth century also brought new religious practices to American shores.[79] In the nineteenth century, health and spiritual trends circulated through transnational networks that introduced a range of practices and beliefs from naturopathic care to Theosophy to yoga. Beginning in towns like Davos and Badenweiler, Switzerland, and extending to the Adirondacks and California, health entrepreneurs developed resorts that catered to middle- and upper-class visitors who wanted to learn exercise, diet, and health practices that would correct their lifestyle errors. At about the same time, in New York City in the 1880s, Russian immigrant Helena Petrovna Blavatsky established Theosophy, a religious movement premised on the existence of an eternal principle rather than a personal god, by drawing on ancient esoteric and modern scientific worldviews as well as Eastern religions such as Buddhism and Hinduism. Blavatsky and her associate, Henry Steel Olcott, traveled to England before relocating to India, where they founded the International Headquarters of the Theosophical Society. By the time Olcott died, there were over six hundred Theosophical lodges in over forty countries. Katherine Tingley (chapter 1) became the leader of the original national wing, renamed the Universal Brotherhood. Transimperial networks also brought South Asian gurus to the United States, especially after the devastation of World War I, when colonized peoples were positioned to critique the West's sense of its "civilizing mission." Both Paramahansa Yogananda (chapter 2) and Jiddu Krishnamurti, the leader of Theosophy's Adyar wing (until his subsequent break with Theosophy), arrived on American soil ready to proselytize to seekers in packed auditoriums.

After World War II, the process of American-led mass globalization included the containment of communism. During this period, American appeals to potential allies in the Global South balanced the contradictory claims of the purported universality of its values with notions of its national exceptionalism. Foreign policy documents like NSC-68 represented communism as a "fanatic faith" that had to be countered through global efforts, and Protestant leaders seized upon this religious framework to position themselves as the guardians—the greater among equals—of American religion.[80] Yet American empire also included integration and development as during the Cold War the United States tried to establish and develop free market capitalism with potential trading partners in Europe, Asia, and the Global South, making economic assistance an important aspect of foreign policy through programs like the Marshall Plan and Point Four.[81] Positive and universalizing cultural forms had a role to play in mobilizing American sympathies.[82] As American empire expanded into the Pacific Rim and Asia, American culture—exhibited in films like *South Pacific* and *The King and I*—at times took on an anti-racist (but racialized) cast that depicted US-Asian relations in familial terms as "an international community that transcends the potentially divisive boundaries of race, nation, sex, and generation."[83] Cultural practices continued to cross and re-cross boundaries, especially in the emerging "Fourth Globalization" of the twenty-first century, which was understood as an era where the movement of ideas, information, and services (including research, design, and engineering) took precedence over manufactured goods that characterized earlier moments.[84]

At home, multicultural practices also influenced Americans. In looking at American cultural hegemony in global context, it is important not to confuse "globalization" with "Americanization." As Penny Von Eschen writes, "It is clear that processes of globalization have transformed US-American popular culture as much as the circulation of American culture . . . ha[s] influenced peoples and nations outside of the United States."[85] In this context, "American" globalization describes a process of intensive crossing and recrossing of borders and frontiers that "speaks across languages in a much more immediate way" due to the technology that intensifies exchange while absorbing and reflecting difference.[86] Practices like yoga had connections to sixties-era critiques of Western materialism and were valued as the cosmopolitan freedom to assemble a hybrid identity from multiple source materials. These examples show how concepts of "mindfulness" and "wellness" have become pervasive in business, schools, athletics, community planning and policy, and scientific discourse. Institutions embraced the concepts as a means for gaining a competitive advantage at the expense of collective action or even awareness. Yet critics worry that the trend toward "mindfulness" is yet another step in "capitalist spirituality" that sought the privatization of religion in Western societies that have valorized individual interests.[87] Chapters 2 and 5 explore the ways that spiritual practices and beliefs have, over time, been contested as they are recontextualized and reinterpreted by businesspeople, corporations, or even entire communities.

The American religious imagination articulated and nurtured transnational attachments as the United States developed a formal global hegemony beginning in the early twentieth century.[88] California has become a site for examining these connections. Scholars of religion have suggested that, since the late nineteenth century, Southern California showed an affinity for a "pluralist" religious culture—defined by scholar of religion Wade Clark Roof as "a recognition and acceptance among the participating groups of the legitimacy of religious and spiritual alternatives" within "normative boundaries" of what constitutes a religious or spiritual group—long before the term characterized American society more broadly. According to this understanding, Southern California's religious history diverged from the Northeast or the South: it lacked a deeply entrenched religious establishment (despite the presence of Catholic missions from the eighteenth century and the historic connections to the Catholic Church for Mexican-American Catholics); its geography allowed it to become a nexus for global encounter; and the fluidity of identities for transplanted migrants contributed to a culture of "openness and acceptance."[89] This "culture of pluralism," in which adherents chose their affiliations and no single faith had "strong cultural dominance," is evidenced in the 1920 survey of faiths in Los Angeles, which counted 147 Roman Catholic churches, 816 Protestant churches, and 860 labeled as "other," with many of these assumed to have "metaphysical leanings."[90] The variety of churches represented the diversity of migrations to California at the turn of the century. In this period, Japanese, Filipino, and Korean migrants brought variations of Buddhism, Taoism, and Shintoism. Protestant and Catholic immigrants from Europe established new congregations and parishes. Migrants from other parts of the United States brought American variations of Protestant traditions. The interracial Azusa Street Revival, which began in 1906, helped found the Pentecostal movement. Jewish immigrants founded both Orthodox and Reformed synagogues. The early twentieth century also witnessed the arrival of migrants practicing Islam and Hindu traditions as well as "new religions" like New Thought and Christian Science, and multiethnic religious communities worked to assimilate as well as resist dominant cultural norms.[91] Nevertheless, Anglo Protestants—fortified by institutions like the Bible Institute of Los Angeles (Biola) and minister Robert Shuler's sermons and KGEF radio broadcasts—sought to assert cultural dominance. In the wake of the Scopes Trial, in 1926 religious conservatives unsuccessfully sought to amend the state constitution to mandate that a copy of the Bible be placed in every public school classroom to be studied or read by any teachers "without comment as a part of the daily school exercises."[92]

In the second half of the twentieth century, forces of globalization linked Southern California to internal and transnational migration patterns while intensifying existing racial and economic inequalities. Depression and World War II–era migrations from the Southwest added to the region's white Protestant revivalist inclinations, as when Billy Graham held his first revival campaign, lasting eight weeks, in Los Angeles. By the late 1950s, white evangelicals in the region, especially in Orange County, helped to define the politics of suburban conservatism surrounding "family values."[93] More recently, historians of religion have documented the challenges to Anglo efforts at hegemony, especially after 1965, by showing how multiracial coalitions of liberal religious and ecumenical organizations contested inequality and how they sought to enact an inclusive vision of human dignity through social and political activism into civic life.[94]

Beyond Los Angeles's history of religious denominations, the region has become an important site for understanding the broader American literature about belief and self-fulfillment. Civic boosters worried that new belief systems and the arrival of non-Anglo migrants endangered the region's brand as the "white spot" of the nation's future.[95] When folded into the promise of reinvention, better living, and present-day multiculturalism, however, spiritual beliefs enhanced the region's lifestyle brand. Even as present-day articles repeat the characterization advanced by the *Life* story with which I began this introduction, scholars hail the region's "remarkably vigorous, diverse, and pluralistic religiosity," which countered the "conventional narrative" about the practice of Catholicism, Protestantism, and Judaism in East Coast–centric histories while matching "contemporary national themes" about migration, diversity, and tolerance.[96] As members of the counterculture experimented with non-Western religions and more migrants from South and East Asia arrived following immigration reform in 1965, scholars saw California as "the laboratory—'the great crucible,' so to speak, where new religious forms are being forged."[97] In the words of religious studies scholars Eldon G. Ernst, beginning in the early twentieth century, Southern California became the place that "stretches our religious imagination and our conception of what it means to be religious" even as religion "also stretches our California imagination and conception of what constitutes California."[98] This included burgeoning notions of what religious studies scholar Bron Taylor calls "dark green religion," which he defined as a set of deeply committed environmental beliefs that assert the intrinsic sacredness of nature. Within this belief system, activities like surfing provide an ecstatic experience that connect humans to nature and other living beings.[99] The expansive definitions of the state's belief systems do not fully account for the ideological work that the concept of religious pluralism does in an uneven global economic structure of exchange that valorizes individual spiritual and secular expression through choice while masking, continuing, and often deepening histories of expropriation, colonialism, and conquest. Rather, this vision of a self-consciously tolerant and diverse California tends to ignore that the full privileges of the "California Dream" were limited by racial and class exclusions.

BOOK STRUCTURE

Golden States highlights the long-range impact of alternative spiritualities on the region's social and cultural landscape. The chapters here are not intended to provide a complete sampling of alternative spirituality in California. Instead, *Golden States* centers on a series of case studies organized around beliefs that, over time, filtered into lifestyle practices. Each chapter is organized, like the 1939 *Life* magazine article, around a religious figure or location that media accounts sought to represent as quirky California spirituality. It is divided into two parts. The case studies in part 1 consider the origins and legacies of religious pioneers whose utopian values established the path to better living—whether for individuals or a broader collective—in the region. Over time, their beliefs and practices became linked to broader cultural systems, including therapeutic routines, business strategies, and environmentalism. Each chapter questions the ways that belief systems navigated the tensions between individual choice and collective identities, especially as they related to racial and economic inequalities.

The first chapter provides an early example of the shifting vocabulary of self-transformation and efforts to foster participatory access to California's restorative leisure. It investigates Katherine Tingley, a Theosophist who in 1900 established a utopian community, the Universal Brotherhood and Theosophical Society (UBTS, also known as Lomaland), outside of San Diego. The group's beliefs often brought them into conflict with civic boosters and skeptical pundits. Lomaland offers entry into early moments through which religious pluralism and restorative leisure became powerful symbols in American culture. Despite its appeals to world brotherhood, the community's cultural imagination—visible in its public programs as well as its involvement in regional boosterism—placed Anglo seekers at the apex of broader transcultural and transhistorical processes of progress.

Turning to the long-term impact of twentieth-century transnational religious encounters, the second chapter contextualizes the American religious imagination within longer histories of imperialism and decolonization, America's deepening economic and political connections to the developing world, and consumer-driven shifts in the religious marketplace by focusing on Paramahansa Yogananda. Arriving in the United States amid the anti-immigrant panic of the 1920s, Yogananda, the founder of the Self-Realization Fellowship, sought to convince Americans that the pursuit of South Asian spiritual "intuition" could provide a means to self-improvement that could be turned toward material ends. Yogananda's legacy endured as "New Age capitalism" came to define Silicon Valley, most notably when Steve Jobs seized upon his concept of "intuition" to help Apple transform the personal computing industry. His efforts to harness spirituality to techno-utopian visions about personal emancipation point to the era's ongoing optimization of individual choice and liberation.

The third chapter turns to a family-owned business to examine a sustained effort to affirm social and ecological solidarities amid shifting historical contexts. The chapter examines Dr. Emanuel Bronner, a German-Jewish émigré and soap maker who espoused an "All-One-God-Faith" on the packaging of his soap. Over time, the family-owned company evolved its founder's message to include guarantees of environmental stewardship and responsible business practices. The history of Dr. Bronner's Soaps allows for an examination of the convergence of modern proselytizing with social activist business practices. In contrast to the individualist impulses that have defined the recent past, the brand's "All One" philosophy espoused what it called "constructive capitalism": a civic and environmental extension of humans' responsibility to both one another and their ecological home.

The second half of *Golden States* examines the long-range impact that alternative spiritualities made on Southern California by exploring how ideas, peoples, and commodities drawn from around the world informed the development of concepts such as wellness, fitness, and multiculturalism. These chapters demonstrate the importance of consumer choice in the contemporary understandings of the community's beliefs. Both chapters show how communities navigated a civic inheritance of what it meant to live right in a religious or spiritual enclave. In doing so, the chapters identify and explore the tension between community and individual health and wellness practices and whether they wished to protect or expand access to the "good" life as defined by their community.

Chapter 4 investigates the concept of "wellness" through an analysis of the health-conscious lifestyle practices of Loma Linda, a Seventh-day Adventist outpost since the 1890s. Over time, the long and healthy lives of Loma Linda residents—linked to Adventist-prescribed vegetarian diets and active lifestyles—brought the city increased national and international attention. Most significantly, in 2005, *National Geographic* designated Loma Linda as one of three global "Blue Zones"—and the only one in the United States—where residents "live longer and have healthier lives than anyone else on Earth."[100] Taken out of its cultural and socioeconomic contexts, however, the concept of the "Blue Zone" ignored broad structural and environmental factors that influenced health and instead repositioned choice as a means for individuals to maximize their life span. As "right living" became a matter of individual choice not a community enterprise, community members had to decide how best to protect their collective health consciousness.

Finally, chapter 5 uses Encinitas, a city in northern San Diego County, to understand how a cultural pluralism based in religious experimentation came to define the city's civic imagination. The chapter explores three controversies where spirituality, including self-consciously therapeutic lifestyle practices, occupied the foreground in community debates about the proper relationship between religion, identity, and public space. The examples convey how a transnational religious imagination harnessed alternative beliefs and practices to a California dream that was increasingly characterized by an exclusionary economy of bourgeois consumption. Despite the celebration of alternative religious and spiritual identity, a culture of individualistic choice and racial privilege inhibited collective consciousness.

Although media accounts—like the *Life* magazine profile described at the beginning of this introduction—frequently characterized spiritual pursuits in Southern California as superfluous fads, they reflected a remarkable shift in the understanding (and self-care) of the liberal subject. In 1946, Carey McWilliams picked up on this ethos of self-actualization in his discussion of Southern California's fondness for "cultism." McWilliams remarked that, because of this therapeutic strain, strangers were, upon meeting, supposed to inquire first, "Where are you from?" and then, "How do you feel?"[101] To answer similar questions about modern-day spirituality, *Golden States* interrogates cultural and economic contexts to find the historic sources of Californians' pursuit of individual wellness.

PART ONE

Spiritual Visionaries, Historical Imaginaries, and Self-Improvement as Therapeutic Leisure

Part 1 examines the long-range influence of spiritual visionaries on social and cultural practices in Southern California. The case studies consider the origins and legacies of three religious pioneers whose utopian values became linked to broader cultural practices or social causes—therapeutic routines, business strategies, and environmentalism—over the course of the twentieth and early twenty-first century. The religious visionaries in these chapters created new parables for living amid globalizing currents that intensified religious encounter and exchange. Although articulated in universal terms, the belief systems were often enacted in racialized ways that limited the applicability of practices to a privileged few. Because belief systems are not static, the second half of each chapter examines the ways that ideas were readapted to new cultural and economic contexts over time. The latter of these chapters touch on a broader theme of this work: although religious figures articulated paths to "better living," over time it was often difficult to navigate the tension between valuing individual choice and collective identities.

In some instances, religious leaders celebrated leisure-based therapeutic experiences that provided new avenues for exploring spirituality and developing one's fullest sense of self—with material benefits for the individual. Chapter 1 examines Theosophist Katherine Tingley and the Universal Brotherhood and Theosophical Society, or Lomaland, the utopian community she founded in San Diego in 1897. At a moment when Americans were exposed to an array of globalized goods and ideas, Tingley's beliefs wed social reform efforts to world philosophies and religions and positioned her ideas as exemplary of notions of "progress." Although many civic boosters thought she was a charlatan preying on foolish rich people, Tingley found a home in San Diego's developing tourist economy. In examining representations of Lomaland and its foundress, the chapter offers entry into early moments where restorative leisure became a powerful symbol—and useful ideological tool—of San Diego's reputation as a space for health and wellness. At the same time, the chapter examines the limits of inclusivity of the developing health and leisure economy. Although the community appealed to "world brotherhood," its cultural imagination placed Anglo seekers at the apex of broader transcultural and transhistorical processes of progress.

The second chapter contextualizes the American religious imagination within longer histories of decolonization, America's deepening economic and political connections to the developing world, and consumer-driven shifts in the religious marketplace. Chapter 2, "'Efficient America,' 'Spiritual India,' and America's Transnational Religious Imagination," shows how Paramahansa Yogananda, founder of the Self-Realization Fellowship, arrived in the United States in 1920 to convince Americans that the pursuit of South Asian spiritual "intuition" could provide a means to self-improvement that could be turned toward material ends. His legacy endured: his most famous admirer, Steve Jobs, later embraced Yogananda's concept of "intuition" to help Apple transform the personal computer and cellphone industries. In doing so, Jobs helped move "self-actualization" from a spiritual practice to a business strategy, a practice that placed personal freedom and cosmopolitan engagement at the service of late capitalist techno-utopianism.

Despite the economic logic of personal and corporate "perpetual growth" in the early twentieth century, not all paths led to greater atomization: some seekers drew upon their spiritual inheritance to renew calls for interdependence and environmental stewardship. Chapter 3 examines the connection of the convergence of urgent moral belief with social activist business practices through an examination of the Bronner family and its brand of soaps. The chapter demonstrates how, over multiple generations, the company altered its spiritual and business mission to fit different existential imperatives and actively affirm—even build—social solidarities.

In seeking personal development, religious seekers did not obey perceived boundaries between secular and sacred, nor did they observe distinctions between scientific and religious authority. Indeed, the paths for

achieving "salvation" expanded considerably in the twentieth century—
and no more so than in Southern California, which was the advance
guard of these changes to a more therapeutic religion in keeping with
an increasingly cosmopolitan consumerist society. Taken together, these
chapters show how religious leaders drew on inherited historical imaginaries and global encounters to create religious visions and how, subsequent to that, religion as a cultural phenomenon was experienced and
renegotiated within new political, economic, and social contexts.

CHAPTER I

"A Paradise for the Healthseeker and Retired Capitalist"

Katherine Tingley and San Diego's
Early Therapeutic Religious Economy

In 1897, Katherine Tingley, a former spirit medium turned philanthropist and religious leader, purchased 132 acres of land at Point Loma for the Universal Brotherhood and Theosophical Society (UBTS). Lomaland, the utopian community she subsequently founded on the site, a peninsula in San Diego, linked the present-day West with distant points in time and space. She later described a childhood vision of a "White City" built in the "Gold-Land of the West," where she "should gather together children of all nations and teach them how to live rightly." Tingley envisioned a school that was "American in center" but "international in character . . . lighting up the dark places of the earth." Students would be "taught the laws of physical life, and physical, moral, and mental health and spiritual unfoldment," and as they gained an understanding of themselves, they would "learn to use [the knowledge] for the good of the whole world."[1] Residents lived according to Tingley's vision, which combined the philosophical elements of Theosophy with popular therapeutic lifestyle practices that wed international aims and classical inspiration to American exceptionalism.

This chapter uses Katherine Tingley and Lomaland's place in the Southern California regional imagination to illuminate the intersection of cultural, religious, and economic understandings of better living in the early twentieth century. As the United States moved away from the sober producerism associated with Protestantism, Southern California became a site for new understandings of self-improvement and belief based in an emerging consumer ethic. Through an examination of representations of Tingley and the Universal Brotherhood in regional and national newspapers and magazines as well as tourist guides and promotional pamphlets, this chapter demonstrates how gendered, racial, and economic understandings of progress and the importance of intense spiritual and therapeutic experience combined to shape Southern California's regional identity. Lomaland therefore reveals the ways that religious, economic, and civic values developed in tandem at the beginning of the twentieth century.

Lomaland was one of many utopian communities or religious orders that took root in Southern California in this period. A few, like the Llano del Rio colony, envisioned a place for communal economic engagement, while others—the Mormons of San Bernardino, the Rosicrucians at Mt. Ecclesia in Oceanside, or the different Theosophist communities in Point Loma, Halcyon, and Krotona—shared a common religious vision.[2] Tingley was among the most flamboyant of the era's religious leaders and therefore a flashpoint for the heralds of both the region's "sunshine" and "noir" narratives.[3] Indeed, no history of utopian religion or lifestyle spirituality in Southern California can rightfully begin anywhere—or with anyone—else. Carey McWilliams described Katherine Tingley, often referred to as the "purple mother" due to her preference for the color, as "the first major prophetess of the region" who helped popularize the yogic and occult influences from which other experimental and utopian movements evolved.[4] Tingley appeared at the moment when elements of a "new religious consciousness" usually associated with the 1960s became established in American culture; historian Philip Jenkins calls this "first new age" a "period of Emergence" for eccentric and mystical religious ideas.[5] The shifting boundaries of legitimacy—informed by racial, class, and gendered expectations of respectability and belonging—provide insight into a different worldview taking shape at the turn of the century. Although often dismissed as "fringe religions," alternative communities like the Universal Brotherhood both drew upon and contributed to understandings of cultural power and identity that became synonymous with California's role in American history and the role of the United States in world history as it emerged as an imperial power.

The Universal Brotherhood represented one prominent strain of Theosophy, which was part of a broader nineteenth-century process that historians have categorized as the institutionalization of the concept of "world religion." Many of these movements consolidated or resisted nationalism through the concept of religious solidarity, but there were also transnational movements, including Theosophy.[6] Although the basic concepts of belief had existed for centuries, modern Theosophy, which drew from "ancient" esoteric thought that valued theories and knowledge practiced outside established religious practices as well as "modern" scientific worldviews, represented a "self-consciously global and intellectual tradition" that built a hybrid religious movement among a growing middle-class in England, the United States, Australia, and India.[7] Scholars of religion recognize South Asian religious beliefs (filtered in part through Transcendentalism) as well as Western esotericism and occultism (meaning "hidden" and accessed via instruction and initiation) in this belief system. At times, Theosophists denied they were a religious movement at all. Theosophical principles overlapped with systems like New Thought, which believed in the human ability to exert control over ailments of mind and body.[8]

Although the Universal Brotherhood was part of a larger transnational movement, it fit neatly into California's emerging religious ethos. The community offered residents an opportunity for self-transformation wherein seekers adopted and modified aspects of an array of religions under the banner of physical and spiritual wellness. Many upper- or middle-class Anglos were ambivalent about the changes wrought by the capitalist developments of the late nineteenth century. Although they benefited from the material progress of the era, the bourgeois class—increasingly managed via internalized self-control as external forms of authority disintegrated—experienced a sense of "unreality." A tier of affluent Anglos sought comfort not through liberal Protestantism, which for them had lost its emotional immediacy and theological rigor, but through an ethic that viewed "growth" and "experience" as paths toward well-being. This belief nevertheless helped construct a hegemonic cultural authority based on a "therapeutic worldview" seeking self-fulfillment acquired through consumerism.[9] The Universal Brotherhood—with its verdant grounds, active performing arts troupes, and international educational and philanthropic mission—exemplified a type of recreational retreat with physical, spiritual, and educational elements to which Anglos might aspire. Their beliefs and practices at times brought them into conflict with civic boosters who viewed the Lomaland's existence as contradictory to the modern city they envisioned, as well as skeptical pundits, who scorned the community for their cosmopolitan pretensions and Tingley herself for her autocratic proclivities. Nevertheless, Tingley envisioned material progress in the future path of the Universal Brotherhood and the city of San Diego. City leaders likewise believed Southern

California could become a "frontier of leisure" where middle-class and wealthy Anglo transplants could become their best selves through spiritual introspection sought within a healthy environment.[10] Tingley aligned Lomaland with boosters' renderings of the region to advance her group's standing in the community. The universalizing language articulated by Tingley and city boosters belied a deeply racialized understanding of who had access to this type of civilizational "progress," a tendency made evident by the 1902 arrival of Cuban orphans after the Spanish-American War. Despite their inclusionary tone, the subsequent "Americanization" efforts undertaken by the community highlighted its sense that universal brotherhood might only be achieved within a hierarchical racial and national structure with the United States—and Anglos—resting at the top.

Tingley's religious, historical, and transcultural imagination—at once expansive and exclusive—was foundational to the identity of the Universal Brotherhood and, as this book argues, to Southern California's brand of therapeutic wellness culture. Battles about religion and spirituality frequently take place outside the institutional structures of organized religion, and they reveal cultural understandings of identity and belonging. Tingley proved to be both an irresistible target and heroine because her religious imagination incorporated a wide-ranging mix of practices and ideas that placed the community at the center of new understandings about self-transformation as well as regional and national progress.

This chapter explores three examples of the way that Tingley's community at Lomaland shaped and was shaped by the region's emerging therapeutic identity. First, both boosters and skeptics placed Tingley and the Universal Brotherhood at the center of debates about the legitimate boundaries of religious and spiritual experimentation. Second, despite attacks from civic boosters and religious muckrakers that castigated the Universal Brotherhood for its autocratic leadership, obscure rites, eclectic architecture, and communal structure, in many ways the organization reflected—and even advanced—the new cultural and religious ethos that was emerging within and about Southern California and the United States more generally. Theosophists placed their belief system within global historical understandings and seemingly sophisticated consumer tastes, but they benefited from pursuing their activities in Southern California at a time when the region envisioned itself at the forefront of an emerging American empire. Third, by tapping into regional and imperial identities, Tingley helped promote Southern California—and especially

San Diego—as a site where a growing therapeutic economy provided restorative leisure. While illuminating the imprint that the "first new age" made on California and its regional imagination, this discussion of Lomaland demonstrates how, even in the early twentieth century, the pursuit of spiritual innovation and health consciousness was limited to a subgroup of affluent white seekers. Despite its appeals to world brotherhood, the community often espoused gendered and racial hierarchies. The community's cultural imagination placed Anglo seekers at the apex of broader transcultural and transhistorical processes of progress. The community's projection of itself as a high-minded utopia that embraced a certain type of lifestyle matched its efforts to advertise San Diego—a city that grew from 17,700 residents in 1900 to nearly 40,000 in 1910 and 74,000 in 1920—as a community built on suburban living, consumerism, and health and wellness.[11] In this sense, Lomaland shaped efforts to create a religious tradition that allowed Anglo practitioners to, in Tingley's words, "live rightly" by combining physical, moral, and mental health with spiritual fulfillment.

THEOSOPHICAL ORIGINS AND LIFE AT LOMALAND

Although Tingley purchased the property in 1897, it took another two years for her to solidify her power within the Theosophical Society and relocate to Lomaland, whose property soon sprawled across nearly five hundred acres. Over the next few years, she opened the Raja Yoga School for young people as well as an orphanage for Cuban children, built a Greek temple and the Temple of Peace, and renovated the Homestead building. Though most residents lived in shared housing, she permitted some members to build permanent bungalows. Beyond physical structures, there was a large-scale agricultural wing that planted fruit groves and vegetable gardens that fed the community and avocado and eucalyptus trees that covered the grounds. In a further effort at self-sufficiency, there was also a refectory, bakery, stables, a carpenter shop, a smithy, and facilities for creating textiles and tailoring clothes.[12] Members tended to dress alike given that their clothes were made within the community. They were prolific in their production of texts: the community had its own printing press and bindery to publish its books, magazines, memoirs, lectures, and conference proceedings. Residents signed an agreement to live by the rules of the community and paid an admission fee of five hundred dollars per family (although the admission and tuition fees varied by family or individual wealth and payment could be waived). All told, about five hundred residents lived there at its peak in 1910.[13] Daily life in the community involved a range of activities. Viewing education and performance as important components of their commission, Tingley supported arts programs, and the Universal Brotherhood drew upon the talents of artists and academics who staffed the music, drama, and education departments. Children lived in a communal nursery, meals were taken in a group setting, and Tingley assigned new vocations to members. Residents gathered for rituals (often held at unusual hours) and for Sunday evening services. Those enlisting in this new lifestyle included sporting goods magnate Albert G. Spalding, diamond broker E. August Neresheimer, and hardware manufacturer Clark Thurston; these member-benefactors bankrolled some of the community's construction projects but did not relinquish their wealth upon joining.

Americans' interest in esotericism—that is, traditions based in locating spiritual awareness and secret metaphysical knowledge through inward reflection—dated to the colonial period, but philosophies like Freemasonry, Swedenborgianism, Transcendentalism, and mesmerism popularized the practice. The imperative to connect science and religion through unconventional means intensified in the late nineteenth century. Helena Petrovna Blavatsky, who was born in Russia in 1831, established the Theosophical Society in New York City in 1875 with Henry Steel Olcott, an American lawyer who shared her interest in spiritualism, the study of the occult, and Eastern religions. In moving explanations of the phenomenon of spiritualism from the dead to more natural forces, Blavatsky's work blended occultism with pseudoscientific and scientific (especially evolutionary) theories, mythological pasts, and racialized imperial assumptions.[14] Blavatsky established the concepts of Theosophy in *Isis Unveiled* (1877) and *The Secret Doctrine* (1888). *Isis Unveiled* sold a thousand copies within ten days of its release (and ultimately more than five hundred thousand). Blavatsky maintained that humankind exists in a multidimensional universe and that world religions were simply elaborations around a common set of ideas.[15] In an effort to expand the society, Blavatsky and Olcott embarked on a tour of England and India in 1878; they appointed William Quan Judge as the chief representative of the Theosophical Society of America in the United States. Judge converted Tingley and then appointed her the Outer Head of the Theosophical Society before he died in 1896. At a tense meeting of American Theosophists in 1898 in Chicago, Tingley changed the name of the society to the Universal Brotherhood and Theosophical Society. Her action resulted in schisms within the American wing of the movement. Blavatsky and Olcott, who largely remained abroad for the rest of their lives, founded additional wings of the movement, including the International Headquarters of the Theosophical Society in Adyar, India. By the time Olcott died in 1907, there were over six hundred branches in over forty countries; this included the so-called Adyar wing, which gave rise to leaders such as Annie Besant (a prominent British socialist and member of the Indian National Congress) and her successor, Jiddu Krishnamurti (who also eventually settled in Southern California and whom Tingley only acknowledged as "a fine chap"), as well as Albert P. Warrington, founder of the Hollywood-based Krotona in 1911. Theosophy never had more than ten thousand members at its most popular moment, although its concepts—like the notion of the existence of a few universal core spiritual concepts that united world religions—disseminated widely through modern spiritual culture.[16]

The key premises of Theosophy included a belief in a universe centered in a "boundless, omnipresent, eternal Principle" as opposed to a personal God; a sense of cyclical patterns that occurred within this principle; and a unity of life. The objectives of the Theosophical Society coalesced around three emphases: first, a belief in universal brotherhood of humanity regardless of race, creed, sex, caste, or color; second, an interest in the study of ancient and modern religion, literature, and sciences; and third, a desire to uncover the hidden mysteries of nature and the powers of mankind.[17] Aside from the name of the Raja Yoga School, Tingley—unlike her counterparts in Theosophy's Adyar wing—was not associated with any South Asian–based spiritual influences or personalities. Under Tingley's leadership, the Universal Brotherhood—as its name indicated—concentrated on the concept of brotherhood and humanitarianism. Before her conversion, Tingley had established philanthropic foundations for the elderly and for orphans. At Point Loma, Tingley combined her interests in esotericism and social work: service-oriented projects like the Raja Yoga School sought to train and develop souls to realize their divine nature across multiple reincarnations; the effort sought to change individuals, not necessarily restructure society.[18]

The philosophy of the Universal Brotherhood aligned with regional boosters' conviction that Southern California would play a key role in the future of the world. Reflecting the new role of the United States as a nation with an overseas empire, the society's worldview combined notions of internationalism under a mantle of American exceptionalism. As nonstate transnational social networks—organized around religion, reform, race, class, and gender—grew in the late nineteenth century, participants often professed an allegiance to universalism in opposition to the particularism of nation-states and empires. These associations nevertheless maintained presumptions of racial and imperial hierarchy.[19]

And so it was with the Universal Brotherhood, whose members were mainly white or European: the group affirmed international solidarity and interdependence, but it sought to achieve its goals within a tiered system of racial cooperation wherein the United States served as a guardian leading toward modern development. The Universal Brotherhood represented itself as a "great educational institution" that united "the best in the practical Occident, the noblest in the East."[20] In this teleological vision, Theosophists believed the world to be on the cusp of achieving a "brotherhood of humanity" with the United States—especially California—at the forefront. California was, after all, "esoterically significant" for Theosophists. Reflecting the Victorian fascination with origin stories and archaeology (the better for articulating narratives of progress), Blavatsky's The Secret Doctrine had outlined an historical cosmology through which seven "Root Races" would evolve.[21] Humanity was in its fifth Root Race (the Aryan era, in Theosophical terms), but Blavatsky saw the Southwest, including California but also parts of Mexico, New Mexico, and Arizona, as important areas in the evolution. As art historian Grace Converse explains, by establishing footholds in California, both Tingley and her Adyar counterpart Annie Besant sought to solidify their claim to be legitimate heirs to Blavatsky.[22]

In California, Theosophists could prepare for the next stage of development, although Tingley and Besant diverged on what this might look like. Tingley's emphasis on the "practical" side of Theosophy put her interventions in line with Victorian social activism.[23] She told one profiler, "I would not say, 'Let us pray,' but 'Let us do'; let us turn from the negative side of knee prayer to the positive side of heart action."[24] For the Universal Brotherhood, "heart action" included international symposia and education. For example, a congress in 1899 brought 525 delegates from European countries as well as India, Egypt, Australia, New Zealand, and Cuba to Lomaland; a Peace Symposium held in 1915 after the outbreak of World War I similarly attracted speakers from around the world. The Raja Yoga School also fulfilled the practical mission of the community by, in Tingley's words, teaching the world's children "the perfect balance of all the faculties, physical, mental, and spiritual."[25] At the same time, the pedagogical tone of uplift mirrored turn-of-the-century imperial discourses that highlighted

American "benevolence" while advancing colonial projects of civilization and racialized power.[26]

In the early years of the community, a few journalists traveled to San Diego to observe how the organization enacted its beliefs by reimagining work and community life. These pieces provide insight into daily life at Lomaland—or at least the routine that Tingley wished to represent or journalists wished to report. A 1903 piece in *Munsey's Magazine*, for example, remarked that Tingley had created a community where, "among other strange things, men work month in and month out for neither gold nor glory," an assertion based on the fact that members received no wages and rotated through jobs as decided by Tingley. The author fixated on businessmen with newly discovered passions for manual labor or artistic work, including a Georgia lawyer who became head gardener while his daughter worked in the kitchen and a wealthy southerner who had become a violin maker.[27] The author did not question why, for example, a young working-class woman who arrived for classical musical training might instead be handed a mop and bucket.[28] It was more compelling to see an accomplished entrepreneur toiling in the fields than to see a talented young woman confined to her existing station in life. Although the Universal Brotherhood's membership skewed female, the experience of a pastoral life fit the quest for "intense experience" that many white Anglo men sought when they believed their bodies had grown weak at desk jobs.[29]

Another journalist, Ray Stannard Baker, published a sympathetic account of the community a few years later. More than any other profile, Baker's piece successfully summed up the stakes for Point Loma and other utopian communities:

> Here was a group of cultivated men and women, inspired or perverted, according to one's point of view, by a faith so ardent, so strange to ordinary knowledge, that they had left their former homes, their business, and even their friends and relatives, had settled upon a far and wonderfully beautiful point of land reaching out into the Pacific Ocean from Southern California and were there seeking the ideal life as they conceived it.

For Baker, the controversies surrounding the community were irrelevant; what mattered was whether the members were "satisfied with their strange life," one that "overturns our settled and customary conceptions of life." Community members had earned the right to live in communal dorms or a bungalow and eat communal meals if that fit their definition of the "ideal life." Although Baker believed that members labored out of enthusiasm for their endeavor, it was not clear they were look-ing for meaning in communal living in and of itself. Feeling useless or unhappy in their previous lives, members perhaps sought revitalization by simulating simplicity and aestheticizing the labor no longer required of them.[30]

THE CHALLENGE OF SKEPTICS

The outside world remained unconvinced. As has often been the case in American religious history, a "marginal religion" like the Universal Brotherhood raised concerns about deviance, whether "authoritarian, deceptive, exploitative," or "violent" in nature. In the early twentieth century, California witnessed the arrival of several new religious move-ments. Opponents articulated fears about "crackpot beliefs" in a range of ways; for example, the term *cult* tended to connote a connection to non-Western religions.[31] To skeptics, the Universal Brotherhood commit-ted heresy not just in its abstruse spirituality (especially its connections, however vague, to Asian beliefs) but often simply in its cultural norms, including its female leadership. A series of scandals and litigation sought to expose the true nature of power and belief within the community. These controversies delimited how the "good life" in Southern Califor-nia ought to be defined, how religion should be practiced, and, moreover, how whiteness should be lived.

From the outset, boosters embraced a particular vision for growth in Southern California, particularly Los Angeles. Groups such as the Los Angeles Chamber of Commerce, founded after the economic bust of the 1870s, relentlessly peddled their vision of the state. After 1900, the chamber focused on attracting white Midwesterners looking for a lifestyle that offered "an easier, more varied, less complicated, and well-rounded life."[32] Transplants arrived with established notions of the proper environment for a comfortable living, and that was a residential suburb: "spacious, affluent, clean, decent, permanent, predictable, and homogeneous."[33] Boosters imagined Los Angeles as the city of the future and conjured this destiny through selective historical memory as well as social and political force.[34] Even when its population hovered around one hundred thousand at the turn of the twentieth century, civic boosters feared degeneracy and believed that Los Angeles possessed an "aesthetic, political, and moral purity" that was absent in Eastern cities. Newspaper-man Harry Chandler captured this sentiment by referring to Los Angeles as the "white spot of America," based on its warm climate, freedom from industrial labor strife, and relative lack of foreign or ethnic populations.[35] As historian William Deverell explains, the city's understanding of itself combined "prophecy, faith, and wide-eyed optimism" with "presumptions of the racial superiority of self-identified Anglo Saxons."[36] Atop the civic power structure, boosters celebrated the arrival of middle-class and elite Anglos as, between 1890 and 1910, the percentage of native-born white Anglos topped 76 percent of the population, a proportion that was higher than that of other large American cities.[37] Anglos viewed ethnic and interracial interaction and accommodation—including its religious "culture of pluralism"—as something to be managed or suppressed. The regulation of culture often involved the "whitewashing" of ethnic relations, conflicts, places, and cultural memory, especially those with or involving Mexican people, whose "adobe" past became the premodern foil to the city's "Anglo" present and future.[38] Erasure was not only achieved through forgetting. On the contrary, as Kelly Lytle Hernandez has shown, the ongoing project of settler colonialism allowed Anglos to eliminate marginalized populations through methods of removal and eradication that included policing, policy, and incarceration. This framework provides insights into the implications of the Universal Brotherhood's construction projects and its enaction of historical memory, even as the organization came into conflict with civic boosters.[39]

Anglo boosters, especially Harrison Gray Otis of the *Los Angeles Times*, were protective of their vision of the city based on "homes, pastoral landscapes, and endless recreation."[40] In many ways—especially its Anglo-dominated membership and its vision of Southern California as a site of destiny and progress—the Universal Brotherhood met these criteria. Yet Tingley also challenged conventional definitions of home and family, and the recreational pursuits of the community proved too risqué for some boosters. The *Los Angeles Times* repeatedly expressed its preference for the region to become a "city of homes," defined as detached, single-family residences with open spaces and gardens. Through these preferences for "aesthetic attractiveness, bucolic setting, and thorough cleanliness," the *Times* created norms of social and moral character that it hoped would function to attract more tourists and like-minded Anglo transplants.[41]

The *Times* was known for its racialized criticism of sects that defied the sober and serious tones of mainline Protestantism. A 1906 article in the *Los Angeles Times*, for example, voiced a revulsion for the "weird babel of tongues" emanating from the Azusa Street mission, an interracial crucible of the burgeoning Pentecostal movement.[42] In contrast, in

1902 the paper characterized Seventh-day Adventists—ironically, a multiracial movement with a white prophetess—as "a zealous, courageous and hopeful people" whose camp meetings were places of "great religious fervor."[43] Despite its proximity to San Diego rather than Los Angeles, the fledgling Point Loma colony violated the norms that the *Times* had sought to uphold for the region. The relatively small community—about three hundred members, including children, at the settlement in 1902—drew an inordinate amount of attention from the paper. It was clear that, as Carey McWilliams later opined, Otis viewed the Universal Brotherhood colony as "bad advertising" for the region.[44]

When the *Times* raised objections to the Universal Brotherhood, it focused on the rites practiced by the community, the autocratic power that its female leader possessed, and the colony's perceived attacks on Victorian domestic structure. The *Times* at first treated them with bemusement. One early story, for example, described "the most unique ceremony ever held in this portion of the country" that accompanied the laying of the cornerstone—made of rock from the United States, Ireland, and Scotland—for the "School for the Revival of the Ancient Mysteries." The piece portended some future themes, as it highlighted both the outfit selected by Tingley (a black robe with flowing sleeves accessorized with a lilac scarf) and the foreign-seeming phrases— "ohm" at one point and "Budham Saranam Gocham" at another—chanted during the ceremony. Before long, stories began to question the rites of the community, and the legitimacy of Tingley's leadership. Fears arose about the timing of ceremonies, allegations of "free love" among community members, and the autocratic nature of her leadership.[45] Given Tingley's uncertain background, the *Times* delighted in alluding to her rumored past as a spirit medium in New York City. The newspaper published a satirical verse aimed at the leader that included the couplet, "Tingle, Tingle little star / What a rotten sect you are."[46] Another piece referred to her as the "Purple Mahatma"; as religious studies scholar Anya Foxen explains, American newspapers often used the label "mahatma" to describe "charismatic white women within the metaphysical circuit" because their invocation of conventional (from a Victorian standpoint) masculine intellectual traits countered the cultural expectations of docile spiritual mediums.[47] These stories showed a proclivity for sensationalist attacks on a strong female religious leader whose enigmatic background, cryptic (at least to outsiders) religious ceremonies, and seemingly subversive communal norms posed a threat to polite society.

To be sure, Tingley and the community's exploits provided great copy, and the *Times* intensified its attacks over the summer of 1901. Tingley successfully sued General Harrison Gray Otis and the *Times* for an article entitled "Outrages at Point Loma. Exposed by an 'Escape' from Tingley." The initial story came about when a *Times* editor dispatched a reporter to interview a Theosophist opposed to Tingley's leadership who alleged "gross immoralities" perpetrated at the colony. In addressing the treatment of women and children, the article enumerated the ways that the community was an affront to Victorian domestic arrangements: an affluent white woman who arrived from the East was put to work in a field doing "hard labor" and then shut in a room at night; girls sent to learn were instead set to "menial tasks" in solitary guarded cells. Children were likewise "quartered in a miserable building" set apart from the main quarters and were "continually on the verge of starvation."[48]

Tingley responded by filing a lawsuit alleging libel. The *Times'* defense team and its courtroom reporters gleefully redoubled their efforts to make Tingley look at once autocratic and absurd. Defense attorneys questioned her past, arguing that "character as well as reputation" was important to the case, so it was vital to interrogate her career and whether she was a "a fake and a fraud." The highlight of the case—and the revelation most often cited in the historical record—was the contention that Tingley considered her dog, Spot, as possessing the reincarnated soul of her mentor, William Q. Judge. The *Times'* attorney characterized her power as "autocratic, un-American and un-Christian" that was more absolute than any "despot that sat at Constantinople." Although the *Times* lost the case with a $7,500 judgment (never paid due to its dismissal during the appeal process), it viewed itself as protecting the public integrity against campaigns of "vice, corruption, and indecency."[49] Yet the explicitly misogynistic and othering objections to Tingley and Lomaland—linking her to forms of religious and political power in South Asia, Russia, and the Ottoman Empire—provided the paper with a morality tale warning transplants against becoming intoxicated with religious experimentation in their new home. In this way, the *Times* safeguarded the straight and narrow path to white Christian respectability. Eventually a series of lawsuits over estates led Lomaland (and therefore Tingley) into a spiral of financial ruin. Following Tingley's death in 1929, the Brotherhood resumed calling itself the Theosophical Society and relocated to Covina in 1942. It eventually moved to Pasadena in 1945 and Altadena in 1951, where it continues to exist.

Historians may have noted the lack of a dominant religious tradition in California, but that did not stop mainstream Protestant ministers from engaging in turf wars over Theosophy's legitimacy.[50] Theosophists had already attracted the suspicion of mainline Protestants in the 1890s when an Episcopal minister in Wisconsin published a book that characterized Spiritualism, Theosophy, and Christian Science as "cults" contrary to Christian religion. The label allowed Christian denominations to enforce doctrinal orthodoxy, especially important when non-Western religions were gaining in popularity in the United States following the 1893 World Parliament of Religion.[51] Amid the negative articles published by the *Times*, a Methodist preacher in San Diego started a months-long feud with Theosophy after the Brotherhood announced its plans to open a nonsectarian Sunday school. In a sermon entitled "Theosophy as a Modern Substitute for the Religion of Christ," the Reverend Dr. Clarence True Wilson denounced the organization, having alerted the media in advance so they—and members of Tingley's cabinet—could be on hand to hear the condemnation in person. In the following weeks, over twenty more mainline Protestant and Catholic clergy—minus a single Unitarian minister—signed on to Wilson's assertion that Theosophy was "the antithesis of Christianity" and "a system of pantheism" that left room for neither "religion nor ethics." The controversy probably drew attention to both organizations: the Methodists acted like beleaguered defenders of the faith, while the Universal Brotherhood spent months clarifying their relationship to Christianity at Sunday meetings.[52]

Confident in their future, some mainstream newspapers and mainline ministers objected to those whose worldview failed to match their plans. They objected to competing visions rendered through past mysteries or projected onto a bohemian future. And yet it was not just the boosters who shunned alternative beliefs. Even muckraking journalists, who countered the cheerful platitudes about the region by exposing the repressive power exercised on communities of color and labor unions, mocked the pretensions of unconventional religions. According to this genre, spiritual seekers advanced through the following life stages: born in the Midwest, migrate to Southern California in midlife (often due to physical frailty), bask in the newfound freedom of a warm climate, establish/join a cult. Although "optimistic faiths" existed in metropolitan areas outside California (Tingley, for example, became a Theosophist in New York City), skeptics saw a set of religious superstitions that blocked progress that they, too, had imagined for the American West. These detractors held a teleological understanding of historical evolution in which the working class was the engine of historical liberation. Muckrakers therefore sought at once to expose spiritual fraudulence and unmask the banal tastes of the gathered petit-bourgeois Midwesterners. Willard Huntington Wright, who was raised in Santa Monica, exemplified this outlook in a piece that appeared in *The Smart Set*, a New York–based literary magazine. Wright used developmental language to describe the city's culture, declaring the desire for spiritual knowledge as "adolescent intelligence." Despite robust civic efforts, the city could not hide its hopeless provincialism; it was a city with "no foundation of culture, religion, habits or tenets." This was particularly true of "faddists and mountebanks" who promised followers wisdom without endeavor. Although Wright did not single out Theosophy, he mocked religious leaders who "dangle the tinsel star of erudition before the eyes of the semi-educated."[53] His criticism of simplistic knowledge echoed critics of camp meetings during the Second Great Awakening who worried that emotional and easy conversions had replaced a depth of religious belief.[54]

Even before the Scopes Trial in 1925, the division between modernism and fundamentalism opened a rift in American society regarding the proper measure of progress. Fundamentalists viewed a damned world bereft of progress. Modernists tended to use science and objectivity as their measure. But this was not a two-sided view. Progressively minded journalists often saw the world in terms of class politics, and they viewed religion as a cover for economic exploitation. For example, Upton Sinclair, the socialist and journalist who sought to expose inequality in fictional and nonfictional accounts of American society, viewed religion as another example of structural economic abuse. Sinclair founded a short-lived commune in 1906 and was a proponent of physical culture, which emphasized the health-oriented benefits of personal diet, fasting, abstinence from alcohol, and fitness. Institutionalized belief systems were another matter. In *Profits of Religion: An Essay in Economic Interpretation* (1917), Sinclair roared that religion provided "income to parasites," making it "the natural ally of every form of oppression and exploitation."[55] Although California was thought to be "a place of freedom," he found the term meant "the ability of ignorant and fanatical persons to start some new, fantastical quirk of scriptural interpretation, to build a cult around it, and even a living out of it." Theosophists were particularly exasperating, as competing wings cultivated "millionaire souls," making it impossible to detect sincerity.[56] Sinclair's work helped establish religious organizations as synonymous with Southern Californian frivolity.

Louis Adamic, another Progressive-era muckraker, focused more narrowly on Katherine Tingley and her followers, asserting that Tingley used "natural and artificial charms" to "lure suckers."[57] His 1927 account exemplified efforts to reveal the shallow intellectualism in new faiths in Southern Californians. Just one year before, he had written a similar account mocking the "half dead" followers of evangelist Aimee Semple McPherson, whom he characterized as "morons, boobs, and suckers."[58] Writing about the Universal Brotherhood as well as its rival Adyar wing, Adamic concluded that "the moribund and absurd theosophic doctrine" was inapplicable to "the vigorous, individualistic life of America and the Occident in general." If Westerners were curious about Eastern thought, Adamic counseled them to read the original sources in translation rather than the interpretations created by Theosophists, most of whom had but "superficial if any knowledge of the systems from which their doctrine has been culled." With science making "old-fashioned religion preposterous," softer minds searched for a comforting panacea. Adamic's religious skepticism caused him to find fault with all types of religious beliefs. Theosophy, Adamic asserted, failed to achieve rational or coherent thought despite its elements of modern scientific concepts. Bewildered more than outraged by her "ordinary, indistinctive personality," Adamic suggested that the "weak-minded millionaires" who funded her building campaigns were "simple suckers."[59] Adamic sneered at the notion that Lomaland's borrowed architectural symbols might bestow legitimacy on the community. For a professional skeptic like Adamic, the Universal Brotherhood—which dressed itself in trappings of international brotherhood, ancient and esoteric learning, and modern rationality—exemplified the collective stunted intellectual development of the region's provincial populace.

LOMALAND AND THE SOUTHERN CALIFORNIA BOOSTER IMAGINATION

Even as journalists criticized the Universal Brotherhood for its autocratic leadership, obscure rites, eclectic architecture, and communal structure, in many ways the organization both reflected and advanced a new cultural and religious ethos that was emerging in Southern California. The *Los Angeles Times* wished for sober and thrifty migrants to avoid partaking of too much of the good life. However, as religious studies scholar W. Michael Ashcraft explains, Tingley grasped the ways that consumer culture had altered the religious terrain of the 1890s. Going forward, religious institutions needed to cater to white middle-class desires for individual fulfillment through leisure and consumption. Deploying modern publicity campaigns, religious institutions might entertain and educate their believers, and engage in light reform efforts. The Universal Brotherhood offered its middle- and upper-class Anglo adherents a "dynamic religious alternative" with "liberal, reformist principles" consistent with a modern scientific worldview and the burgeoning cosmopolitan tastes offered by the commercial marketplace.[60] Theosophists placed their belief system within global historical understandings and seemingly sophisticated consumer tastes, but they benefited from setting their activities within a regional context.

Tingley possessed an astute understanding of civic engagement and identity. Under her guidance, the Theosophical Society of America was to organize, in the words of one scholar, "a worldwide cultural and ethical renovation of the next generation through education."[61] Although at times combative with reporters, she nevertheless knew how to earn positive press. She placed her colony at the center of a historical narrative that projected a new era of growth based in Anglo-centered progress that intersected with developing regional and imperial imaginaries. For example, a pamphlet created in 1913 for the Panama-California Exposition by the Board of Supervisors and the Chamber of Commerce, titled "The Harbor of the Sun," captured how San Diego envisioned itself. The cover image depicted lines emanating out from San Diego toward the East Coast, Central and South America (including via the Panama Canal), and across the Pacific Ocean to Asia. The text of the pamphlet suggested that San Diego was at the edge of empire, a city whose climate and scenery made it ideal for "the healthseeker and retired capitalist."[62] This outlook begged for synergistic enterprises, and Tingley exploited them. Theosophical teaching viewed human development as cyclical, with moments of renewal. The turn of the century marked "the dawn of a new cycle"; indeed, the final two lines of the cornerstone that Tingley laid in February 1897 read,

UNIVERSAL BROTHERHOOD
NEW CYCLE. YEAR ONE.[63]

Flattered by Tingley's decision to make it the "world center" of universal fraternity, the mayor recommended the city council pass a resolution thanking Tingley.[64] The *San Diego Union* highlighted the community's events and published supportive accounts of her work.[65] In an early interview, Tingley explained that she selected California because it possessed "rare advantages for the development of the physical, mental, and spiritual powers of man. The equable climate, the glorious touch which Nature has given to shrub, flower and field, the beauty of sea and sky and the rare atmosphere, afford marvelous opportunities" for the organization's international humanitarian work.[66]

Tingley's efforts in Southern California fit into broader patterns of social activism in the early twentieth century, when female Anglo middle-class reformers found public roles for themselves in civic campaigns in public health and sanitation, parks, and Americanization efforts.[67] Pundits noted that Anglo women in Los Angeles were strivers who eagerly circulated petitions, attended meetings, proposed ordinances, and formed political clubs.[68] Although the Besant-led Adyar Theosophists were more radical in their politics and outlook, the Point Loma community in many ways reflected the broader type of reform-related activism that was emerging among prosperous white women. Women constituted about 60 percent of the community during most of its existence. The community appealed to middle- and upper-class women with backgrounds in Christianity, Judaism, or Spiritualism and rewarded its female members with prominent cabinet positions.[69] Tingley recruited women through the Women's International Theosophical League and "women only" lectures during speaking tours.[70] In addition, the organization engaged in education and prison reform; it opposed capital punishment; it provided relief to victims of natural disasters; and it offered support to working-class women. Tingley herself had a history of such actions; while still based in New York City, she had helped establish both an orphanage (the Lotus Home) and a gardening system for the poor in Buffalo and had collected aid for soldiers fighting in Cuba during the Spanish American War.[71] To cynics, the region's parochial tastes derived from the strong female hand guiding cultural affairs. Willard Huntington Wright, for example, complained that the female leadership in politics and culture reeked of "the aggressive cologne of a village trying to improve itself."[72] Anglo women nevertheless had an important role in creating middlebrow taste in Southern California.

At the same time, it is possible to contextualize these efforts within the emerging understandings of California as the new center of American empire. Although Los Angeles and San Diego competed for primacy during the late nineteenth century, the Southern Pacific railroad's expansion into Los Angeles and surrounding communities spurred migration and development and allowed the city to establish itself as the "regional metropolis" by 1885.[73] Nevertheless, a "Southern California" regional identity emerged that cast the area as an engine of progress. At the turn of the century, Anglo boosters in Southern California invented a Mediterranean—especially Spanish but also Greek and Italian—tradition of climate, vegetation, and architecture.[74] Even as the booster literature sought to attract industrious people, the Mediterranean vision in these renderings highlighted an obtainable life of "beauty and leisure" for migrants that blended American efficiency and productivity with Mediterranean leisure. In 1891, Charles Dudley Warner published *Our Italy*, in which he wrote longingly about California's promise for achieving a lifestyle where "there will be a little more leisure, a little more of serene waiting on Providence, an abatement of the restless rush and haste of our usual life." Having reached the West, Anglos might find that "conditions of life will be somewhat easier there, that there will be some physical repose."[75] Bolstered by racial and ethnic privilege, Anglos safeguarded which identities could exist and the stories that could be told in this location. Historian Carey McWilliams subsequently identified this tradition as the Spanish fantasy heritage (or Spanish fantasy past).[76]

Although historians have associated this racial imaginary with regional narratives (and real estate promotion), it might also be connected to broader imperial discourses that emerged in the same era because, as historian Paul Kramer explains, "histories of U.S. race making . . . belong in the transnational frame from which they have long been isolated."[77] Whether it was novels, parades, plays, public histories, world fairs, or architectural styles, this Anglo ideology of racial dispossession, displacement, and erasure ascribed agency and historical action to Europeans. The tradition rendered indigenous peoples and Mexicans within a Spanish past of "romantic chivalry, preindustrial innocence, and harmonious hierarchy" while rationalizing historic and contemporary containment or removal of these groups and, ultimately, excluding them outright or giving them only a limited role in defining their own or the region's history or its future. As Phoebe Kropp has shown, these regional tales foretold Southern California's role as "the vanguard of American progress and civilization." Elite Anglo women organized clubs that took up the cause of historic preservation, especially reviving awareness of the Camino Real, a historical route that restored missions and other Spanish-era sites and linked them along an improved road. In valorizing the Spanish conquest, thereby erasing Spanish violence as well as indigenous claims to the land, they positioned themselves as the heirs of earlier efforts at transplanting European civilization. Moreover, they helped create an exclusionary tourist economy based in a racialized nostalgia that allowed for a reinvention of California history; people of color appear in the historical narrative only when called upon by Anglo settlers, who served as the heralds of progress.[78]

The Spanish fantasy heritage was but one example of the historically based imaginaries of belonging and exclusion in which Anglo boosters validated their past and present existence and erased or minimized those of marginalized others. Allusions to Mediterranean classical antiquity—rich with metaphors about the upward trajectory of American power and cleansed of the racial or ethnic diversity or socioeconomic hierarchies of those historical societies—emerged in the state seal, marketing campaigns, landscape design, public works projects, architecture, and theatrical performances.[79] Enthusiasts characterized these efforts as self-reinvention with a propensity for lavish spectacle; detractors dismissed them as pretentious scams that preyed on aspirational identities. Even if it seemed paradoxical, middlebrow bohemianism was a bankable strategy. Aimee Semple McPherson, a Pentecostal minister and the founder of the Foursquare Gospel, and Katherine Tingley excelled at the emerging spectacles of "edutainment" that edified while it entertained. Born in Canada, McPherson, like Tingley, first relocated to San Diego, where she gained notoriety by dropping tracts from an airplane and by holding revival meetings in Balboa Park and at Dreamland, a boxing arena. Carey McWilliams suggested that McPherson drew inspiration for her church from Tingley before moving to Los Angeles in 1922 and building the Angeles Temple. McPherson transfixed members of the press, many of whom developed a morbid fascination with her antics, by employing early public relations tactics.[80] Her personal charm, flair for pageantry, and relentless positivity attracted droves of fellow transplants.

Like McPherson, Tingley had a knack for institution building, having honed her skills in the parlors of wealthy New York City donors. The Theosophists' lifestyle fit within the booster vision for attracting white migrants from the East. Critics dismissed Tingley as a petty autocrat, but admirers saw a "Master Builder" worthy of adulation.[81] For example, a profile in the Los Angeles Herald observed that William Q. Judge, Madame Blavatsky's successor, was "pre-eminently a philosopher," but Tingley was "pre-eminently an accomplisher," with an entrepreneurial spirit that captivated entrepreneurs themselves.[82] Tingley's programming offered educational uplift at a higher register of prestige than McPherson's Angeles Temple. Whereas McPherson delivered "illustrated sermons" by, for example, dressing as a motorcycle policeman or as a maiden threatened by the "gorilla" of evolution, Tingley's symposia served a similar purpose of attracting and engaging audiences with accessible but more highbrow cultural forms. Tingley asserted this was a key intervention of the Universal Brotherhood in comparison to both its predecessors and rival factions. The organization purported to have dispensed with "Sanscrit [*sic*] terms and metaphysical expressions" in an effort toward accessible and "practical realization" of its goals.[83] The notion of practical philosophy aligned with the Progressive Era's understandings of applying sciences to solve social issues. In the words of one visitor, Theosophy was a system of "pure science applied to daily life."[84] Beyond humanitarian concerns of teaching "brotherhood," the organization declared its subsidiary purpose "to study ancient and modern religion, science, philosophy and art" and "to investigate the laws of nature and the divine powers in man."[85] In other words, the organization engaged in the type of cultural taste-making that skeptics mocked. The arms of the organization included the Theosophical Society (its literary department), the Isis Conservatory of Music, the Isis League of Music and Drama, the Raja School of Yoga, the School for the Revival of the Lost Mysteries of Antiquity, the Eastern and Esoteric School, and the Theosophical Publishing Company. The colony planted fifty thousand trees, experimented in fruit growing, and produced honey. It had literary magazines, dramatic productions, symposia, correspondence courses, international crusades, and local bureaus to disseminate its material. Many of its residents, such as painters Maurice Braun and Reginald Machell, were well-respected artists, writers, or musicians known for incorporating Theosophical themes into their work.

Even the architecture served a pedagogical function rich in historical fantasy. When the community arrived, there was already an on-site hotel-sanitarium built by a member a year or two before. Drawing on the resources of her wealthy members, Tingley added the aquamarine glass dome above the rotunda and plastered the exterior with a stucco that made it appear to be stone. This building became known as the Homestead Building. The nearby Temple building was often described as "Moorish" in its architectural influences. To demarcate the transition from the outside world to the community, Tingley added an "Egyptian gate" at an entrance that led to the Greek Theater and named the tents housing literary staff "Camp Karnak" after a famous temple complex in Egypt.[86]

Classical Greek and Roman cultures were the most important pieces of Tingley's plan for enlightening the masses. The celebration of antiquity existed in tension with contemporary racial and ethnic hierarchies: in the late nineteenth century, white nationalists were loath to accept

FIGURE 1. Visitors to Lomaland entered through either the Egyptian Gate or, pictured here, the Roman Gate. In early images like this one, taken in the community's first decade of existence, the main buildings are fully visible; however, photographs taken a decade later show that the community's gardens, including the palm plants along the road visible here, had grown enough to create a lush entranceway, nearly obscuring the Raja Yoga Academy. Photo from contemporary postcard.

immigrants from southern (and eastern) Europe, yet Americans positioned the United States as the inevitable heirs of Mediterranean classical antiquity. Based in part on archaeological discoveries, the nineteenth century witnessed a renewed interest in antiquity as references flourished in architecture, landscape design, literary and visual culture, and performance. Mediterranean antiquity filled in for the assumed absence of a premodern and pre-European past in North America, further erasing indigenous and Mexican existence in the past and present.[87] Through these cultural and architectural markers, Tingley created an air of seriousness while also bestowing world historical legitimacy on American global power. And, as with the racial whitewashing that occurred within Californian notions of progress, participants recreating classical antiquity imagined a monochrome "white" society. Visitors to Point Loma were immediately aware of the influence when, upon their arrival, they stopped at a sentinel house called the "Roman gate" (figure 1). Art historian Peter J. Holliday explains that Lomaland's Greek Theater (figure 2) and its productions helped cement the community's reputation. Tingley claimed to have based the theater on the ancient amphitheater built at

FIGURE 2. Built in 1902, the Greek Theater at Lomaland offered a view of the Pacific Ocean. The theater was the site of many of the community's productions, including *Aroma of Athens* and *A Midsummer Night's Dream*. Photo from the Clark B. Waterhouse Photograph Collection, Smith-Layton Archives at the Sourisseau Academy for State and Local History, San Jose State University.

Taormina in Sicily in the third century BCE. The Lomaland theater sat twenty-five hundred with eleven steps of cement seats set around the stage. Audience members had a spectacular view of the Pacific Ocean. Productions met the popular demand for outdoor performances.[88] A syndicated piece raved about the revival of "old Greek mystery plays and symposiums" performed not out of professional ambition but out of the community's "altruistic and humanitarian work" to educate the public.[89]

Live performances were among the most well-known events staged by Lomaland. Performances at the Greek Theater and the Fisher Opera House, a performing arts center in downtown San Diego that Tingley purchased and renamed the Isis Theater, became an important springboard for Theosophists' community engagement in San Diego. The opening of the dramatic season was community news.[90] The performances met a popular demand for content about antiquity. Although college campuses at the time presented Greek plays in the original languages, Tingley offered translated "classical" performances with elaborate costumes as well as crowd-pleasing dancing and singing numbers—a kind of vaudeville mixed with classical

FIGURE 3. Cast of the 1912 production of *The Aroma of Athens* performed by Raja Yoga students at the community's Greek Theater and directed by Katherine Tingley. Photo courtesy of the Theosophical Society Archives (Pasadena, CA).

content that aimed to be "elevating and instructive."[91] Tingley closely supervised every detail—from dialogue to scenery to costume to props like weaponry and chariots—of each production and sent scripts to affiliated lodges across the country.[92] Even when locals were not present, residents frequently dressed for gatherings in modified "Greek" costumes described as a "cheesecloth garment without sleeves, belted with a cord around the waist."[93] The performances were consistent with the Brotherhood's claims that they were unlocking common truths known in earlier iterations of history, creating a kind of archaeology of the universal intellect that elevated certain traditions—and enacted it on the site—and relegated others to the historical dustbin. It also allowed the Brotherhood to exploit understandings about the American inheritance of classical values, which provided an air of dignity to what might otherwise be characterized as community theater for wealthy colonists—or, to contemporary audiences, as "cosplay." Members of the troupe, often including children, staged productions of Aeschylus's *Eumenides*, and Shakespeare's *A Midsummer Night's Dream* (set in Athens with mythical Greek characters).[94] Their most famous production was *Aroma of Athens*, a dramatic

FIGURE 4. Children of the Raja Yoga School with the caption "Point Loma Children in One of Their Fairy-Plays." Profiles of the Point Loma community often featured photographs of the community children in historical dress receiving training in music, drama, or other fine arts. Published in *Out West* magazine, 1903.

symposium that conveyed Theosophist concepts through philosophical discussions interspersed with dances and recitations (figure 3). Lest anyone miss the connection between Lomaland and ancient Greece, Tingley solicited testimonials for the 1911 staging of the symposium from classics scholars, some of whom were Theosophists.[95]

Photographs from colony productions provide visual evidence of the organization's sense of cultural and historical inheritance. When the Isis League performers presented scenes of "Socrates and His Disciples" and *The Iliad*'s "Parting of Hector and Andromache," the photo and engraving department captured scenes on film for souvenir albums. A photograph of the cast in full costume was even available as a postcard for visitors. The prominence of children in community photographs, however, offers some of the clearest evidence of the colony's expansive historical imagination. The changing world may have inculcated a sense of "weightlessness" for this generation of adults, but children retained their wholeness. Educational experiences were therefore imbued with new significance while also providing a justification for notions of civilizational development as the United States became an imperial power.

Given Tingley's focus on achieving utopian progress through the education of the next generation, it is no surprise that feature articles about the organization were often accompanied by photographs of children's activities at the Raja Yoga School (figure 4). The school opened with five students in 1900 and over the years educated at least six hundred to seven hundred students from twenty-six nationalities by 1929. Scholars of Theosophy have noted that educational experts praised the progressive orientation of student education, which sought to cultivate the "higher nature" of the soul while disciplining the "lower nature," which included instincts and hereditary features, to create a balanced nature and bring out the child's inner "soul-qualities." Children began their education by age eighteen months, although full-time schooling did not begin until a few years later. Their days were regimented with a mix of meditation, classroom schooling, practical labor for the community or gardening, and sports. In the evening, students had music or drama rehearsal or studied.[96] Parents visited children on Sundays. Virtually every story about the school presented a similar didactic tableau wherein children were coaxed into adapting necessary dispositions to achieve modern "development" and "progress." Photographs connected children, known to be from around the world, to historical events that suggested they were being provided with correct social and cultural training. For example, one early profile—a defense of recently arrived schoolchildren, many of them orphans, from Cuba whose immigration was slowed by officials in New York City—showed children in fanciful outfits: girls wearing light flowing gowns and laurel wreaths, boys dressed as ancient Greek soldiers with spears and shields, all standing by a May pole as evidence of the value of the education children received.[97]

The Raja Yoga children's pageants depicted in a 1909 *San Diego Union* story provide another representation of this imagined inheritance of American-led excellence. In the photo spread, young boys stood at attention before an American flag; children were dressed as Amazon attendants of Queen Hippolyta in a production of *A Midsummer Night's Dream*; a very young boy and girl wore elaborate George and Martha Washington costumes; and a young boy outfitted as "Father Christmas" received the "heralds of all nations" at the annual holiday pageant.[98] Although it was common at the time to engage the heterogeneous population of school-age children in the United States in public commemoration rituals, such depictions—influenced by Romanticism's renderings of ancient civilizations—offered Point Loma, and California more generally, as a place where Anglo migrants united nature and culture into a bucolic future civilization based on acquired (or unlocked) wisdom. The content showed the ways that the school exposed its students—vessels for knowledge—to the world's inherited wisdom regardless of time or space. The effect was to flatten the passage of time and to create a narrative of a bountiful, inexhaustible reserve of American-led cultural inheritance with no awareness of an unequal power dynamic. It also showed a community hard at work at pursuing outdoor leisure and classical erudition. This vision of education may not have depicted a city of suburban homes, but it did match San Diego's boosters' vision of "genteel consumption" lived in the great outdoors.[99]

In fact, although the *Los Angeles Times* centered part of its defense in the libel case on the separation of children from parents, the education and training of children was the basis of much of the positive coverage that Lomaland received. The coverage also reveals the hierarchies embedded within Theosophical (and booster) visions of racial inclusion. Madame Blavatsky had blended American exceptionalism with emerging notions of internationalism by positioning the United States as the "racial nursery" that would become the "vanguard" of a new "subrace" through a progressive process of reincarnation. These beliefs underpinned the efforts to educate children at the Raja Yoga School. As W. Michael Ashcraft explains, Theosophical thinkers approved of racial mixing in theory but were ambivalent about the practice. There were no African Americans in residence, and the community often featured the Cuban children as exemplars of its reform work. The United States was not merely a rising empire in a world of empires. Tingley founded the Universal Brotherhood just as the United States acquired territories via the Spanish-American War and as it debated the terms of Cuban independence, underlining the relevance and inculcation of "self-government" for territories and the individuals that lived within them. The photographs implied that the United States was the "birthplace for greater brotherhood" achieved through "higher patriotism."[100] Tingley's work typified the contradictory impulses operating in the United States between paths to "good citizenship" and hierarchies of race and national origin.[101] Articles noted the students from England, Germany, France, Ireland, Sweden, Finland, Hungary, Greece, Japan, and Spain, but most of the attention focused on the Cuban children. Some of the Cuban children were orphans; others were—at least according to reports—members of intact wealthy and middle-class families.

Charles Fletcher Lummis, one of the region's most famous boosters, was among those who viewed the Universal Brotherhood's Raja Yoga as a forward-thinking cultural nursery. As editor of *The Land of Sunshine* (later renamed *Out West* and then *Overland Monthly and Out West*) from 1895 to 1905, Lummis expounded on the importance of leisure and recreation as a place for white Americans to restore their mental and physical powers.[102] An episode in 1902 allowed Lummis to opine on the work of Tingley's utopian community and its role in bringing about a regional culture of healthful outdoor living. Treasury Department officials—along with members of the New York Society for the Prevention of Cruelty to Children (also known as the Gerry Society)—detained Point Loma–bound Cuban orphans at Ellis Island pending an investigation of the school. Lummis leaped at the opportunity to defend a convert to California charms—Tingley was born in Massachusetts—against the East Coast establishment.

Lummis argued that there were artistic and altruistic lessons to be learned from California's civilization. An examination of the community's publications demonstrates an aesthetic affinity—or perhaps cribbing—between Lummis's *Land of Sunshine/Out West* and the Universal Brotherhood's publications. As art historian Jennifer Watts explains, under Lummis's supervision, *Land of Sunshine* used gardens and children—especially in photographs—as stand-ins for Southern California's regional identity.[103] Similarly, he argued that Tingley had carved out a garden space for recreation for her Anglo followers and, moreover, a place for the edification of children who arrived to study there. Lummis used his "California Babies" column to project the dominant regional imagination of a white future by featuring Anglo offspring. His feature about the Raja Yoga School showed the recently arrived Cuban children and visiting Cuban dignitaries with the same aesthetic, demonstrating that Tingley's community worked within the dominant cultural ethos.[104] The article included seventeen photographs in a fourteen-page spread depicting the "Lotus Buds and Blossoms of the Raja Yoga School" (figure 5). Reflecting *Out West*'s theme for setting children in nature, one photo depicted the children eating lunch outside under newly planted eucalyptus trees; in a detail that reveals the disparity between the community's representation of children in "natural" garden settings and the constructed reality of that rendering, the most common eucalyptus, the blue gum, was a nonnative tree first introduced to California during the Gold Rush and now considered an invasive species. The Raja Yoga School had clear notions regarding how to induce discipline and health; even non-orphans lived apart from their parents in the dorms.[105] Although Lummis did not

FIGURE 5. Students outdoors with their teacher. Reflecting California's regional identity, the photo depicted the children eating lunch with their teacher under eucalyptus trees. Published in *Out West* magazine, 1903.

advocate separating children from parents, he believed that California's atmosphere spawned children who were physically robust and mentally fit (depicted with books or with reflective gazes). Through these depictions of children in nature, *Out West* argued that Los Angeles was "an incubator for a better, more productive race," which matched Tingley's ideas about the formation of a new cycle of history.[106]

The Universal Brotherhood showcased children in demonstrations that exhibited its cosmopolitan view of humanity, yet its assimilationist tendencies also exhibited what historian Paul Kramer has referred to as "inclusionary racism" that placed non-Anglos along a slower-moving track of development and in need of guidance.[107] As with the *Out West* feature, journalists frequently reported seeing (no doubt preselected) uniformed children of different ethnic and economic backgrounds engaged in learning a musical instrument, marching to or singing a tune, performing a play or a precocious recitation, or engaged in structured outdoor activities. Girls were dressed in uniform white dresses with laurels and were surrounded by flowers; to reinforce the notion that the girls themselves were part of nature's bloom, the caption read "Raja Yoga Sunbeams." (See figures 6 and 7.) The photographs, however, told a specific story of historical succession, hierarchy, and uplift. The photographs in

FIGURE 6. The children's string orchestra at Point Loma in 1902 with several interesting figures, identified as Albert Spalding (standing at far right), the son of the founder of Spalding sporting goods; E. August Neresheimer, a diamond broker and leader of the society; and several of the Cuban children who lived in the community (seated on floor). Magazines often commented on and featured photographs of the classical learning, and it was significant that the photo depicted Cuban children receiving the same education as the children of wealthy members. Photo courtesy of the USC Digital Library, California Historical Society Collection.

the Lummis story showed eleven Cuban children in their Raja Yoga uniforms. The images hinted at an imperial ideology: having defeated Spain in the Spanish-American War, the United States had taken in the children of its empire and assumed responsibility for their education. Other stories provided a bit more detail about the children's education, although they were still not named. For example, a 1901 article described a group of nine- to fifteen-year-old boys, including several recently arrived "Cuban" and "Spanish" boys, as they performed military drills. The piece claimed that, while the Cuban and Spanish children arrived with antagonistic feelings toward one another, their discipline had improved and, according to Tingley, they had "nearly lost all feeling of animosity toward each other."[108] The uniforms and education erased the Spanish cultural influence the Cuban children might have carried,

FIGURE 7. Girls from the Raja Yoga Academy, ca. 1910–1915. The written caption read "Children at Raja Yoga Academy, Point Loma," but a typed caption underneath identified the girls as "Raja Yoga Sunbeams." The community frequently took photos of girls surrounded by flowers to highlight the connection between children and nature. Library of Congress, Prints and Photographs Division, LC-B2-2378-6.

mirroring broader educational efforts of "Americanization" of racially disparate groups that created "competing, complementary, and unequal forms of 'good' citizenship'" under Anglo tutelage.[109] Children therefore underscored the premise of a universal brotherhood achieved within a hierarchical racial and national structure with the United States—and Anglos—resting at the top.

TOURISM AND LEISURE

The sense of racial hierarchy and historical succession started in the American East but achieved most distinctly in the West was even clearer in the religious and historical imagination rendered by Southern California's tourist economy. Restorative modern leisure allowed seekers to look to bygone eras to cure the fragmented modern self. If appeals to brotherhood allowed Lomaland members to imagine transcultural solidarities with other regions of the world, the community's historical imagination provided transhistorical mastery across multiple ancient pasts. This aligned with efforts among some late nineteenth-century elites to turn to historical practices—for example, medieval pastoralism and "ancient" Asian religious ideas—in a search for intense experience.[110] The experiential culture at Lomaland perhaps offers another example of this longing for authenticity and a connection to a historical past. At the same time, these efforts complemented civic boosters' work to cultivate Mediterranean traditions that promised to alleviate modern ailments through robust experience lived in a healthful climate. Contemporary geographers linked prevailing climate to issues of "character, constitution, and productive energy" and believed, as one leading textbook author asserted, that when European or Anglo peoples had expanded or settled in temperate regions, the "influence of warm ocean currents and warm winds" had created a "great number of powerful civilized nations." These educational currents meshed with civic fantasies that considered San Diego (and American) history to be a story of racial succession in which, in the words of a *San Diego Union* column, the "Saxon" and "Latin" converged, and "the weaker was absorbed by the stronger, but with the passing of the weaker they left a legacy of their art and culture, which the survivor has gladly possessed to beautify and decorate his own."[111] Anglo settlers imagined themselves as part of a historical continuum that carried progress into the region after the Mexican War while displacing or relegating people of color to the past. The heritage allowed visitors to envision themselves as actors within an unfolding historical drama with rich cultural inheritance; at the historical end point, Anglo-Saxons in the United States became a world power. In his 1908 proposal for San Diego's city plan, John Nolen, the landscape architect hired by the city's Civic Improvement Committee, described his plan to summon "the peculiar opportunity for joy, for health, for prosperity, that life in Southern California, more especially in San Diego, offers to all."[112]

Lomaland did not build in the Spanish revival style, but its proximity to coastal resorts and "Spanish" sites as well as the accessibility of its architecture, gardens, and public performances made it a popular side trip in tour books. Lomaland's embrace of classical antiquity, in fact, allowed tourists to envision themselves within a range of Mediterranean pasts. San Diego–based newspapers offered favorable copy that amounted to human-interest features. In these accounts, Point Loma—dismissed as "a dreary and almost desolate spot" in an early *Los Angeles Times* account—emerged as a lifestyle paradise.[113] These accounts matched efforts among San Diego boosters to build the economy around suburban living, consumerism, and health and wellness.[114] An interview with

Tingley by a tourist, recently departed from England in December—
ebulliently described the cross-country trip to California, noting the
change in "climate and aspect" as fruit and olive groves and fields of
flowers and exotic plants appeared on the landscape near Los Angeles. The author affirmed author Charles Dudley Warner's designation
that the region was "Our Italy"—though superior due to the absence of
malaria—and compared the view at Point Loma to Vesuvius and the bay
of Naples. The report described the architecture in similarly animated
terms.[115] A profile showed sporting goods magnate Albert Spalding,
"in the full of vigor of life," comfortably living out his years in a mansion
that overlooked the ocean and combined "the Egyptian, the Greek and
the Mexican" types of architecture. The aroma of the rose garden and
nearby lemon and orange groves along with date palms swaying in the
breeze provided the backdrop to an interview where Spalding explained
that he had arranged his business affairs so they only required him to be
in Chicago or New York once a year, allowing him more time for gardening, fishing, horse riding, and golfing at the nine-hole course that he
installed at his residence (he had also become involved in real estate development in nearby neighborhoods like Sunset Cliffs).[116]

Other articles marketed the aspirational qualities of the good life
available to those who settled in the colony or the surrounding community. An article in the *San Diego Union*'s annual year-in-review edition
suggested that Point Loma's members were "front rank" in the fields of
medicine, journalism, arts, and law but had earned a right to learn and
to train in the accumulated wisdoms (i.e., "the science of life") of earlier cultures in a natural environment that had been made into "a fairy-
land."[117] Local entrepreneurs took note of the prestige that Theosophists'
famous residents provided. In 1910, a developer heralded the opening of
"Point Loma City," promising that he would create affordable "estates"
at modest prices—like suburban homes. Like many lifestyle features, the
ad mentioned Charles Dudley Warner's affinity for Point Loma's views
in *Our Italy*. In Point Loma, "the skies are bluer and kinder, with their
incessant health-giving sunshine; the waters below are more sparkling,"
and nearby San Diego was "springing magically . . . into being one of the
great business centers of the new Pacific West, where is being made the
money that will reproduce upon these slopes for its owners all that is
entrancing in the architecture and outdoor art of the Old World Italy,
combined with what is best of the New World."[118]

Utopian communities in American history have often set themselves apart from the rest of society to achieve their goals.[119] Lomaland,

however, saw opportunity in outsiders. The community positioned itself as part of the California tourist economy—or, at the very least, believed it could recruit among novelty-seeking tourists. The society maintained the Theosophical Information Bureau at the U.S. Grant Hotel, San Diego's flagship luxury hotel, to provide literature to the curious and sell tickets to productions at the Isis Theatre.[120] The community also partnered with a local sightseeing company, the Clover Leaf, to provide accompanied excursions on the grounds during high tourist season and claimed to have hosted one hundred thousand guests in 1915.[121] The grounds were open for several hours each day to visitors who paid ten cents for admission; school-aged children put on a special program every weekday from 3 p.m.–4 p.m.[122]

In establishing its place in the tourist economy, the Universal Brotherhood extended hospitality to a wide range of visitors. Early on, the Universal Brotherhood became a fixture in press junkets—alongside visits to Fort Rosecrans, the Hotel Coronado, and visits to the ocean—hosted by the Chamber of Commerce. In the leadup to the Panama-California Exposition in 1915, the city hosted members of the Southern California Editorial Association and their families on multiple occasions (Tingley seemed to serve as the vice president of the association in 1913).[123] In hosting the journalists, the Chamber of Commerce secured positive coverage of the "marvel of achievement" and "future promise" of the "City of Bay 'n' Climate."[124] Tingley also welcomed a range of visiting dignitaries—American and foreign politicians, educators, writers, thespians, nurses, and even solitary sojourners from Northern California—for tours of the grounds and performances by the schoolchildren.[125]

The cooperation brought the Universal Brotherhood positive local coverage. For several years, the *San Diego Union* published a special New Year's edition that highlighted aspects of the city's economic growth including agriculture, manufacturing, education, public infrastructure, and construction; seemingly every piece—whether addressing lumber, honeybees, or precious stones—invited readers to marvel at the "great activity," "exceptional opportunities," "splendid progress," and "exceedingly bright" future of the city. Point Loma was no exception, as it was consistently included in the annual feature.[126] The 1907 edition opened with dramatic photographs of the Brotherhood's properties in Sweden, Cuba, England, and Point Loma, allowing readers to imagine San Diego as the cosmopolitan center of a broad international movement. The author linked growing interest in San Diego with Lomaland's international reputation. The accompanying text compared the climate and setting in Point Loma to Greece and Rome in the Mediterranean "Golden Age." The author—and, according to an accompanying headline, Tingley herself—promised the site was certain to become "an Athens, a sacred and high place" where the "slums, divorce, courts, crime, vice, poverty, misery" of Eastern cities vanished amid the innovations of the Universal Brotherhood. This new Athens promised to become a flourishing center for education, the arts, music, and literature.[127]

Over time, so many dignitaries visited the colony that it became part of the broader San Diego tourist circuit. Although early guides mentioned it as a side attraction, auto touring guidebooks eventually invited readers into more romantic and interactive itineraries through multiple Mediterranean pasts etched into the built environment. The terrain became infused with more mystery and historical significance, not just outdoor pleasures and tourist amenities. The community therefore became a stop for those seeking out historical sites associated with John Steven McGroarty's *The Mission Play* (1912), a pageant drama that, in the words of the author, presented "the sublime story of the founding of the white man's Christianity and civilization on the western shores of America."[128] Reflecting the prevailing racialized view of white boosters, the opening act of the play, "The Founding of the Missions," presented the arrival of a galleon in the Bay of San Diego to intervene in an encounter between Junipero Serra, Spanish soldiers, and indigenous people. The 1913 rebranding and restoration of the Point Loma lighthouse, which was originally built by the United States government in 1854, as the "old Spanish lighthouse"—along with the surrounding area's designation as the Cabrillo National Monument—improved its historic luster.[129] Lomaland specialized in scenic and historic flights of fancy. *The Tourist's California* (1914), a guidebook that firmly positioned San Diego within the mission narrative, mentioned the colony's outdoor playhouse, its staging of Greek classics, and the "turrets and domes" of the headquarters.[130] *Across the Continent by the Lincoln Highway* (1915) remarked upon the "beautifully kept grounds of the fine property belonging to the School of Theosophy" as an attraction on the way to the vista at the "little old Spanish lighthouse."[131] *On Sunset Highways*, a travelogue published in 1915, included a brief tour at the Theosophical Institute provided by a member. The author, Thomas D. Murphy, was relatively unconcerned with the merit of the colony's belief system but admitted that his companion found them attractive. From a tourist's perspective, however, the appeal of the community rested in its romantic setting, manicured grounds, and peculiar architecture:

Everything about the establishment speaks of prosperity and it would be hard to imagine more beautiful and pleasing surroundings. The buildings are mainly of oriental design, solidly built and fitting well into the general plan of the grounds. Among them is a beautiful Greek theatre where plays open to the public are sometimes given. The grounds evince the skill of the landscape-gardener and scrupulous care on [the] part of those who have them in charge. ... Through these gleams the calm deep blue of the ocean, which seldom changes, for there are but few stormy or gloomy days on Point Loma. ... It is a glorious spot, well calculated to lend glamour to the—to our notion— fantastical doctrines of the cult which makes its headquarters here.[132]

The grounds may not have matched efforts underway to link Southern California to Spanish colonizers via the cultivated mystique of El Camino Real. But by offering romantic natural landscapes and an eclectic built environment, Lomaland provided a parallel curiosity that helped sell the regional historical imagination.

The Universal Brotherhood even participated in official booster activities such as the San Diego Panama-California Exposition. This was perhaps not surprising given that one of their most prominent members, Albert G. Spalding, was a key member of the organizing committee. After the event's first year, the Theosophists took over what was originally the Kansas State Building. To commemorate the exposition, the Santa Fe Railroad commissioned an essay by John Steven McGroarty, author of *The Mission Play*. The resulting essay appeared in a thirty-page booklet that documented the rise of San Diego, a city "very old in history yet very young in destiny." McGroarty managed to fit a contemporary tourist guide amid his sweeping historical narrative, including a description of the Universal Brotherhood. Following the Exposition's theme of "becoming," McGroarty connected Cabrillo's vision with the present-day development of the institute. The group transformed the grounds from "a bare waste" to "a paradise of gardens and fruitful fields" with every space "put to some use with the most exquisite taste."[133] McGroarty therefore located the community within a longer American imperial mythology that discounted indigenous land use and praised Anglo settlers' knowledge of agriculture and efforts to put "unproductive" land to cultivated use.

Theosophist literature demonstrates the degree to which the colony aligned its interests and destiny to those of the region. In October 1914, the community's magazine for children, *The Raja-Yoga Messenger*, highlighted the upcoming Exposition. The feature echoed many of the talking points advanced by civic boosters who sought to elevate the city's profile. Promoters made San Diego a symbol of California but also, more importantly, of the empire the United States was poised to become.[134] In doing so, both the *Messenger* and the Exposition it described linked the first American empire, marked by territorial expansion and settler colonialism, to the next phase of the American imperial project. The opening paragraph heralded San Diego as the "mother-city of the West, where the history of California had its beginning, San Diego preserves the flavor of ancient days without forgetting that it is a twentieth-century community." The city was connected to the nation's origins and its future trajectory, yet it also matched the Universal Brotherhood's self-imagined role; its cornerstone, after all, had established that it was "year one" of a "new cycle" of history. The unsigned article praised every aspect of the Exposition, from the way the "Exposition Idea" inspired cooperation among citizens and fostered population growth to its celebration of the completion of the Panama Canal, "that stupendous engineering achievement," to its architecture, which hewed closely to the "Spanish-Colonial type ... in keeping with the traditions and romance of California." The author promised the Exposition would show *processes*, not finished products, to improve its educational value. Most important among those processes, perhaps, was *settling* the West. The suggested aim of the Exposition was "to exploit the great West—to bring from the over-crowded cities hundreds of thousands of men and women and aid them in locating on the millions of idle acres" in the West, especially the Southwest. The Exposition could mean much to "the farmer, the manufacturer, the home-seeker, and the tourist" in highlighting the opportunities of "the Great West," adding seekers of therapeutic leisure to established methods of settler colonial processes of removal and displacement.[135] The emphasis on opportunity and development highlighted transformation. The notion of becoming—the unfolding of, say, engineering or agricultural feats but also of history—matched Anglo Americans' sense of itself as an empire of destiny and Southern California as the edge of that empire. It also matched the Universal Brotherhood's sense of a new cycle of history.

CONCLUSION

Even after Lomaland closed, the area—and the community—remained a site for signaling utopian visions. For example, in December 2012, Jacob McKean left his job as the social media coordinator at Stone Brewing Co. to fulfill his dream of opening a craft brewery.[136] He spent the next several months testing formulas and touring potential locations for a fermentorium. He ultimately selected a space in Point Loma, just a few minutes from Lomaland. McKean, who had studied the history of religious utopias as an undergraduate at Columbia University, named his brewery Modern Times after one such community founded in 1851 in Suffolk, Long Island, by Josiah Warren based on "equitable commerce" and a belief that individuals should follow their conscience rather than the dictates of any external authority.[137] In the following years, McKean's brewery named most of its products after either utopian experiments or mythological utopias. This included its first beer, a Belgian-style ale, Lomaland, a "brilliantly crazy utopian community" according to the Modern Times website. Other beers followed, including Oneida (a perfectionist community established in 1848 by John Humphrey Noyes), Fruitlands (an agrarian Transcendentalist commune established in 1843 by Bronson Alcott, the father of Louisa May Alcott), and Orderville (an LDS community founded in 1875 to restore Joseph Smith's collective-based United Order). Beers named after mythological utopias included communalist visions from around the world: Fortunate Islands (a paradise described in Greek mythology), City of the Dead (the Cairo necropolis built by Arab Muslims who conquered Egypt), City of the Sun (a description of an ideal community written by Italian philosopher Tomas Campanella in 1602 after his imprisonment for heresy), Blazing World (a 1666 satirical work by Englishwoman Margaret Cavendish describing a utopian kingdom), Space Ways (after "We Travel the Space Ways," a 1967 album by jazz musician and Afrofuturist Sun Ra), and Star Cloud (a science fiction collection of the same name published in 1980 by Taiwanese-born computer scientist Chang Hsi-Kuo); a "Hazy IPA" edition named each product in the series after a mythic figure (e.g., Caliban, a character in *The Tempest*).

McKean saw religious utopias as "colorful, ambitious little pockets of history that develop in the folds of progress, the forgotten little paradises" made up of colonists who were trying "to live, right now, in a world of enterprising, fulfilling hedonism." He hoped to make his brewery "one of those little pockets" by establishing a place that would "make beer for beer enthusiasts" and "talk largely about the process of trying to make great beer, which—absurdly—feels like something of a radical proposition in the current craft beer environment."[138] By the end of the decade, Modern Times had added coffee roasting to its business and had become a mid-sized brewery with out-of-market distribution deals across the Pacific and Mountain West and tasting rooms in San Diego, Anaheim, Los Angeles, and Portland, Oregon.

When McKean opened his storefront, craft breweries had become as numerous in San Diego as church revivals were in western New York's Burned-Over District in the 1830s. Beginning in the early 1990s, the city's craft brewery scene attached itself to the hospitality industry in San Diego. Although the city's economy owed much to the presence of military installations and sun-seeking conventioneers, in the late twentieth century a rising high-tech sector attracted affluent professionals who defined themselves by their discriminating consumer tastes. The craft brewery scene, along with surfing and yoga lifestyles of coastal areas like Point Loma as well as Encinitas, came to define this generation of the San Diego lifestyle. By 2018, when the state of California boasted over 900 craft breweries, San Diego alone had 155 such businesses that generated $848 million in revenue and had an economic impact of $1.2 billion.[139] As the industry continued to expand in the early 2010s, local beermakers lobbied for the city's high-profile sports and entertainment venues to "drink local"—that is, to feature local brews on tap to highlight the growing scene.[140] San Diego's Economic Development Corporation touted the city's status as the "Craft Beer Capital of America," citing the regional convergence of "life science and lifestyles" for industry growth; the state's tourism website likewise offered prospective visitors an itinerary of tasting rooms and award-winning brews for every palate.[141]

Craft breweries often draw upon community and regional histories for inspiration in names and labels (indeed, another local brewery, Pizza Port, had a product, Swami's IPA—named for a surf spot and Paramahansa Yogananda's seaside retreat—which will be discussed in chapter 5). These references highlight their hyper-local roots, especially in comparison to internationally known and distributed corporate brands. But perhaps we can find something else in McKean's desire to connect (often teetotalling, mostly abstemious) utopian communities with craft beers. Thanks to the naming protocol at a craft brewery like Modern Times, we see the continuity in the religious imagination from the turn of the twentieth century to the turn of the twenty-first century. Set apart from society, American utopias have historically allowed members to restructure social and cultural patterns of community, family, work, and leisure. They drew on past traditions to modify their present and, perhaps, realize their desired future, which involved gendered and racialized understandings of power. In founding Lomaland in 1897, Katherine Tingley sought to reconceptualize a community of belief around access to better living. Beyond merely recalling a usable past, Tingley sought to reanimate history at the "School for the Revival of the Lost Mysteries of Antiquity." Although her ambition raised suspicion among regional elites and muckrakers alike, her vision aligned with San Diego's booster imagination, which heralded the rise of a city based on restorative leisure for Anglos while requiring a particular hierarchy of power. In the early twenty-first century, San Diego and its craft breweries continued to invoke this vision of the health-conscious outdoor lifestyles available to residents and visitors. By drawing on multicultural historical and fictional religious pasts to sell a lifestyle commodity, McKean's language suggested the extent to which concepts of "better living"—including those based in religious belief—had become deeply engrained in consumer culture.

When Jacob McKean based his brews at Modern Times on real and mythic utopias, he continued a Southern California tradition of searching for usable pasts and idealized futures. In the early twentieth century, religious seekers came to California to find authentic experience through a glamorized—even curated—experience of self-betterment based in racial and class hierarchies. In doing so, they defied efforts by boosters to promote a sober and hard-working Protestant experience. The early religious activists of the "first new age" like Katherine Tingley and her followers helped establish Southern California as a place that combined refined living and intense spiritual experience in the pursuit of personal growth. They created an early example of an alternative—yet still officially endorsed in some circles—vision of Southern California as a place of therapeutic lifestyles and an endless cycle of personal and historical development often realized through consumer choice. In the future, others would increasingly search for—and find—more commercially available forms of restorative leisure.

"Efficient America," "Spiritual India," and America's Transnational Religious Imagination

In his 1946 autobiography, Paramahansa Yogananda, an Indian yogi and charismatic guru, offered insights to his American audience seeking a path to world progress. Yogananda described how his organization, the Los Angeles–based Self-Realization Fellowship (SRF), had established an exemplary "world civilization," defined by a multicultural synthesis located somewhere between what he called "efficient America and spiritual India." Beyond that lofty goal, *Autobiography of a Yogi* also focused on the individual's spiritual progress, including advice for those seeking greater mental acuity and focus. "Intuition," Yogananda wrote, "is soul guidance, appearing naturally in man during those instants when his mind is calm."[1] Yogananda's teachings and the allure of "a mystical, otherworldly India," attracted followers who sought to pair spiritual and material progress.[2] In the late twentieth century, the work became a foundational text in the emergence of "New Age capitalism" in the Silicon Valley, where entrepreneurs—including Apple CEO Steve Jobs—found in it a perfect wedding of Eastern spirituality with contemporary business acumen.[3]

Yogananda's autobiography—and its journey from Gorakhpur to Steve Jobs's tablet—reveals the consequences of the deepening of American experimentation with non-Western religions that, while providing an influx of new beliefs, nevertheless obscured the quasi-colonial power dynamic inherent in these encounters. Yogananda, one of many Indian gurus based in the United States in the twentieth century, offered an interesting bridge between Indian spirituality and American business. He spent nearly three decades synthesizing the spiritual elements of *kriya*, a meditation-based form of yoga, with liberal Christianity for American audiences.[4] He worked throughout his career to frame Indian spirituality as a complement to American business acumen. The result was a pursuit of spirituality that provided a means to self-improvement that could be, at the same time, turned toward individual material ends. Yogananda's efforts to assuage growing anxieties about the technocratic tendencies of American business proved useful for entrepreneurs like Jobs as they sought to characterize their accomplishments in novel ways.

Drawing on the writing of Yogananda and *Self-Realization Magazine*, the in-house publication of his organization, this chapter first examines how Yogananda's missionary work promised to advance the American way of life while reaffirming the traditional and authentic nature of his message. By contextualizing Yogananda's career within processes of imperialism and decolonization, America's deepening economic and political connections to the global South, and consumer-driven shifts in the American religious marketplace, we can see how, within transnational networks of ideas, "seemingly binary poles" often worked not as opposites, but as what historian Emily Rosenberg calls "nested complements that operated in creative tension with each other."[5] Yogananda provided a means for managing difference—wherein Indian "spiritual science" provided a balance with American "material science"—while seeking to forge greater sentimental, cultural, and commercial connections between the nations.

Having shown how Yogananda's career sought to reconcile American and Indian notions of civilizational "exceptionalism" at a moment of American imperial expansion, the second half of the chapter demonstrates Yogananda's legacy on American business practices in service of a California brand of capitalist cosmopolitanism. Yogananda correctly anticipated an intensified crisis in confidence surrounding Western-based material knowledge. After his death, devotees found new uses for his message about material and spiritual progress. "New Age capitalism" devotees drew from his ideas as well as sixties-era countercultural ideas to describe their techno-utopian visions for the information age economy that promised self-actualization through personal technology. Seeking to defy the button-downed rationality of mid-century institutions, Silicon Valley figures like Steve Jobs deployed concepts like "intuition" to describe their desire to use personal technology as a tool to drive economic growth and social change.

Over the course of the twentieth century, global exchanges informed the development of the American transnational religious and spiritual imagination. As the United States developed a more formal global hegemony, American beliefs articulated and nurtured transnational attachments that "pulsed above, below, and through the more formalized structures of national states, empires, and international institutions."[6] Scholars in several disciplines have questioned the power relationships that emerged within American-style multiculturalist globalization. Stuart Hall describes this American-led process as "a homogenizing form of cultural representation, enormously absorptive of things, . . . but the homogenization is never absolutely complete, and it does not work for completeness. . . . It is wanting to recognize and absorb those differences within the larger, overarching framework of what is essentially an American conception of the world." This type of hegemony works through, rather than against, difference while still shaping the terms of that difference. The United States, according to Hall, created a globalized sense of "difference" that appropriated "new exotics" in the production and sale of postwar mass culture.[7] Although participants in transnational networks sought to advance universalism in opposition to the particularism of nation-states and empires, their presumptions at times drew upon implicit racial and imperial understandings of superiority. The religious transnationalism of the early twentieth century navigated between universal and particular claims; indeed, Yogananda excelled at reconciling these types of "differentiated commonalities."[8] We must therefore examine how shifting historical contexts and imperatives altered the claims and how ideas that in one era articulated universal concepts in the longer term became wedded to dominant power structures.

Yogananda's civilizational imaginary exemplifies a broader trajectory of American Orientalism that unfolded within American religious culture over the course of the twentieth century. Modern yoga emerged from a long history of transnational exchanges rather than a transplantation of an "authentic" process from one culture to another.[9] American Orientalism, according to critic Vijay Prashad, associated "American" as "practical" and "worthy" in contrast to Indian values of "spiritual" and "ethereal"; Swami Vivekananda outlined the parameters of this dynamic when, at the World Parliament of Religions in 1893, he critiqued the West's materialism by noting, "You of the West are practical in business, practical in great inventions, but we of the East are practical in religion. You make commerce your business; we make religion our business." The notion of a morally exceptional and ancient Hindu ethos continued in the twentieth century.[10] Yogananda, in popularizing his system of *kriya* yoga, presented similar assurances to Americans to soothe concerns about their modern condition. Emerging from and refined by ongoing complex connections with the West, these beliefs were "modern, reformist, and designed to appeal to Western audiences."[11] Both Vivekananda and Yogananda exemplify early instances of what scholar Srinivas Aravamudan characterizes as "Guru English," which, while asserting South Asian spiritual superiority in the face of imperialism and the possibility of a positive East-West encounter, also came to signify a "commodifiable cosmopolitanism" accessible in the marketplace.[12]

Ideas morph over time and cannot be confined within any "original" cultural sphere; we can, however, historicize the ways that ideas became affixed to hegemonic structures.[13] This chapter interrogates one such trajectory, which eventually allowed "New Age capitalism" to connect the value of spirituality to technological and entrepreneurial innovation. The late twentieth-century efforts to harness spirituality to techno-utopian visions about personal emancipation tie to broader themes in this work regarding the ongoing optimization of individual choice and liberation. The material benefits of "spirituality" thus represented continuity, not change, in the desire to capitalize on, as Vijay Prashad has said (echoing W. E. B. Du Bois), the "karma of brown folk."[14]

YOGANANDA'S CIVILIZATIONAL MISSION

In the late nineteenth and early twentieth centuries, international conferences played an important role in the development of "cultural internationalism" that sought to foster cross-cultural understanding. Although political and economic organizations tended to exclude non-Westerners, religious and cultural symposia allowed colonized participants from places like India to articulate their vision of "civilization" and modernity to the international community. There were forty-two such exhibitions and symposia between 1851 and 1914, held to celebrate the technological and scientific advancements of modernity achieved by the United States and European nations.[15] The Universal Brotherhood documented in chapter 1, for example, held two such conferences. Cultural internationalism became more inclusive after the devastation caused by the First World War, as a "new cosmopolitanism" embraced "the whole of humanity" and worked in tandem with concepts of civilizational and national character.[16] Early twentieth-century projects to locate universal religious truths, however, existed in tension with simultaneous efforts by

American white supremacist groups to preserve a vision of "America" founded solely on Anglo-Saxon Protestantism. Newspapers like the *Washington Post*, for example, warned readers about the dangers that "Hindu mysticism" posed to women interested in non-Western spiritual pursuits, which led to a panic about the influx of yogis and a more general xenophobic antagonism toward South Asian immigrants.[17] In 1923, the Supreme Court rejected a South Asian's eligibility for citizenship in *United States v. Bhagat Singh Thind*. A year later, white nationalists—fearful of non-Protestant populations—achieved their long-term goal of excluding Asian immigrants from entry into the United States through the passage of the Johnson-Reed Act.[18] The hostility to Asian immigration continued with the publication of *Mother India*, a 1927 exposé by Katherine Mayo, about the abasement of women in India that affirmed Anglo-Saxonism in the United States and justified continued British rule based on its allegations of Hindu backwardness.[19] Yogananda therefore had every reason to carefully balance his claims for universal beliefs with civilizational claims. He nevertheless chose to settle in Los Angeles, where Progressive-era developers and boosters suppressed social and cultural diversity in pursuit of an Anglo-dominated "white" city.[20]

Yogananda arrived in the United States in 1920 for the International Congress of Religious Liberals, after which he embarked on a three-decade-long missionary career in the United States. He made claims regarding the universal truth of scientific knowledge while also asserting that particular civilizations had specialized in certain areas. As he explained in an early issue of *East-West* (later *Self-Realization*) magazine, his organization sought to present "the different good traits of Eastern and Western life in general" and to concentrate on the "universal principles for making life more beautiful," thereby minimizing "our minor differences."[21] According to Partha Chatterjee, this rhetorical framing—common among anticolonial nationalists—allowed activists to point to a material "outside" and spiritual "inside" that marked essential qualities of cultural identity, which often included ancient civilizational roots or languages.[22] The language, though essentializing, created space for the claims of gurus like Yogananda.

Transnational networks of this era tended to function along elite connections, and Yogananda was no exception.[23] Yogananda, a graduate of Calcutta University and the son of a railroad executive, was "a Westernized Hindu" before he embarked on his religious career in Los Angeles.[24] Indeed, he later recounted that his guru had urged him to finish his college degree because Western audiences would be "more receptive to India's ancient wisdom if the strange Hindu teacher has a university degree."[25] His background informed his sense of mission. Yogananda came of age during the Bengal Renaissance, when educated Indians made claims about the universal applicability of "Vedic science."[26] England tended to view India as a "lab" for the application of science and technology that proved the superiority of Western "modernity." Recent historical research, however, emphasizes "co-production" of expertise that highlights "contextualized and local knowledge" rather than "imposed" imperial knowledge.[27] Science—blended within Hinduism's universal truths and applicability—became an avenue for Indian elites to stake their claim to concepts of rationality, progress, and modernity. They used science as an instrument for religious renewal. The resulting "neo-Hinduism" had an important impact on elites and Western perceptions of Hinduism via meditation movements but was less important to denizens of rural India.[28] Yogananda's arrival in the United States to teach the "Science of Religion"—the title of his speech in Boston—was therefore the result of a long process of encounter and exchange; in his system, *science* was a term used to connote that "the techniques are based on the laws of nature and are thereby reliable."[29] "Truth," according to Yogananda, was "neither Eastern nor Western," and he promised to deliver superior scientific techniques for accessing spiritual power.[30]

Yogananda arrived in Los Angeles at a moment when American consumers were growing more receptive to the goods and ideas of other cultures. Civic leaders hosted a private reception for Yogananda at the Biltmore hotel, and his lectures filled the Music Arts Hall in 1925.[31] In the midst of anti-immigrant fears of the 1920s, Yogananda positioned himself as an antidote—steeped in antiquity but also reconciled with Christian beliefs—to modern alienation for seekers looking to connect to the wider world.[32] A *Los Angeles Times* reader in 1925 looking to attend a religious service could choose among Yogananda's lecture about "Healing by Christ-Power" at the Mount Washington center, a lecture by Swami Paramananda, a presentation about New Thought, a "gospel presentation" about "Slavery Days: Scenes from the South" by Aimee Semple McPherson at the Angeles Temple, or more traditional services by mainline Protestant denominations. Those perusing the ads for a movie or a show could select from among Yogananda's "Miracles of Yoga," Charlie Chapman's *The Gold Rush*, a production of *Madama Butterfly*, a new adventure of Rin-Tin-Tin, or various vaudeville acts.[33] Audiences received Yogananda, by all accounts an effective speaker, as a fantastic specimen: descriptions of his lectures noted his physical appearance that included "an orange robe with a Roman collar, a turban, and . . . enough long, black hair to make any of the Sutherland sisters jealous" (the Sutherland sisters were a family singing troupe known for long locks).[34] If he was aware of the Orientalist tropes that established his appeal with one segment of Americans, anti-Asian immigrant sentiment nevertheless fomented fears that he was a confidence man seducing women. Amid the broader panic generated by the publication of *Mother India* in 1928, a Miami newspaper referred to Yogananda, on tour in the South, as an "East Indian love cult leader," and Yogananda sought an injunction against a police order that demanded his departure based on alleged complaints from husbands; back in Los Angeles, the district attorney announced plans to investigate Yogananda.[35]

Yogananda sought to build on the successes of earlier gurus by appealing to liberal Christians—most often well-to-do Anglo women—who were already familiar with metaphysical traditions.[36] The third president of the SRF, Daya Mata, was a white woman born to an LDS family who joined the ashram at age seventeen and later served as president for fifty-five years; her mother and siblings also joined the order. Yogananda introduced American audiences to *kriya* yoga, a meditation system taught to him by Swami Sri Yukteswar Giri (1855–1935), an Indian guru interested in the Bhagavad-Gita and familiar with Christian doctrine based on his education at a missionary school.[37] Continuing in the universalist tradition of Indian intellectuals like Rammohan Roy, Keshab Chandra Sen, and Swami Vivekananda, Yogananda combined his beliefs with modern science as well as elements of Christianity.[38] Americans at this time tended to be receptive to meditative and philosophical more than postural styles of yoga, and Yogananda's early repertoire in the United States included a practice that wed "muscle control" to mental and spiritual techniques.[39] He explained to audiences that self-realization was "a combination of the original Christianity of Jesus and the original Yoga of Krishna."[40]

Yogananda valued "the art of spiritual living"—a consciousness of God's presence over doctrine. His approach fit within the framework of "perennial philosophy," a theologically open disposition that minimized the difference between "ritual, doctrine, and institutional reality" and played an important role in yoga's global diffusion.[41] Debates in the 1920s between modernist and fundamentalist interpretations of the Bible created an opportunity for Yogananda to establish his scientific credentials. Anthropologist Susan Harding has argued that the 1925 Scopes Trial helped define modernity through a set of oppositions "between Fundamentalist and Modern—between supernaturalist and reasoning, backward and progressive, ignorant and educated, rural and cosmopolitan, anti-intellectual and intellectual, superstitious and scientific, duped and skeptical, bigoted and tolerant, dogmatic and thinking, absolutist and questioning, authoritarian and democratic."[42] The Self-Realization Fellowship positioned itself as modern by, for example, publishing an article by botanist Luther Burbank criticizing "those who take refuge behind theological barbed wire fences" based on their fear of "scientific truth," which he found to be "exhilarating, tonic, healthful, and life giving" and which removed "the debasing sin of ignorance, the mother of misery, crime, inefficiency, superstition, bigotry, disease, and death." He protested that Americans opposed to the teaching of evolution "should also legislate against gravity, electricity, and the unreasonable velocity of light."[43]

Once settled in Los Angeles, which he called "the Benares of America," Yogananda set about creating a bustling mail-order meditation course and a network of temples.[44] By 1952, the year of his death at age fifty-nine, the Self-Realization Fellowship included seventy-two centers around the world, including several in India and Southern California, and a membership of approximately one hundred fifty thousand.[45] At that time, there were sixty renunciate monks living at the organization's Mount Washington center and another forty living at its ashram in Encinitas.

TRANSNATIONAL CONNECTIONS

Yogananda liked to tell a story that when he departed India in 1920, his father asked when he would return from his trip. Yogananda replied, "In four months, unless America needs me."[46] As it turned out, he returned to India once, in 1935, when he built a headquarters for his foundation outside of Kolkata; otherwise, he continued to expand his mission in the United States. He sought to foster closer ties between the United States and a soon-to-be postcolonial India. Yogananda's ideas found resonance at a moment when the United States sought closer economic and political ties to the Global South and as India sought and then attained its independence, established itself as the world's largest representative democracy, and sought to define its place among other nations.

There were national repercussions to Yogananda's ongoing efforts to forge global human awareness in the context of the Cold War. While white evangelical Protestants made family a site for regulating the home and unifying—or "containing," as Elaine Tyler May explains—core concepts of Cold War nationalism, individualism, and normative white heterosexual values, figures like Yogananda sought to foster positive connections between the United States and potential postcolonial allies.[47] Yogananda's vision of the American and Indian civilizational partnership worked within an imaginary of American benevolence and connectedness to the "free world"—a process of solidifying American economic and cultural hegemony that historians call "integration." As the historian Christina Klein explains in her work on Cold War Orientalism, although integration spoke to American goals of free-market capitalism—efforts that began well before the postwar era—it also included Americans' need to feel a sense of kinship or responsibility with the peoples of other nations—often expressed through a pedagogical tone. Within this process, American cultural texts articulated "narratives of anti-conquest" that formed the justification for America's new global power. Nominally tolerant and inclusive, these texts sought to establish connections between nations and peoples based on fantasies of reciprocity and commonality, often fostered through feminized or childlike tropes. "Global imaginaries" therefore played important roles in achieving both containment and integration. The former helped Americans understand the conflict in terms of "Otherness and difference" and to develop everyday social and cultural anticommunist practices rooted in fear. The latter aided in understandings of cooperation and mutuality while nevertheless relying on racial and gender hierarchies that positioned the United States at the apex of modernity.[48] Although containment sought to defend American values from exterior threats, integration sought to spread them through programs with an "expansive, optimistic, open quality." The language mirrored developments in postwar domestic life, where understandings of Asian ethnic assimilation and the creation of the "model minority myth" helped downplay concerns about American racism at a moment when the United States sought to advance its interests along the Pacific Rim. All told, this ideology fit with Americans' self-perception of their status as the "Empire of Liberty"—a nation leading other nations like Korea and Japan toward modernization and development based on mutual interests rather than conquest—in a postcolonial world.[49]

Postwar attempts at economic and cultural integration provide a context for understanding Yogananda's continued efforts at popularizing his spiritual practices by wedding meditation practices to liberal Christianity. Yogananda and *Self-Realization* voiced concerns about communism, but—given his efforts to proselytize in the United States—more often the organization's message sought to elaborate on its connections to and commonality with American culture. Until this era, proponents of postural yoga were considered "countercultural, elite, or scandalous."[50] By the time that Tirumalai Krishnamacharya and his students, B. K. S. Iyengar and K. Pattabhi Jois, brought modern postural yoga to the West, it had already been adapted to Western fitness practice. Meditative practices were, in comparison, more accepted but also considered countercultural.[51]

Since the United States lacked the long-term institutional networks of a formal empire at the outset of the Cold War, Yogananda's lectures and publications filled an informational gap about the decolonizing world.[52] In the wake of World War II, Yogananda published his memoir and most popular work, *Autobiography of a Yogi*. Having ministered to American audiences for over a quarter century, Yogananda knew how to weave a compelling and popular narrative in the tradition of what Mary Louise Pratt calls "autoethnography"—that is, "a text in which people undertake to describe themselves in ways that engage with representations others have made of them." It was, after all, Yogananda's stated intention to engage Americans regarding terms such as *modernity, civilization, science,* and *spirituality*.[53]

Told in episodic encounters that spanned from his childhood in India to his career in the United States, *Autobiography of a Yogi* narrates Yogananda's spiritual journey as well as those of his mentor (Swami Sri Yukteswar), his mentor's guru (Lahiri Mahasaya), and his mentor's mentor's guru (Mahavatar Babaji), while also relating the personalities to biblical figures like Jesus and John the Baptist. Early chapters include his interactions with living saints and significant historical individuals like Rabindranath Tagore who gladly hosted the pious, inquisitive youth. A few of the gurus, according to Yogananda's account, anointed him as a prophet ready to evangelize India's accumulated wisdom in the West, a culmination of *kriya*'s break from asceticism; an SRF pamphlet of the same era noted that Yogananda received his "Divine Mission" to the world, but "especially to the West," from God and Jesus as well as his more immediate masters.[54] Yogananda relates the tale of how Mahasaya received permission from Babaji to make the "spiritual solace" of discipleship open to "earnest seekers" who lived in the material world. In a phrase that echoes a popular Christian gospel verse (John 17:14–19), his mentor informed him, "Not of this world, you must be in it."[55] In subsequent chapters, Yogananda encounters Mahatma Gandhi and botanist Luther Burbank.

The desire to link the United States and India aligned the Self-Realization Fellowship with American foreign policy objectives that imagined international cooperation through economic and political as well as sentimental and cultural means. Readers learned about India through an array of methods. The magazine offered updates on developments at its centers across India, the world, and the United States but especially in Southern California, which included the Mt. Washington center, the Encinitas colony, an "India House" that opened in Hollywood in April 1950, and the Lake Shrine Temple that opened in Pacific Palisades in August 1950. The magazine's "Notes from the News" section offered news about contemporary India during the post–World War II period—more so than before the war—to generate awareness among its largely American audience. For example, after a series of famines hit India in the early 1940s, especially parts of Yogananda's native Bengal, *Self-Realization* lamented, "the average American is familiar with and sympathetic toward the needs of Europe, but vague and apathetic concerning the needs of 'distant Asia.'"[56] At other moments, the magazine emphasized the closeness of India and the United States by noting new flight routes between New York and India that took a shade less than forty-two hours to travel.[57] In the early postwar years, the magazine also followed the trajectory of citizenship laws through the US Congress that allowed legal entry of native Indians (rather than just Europeans born in India) to immigrate.[58]

The magazine's coverage about Partition, decolonization, and early nationhood created a narrow understanding of South Asia, minimizing the representations of India toward singular and teleological ends. Even as the 1947 Partition brought sectarian violence—including estimates of deaths that ranged from several hundred thousand to a million and the migration of 12.5 million people—and the creation of a militarized border between India and Pakistan, the tone and content of *Self-Realization Magazine* steadfastly maintained India's innate nonviolence and spirituality.[59] The magazine focused on Gandhi—even after his death—as a symbol of Indian culture. The leaders of modern-day India and Pakistan received less, if any, attention, even as they sought assistance from the United States following independence and as Jawaharlal Nehru, the prime minister of India, and Liaquat Ali Khan, the prime minister of Pakistan, made state visits to the United States in 1949 and 1950; Yogananda in fact met Nehru when he arrived in San Francisco.[60] The magazine highlighted visits from other visiting Indian dignitaries, especially the Indian consul based in San Francisco, which underscored the organization's authority in establishing links, whether diplomatic or cultural, between a newly independent India and the United States.

Self-Realization hailed the affinity between American and Indian culture. Representative democracy offered an obvious place for finding common ground.[61] For example, the magazine printed the statement from the Indian ambassador to the United States, who—while reaffirming that India was a constitutional democracy and a nominally secular state—also noted the nation's opposition to "every form of imperialism—whether economic or any other kind" and its antagonism to "all kinds of totalitarianism—colonialism or communist aggression," indicating American efforts to downplay its imperial ambitions.[62] Similarly, a lecture given by Dr. Haridas Chaudhuri, soon to become the founder of the California Institute of Integral Studies in San Francisco, observed the common commitment to democracy as well as individual and national freedom, making communism antithetical to both cultures. Like Yogananda, Chaudhuri hoped for a closer relationship between the United States and India based on exchange of the American "practical drive and initiative" and the "inner poise and balance of the Indian mind."[63]

As an organization, the SRF presented Yogananda as having an intuitive understanding of the complementary relationship between the United States and India. Yogananda positioned himself as a civilizational translator and facilitator. One pamphlet stated one of the organization's main goals as furthering "the spiritual and cultural understanding between East and West" and promoting "the constructive exchange of their finest features."[64] Yogananda fit the model of what the religious studies scholar Jane Iwamura has called the "Oriental monk," a long-established figure that provided American audiences with a "stable frame" with which they could sympathize during a moment of postcolonial change. This narrative "credentials the monk as an *ideological caregiver* who gains recognition by helping dominant white Americans gain spiritual insight and, often, political mission as they work out the meaning of their existence in modern life."[65] Although Yogananda often invoked the cause of "world brotherhood," he particularly sought to align American and Indian "civilizations" whose citizens would benefit from cultural exchange. Indeed, after his death, officials singled out these efforts for recognition. Mulk Raj Ahuja, the consul general of India based in San Francisco and a frequent visitor to the SRF centers, eulogized Yogananda as a man who saw India and the United States not as "two separate countries but the two component parts of one single plan for the development in harmony of both material and spiritual values of man." The letter repeated the

FIGURE 8. Although Paramahansa Yogananda emphasized meditation-oriented Kriya yoga, his temples also offered instruction in postural yoga, as in this 1949 photograph of him instructing students in a headstand lotus position. Photo courtesy of the *Los Angeles Daily News* Negatives (Collection 1387). Library Special Collections, Charles E. Young Research Library, UCLA.

reported last words of Yogananda—"My America—My India" which for Ahuja captured the swami's dual mission.[66] A letter from Binay R. Sen, the Indian ambassador to the United States who was present at his passing, noted, "No one has worked more . . . to bind the peoples of India and America together."[67]

Matching Yogananda's long-standing missionary message, *Self-Realization* also stressed the usefulness of Indian spirituality for improving mental and physical well-being as a means for valorizing "Indian" culture within American society. Historians already note the way that Americans viewed physical fitness as a national security issue that prevented its citizens from becoming "soft" on communism.[68] Postural yoga, as reshaped by practitioners like Indra Devi (a student of Krishnamacharya), became part of the postwar fitness culture that sought to create a healthy national body (figure 8). Yet fitness culture—not to mention international cultural exchange—included mental as well as physical practices to induce fortitude. Yogananda emphasized mental rather than physical aspects of yoga, although the magazine and yearly SRF convocations included demonstrations of postural yoga.[69] He represented his practice in a similar manner as other gurus, which was to construct yoga "as both timeless and beyond time."[70] While emphasizing *kriya* yoga's ethereal roots, Yogananda heralded its beneficial applications in modern contexts. "The goal of yoga science," he suggested, "is to calm the mind, that without distortion it may hear the infallible counsel of the Inner Voice."[71] Yogananda invoked concerns about the atomic bomb—he gave at least one talk entitled "Averting the Coming World Atomic War" in 1948—when he highlighted the potential significance of meditation in an age of anxiety.[72] In the *Autobiography*, he wrote that the dawn of the "Atomic Age" necessitated an improved "inner science of self-control" as well as "the outer conquest of Nature." The "science of yoga" might, in fact, provide the best "bombproof shelter" against "mindless destruction."[73]

SPIRITUAL AND MATERIAL PURSUITS

Over the course of his career, Yogananda's work helped Americans make sense of the dramatic economic and cultural changes they were experiencing. Historians have long observed the parallels between emerging social and economic formations and malleable American religious beliefs. These material-religious alliances have ranged from the piety of small businessmen inspired by evangelist Charles Grandison Finney during the Market Revolution to Walmart's Christian free-market ethos in the Sunbelt of the late twentieth century.[74] Efforts to redefine religious truth around "subjective religious experience" stretch back to the turn of the century, when religious thinkers shifted their end goal from "salvation to self-realization" by working within a "self-help paradigm" to guide seekers toward greater empowerment, especially within the modern consumer marketplace.[75] Yoga became part of this modern effort to reconceptualize the relationship between body, mind, and spirit; indeed, the terms "self-realization and "God-realization" were key neo-Vedantic terms that became pillars of New Age religions based in human potential.[76] New Thought and yoga practitioners also asserted that the pursuit of health and spiritual awareness could advance material goals.[77]

Yogananda was among those redefining the religious landscape according to the therapeutic needs of individual seekers.[78] His efforts coincided with the "paperback revolution" of popular psychology works in the late 1930s, which further advanced notions of mutable self-actualization.[79] From the start, Yogananda's originality rested in his "ability to sell a system that linked spiritual and material elements while allowing people to foreground one or the other, taking away the message they needed or wanted to hear." His version of *kriya* yoga promised practitioners authentic insights into the "spiritual nature of reality" that could then be turned into self-empowerment, whether in one's personal life or professional endeavors.[80] An ad in *Inner Culture* in the midst of the Great Depression told readers that they had "many untold and hidden talents" that would allow them to be "lifted from the ranks of mediocrity" if they learned to access them through self-realization. Upon finding their inner truths, they would receive "health, abundance, and happiness."[81] This messaging continued even after the economy recovered. At a time when Americans worried about becoming drones within an increasingly bureaucratic society, Yogananda's teachings offered Indian culture as a means for purposeful "self-realization."

Indeed, the Self-Realization Fellowship, like the Universal Brotherhood in Lomaland (chapter 1) and the Seventh-day Adventists in Loma Linda (chapter 4), offered potential visitors the promise of peaceful leisure that blended mental and educational uplift, physical well-being, and a salutary climate. There was something aspirational to the Self-Realization Fellowship properties—especially Encinitas hermitage, which was designed and built by devotees to provide Yogananda with a place for full-time meditation and writing. The pages of *East-West* and later *Self-Realization* updated readers on the daily activities at the Southern California locations and invited them to join in the lifestyle. Visitors received intellectual edification through a variety of dance, music, and theater programs as well as international symposia. Beginners could attend guided meditative study on Tuesday evenings. There were also "Hindu and Christian Bible classes." The locations were also able to offer accommodations for longer-term visits. The Mount Washington location, a "hilltop paradise" that featured tennis courts, a stadium, and an orchard, offered rooms that could be booked by the day or month with vegetarian meals on offer. Acolytes could sign up for all-day meditation retreats or sustained "summer training" for "spiritual and healthful influence" where they could stay for a week, two weeks, a month, two months, or longer to enroll in courses that would teach how to attain the "highest conscious contact with God" through lectures by Yogananda and demonstrations by other leaders at the Center.[82] If they could not visit the seaside retreat in Encinitas for lessons in advanced meditation, readers could at least correspond with devotees, who would send Praecepta lessons to out-of-town seekers.[83] Those who visited might actually hear Yogananda speak at public lectures offered on Thursday or Sunday evenings over the years.

Like other spiritual leaders in California who linked mental and physical wellness, Yogananda experimented with restaurant and hotel commerce as well as health foods. The hermitage in Encinitas originally featured a Golden Lotus Hotel and Cosmopolitan Café that had "unusual health meals" with "East Indian recipes" and "American dishes"; this location, which Yogananda preferred to describe as "cleansitarian" rather than vegetarian, was known for its juices and mushroom burgers. A 1948 profile in the *San Diego Union* interviewed permanent residents of the Golden World Colony from Egypt and British Guiana as well as a handful of local converts gamely working at the restaurant despite a lack of previous experience in the field.[84] Some of the produce for the restaurant was grown in gardens at the colony. An ad for the hotel highlighted access to the beaches and—in keeping with Southern California boosterism—made an appeal to retirees, especially those who were "financially stable." The goodies available at the café were also available for mail order: the fellowship's Ora-Mint Alfalfa Tea, "nutritive nuggets," and India nut steak (a meat substitute made of nuts, grain, and vegetable seasoning) were advertised alongside a section on diet and health; the same issue featured an advertisement for Carque foods, an original Southern California purveyor of "natural foods" established in the 1920s, as well as a pamphlet for "Hindu dietetics for Body Building' offered by a vendor in San Francisco.[85] Merchandise included incense sticks and cubes in different scents as well as malas (Hindu prayer beads), SRF lotus pins and buttons, a psychological chart, and a library of meditation pamphlets, prayer books, and chants. The Hollywood center featured an Indian restaurant where the female renunciate servers wore saris as well as an array of cultural programs and speakers such as the consul general of India, the Indian ambassador to the United States, and visiting scholars.

The retreats, courses, symposia, and even the hotel/restaurants provided a way for Yogananda to offer Indian religious practices as an everyday system for American lives. A popularizer, he offered meditation courses via mail order so that the multitudes might experience the "liberating science" of guru-directed yoga at home.[86] He used signifiers of "Western" science and technology to suggest the "modernity" and practical applicability of SRF teachings in the search for the self. For example, he frequently characterized his efforts to create a faith that would "lead one to a common highway of spiritual realization, above dogma or creed."[87] A pamphlet entitled "Follow the Self-Realization Highway to the Infinite" expanded the metaphor. Under a heading heralding "One Basic Truth," the pamphlet boasted that SRF teachings "show that all true religions are expressions of the same basic truth and that this truth is the foundation of all science and all knowledge." The underlying truth of SRF teachings brought "clearer understanding" of "religious" people to "religion" but also to "the scientist of his sciences" and "to the business or professional man of his activities." In the spirit of the conveniences of modernity, SRF's meditation provided "the quickest conveyance" to God via "the highway . . . where all religions meet."[88] In other words, meditation should not be confined to the spiritual ends of an ascetic believer; on the contrary, it could enhance the performance of scientists, professionals, and businessmen. The organization distributed small prayer cards, called "Par-a-grams," that described esteemed values such as "Kindness," "Wisdom," "Generosity," "Perception," "Tolerance," "Will," "Joy," and "Calmness." The chosen topics provide aphoristic insight into positive values that might be achieved through greater self-mastery. A card for "Intuition" advised readers as follows:

> You must develop the intuitive faculty, which can grow only through meditation. Develop your latent intuition and let it guide your thinking, and then march in any direction you wish and you will succeed. Your will and intuition must go hand in hand. A person with a strong will usually has an active intuition. . . . Intuition tells you that certain reasoning is correct. That faculty by which you decide between two reasons, as to which is right, is intuition, which will make you master of all knowledge.[89]

The authoritative self-help advice paralleled the self-interested altruism offered in contemporaneous positive-thinking manuals like Dale Carnegie's *How to Win Friends and Influence People* (1936), perfected by works like Norman Vincent Peale's *The Power of Positive Thinking* (1952; his radio show, "The Art of Living," began in 1935) and, later, Rhonda Byrne's *The Secret* (2006). These "mind-cure" methods suggest that individuals adapt themselves and their expectations to the changing world rather than changing the unequal power structures of the world: they make demands of the self, not of institutions.[90] It also fit an enduring theme of the relationship between well-being and prosperity in Yogananda's speaking tours, which included presentations to civic and business groups as well as the SRF congregation with titles like "How Oriental Methods Help Occidental Business," "Self-Realization in Advertising," "Attracting True Abundance," and "The Divine Way of

Increasing Your Earning Power."[91] In this sense, the pursuit of spirituality could valorize—or sanctify—material achievements. Yogananda therefore engaged in a broader conversation about the changing characteristics needed to succeed in an economy that valued mental engagement; physical and psychological elements became entangled in ideas of "health," "happiness," and "productivity."[92]

Self-Realization expressed distaste for difference along the lines of race, language, nationality, religion, or culture, yet the magazine asserted that modern advancements and progress would be made through different—and essentialized—civilizational contributions.[93] Elite South Asians like Keshab Chandra Sen (1838–1884) and Rabindranath Tagore (1861–1941)—as well as Yogananda—traditionally emphasized India's civilizational heritage as response to British colonial framings that diminished it.[94] The language fit within conceptions of "national character" that became popular in the 1930s and culminated in postwar thinking about "modernization theory," which for liberals explained the direction and development of postcolonial nations.[95] Postwar social scientists distinguished between traditional societies, where culture and religion shaped economic, political, and social life, and modern societies, which favored individualism, capitalism, and complex institutions. The theory identified the United States, with its "liberal values, capitalist economy, and pluralist democracy," as the "first new nation" to reach the "universal end point."[96] The language of development used "neutral-sounding language" of progress and culture to perpetuate long-standing practices and perceptions. It positioned the United States at the apex of Western civilization while questioning whether other cultures were malleable enough to follow the same course of "development."[97]

Working within this context, Yogananda countered that India was not a "new" nation but rather a "mature" civilization with a "spiritual science" that had something to offer in terms of modern material progress. Despite being "materially poor," India had "an inexhaustible fund of divine wealth" from which to draw; it was "especially fitted to make great contributions" through its powers of concentration.[98] As a back-page advertisement explained, "America has specialized in industrial expansion, England in political science, Germany in mechanical inventions, France in art, Italy in music, China in social relations. INDIA FROM TIME IMMEMORIAL HAS SPECIALIZED IN THE SCIENCE OF THE SOUL."[99] Yogananda viewed himself as an important agent in securing a close bond between the United States and India. *Self-Realization* suggested that his final moments encapsulated his destiny. With the Indian ambassador to the United States in the audience, Yogananda's final speech included many of his favorite themes: he noted that he liked to be an American (he had become a citizen) when he thought of American "energy," but news of the premature deaths of successful American businessmen made him "like to be a Hindu—to sit on the banks of the Ganges and concentrate on the factory of Mind from which spiritual skyscrapers can come. . . . Somewhere between the two great civilizations of efficient America and spiritual India lies the answer for a model world civilization."[100] The goal for American audiences, of course, was to bring the two pieces together, with individual practitioners the beneficiaries of the convergence.

Yogananda's valorization of Hinduism and India's past represents an effort that highlights difference to articulate a place for India within the global imaginary that would complement, not challenge, America's sense of its "benevolent supremacy."[101] Such efforts represent the power of religious ideas within progressive ideas of diversity in constructing American hegemony. The progressive adoption of multiculturalism after the war paradoxically helped create a globalized sense of "difference" that appropriated "new exotics" in the production and sale of postwar mass culture.[102] Rather than understanding the importance of histories of encounter, exchange, and domination, this type of civilizational multiculturalism belonged to a view of culture wherein, in the words of Prashad, "culture is bounded into authentic zones with pure histories that need to be accorded a grudging dignity by policies of diversity."[103]

Even as Yogananda and members of the SRF highlighted the inherent modernity of India, they romanticized elements of India's premodern origins. This emphasis followed the magazine's tendency to characterize India along monolithic religious and cultural lines as opposed to, say, a broad array of cultural processes or the political or economic desire for self-sufficiency articulated by Jawaharlal Nehru during the early years of post-Partition India. The magazine's editors accentuated the significance of the rural village to "Indian civilization." In 1946, the magazine reprinted an interview with Gandhi that lauded the purity of villages in India untouched by Western markers of modernity like the telegraph or railroads; there, according to Gandhi, "the spirituality . . . is unconscious of herself. It is an inherited culture."[104]

Yet if Gandhi sought to construct a usable past of Indian authenticity and self-sufficiency in pursuit of independence, the magazine perhaps had a different goal: the SRF had to create a saleable, consumable, and unchanging "India" that would appeal to American audiences. The organization's pluralist imagination empowered American audiences to construct a modern identity through the consumption of a rural, ancient, and spiritual India. The SRF center in Long Beach captured this imaginary world with its production of "A Night in India" at the Wilma Hastings Auditorium in June 1952. As with most SRF events, the program sought to blend "Western" and "Indian" cultural achievements: musicians played "Come unto Him" (from Handel's *Messiah*) and a rendition of Nikolai Rimsky-Korsakov's "Song of India" before the performance of a play entitled "The Song of the Sadhu," penned by a devotee, which included a cast of SRF monks as well as children from its Sunday school. The program assured audiences that the play portrayed "the true India, an India composed mostly of the villages, where daily life and eternal God are brought into effortless harmony by the humble magnet call of a deep faith such as one encounters everywhere among the noble country folk of that land." A section entitled "A Word about Our Program" captured the essentialism at the heart of the contrast between the "modern" and "urban" West and the "rural" East, even as it acknowledged India's urban growth:

> In the light of the present world conditions, that presentation is rare which attempts to unite East and West through appreciation of spiritual virtues, often dormant within a nation's culture.
>
> It is fitting that when we think of India we immediately envision, not the skyscrapers and television studios of our western civilization, but rather a simple people of outer and inner simplicity, whose spiritual ancestry brooks no comparison.
>
> True, India's outward culture is now becoming more modern, in the Western sense, but tonight we wish to wend our way with you in thought beyond the metropolises such as Bombay and Calcutta, to the romantic simplicity of the India village where the spiritual fragrance of ancient India is still apparent in the face of her rapid material advancement.
>
> As we walk through this ancient land, gazing upon the vast fields of grain, the shepherds tenderly watching over their flocks, the golden beauty of the sky, the hoary majesty of the mountains, we drink deep of a spiritual atmosphere which penetrates the very soul of man. . . .
>
> Thus a true oriental devotee looks at life. Let us tonight look through his eyes, as we visit the real India. Perhaps we too shall see the subtle beauty of Spirit hiding behind the forms of art and nature.[105]

The note instructed audience members to ignore the visible traces of India and instead use their imagination to see, taste, smell, and hear a "real" (and timeless) India of the spirit. "A Night in India" acknowledged an "outward culture" of modern India but invited audiences to consume the "ancient India" of the villages to "unite" the "East" and "West" through a mutual appreciation of spirituality.

FIGURE 9. Ceremonies at the Self-Realization Fellowship often attempted to blend Eastern and Western cultural elements. Here, at the August 1950 dedication of the organization's Lake Shrine Temple in Pacific Palisades, women wear white saris and prayer beads. Photo courtesy of the *Los Angeles Daily News* Negatives (Collection 1387). Library Special Collections, Charles E. Young Research Library, UCLA.

Other Self-Realization Fellowship events sought to model an inclusive religious imaginary that brought different beliefs into harmony. A description of the Lotus Festival Concert in 1951 at its Lake Shrine exemplified the organization's cultural eclecticism. The orchestra selected renditions ranging from Schubert's "Ave Maria" to a Finnish folk song to "Blue Danube" and Brahms's "Lullaby" to another rendition of "Song of India." At the end of the musical program, according to a reviewer, "a dramatic and extremely artistic effect was achieved ... with the slow and silent passage across the lake of a large junk decorated with Chinese lanterns"; the author then noted, "High up on the hillside of this natural amphitheater an illumined statue of Christ looked down upon the scene." The author also provided a tour of the recently opened grounds in Pacific Palisades. Yogananda designed the Golden Lotus Archway at the location to be a wall-less temple (figures 9 and 10). The SRF shrine included statues of Buddha and Kwan Yin, a statue of Jesus, and the Gandhi World Peace Memorial, which included some of the ashes of Mahatma Gandhi

FIGURE 10. An overhead view of the 1950 dedication ceremony of the Lake Shrine Temple shows the "wall-less temple" created by the Golden Lotus Archway. A Mississippi houseboat and a wooden boat were installed by a previous owner, who also built a windmill that remains on the grounds. Photo courtesy of the *Los Angeles Daily News* Negatives (Collection 1387). Library Special Collections, Charles E. Young Research Library, UCLA.

donated by J. V. Nawle, a journalist from Bombay. Even the plants—from Chinese rice-paper plants to bamboo and ginger plants to mango, papaya, guava, jujube, cherimoya, pepino, banana, fig, and rose-apple—sought to convey the shrine's ecumenical spirit.[106] Within five years, the SRF constructed a "Court of Religions" on the site that included five concrete monuments dedicated to each major world religion, including those that seldom received mention in *Self-Realization*: a star of David, a wheel of the law for Buddhism, the Sanskrit character for "om" in Hinduism, a cross for Christianity, and a star and crescent for Islam.[107]

EMBODYING THE CIVILIZATIONAL CONNECTION: YOGANANDA AND SAINT LYNN

Yogananda's argument that meditation could lead to greater productivity took root at a moment when American cultural critics worried that the expansion of the white-collar economy imperiled white masculinity. Given its location in Los Angeles, the SRF drew an array of artists and entertainers into its fold, but its most celebrated convert was a businessman, James J. Lynn, whose friendship with Yogananda epitomized the goals of his mission. The representations of Yogananda and Lynn's friendship in *Self-Realization* capture the organization's efforts to nurture sentimental and material connections between the nations and point us to the organization's business-friendly ethos. Their relationship also provides an outward-looking intervention at a moment when business activists sought to define the United States as a "Christian" nation that stood for faith, freedom, and "free enterprise."[108]

Much of Yogananda's writing described civilizational deficits that could be met through encounter and exchange, as in the way Yogananda sought to forge an alliance between "spiritual" India and "industrial" America. In a message reprinted after his death, Yogananda noted that "the West" suffered from "over-production" due to its "concentration on unnecessary objects of luxury" while "the East" suffered from lack of production, which he associated with lack of factories as well as "inactivity and laziness." Yogananda argued, "Comfort can be acquired only by a balanced attitude" through self-mastery. He believed that the "astute man" should "apply system and science to better his health, prosperity, and social and international life." He remarked that while business was important, "your appointment to serve others is more important, and your engagement with meditation, God, and Truth is most important."[109]

The SRF's publications frequently lamented the imbalance between the material and spiritual achievements in the United States and India—whereas America possessed "more millionaires than any other country," India had more "actual saints."[110] No sermon or pamphlet could convey Yogananda's desire for balance better than his friendship with Lynn, a Midwestern insurance businessman who became his disciple and, from 1952 until his death in 1955, successor at the SRF. In many ways, their friendship conformed to the typical trajectory of the "Oriental Monk" relationship with spiritual seekers. The history of American encounters with Eastern spirituality frequently follows a formalized narrative in which a "lone" monk figure nurtures a white child—often with an "ambivalent" relationship with the dominant culture—and causes a transformation of both the child and the West, saving them from "capitalist greed, brute force, totalitarian rule, and spiritless technology."[111] Lynn, whose SRF name became Rajarsi Janakananda, first met Yogananda at a lecture in Kansas City in 1932 and became a disciple immediately thereafter. A successful businessman, Lynn nevertheless fit Iwamura's characteristics of a white man with some ambivalence toward his economic and cultural moment. Like many white-collar workers of the era, he complained of a generalized anxiety. Over the course of the twentieth century, anxiety or "stress"—a term first used in scientific discourse in 1914—became associated with high achievers like Lynn.[112] Lynn credited Yogananda with curing his nervousness by providing a "healing light" and entrance into a "spiritual realm."[113]

At a moment when the United States' relationship with Pacific Rim allies was often cast in terms of a parent-child or male-female hierarchies, the Yogananda-Lynn friendship emphasized balance.[114] In the relationship between Yogananda and Lynn, the SRF found its test case: Lynn received India's "Sacred Teachings," and Yogananda had, according to the pamphlet, his Henry Ford or Thomas Edison who represented "Western business ability."[115] Just a few years before sociologists like William Whyte questioned the bureaucratic focus of the Organization Man and Sloan Wilson documented the travails of *The Man in the Gray Flannel Suit*, the organization presented James Lynn as an object lesson in the benefits of self-realization. Unlike the Beat poets, the era's most famous spiritual experimenters, Lynn's business acumen had the potential to position the SRF as a legitimate belief system for middlebrow audiences.

Yogananda was aware of Lynn's usefulness to his mission; he referred to his disciple as "Saint Lynn" and noted that he filled the promise of "potential saints" in America, a mission that had summoned him to the West. Americans and Indians were "alike in soul though diverse in outer experience," yet "neither West nor East will flourish if some form of disciplinary yoga not be practiced."[116] Yogananda highlighted Lynn's success while also noting their common spiritual dedication. He noted that Lynn was "more than most of us, busy with many large affairs" but that he and Lynn meditated together rather than speaking of business or worldly affairs. With his "simple habits" and "balanced life," Lynn became a Westerner who proved the "worth" of kriya yoga.[117] In addition to his monetary support to the SRF—Lynn purchased and built the Golden World Colony while Yogananda traveled in India—he echoed Yogananda's appeal to balance the material and spiritual.

Over the years, the magazine published photographs of Lynn and Yogananda that depicted the desired harmony between "Eastern spirituality" and "Western materiality." The photographs ranged from showing affinity to hybridity to antithesis. One photo, which depicts the men holding hands with Yogananda in a Western-style jacket and pants and

Lynn in white pants with no shirt and a shaved head, featured a caption with words from Lynn's successor, Sister Daya, who commented,
"Seldom has the world seen such a perfect friendship."[118] Other photographs suggested a convergence of cultures: a photograph captioned "A
Great Hindu Yogi and a Great American Yogi—Masters of Themselves"
showed both men in Encinitas in 1952 dressed identically in short
dhotis.[119] Still another photo showed Lynn in 1954 in a meditative pose
dressed in a business suit with a caption from Yogananda stating, "I am
proud that in Mr. Lynn . . . a Westerner stepped forth to show the world
the worth in daily life of yoga training."[120] Yet another photo published
(posthumously) in 1957 showed Yogananda and Lynn "hand in hand"
with Mr. Lynn in a business suit and Yogananda in robes. The caption
quotes Yogananda as saying that Mr. Lynn "represents the best in American business principles as well as in universal spiritual principles."[121] In
the representation of this relationship, *Self-Realization* found a metaphor
for a civilizational partnership that worked within the imaginary of harmonious integration of spiritual and material principles.

DISRUPTION AND INTUITION

Yogananda identified the early signs of American disillusionment within
alienated seekers like James Lynn and presented his spiritual message
as an antidote to material pursuits. Decades after Yogananda's death, a
range of people continued to cite the guru's work as inspiration: for example, even before the Beatles met Maharishi Mahesh Yogi, Yogananda,
Sri Lahiri Mahasaya, and Sri Mahavatara Babaji appeared on the cover
of the Beatles' 1967 album *Sgt. Pepper's Lonely Hearts Club Band*. Yogananda surfaced in popular culture once more when, in the wake of
Steve Jobs's death, guests at his self-choreographed October 2011 memorial service received a box containing Yogananda's *Autobiography*.
Marc Benioff, the CEO of Salesforce.com, declared that the gift captured
Jobs's message to his business associates: "Actualize yourself." According to Benioff, "[Jobs] had this incredible realization that his intuition
was his greatest gift, and he needed to look at the world from inside
out."[122] The memento resonated with revelations in Walter Isaacson's
authorized biography of Jobs, published within weeks of the entrepreneur's death, that emphasized his early and life-long experimentation
with Eastern spirituality, including Zen Buddhism and the eponymous
Autobiography, a volume he read as a teenager while staying at a hostel
in India and revisited once a year on his iPad.[123]

As the cofounder of the most successful personal computer company, a self-professed adherent of Zen Buddhism, and an admirer of Yogananda, Steve Jobs provides an excellent opportunity to explore the "East washing" created by the confluence of the sixties counterculture with the economic changes wrought by Silicon Valley in the late twentieth century. A little more than a decade after Yogananda's death, the United States experienced a crisis of technocracy that had informed its twentieth-century society and economy. For many involved in sixties-era movements, spiritual practices like those offered by Yogananda provided an experiential vocabulary, a new method for achieving consciousness, and a balm for their alienation from a society dominated by centralized bureaucracies. Although many in the counterculture pointed to technology as a symbol of oppression, the generation of technology researchers and entrepreneurs who came of age in the 1960s viewed information technology as a source of personal liberation. As leaders of the "information economy" that took shape in northern California, some created a form of what Kimberly Lau calls "New Age capitalism" by combining computer technology, contemporary business judgment, and Eastern thought—including Yogananda's autobiography.

The rest of this chapter will examine Silicon Valley—and especially Steve Jobs—as a window for understanding how domestic American culture adeptly absorbed non-Western cultures to soften the edges of capitalism and empire. Yogananda offered his practices as complementary, not necessarily oppositional; his work provided a "commodifiable cosmopolitanism" that helped adapt spiritual language to market terms.[124] White baby boomers melded sixties-era rhetoric of discontent and Eastern vocabularies of spirituality to describe the technology and manufacturing economies of late capitalism. This was not an issue of simple appropriation or homogenization during globalization; it instead represented the ability of a hegemonic American empire to absorb and operate through difference. As Jane Iwamura explains, this type of cultural transfer allows white Americans to reposition themselves as the "protectors, innovators, and guardians of Asian religions and culture and wrest the authority to define these traditions from others."[125] Over the long term, late capitalism proved adept at advancing through—not against—the commodification of variation and differentiation.[126] By incorporating ideas of Zen Buddhism and Yogananda's *kriya* yoga, Jobs represented a "new prophet of capitalism," which sociologist Nicole Aschoff characterizes as a generation of elite "storytellers" who created legitimating narratives for late capitalism through visions of how to improve the economic system.[127]

Silicon Valley originated in the military Keynesianism of US Cold War–era science and aerospace engineering. In many ways, the region exemplified the achievements of technocracy. Historian Fred Turner has explained that the research projects of the military-industrial complex gave rise to a "free-wheeling, interdisciplinary, and highly entrepreneurial style of work" that, over time, also produced the techno-utopian world of Northern California, especially when contrasted to more conservative Eastern tech centers in New York State and Massachusetts.[128] Silicon Valley's iconoclastic self-perception matched the anti-government political ethos that emerged during the Reagan era. In a speech to computer science students at Moscow State University in 1988, Reagan characterized the 1980s as the "decade of the entrepreneur," citing Silicon Valley and the "computer revolution" as cogs for a "free-market society." Given his propensity for positive psychology, it is not surprising that Reagan also gave a nod to self-actualization, arguing, "In the new economy, human invention increasingly makes physical resources obsolete. We're breaking through the material conditions of existence to a world where man creates his own destiny."[129] Although praised by Reagan as a crucible of economic freedom, Silicon Valley's roots were, according to historian Margaret O'Mara, better understood as stemming from historical conditions in which government programs and public spending on science and technology combined with entrepreneurship, deregulation, and globalization. It is nevertheless illuminating to unpack how businesspeople imagined themselves and their roles in reshaping American society and how they deployed the language of Eastern spirituality to characterize their actions.

In the 1960s, many Americans expressed dissatisfaction with the rationality and large centralized organizations that characterized American life. These sentiments most frequently became associated with the generation of white college-aged students who, while seemingly on track to succeed in a meritocratic social and economic system, nevertheless rejected centralized social institutions in pursuit of personal freedom. Early student campaigns viewed technology as an engine of oppression. For example, the Free Speech Movement at Berkeley, which began in 1964 as a campaign against the campus ban on political activities, expanded to include a broader critique of the role of the university in the nation's military-industrial complex. The university chancellor, Clark Kerr, believed it was the university's role to create workers (specifically professionals and managers) for an "information society," but student activists countered that the university was a "knowledge factory." They used punch cards—important to class registration at the university but also emblematic of the broader symptoms of bureaucratic organization, standardization, and automation through their use in IBM processing systems—at their demonstrations, perhaps most famously when a protestor, echoing the handling instructions on every card, pinned a sign to himself reading, "I am a UC student. Please don't bend, fold, spindle, or mutilate me."[130]

Throughout the 1950s and 1960s, intellectuals sought to identify the dissatisfaction with rationality, depersonalization, and automation that had emerged in Western society. Authors like Jacques Ellul (*The Technological Society*), John Kenneth Galbraith (*The New Industrial State*), Herbert Marcuse (*One-Dimensional Man*), Lewis Mumford (*The Myth of the Machine*), and Charles Reich (*The Greening of America*) identified the hierarchical organization of military, industrial, and academic institutions run by, in the words of C. Wright Mills, a "power elite" that pervaded ordinary existence. According to these intellectuals, the path to social change rested in reclaiming consciousness.[131] Writing in 1969, historian Theodore Roszak explained how Eastern beliefs became part of the battle over consciousness. Roszak located the heart of the sixties-era protest in the alienation among young adults, which he famously called the "counterculture." He argued that this opposition was at its core a critique of American technocracy, which he defined as "that social form in which industrial society reaches the peak of its organizational integration. It's the ideal men usually have in mind when they speak of modernizing, up-dating, rationalizing, planning." In this moment of perfected social engineering brought about by a "regime of experts," "entrepreneurial talent broadens its province to orchestrate the total human context which surrounds the industrial complex."[132] Science and notions of progress had fundamentally come to dominate the domain of "reliable knowledge" characterized by objectivity that defined ideas about "human needs, social engineering, economic planning, international relations, invention," and "education." "Technocracy" was the terrain of "objective consciousness" and provided the only legitimate means for accessing reality in the dominant culture.[133] In its critique of this regime, the counterculture embraced concepts of the "mystical," including those that originated in Eastern traditions like Zen Buddhism. These traditions had also proved popular during the late Victorian era when a generation of affluent Americans had also looked to Asian religions as a means for addressing the "weightlessness" of modern life.[134] Roszak attributed the "Journey to the East" to the totalizing nature of scientific discourse in American society. As historian Fred Turner has explained, as "consciousness" became a site for enacting social change, "information"—and by extension information technologies—became an important component of countercultural politics.[135] It also became the basis for new descriptions of Silicon Valley capitalism.

The critique of technocracy and rational knowledge expressed by the counterculture, along with the era's urgent demands for revolutionary change and personal transformation, gradually became absorbed within broader cultural conversations of late capitalism that valued personal freedom and cosmopolitan engagement. During the 1970s, computer technology changed as room-sized mainframe computers became desk-sized and then laptop-sized minicomputers, and, aided by improved software and operating platforms, their functions expanded to include facilitating networked communication rather than simply performing calculations. Although military and defense projects created the conditions for the computer revolution, Silicon Valley entrepreneurs deployed revolutionary and antiestablishment metaphors for describing their ventures, which they saw as upstart projects that would wield market-based technologies in place of government-based social policies.[136] Drawing on countercultural language of personal autonomy, creators characterized PCs as tools of liberation that could repurpose data to free citizens from totalizing technocratic and scientific oppression, rather than enchain them to it.[137] Apple's *1984* ad introducing the Apple Macintosh computer, which referenced George Orwell's dystopian novel when it aired during the 1984 Super Bowl, encapsulated Apple's utopian vision of personal technology.

Since the 1960s, researchers had believed that computers might amplify human potential.[138] A gifted storyteller and a popularizer like Yogananda before him, Jobs helped define the cultural contours that portrayed the personal computer as an engine of freedom and creativity for home customers. The initial Apple Computer logo was, after all, a bitten apple with a rainbow logo, an early promise that the company would find hope and progress out of human failure.[139] From the beginning, Jobs demonstrated an ability to market personal computers to middle-class American knowledge workers. In a 1980 *Wall Street Journal* advertisement, Jobs compared the personal computer to the bicycle because the Apple computer "can amplify a certain part of our inherited intelligence. There's a special relationship that develops between one person and one computer that ultimately improves productivity on a personal level."[140] The blended language of freedom, radical transformation, and consumer technology achieved its apotheosis in 2011 when Jobs described the new iPad as "our most advanced technology in a magical and revolutionary device at an unbelievable price."[141]

In the 1980s, computers helped to enumerate imagined understandings of American creative exceptionalism during globalization. Free Speech Movement activists protested the role of computers in university life, yet Apple argued that technology was indispensable to education. As the Japanese economy challenged American economic dominance in the early 1980s, the California Commission on Industrial Innovation cited access to computers as a method for combating international competition. By suggesting that computers were tools that fostered independent thinking, Apple persuaded legislatures to institute mandatory computer education and to purchase computers for classrooms—key strategies that underwrote the company's dominance of the American education market.[142] Other characterizations of the personal computer evoked American myths about "frontiers" and "pioneers" that characterized narratives of American exceptionalism and open opportunity. As American empire expanded in the late twentieth century, businesses became the new engines of conquest. In 1987, for example, Jean-Louis Gassee, a French-born executive at Apple, drew a familiar distinction between the United States and France in an opinion piece entitled "Business: The New Frontier." Europe had "its discreet charms and measured joys," but the American West Coast had "futuristic attractions and brassy hedonism" as well as a "pioneering spirit" that fueled "desire, adventure, enterprise" and allowed Americans like Jobs to become innovators. By drawing from well-established American narratives of rugged individualism and pioneer mentalities, Gassee established Apple products as objects of art and pleasure rather than technocratic inventions.[143]

The counterculture sought personal authenticity based in a sense of individual originality. As Roszak and others have shown, those who adhered to "countercultural" attitudes often followed alternative, bohemian, and mystical paths toward enlightenment and away from the "verifiable descriptions of reality" offered by the objective knowledge of technocracy.[144] The desire to alter or enhance consciousness explains why many Bay Area tech pioneers who believed computers might "augment" human intellect, including Steve Jobs, also experimented with LSD.[145] Yogananda as well as practitioners of Zen Buddhism, Transcendental Meditation, and other Eastern spiritual practices offered another vocabulary for their critique. The early "disrupters" of Silicon Valley who founded the personal computer startups were among those who used the language of Eastern spirituality to explain their intervention in the tech economy. As in previous eras of modernity, these late capitalists differentiated themselves through ideas of radical breaks with the past rather than incremental changes, in this case by maintaining that the machines they built were smart, not strong.[146] Beginning in the late nineteenth century, Frederick Taylor's scientific management had, in the name of productivity, taken technical knowledge out of the hands of manual laborers and placed it within a machine. Managers and engineers might then use specialized knowledge and calculations to measure and improve the efficiency of the machine. The shift to a knowledge economy supposedly required the dematerialization of work. Yet in its early years, despite the company's emphasis on its progressive workplace values, Apple manufactured its Apple II computers via contracted piecework in nearby Saratoga, where housewives and Filipino immigrants stuffed chips into circuit boards and soldered pins in place while watching soap operas.[147] When Apple introduced cellphones in 2007, this trend continued—offshore—as the company manufactured iPhones utilizing complicated supply chains with contracted labor at the Foxconn campus in Shenzen, China. Apple's profit mainly derived from the intellectual property of the device and its design, packaging, and marketing.[148] This era of supposed "immaterial labor" produced "knowledge, information, meaning, symbols, and affects" that easily crossed borders through interconnected networks.[149] The "creative class" that came to dominate the American economy in the recent past celebrated the acquisition of knowledge and their value system that went into "forming ideas and making choices" rather than on pure material economic capital.[150]

As historian Malcolm Harris argues, although Americans like to think of the microcomputer industry as a story of "invention" initiated by "visionaries," it is instead important to contextualize figures like Jobs within broader postindustrial economic changes.[151] Inventors and tinkerers, including both Apple cofounders Steve Wozniak and Steve Jobs, characterized themselves as "thinkers" presiding over the "Age of Information" rather than "manufacturers" in a later stage of an industrial economy. In the minds of Apple's leadership, "mode of thinking" simply replaced "mode of production." It is also critical to consider how these figures weaved a mythology of economic innovation in what was a highly favorable business environment fueled by public investment and a globalized and exploited labor force. As personal computers developed the ability to process data, there was an imperative for distinguishing human from mechanized intelligence. They sought a language outside of the linear objectivity that characterized the shift away from technocratic regime to networked information technology. Yogananda's decades-long efforts provided a usable vocabulary for civilizational ideas about "progress" and "science" for those who wanted to, in the words of the famous Apple ad campaign that ran from 1997 to 2002, "think different." Not everyone believed Jobs's hype. In his 1985 history of Silicon Valley, for example, journalist Michael S. Malone described Jobs as "P.T. Barnum with cool, Aimee Semple McPherson with a secular product, . . . an eighties high-tech version of the yogis he followed in India, but in a tailored suit and tennis shoes" who "mixes young-executive patois and the shaman jive of utopianism, poster-caption philosophy and the youthful colloquialism of a self-proclaimed prophet."[152]

Although Steve Wozniak was known for his technical expertise, even in the early years of his leadership Steve Jobs sought to distinguish his vision and leadership from those of other corporate leaders. His actions were part of a much larger push among business leaders to fashion themselves as "charismatic visionaries" who rejected conventional business practices in favor of New Age-tinged wisdom; magazines like *BusinessWeek* and *Fortune* took note of this spiritual turn in corporate culture.[153] Pundits suggested that, whenever he took the stage at Apple events to introduce his company's latest product innovation, he propagated "the gospel for a secular age."[154] Unlike corporate press releases churned out on predictable calendar dates, Apple "keynotes" at product releases became news events for tech economy obsessives, many of whom were part of what sociologist Elizabeth Currid-Halkett calls the "aspirational class." These consumers valued items that signified their productive behaviors and practices; these items might include inconspicuous goods and services like education, but they also included consumables that reflected a sophistication acquired through a person's cultural facility and knowledge. Apple products were mass produced in China, not batch-made by local craftsmen, but their marketing techniques had much in common with smaller retailers who fashioned narratives around their products to make them more unique. By carefully curating its brand identity, Apple convinced consumers that its products were incomparable to other personal computers. This type of storytelling, which Currid-Halkett calls "conspicuous production," helped consumers feel invested in the product.[155] In short, when Jobs took to the stage at Apple keynotes to explain how his knowledge acquisition informed a particular product's development, customers found the ensuing mythology to be compelling.

Jobs's messaging drew not only from the counterculture's language of individual liberation but also its appreciation of subjective experience and insight. His Zen Buddhist practice became fodder for journalists looking to explain Jobs's approach to technology and business leadership. This vocabulary set his work apart from the technocracy that preceded it. In the wake of Jobs's death, his biographer, Walter Isaacson, claimed, "The simplicities of Zen Buddhism really informed his design sense."[156] Jobs in fact told Isaacson that at one point he hoped to go to Japan to become a Buddhist monk but was convinced by his spiritual advisor not to go. Jobs also reminisced about his seven-month expedition through India in 1974. In an interview with Isaacson that appeared in the biography, Jobs recalled his journey in Orientalized ways that drew sharp and deeply racialized distinctions between Indian and Western thinking processes:

Coming back to America was, for me, much more of a cultural shock than going to India. The people in the Indian countryside don't use their intellect like we do, they use their intuition instead, and their intuition is far more developed than in the rest of the world. Intuition is a very powerful thing, more powerful than intellect, in my opinion.

Western rational thought is not an innate human characteristic; it is learned and is the great achievement of Western civilization. In the villages of India, they never learned it. They learned something else, which is in some ways just as valuable but in other ways is not. That's the power of intuition and experiential wisdom.

Coming back after seven months in Indian villages, I saw the craziness of the Western world as well as its capacity for rational thought. If you just sit and observe, you will see how restless your mind is. If you try to calm it, it only makes it worse, but over time it does calm, and when it does, there's room to hear more subtle things—that's when your intuition starts to blossom and you start to see things more clearly and be in the present more. Your mind just slows down, and you see a tremendous expanse in the moment. You see so much more than you could see before. It's a discipline; you have to practice it.[157]

Jobs, like many other Silicon Valley entrepreneurs, broadly embraced both South and East Asian practices in the early twenty-first century that, as scholars note, have been introduced as a means for greater workplace control and productivity.[158] Anthropologist Susannah Crockford defines "intuition" as "guidance of the soul" that comes from "the higher self" rather than "the mind or ego," thus serving as a "radical inversion of scientific empiricism."[159] When invoked by Jobs, "intuition" provided a language to critique the objective mindset of "Western rational thought" and logic that characterized the technocracy of the early post-war era. According to Jobs, "intuition"—long cultivated by the people in the Indian countryside, he maintained, but not in its urban centers—helped Jobs improve his entrepreneurial self. Yogananda had similarly critiqued the West's material science and had offered India's soul science as a complementary mechanism to achieve balance. Jobs turned these "civilizational" thought processes into commodifiable personal characteristics. A notoriously demanding and imperious boss, he used the term in its most individualistic sense to promote his inner vision.

"Intuition" became Jobs's signature refrain for characterizing his leadership style. This method favored self-improvement, self-help, and positive psychology achieved through consumer practices that valorized motivation, competition, optimization, and initiative.[160] During this era, entrepreneurs in the world of finance capitalism as well as Jobs began to replace the "science" of professional management that dominated the business world for most of the twentieth century with "intuition, snap judgments, and hunches."[161] In one of the time-honored genres of self-help advice, the commencement speech, Jobs urged others to hone the ethereal, unmeasurable trait of "intuition," which was a theme of his advice for young people as early as 1996, when he spoke to graduates at Palo Alto High School. After being asked in January 2005 to give the upcoming commencement speech at Stanford, Jobs emailed notes to himself. One early note about "curiosity" read, "Autobiography of a yogi quote 'what is miraculous is all around us.'"[162] Although the quotation did not make it to the final draft, the speech included references to some of Yogananda's ideas (as well as specific mention of Stewart Brand's *Whole Earth Catalog*, which was influential in uniting ideas of the counterculture to information technology). When he addressed the graduating class, who were otherwise to be sent into a booming tech-oriented economy armed with nothing but their degree from one of the world's top private research universities, Jobs counseled: "Don't be trapped by dogma—which is living with the results of other people's thinking. Don't let the noise of others' opinions drown out your own inner voice. And most important, have the courage to follow your heart and intuition." In this usage, *intuition* became a term that connoted highly individualistic acts of ingenuity and innovation in a competitive world of markets. In the same era, George W. Bush's claim to trust his "gut" was interpreted as his trust in religious faith in retrograde defiance of empirical evidence.[163] The East-washing context of his language allowed Jobs's preference for trusting his instinct to be cast differently.

The notion that Jobs followed Eastern "intuition" rather than Western "analytical rigor" became part of his mystique as a genius of the business world. After Jobs's death, scores of obituaries quoted this line urging young adults at the top of the American meritocracy to trust their "intuition." It was less clear how "intuition" might have worked as a tool of collaboration or social solidarity.

Six years after his commencement speech at Stanford, Jobs passed this message of self-actualization to associates at his memorial service. The story of Steve Jobs's funeral represents a point in a longer trajectory of ways that religious pluralism informed the emergence of a transnational imaginary that empowers white elites to adapt and redeploy cultural practices from around the world in a way that, as Sarah Banet-Weiser explains, repurposes a practice in a way in which the practitioner, not the actual practice, is "authentic."[164] Jobs's death also coincided with a moment of soul-searching in the American economy, as questions arose regarding not whether but when the Chinese and Indian economies would overtake the US economy. Optimists suggested that the nation's creativity—its ability to cull the best ideas from scientific, technological, and cultural sources from around the world—might assure America's continued economic hegemony. Isaacson, Jobs's biographer, concluded in a *New York Times* opinion piece that while "China and India are likely to promote many rigorous analytical thinkers and knowledgeable technologists," "smart and educated" thinking was not enough. Rather, if "America's advantage" in the global economy were to continue, it would have to derive from "people who are also more creative and imaginative" and who appreciated both the humanities and science.[165] In the earlier era of industrialization, imperial thinkers questioned the capacity of non-Western peoples to acquire technical skill or grasp Western scientific thought.[166] In this new rendering, China and India were portrayed as unimaginative and technocratic economies while the United States had embraced creativity and imagination. Yet, as this chapter has shown, businessmen like Steve Jobs commodified Eastern and South Asian cultural concepts to portray their thinking as innovative.

In the bigger picture, the suggestion that technical devices could be a path for creativity suggests a way for casting "New Age capitalism" as an effort to manage difference. In the *New Yorker*, Malcolm Gladwell concurred with Isaacson's estimation of Jobs as a master "tweaker" whose sensibility ran toward the "editorial, not inventive."[167] In this type of hagiographic account, Jobs's genius derived from his ability to wed Eastern "intuition" through belief systems like Zen Buddhism with Western technological advances. This outlook cast American empire, with its ability to absorb difference, as the master of all it encountered.

CONCLUSION

Yogananda arrived in the United States at a moment when cultural internationalism sought to foster an inclusive global solidarity, yet he also proselytized over a period when the consumer marketplace increasingly mediated spiritual and religious beliefs. In his commitment to creating a forgivable modernity that blended scientific truth, material gain, and a broad sense of altruism, Yogananda illuminates the accommodationist relationship between spiritual beliefs and capitalism characterized as "New Age capitalism" that, while often linked to the counterculture of the 1960s, has its roots in longer strands of encounter. At the same time, the process of harnessing concepts like "intuition" to utopian visions about personal emancipation through technologies exemplifies the ways that free market capitalism empowered individuals like Steve Jobs to cast themselves as liberators who challenged earlier orders, traditions, and hierarchies.

In closing, we should perhaps think more about the ways that, from the start, the emergence of American economic hegemony stemmed from managing difference, even within claims of universal truths. Religious pluralism informed the emergence of a transnational imaginary that empowered white elites to adapt and redeploy cultural practices from around the world. During the twentieth century, the vision of universality and multiracial cooperation became commodified within a pluralistic logic of contemporary capitalism that prioritized personal therapy and self-transformation. Yogananda's rhetoric indicated an unequal sense of partnership between the "civilizations" in which ancient India could safely supplement, but not supplant, modern American productivity. Yogananda helped translate "civilizational" wisdom into individual practice acquired within the consumer marketplace. He helped to repackage Eastern spirituality as a path to personal success—which, when adapted by white Americans, became, perhaps, a replacement for the Protestant ethic within the global economy.

CHAPTER 3

Message on a Bottle

Dr. Bronner's Magic Soaps and
the Evolution of a Spiritual Vision

In 1947, Emanuel Bronner, a German-Jewish immigrant and third-generation industrial soap maker, escaped for the third time from a mental hospital in Illinois and hitched a ride west with a driver he met via a classified ad. Once he arrived in California—another face in Los Angeles's postwar noir landscape—he slept on the roof of a downtown YMCA. To make money, he fought forest fires and gathered spices for Los Angeles health food stores.[1] He eventually rented a tenement in Bunker Hill at 447 S. Hope Street, where, beginning in 1948—"typically wearing nothing more than a leopard-skin bathing suit"—he brewed soap stirred with a broomstick in twenty-gallon batches to sell on street corners.[2] During this time, he began to refer to himself as a doctor and rabbi. He also started to speak about his religious visions. While lecturing in Pershing Square in 1950, Bronner noticed that audience members were taking the soap he gave away and leaving without listening to his religious ideas, so he began to put his "All-One-God-Faith" message on bottles (figure 11).[3]

Bronner spent the rest of his life tinkering with this creed. Citing inspiration over time from the New Testament, Mohammed, Thomas Paine, and US Olympic swimmer Mark Spitz, the company's labels became famous for their eclectic dedication to an "All-One-God-Faith" that proclaimed, "Absolute cleanliness is Godliness! Teach the Moral ABC that unites all mankind free, instantly 6 billion strong we're All One." The original, versatile peppermint soap—and its inclusive

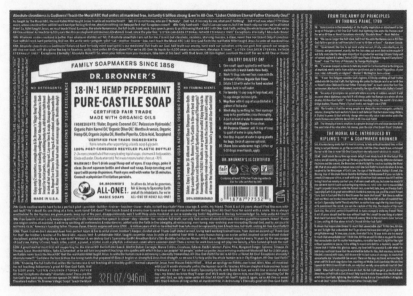

FIGURE 11. The contemporary label for Dr. Bronner's All-One Peppermint Castile Soap. The label incorporates elements of Dr. Bronner's *Moral ABC*, including the exhortation that we are "All-One or None! All-One!" while also including new fair-trade, organic, and no-animal-testing certifications, and information about recycling. Each scent includes a different excerpt of the original *Moral ABC*. Photo courtesy of Dr. Bronner's.

thirty-thousand-word statement of belief—became popular with members of the 1960s counterculture. In recent years, the family-owned company, now based outside of San Diego in Vista, evolved its mission to include guarantees of environmental stewardship and socially responsible business practices. The "All-One" goal of unity, which originated in Holocaust- and Cold War–era concerns about genocide and nuclear destruction, evolved into calls for social equality and efforts to halt climate change.

This chapter uses the history of Dr. Bronner's Soaps to examine the convergence of religious and spiritual visions and social activist business practices over time. Recent interventions in American religious history have shown the intersection of religious beliefs and consumer capitalism, demonstrating that religious values do not occupy an "authentic" space in American culture outside the consumer market.[4] Consumer culture linked ideas of religiosity and materialism. Sarah Banet-Weiser has argued the need to look at the "branding" of religion, which refuses to make the distinction between religion (or spirituality) and commerce. The consumer marketplace—and the burgeoning availability of therapeutic, bohemian, and alternative products—provided a framework for reconsidering concepts such as spirituality and the sacred.[5] By contextualizing American spirituality within consumer affluence, we can see how self-actualization worked through, not in opposition to, consumer lifestyles. This concept provides an opportunity to see how Dr. Bronner's original vision became reinvoked, reshaped, and reimagined within new economic and cultural contexts.

In the twentieth century, the language of American belief began to emphasize concepts of "spirituality," which connoted concepts of femininity, environmental consciousness, and self-realization.[6] While empowering the practitioner, the language also overlapped with other spheres of American life, including emerging consumer capitalist lifestyles and products during the second half of the twentieth century as they transitioned from a marginal or countercultural to a widespread popular practice.[7] As the United States became "a consumers' republic," the market mediated how citizens participated in democracy but also how they experienced everyday life, including spirituality.[8] Even as the countercultural and New Left movements of the sixties protested the dominant culture, the era provided consumers with a greater range of cultural practices with which to identify and critique their own modern condition.

Critics disagree about the extent to which the resulting cultural forms represented a challenge to American capitalism in either the short or long term. Alternative and bohemian values were not necessarily oppositional. Their critique of standardization advanced late capitalism through the commodification of variation and differentiation.[9] As Thomas Frank demonstrates in *The Conquest of Cool*, even rebellion could be commodified: as early as the 1960s, corporations created marketing campaigns that aligned their products with the "counterculture" in what eventually became known as "lifestyle branding."[10] The sixties, in fact, witnessed the creation of new forms of "countercultural capitalism" that wedded business goals to political objectives and worked to advance political goals within a capitalist framework.[11] These "activist entrepreneurs," as Joshua Clark Davis calls them, viewed their endeavors as primarily means for pursuing "social and political change" rather than profit. Their interventions—originating in, for example, Black Power, feminist, or environmental movements—sought to make consumer experiences in American society more "humane, authentic," and, in some instances, "politically progressive or radical." They were part of what Davis calls a "forgotten experiment" in the 1960s and 1970s "to create businesses that advanced the goals of political change and social transformation" and that helped introduce the language of liberation and social change to American industry.[12] Other works in the history of consumerism and capitalism have shown, however, that the commercial origins of Americans' understandings—and critiques—of health care, wellness, and natural foods originated in the nineteenth century.[13] Dr. Bronner's Soaps fits within both of these timelines.

Over the longer term, consumerism continued to shape and alter sixties social movements like environmentalism. In the neoliberal era, environmentalism, combined with the decline of the regulatory state, witnessed the emergence of "green" branding and "ethical" or "radical" consumption, corporate responsibility as marketing strategy, and consumer activism; religious studies scholar Sarah McFarland Taylor refers to the marketing, representation, and mediation of consumer practices of environmental virtue as "ecopiety."[14] This change shifted the onus of environmentalism away from government-led solutions toward "market-led" management and consumer discernment.[15] As the state moved away from regulation, "individual consumers were framed as best able to protect themselves and discipline market actors through their purchases." This had the effect of curbing a radical critique of capitalism, substituting in its place an ameliorative and liberal goal of encouraging individuals to become "critical consumers."[16] It also favored knowledge. Within this structure of consumption, upper-middle-class consumers, who had access to more information and resources, tended to receive a disproportionate amount of the protections.[17] In this context, corporate social responsibility became "an instrument of profitability": an opportunity for corporations to "act virtuously," thereby currying favor with customers looking to identify with green causes.[18] In a process known as "green washing," corporations co-opted the language of environmentalism.[19] These strategies were a consequence of the "fragmented niche markets of post-Fordism," which relied on consumer-led manufacturing.[20] And yet, as this chapter will show, some companies voluntarily structured themselves to commit to a common good.

The history of Dr. Bronner's Magic Soaps allows for an examination of the convergence of modern proselytizing with activist entrepreneurship and, moreover, how companies both embrace and alter their ethical and business missions over time. Documenting the company history and the "constructive capitalism" espoused by Dr. Bronner's Soaps, this chapter interrogates the intersection of spiritual beliefs with progressive causes and environmentally conscious consumer branding in the recent past. More than any case study in this work, this chapter demonstrates the renewal of a commitment to social—and ecological—solidarities amid shifting historical contexts. Models such as the "marketplace of religion" and the "consumer marketplace" privilege choice in the construction of cultural and religious identities. Yet, as the history of Dr. Bronner's Soaps reveals, it is possible, if rare, for concepts like ethical consumption and corporate social responsibility to access broad understandings of what "all-one" might mean.

BACKGROUND: EMANUEL BRONNER

Born Emil Heilbronner in 1908 to a family of Jewish soap makers who owned a large factory in Heilbronn, Germany, Emanuel Bronner apprenticed with another Jewish soapmaking family, attended a guild system trade school, and received a university degree in chemistry. In 1929, Bronner immigrated to the United States after a disagreement with his father about mixing politics—specifically his Zionist beliefs—and the family business.[21] Living mostly in Milwaukee and Chicago for the next fifteen years, according to the biographical note in *The Moral ABC*, "soapmaker/master-chemist Bronner built 3 American soap plants, trained 9 chemists, licensed 6 of 53 patents for $60,000!"[22] He invented the famous peppermint formula in 1935 in an effort to deodorize his children's diapers.[23]

During his first two decades in the United States, Bronner endured a series of personal tragedies—connected to global events—that came to inform his moral philosophy. Although one sister emigrated from Germany to Palestine in the 1930s and another departed for the United States, Bronner's parents, Berthold and Franciska, remained in Germany despite their son's efforts to get them to leave. They later died in the Holocaust (Berthold in Theresienstadt; Franciska in Auschwitz) just a few years after the Nazis Aryanized the family soap business. Bronner's wife, a Catholic maid named Paula, died at a mental hospital in 1944, and Bronner put his three children into an orphanage (they grew up in a series of foster homes). As Bronner endured these tragedies, he relocated to Chicago and began to speak publicly about his plan for world unity. In 1945, as the Allies crossed the Rhine into Germany at Remagen, the *Chicago Tribune* took note of "the first crucifixion mystery in Chicago police records," which occurred beneath the elevated train line and involved an Austrian-born lens grinder, Fred Walcher, who had called for a crucifixion to bring attention to his world peace plan, American Industrial Democracy. Much to Walcher's surprise, his followers designated him as the chosen messiah. They strapped him to a cross with ropes and fastened his palms and feet to the structure with tenpenny nails, then placed a crown of rose thorns on his head. Police found a placard fashioned out of a paper bag above his head that read, "Peace on earth. This good man is choosen [sic] in sacrifice by the noblest and greatest and finest inspiration for world peace. Let's all foolow [sic] for the good of mankind. God bless him. Amen. By the Unknown World Controllers."[24] Bronner, named as "Emil Bronner" in the ensuing news coverage, explained that he had worked with Walcher for months on a universal brotherhood plan.[25] A syndicated story about the episode appeared in local newspapers across the nation. After that episode, Bronner continued his efforts to unite humanity. A year later, he was arrested at the University of Chicago while trying to secure a speaking slot for his "one world peace plan" at the school's International House. In the wake of this incident, Bronner was jailed and, with his sister Luisa's assent, committed to an asylum in Elgin, Illinois, where he reportedly endured forced labor and twenty shock treatments; Bronner later attributed the onset of his blindness to these treatments.[26]

The trauma of both the death of his wife and parents during World War II and his subsequent institutionalization make it easier to empathize with his eclectic preoccupations and prevarications about his credentials. Bronner spent the rest of his life revising the "All-One" message that made his soap distinctive on the grocery store shelf; his family later codified the message in a tract entitled *The Moral ABC* and, more recently, have begun researching the family and company's history. (By all accounts, Bronner worked continuously on the "All One" message, so it is difficult to identify when he wrote many of the sections.) After losing his sight in the 1970s, he hired a series of secretaries to transcribe his ideas or required his visiting son to do so (his son Ralph recalled, "He'd ask me to retype the whole thing, over and over. . . . There's only so much you can do with white-out").[27] In the 1970s, he provided lodging for employees at an apartment building near his home and purchased dinner at The Fireside, a steakhouse in Escondido, for anyone willing to listen to his ideas. He also seemed to have searched for a college-aged assistant who could type.[28] When bereft of companions, he recorded himself. A *Los Angeles Times* reporter who was invited into his home in 1987 noted at least a dozen tape recorders placed in different rooms.[29] His son left behind about four hundred reels of tape that amounted to approximately two hundred hours of his father's monologues dating to 1968;

the company edited and released a limited edition album for charity in 2016 and again in 2021 as a vinyl LP, *Sisters and Brothers*.[30] Reflecting on some of the more controversial statements that Bronner put in his treatise, Ralph remarked, "He put on that label everything he thought would help the Earth."[31]

BRONNER'S CONTEXT

The Moral ABC was not simply the heartbreaking ramblings of a man who experienced a series of deep personal traumas. In fact, Bronner's religious mission, his environmental concerns, and his product fit within three broader currents of mid-twentieth-century history. First, like other members of his generation, the Second World War, the Holocaust, and the atomic age traumatized his memory but heightened his appeals for human solidarity. Second, Bronner's apprehension about environmental degradation connected him to a mid-twentieth-century environmentalism based in alternative health experimentation but also to rightward-leaning politics. Third and finally, his soap found an audience among the left-leaning youths of the counterculture who sought natural and ecologically conscious products. Although Bronner's ideas fit within each of these contexts, his grandsons later adapted these mid-century visions to new historical conditions.

Like many other religious visionaries, Bronner experienced a series of personal misfortunes, and he connected these experiences with broader social causes. His "All One" message sought solidarity in a world fractured by the profound loss of the war followed by the threat of greater destruction caused by bipolar politics of the global Cold War. Bronner adapted his Orthodox Judaism, which he claimed was influenced by Rabbi Hillel, to his American context, which was characterized by crisis and loss. Indeed, starting in the early 1950s Bronner frequently took out classified ads in local papers, and the first reference to the "Moral ABC" in 1966 read, "Stay free. Teach the Moral ABC of Essene Rabbi Hillel to unite mankind in One-God State, not ½ true intolerant hate"; after a few different iterations, he added "ALL ONE GOD FAITH IN ONE— GOD'S STATE" to his ads.[32] Throughout the tract as published by the company, Bronner alludes to his suffering and his mission to carry forward in the face of adversity, including the torture of the asylum and his late-life blindness. For example, in a section subtitled "To Dream the Impossible Dream," he writes,

For this is my goal: To reach that unreachable star, no matter how hope-less, no matter how far! To fight for the Right without question or pause, to be willing to march into hell for a heavenly cause. For I know if I follow this glorious quest, that my heart will lay peaceful & calm when I'm laid to my rest. For I know that all will be better for this: that one man, tortured, blinded, covered with scars, still strove with his last ounce of courage, to reach that unreachable star, 'til united All-One we are, the whole human race in Astronomy's eternally tremendous All-One-God-Faith![33]

The passage references the 1965 musical *Man of La Mancha*—itself an adaptation of *Don Quixote*, an early seventeenth-century novel about a protagonist's idealistic mission—and its most popular musical number, "The Impossible Dream (The Quest)." Just a few pages later, in a section subtitled "How to Love," Bronner repeats his dedication to his mission and the personal trauma he endured to carry it out:

For God alone knows man's far distant future, towards which love's unfail-ing light shows clear the upward path to brotherhood-progress-Unity! Great tasks to nurture! With strength and knowledge, happiness can last!

To keep my health, to do my work, to love, to live; to see to it I gain and grow and give and give; never to look behind me for an hour, never to wait in weakness, nor to brag in power, always working, searching for more truth, more light, always writing, teaching what I found good and right!

Robbed, starved, beaten, blinded, fallen, wide astray, back with the full truth I've learned, back to the way! Smile! Help teach the Moral ABC's All-One-God-Faith, that eternally unites the human race! For we're All-One or None! All-One! All-One![34]

The religious studies scholar Roger Chapman argues that Dr. Bronner's beliefs should be positioned within the historical and cultural context of the Holocaust, the early years of atomic weaponry, and the Cold War. Chapman locates Bronner's unconventional ramblings within the be-havior of a "prophet" or "holy fool" (which also resonates with *Don Quixote*). At the same time, he argues that Bronner's message sincerely sought an "ecumenist response to the violence associated with the Holo-caust, World War II, and the Cold War."[35]

In the midst of these personal and global crises, Bronner developed a "peace plan" around his "All-One-God-Faith" that emphasized the "Moral ABC"—a code of ethics and personal conduct that, according to Chapman, blended Jewish traditions with American ideas of universalism and pluralism.[36] Specifically, he argues that Bronner's beliefs fit within the Jewish tradition of *tikkun olam*: "Fixing the concrete world of objects, animals, and persons through everyone's efforts to prevent harm to, or to restore, the environment and social and familial ties."[37] This philosophy coincided with other efforts among Jewish Americans in the 1950s to "be in partnership with the Creator in healing or restoring the world by promoting moral and ethical responsibility." In this interpretation, Bronner's advancement of his "All-One-God-Faith" was a latter-day plea for human unity in the face of nuclear disaster.[38] Bronner's thirty-thousand-word treatise concludes with this urgent message of present-day dangers:

> FINALLY: THERE IS NO SUCH THING AS 'PEACE.' IT'S UNITY OR DIS-UNITY! FOR ON GOD'S SPACESHIP EARTH, WITH BOMB & GUN, WE'RE ALL-ONE OR ALL-NONE! ALL-ONE! ALL-ONE! ALL-ONE! EXCEPTIONS ETERNALLY? ABSOLUTE NONE![39]

In the aftermath of the Holocaust and amid the Cold War that threatened nuclear annihilation, Bronner sought to remind users of a common humanity. In his invocation of "spaceship earth," a phrase coined by Buckminster Fuller in *Operating Manual for Spaceship Earth* (1969), Bronner also incorporated one of the environmental movement's most enduring catchphrases for capturing the earth as an enclosed machine operated by human "astronauts" charged with steering the machine without destroying it; this metaphor, of course, also fit with Bronner's apocalyptic fears.[40] At the same time, critics have noted the limitations of the metaphor, as it privileged notions of human stewardship in understandings of conservation.[41]

Bronner distilled much of his belief system onto the packaging of his soap, but the manifesto did not represent the extent of his energies. His activism connected him to remote corners of Cold War public health and environmental causes. As Brian Allen Drake explains, prior to the advent of the environmental movement in the late 1960s, a range of Americans—not just those on the Left—had deep-seated and intermingled concerns relating to "pollution, contamination, bodily health, and the power of the state."[42] Americans experienced a series of environmental crises that cast doubts on the promise of technology, whether achieved through physics, chemistry, or public health. Although Rachel Carson's *Silent Spring* (1962), an exposé about DDT, is the best known, other works like William Longgood's *Poisons in Your Food* (1960) and Murray Bookchin's *Our Synthetic Environment* (1962) fit within calls for a "right to know" about environmental effects on the body as well as a tendency to associate human and environmental health.[43] Revelations about radiation, thalidomide, and the pesticide aminotriazole also triggered fears about "unnatural" substances in everyday life and heightened anxieties about the government's complicity in introducing these dangers into citizens' daily lives.[44] These concerns were well founded, as a USDA report issued in the wake of Carson's revelations noted the increase in the use of chemicals as fertilizers, disease killers, defoliants, desiccants, and growth regulators over the previous decade and a half. The report, influenced by agribusiness interests, notably downplayed the significance of this growth because it had been enacted under federal controls.[45]

Bronner was an exemplar of the type of activist who sought to restore human health by challenging mid-century bureaucratic decisions that contaminated human bodies. He considered himself a purveyor of natural food and hygiene products. He had contradictory impulses about notions of unity and progress: he pleaded for solidarity under the banner of "All-One-God-Faith—Unite the Human Race" but remained staunchly opposed to communism as well as the expanding power of the federal government. He was also enamored with the prestige of academic expertise and routinely referred to his (self-inflated) scientific credentials to protest these actions while remaining suspicious of mainstream campaigns to use science to improve public health (Nazis, of course, had used science as well).

Bronner was deeply involved in the anti-fluoridation movement of the era, which, according to Brian Allen Drake, "offers a spectacular example of what could happen when the environmental concerns of the postwar period crossed paths with the era's growing mistrust of the federal government, particularly of the conservative/libertarian variety."[46] Although scientists initially began to hypothesize about the effect of naturally occurring fluoride on preventing tooth decay in the early twentieth century, the United States Public Health Service did not endorse the public fluoridation of water until May 1950. Within a year, the American Dental Association (ADA) and the American Medical Association (AMA) also approved of the public health measure. Although mainstream doctors, dentists, public health advocates, and hundreds of American communities fell in line behind the initiative, a network of antifluoridation activists—including Dr. Bronner—provided pockets of resistance that frustrated these efforts for decades. Already alarmed about both exposure to contaminants as well as the growing reach of the federal bureaucracy into everyday life, activists tended to fall within the following (often overlapping) spectrum. First, there were proponents of alternative medicine, diet, and health practices, who were concerned with issues of purity; this group included Christian Scientists, Jehovah's

Witnesses, and Seventh-day Adventists, who asserted that fluoridation was medication. Second, there were anti-statists who objected to government initiatives on ideological grounds.[47]

Even so, once again defying clear characterization, Bronner's opposition to fluoridation drew from both the alternative medicine and ideological threads of conservative environmentalism. On the one hand, he viewed the practice as a "mass poisoning" that hardened arteries, brains, kidneys, and hearts in a way that was enough to "make atomic bombs superfluous."[48] Most of the time, he referred to sodium fluoride as "rat poison."[49] In 1952, he briefly considered moving his production to Hereford, Texas, the so-called "town without cavities," which had a water and vegetation supply with a high percentage of *naturally occurring* sodium fluoride because he considered the mineral salts in the local farmland to be conducive to his line of health foods.[50] On the other hand, he also advanced claims of a sinister government plot, which brought Dr. Bronner in line with libertarian views of environmentalism. At times, he tied the threat to anticommunism, as when he described fluoridation as "chemical warfare . . . as taught by Lenin, who said Marxist Communists must infiltrate capitalist institutions and destroy them from within."[51] At other moments, Bronner's work coincided with anti-New Deal rhetoric about state impingement on individual liberty. A 1966 letter to the editor in the Santa Ana *Register* heralded Bronner's upcoming speech about fluoridation, a "false doctrine of human welfare," to a chapter of the Freedom Club.[52] In 1968, Bronner gave a series of lectures at the University of New Mexico entitled "Freedom and Fluoridation."[53] A *Kenosha Evening News* paid advertisement from 1955 neatly ties these threads together. The header proclaimed recent victories over the "rat poison gang" and proclaimed, "Fellow Americans, fellow human beings, remember atom bombs destroy everything, sodium fluoride only the people!" It listed reasons to oppose fluoridation:

1) It is a deadly poison.
2) It is accumulative in the system.
3) It will inure other parts of the body.
4) It causes fluorosis (mottling of the teeth which never comes off).
5) It is against the constitution of the united states.
6) Communism is one of the factors behind it.
7) We have enough poisons in our foods now without putting an extra dose in our drinking water.

The list cycles from environmental to ideological objections to fluoride before returning to environmental concerns. The ad purported to be from the Citizens' Committee against Fluoridation, but it also detailed Bronner's persecutions by "politicians" who had "suppressed any and all scientific opposition," especially by institutionalizing Bronner in the 1940s.[54]

Dr. Bronner's claims to being a research chemist created a scientific ethos for his allegations against fluoridation. In 1952, he published a letter to the editor in the Springfield, Massachusetts, Catholic diocesan newspaper that subsequently went viral and became the basis of a pamphlet he self-circulated. Bronner wrote to, was cited in, or lectured in the local reporting range of papers covering areas of New Mexico, Texas, Minnesota, Iowa, Pennsylvania, Idaho, Wisconsin, Tennessee, New York, Nevada, Kansas, Ohio, and North Carolina. In places as far as Kilmarnock, Scotland, medical officers had to refute the doubts about fluoridation sowed by Dr. Bronner's relentless campaign.[55] Small local papers only occasionally fact-checked his claims about his credentials or the reputation of water fluoridation among academic chemists, although a reporter in Ohio once phoned the Elgin State Hospital to confirm that he had escaped.[56] Articles and letters invariably referred to Dr. Bronner as a "research chemist." When the city of Long Beach, California, held a referendum in 1957 to determine whether to fluoridate the city's drinking water, the Long Beach Committee against Fluoridation invited Bronner to speak. The Long Beach Press Telegram noted his credentials as a "research chemist" (debatable) a graduate of Heidelberg University (true), and his relation to Albert Einstein (false).[57] Not surprisingly, he was most active in Southern California. In 1973, he claimed to have spoken against fluoridation every Friday night at the Embassy Auditorium in Los Angeles for a period of seventeen years. There is some evidence for this assertion: multiple classified ads for talks at an address on South Grand about "Health & 'One World Religion'" by Dr. Bronner appeared in the Los Angeles Mirror in the early 1950s, and in 1951 the California Eagle featured an ad for a "health class" held weekly on Fridays at the Embassy featuring "Dr. Bronner's Organic-Mineral-Salts" and— evoking FDR's World War II–era slogan—promising "4 Freedoms" including "FREE, All You Can Eat," "FREE, Speech—FREE, Prizes," and "FREE Admission" ("All Human Beings Welcome").[58] In 1966, Bronner was "shut off" at a joint hearing of the city council's Water and Power Committee and Public Health and Welfare Committee to investigate whether the city should authorize water fluoridation for Los Angeles residents. He had spoken continuously for twenty-one minutes.[59] His notoriety culminated in 1970, when he briefly appeared discussing the topic in *Rainbow Bridge*, a film about countercultural figures in Hawaii that became better known for its brief performance by Jimi Hendrix (and, many years later, Dr. Bronner).[60]

Although Bronner's anxieties about pollution and government over-reach brought him into contact with conservative environmentalists in the 1950s, by the late 1960s his soap's "natural" ingredients endeared it to a kind of environmentalism more closely identified with the Left. The roots of the convergence of Bronner's Soap with the counterculture and the environmental movement stretch back to the nineteenth-century body-reform movements that were, in a sense, revisited in the sixties. Historian Ruth Clifford Engs has characterized the era—with its calls for natural living, physical fitness, improved diet, and experimentation with alternative medicine—as the dawn of a third "Clean Living Movement" in American history.[61] The movement inspired a new wave of prescriptive literature. Bronner's manifesto, in fact, fit squarely within an emerging West Coast grassroots print culture of "lifestyle publishing" producing amateur magazines, catalogs, and journals in the early 1970s—including well-known countercultural publications like Stewart Brand's *Whole Earth Catalog*, first published in 1968—that affirmed the need for a new and different way of organizing life in late modernity.[62] Many within this lifestyle movement were in search of self-meaning quite apart from the scientific and rational sense of progress that had come to character-ize modern life. Bronner's "All One" message complemented the radical critique of technocracy that authors like Theodore Roszak saw emerging within the counterculture.[63]

Soap was not always important to washing. When John Wesley noted that "Cleanliness is next to Godliness" in a 1778 sermon, he was, ac-cording to historians Richard and Claudia Bushman, referring to "neat-ness of apparel" rather than a scrubbed body. In the eighteenth century, a basin of water and a towel provided the means for bathing. Soap (made with tallow and ash) was primarily used for washing clothes. Men lath-ered with soap to shave, and women used toilet soaps with natural in-gredients to treat—but not necessarily clean—skin.[64] Health proponents highlighted the medical, rather than moral, benefit of cold-water bath-ing. The idea of a "cleansing bath" became more accepted at the end of the eighteenth century before being popularized over the course of the nineteenth century. Even then, authorities tended to assign baths as im-portant for their healing properties rather than cleansing impact, and medicinal waters and spas were revived, especially in Europe.[65] As critic

Anne McClintock has noted, during the Victorian era soap became an important commodity for mediating middle-class values about sex, industrial capital, Christianity, social class, and empire.[66]

A combination of factors—including scientific understandings of germ theory, a new emphasis by public and private authorities on personal hygiene, and the advent of industrial soapmaking—created the "cleanliness crusade" of the late nineteenth century. The notion of "hygiene" as a discipline of medical science emerged to dictate both principles and practices for individuals and the broader community.[67] Cleanliness, including adequate sewage as well as access to public baths, became a hallmark of Progressive-era municipal sanitary reform.[68] In urban centers, attitudes about cleanliness signified more about aspirations to gentility and the politics of respectability than piety.[69] Nevertheless, it can be difficult to parse the line between morals, health, and class standing made in advertisements and by middle-class reformers. As religious studies scholar Kathryn Lofton explains, nineteenth-century soap companies created a nation of bathers through their use of the "ritual imagination" that prescribed a certain method of and urgency in achieving cleanliness. At the same time, as Lofton shows, Protestant denominations seized upon shifting imperatives and began to equate individual moral and physical cleanliness in pamphlets, children's books, and curricular materials.[70] Pears Soap, an English brand best known for linking its product to the "civilizing" mission of imperialism at the turn of the century, also used testimonials from celebrities, medical professionals, and clergy. In the 1880s, Henry Ward Beecher extended Wesley's logic in a Pears endorsement that read, "If Cleanliness is next to Godliness, soap must be considered a Means of Grace and a Clergyman who recommends moral things should be willing to recommend soap."[71] The endorsement then noted the soap was the "*purest* and *cleanest*" and was used by "intelligent mothers throughout the civilized world."[72]

Industrial innovation allowed cleanliness to become a generalized aspiration for the middle classes. Steam power and mechanization, advancements in obtaining alkali from salt, and new understandings in the chemical processes of saponification facilitated the expansion of soap manufacturing.[73] Household manuals began to prescribe the use of toilet soap to wash the body. American brands such as Procter and Gamble, established by two immigrants (one a candlemaker and one a soap maker) in the slaughterhouse hub of Cincinnati, used the emerging tools of mass-market advertising to emphasize the importance of hygiene in an urban world of strangers.[74] In 1879, they introduced Ivory, advertised as the first product to work as a soap for both laundry and skin.[75] In the years that followed, the manufacture of toilet soap in the United States became an industrial and national affair rather than a local endeavor among tradesmen.[76] Due to geography, soapmaking remained a regional endeavor dominated by small and mid-sized firms—including that of Bronner's ancestors—for a bit longer in Germany. In the 1880s, there were over two thousand manufacturers with five or fewer employees and six manufacturers with over fifty employees. Henkel—a company that created a laundry wash powder—used the German advantages in the chemical revolution to gain a foothold in the market. By the late 1920s, the global soap trade had consolidated around Proctor and Gamble (United States), Colgate-Palmolive (United States), Unilever (England), and Henkel (Germany).[77]

The desire for hygiene and the advances of the second industrial revolution also became tied to body reform movements—influenced by French physiological theory, the work of Benjamin Rush, and "folk wisdom dressed up as science"—that developed diet and personal hygiene regimens as well as prescriptions for exercise, fashion, ventilation, and chastity as they sought a kind of salvation based on "freedom from illness and infirmity."[78] Health reform became a moral crusade.[79] The emergence of the modern industrial economy occasioned a further reconsideration of health in the United States and Germany. In the United States, a new type of reform movement began to adopt secular and scientific rhetoric that valued the advancement of expertise. Even religious reform movements tended to focus on perfecting or improving the physical body as well as ensuring the purity of the soul.

Meanwhile, in Bronner's native Germany, the late nineteenth century witnessed a moment when lay people and medical experts—like their American counterparts—reenvisioned "popular hygiene culture" within a "shared and contested" category of "life reform" that included both developing medical practices and natural therapies to induce a healthy lifestyle.[80] The "health-mindedness" that materialized among the German middle class included a dedication to "following dietetic rules, a regime that stressed sound nutrition, fresh air, sunlight, exercise, work, and rest as well as a balanced emotional life."[81] These ideas, evangelized in the United States in the twentieth century by German immigrant health food and naturopathy reformers such as Arnold Ehret, Benedict Lust, and Gayelord Hauser (whose diet devotees included Greta Garbo and the Duchess of Windsor)—represent the transcultural diffusion of the conversation about health and diet.[82]

The legacy of the life reform movement is seemingly built into Dr. Bronner's Soaps. Bronner's grandfather established a soap company in the family home in 1858 in the Jewish quarter of Laupheim, Germany (they also made candles for the Jewish Sabbath). By the late nineteenth century, the Heilbronners—Emanuel and his three sons, including Dr. Bronner's father, Berthold—had invented a liquid castile soap used in German washrooms as well as a bar soap sold under the name Madaform.[83] With his penchant for scientific and moralistic language (but implicit distrust of modern science), his desire to be referred to as a "doctor" of chemistry while disavowing synthetic ingredients, and his belief in the restorative nature of his products, Dr. Bronner embodied the contradictions within the life reform movement between alternative medical practitioners and modern physicians. Although the health and moral reform movements of the nineteenth century had prescribed changes to dietary regimes based largely on a vernacular wisdom rendered in scientific language, Dr. Bronner used the mantle of science to render claims about the immorality of the technocratic Nuclear Age. As already evidenced in his antifluoridation activism, he was a "scientist" who was suspicious of modern science and called for a return to nature. In a different moment in history, Dr. Bronner might have been known as a "health entrepreneur."[84]

Bronner's interest in health food as well as soap exemplified his opposition to processed food and chemically rendered hygiene products. At least one newspaper item referred to him as both a "research chemist" and a "nutritionist."[85] The "natural" simplicity of his soap and health foods followed the philosophy outlined in the *Moral ABC*, which decried the changes that modern scientific advancements had wrought in alienating humans from one another. In California Dr. Bronner found an environment that had, since at least the 1880s, proven amenable to entrepreneurial German health reform immigrants. Many of these enterprising men helped build the market for natural foods and products through traveling lectures that were particularly popular in Los Angeles in the 1930s and 1940s among audiences seeking a combination of education and entertainment (Yogananda and, in an earlier moment, Katherine Tingley were in-demand speakers on the Los Angeles lecture circuit).[86]

According to one account, Bronner learned of the health food movement in 1948 from Dr. M. O. Garten, a naturopath and fellow transplanted German also known for his health lectures in downtown Los Angeles. Garten told Bronner to apply his knowledge of chemistry and manufacturing to health food, which was "the coming thing."

Bronner soon concocted his first food product, a mineral seasoning crafted from herbs collected from local hillsides.[87] Brief ads for the "organic mineral salt" and bouillon appeared in West Coast newspapers as early as 1951.[88] His products, including his soap within a few years, found a market within the expanding natural foods economy of the early Cold War era. The mineral salts, which he had often claimed would have been a more natural solution to tooth decay than water fluoridation, were available in Iowa in 1962.[89] Products also included corn and sesame snack chips, chia soup, and calcium carrot powder. In 1956, Balzer's, a grocer in Central L.A., advertised Dr. Bronner's "organic cocktail wafers," which were made from "organic stone ground corn" that were "mineral salted" and "high in protein, low in fat," making them "a perfect appetizer or accompaniment to salads, soups, and fruits" (the chips were still made as late as 1990).[90] An ad for Haseltine Nutrition Center in Long Beach offered Dr. Bronner's "Calcium Food," which promised to "replace sugar and help prevent calcium, phosphorus and mineral deficiencies."[91] A 1959 advertisement for Full O'Life Foods ("for modern nutrition") in Burbank featured products from the Adventist-inspired company Battle Creek Foods (the founder's great-grandmother was Ellen G. White) as well as Dr. Bronner's High Protein Foods featuring "Organic Mineral Bouillon with Vegetable Base Broth" and "High Protein Instant Soup Vegetable Amino Acids."[92]

For the first fifteen years of its existence, Bronner ran company operations out of his home (figure 12). In 1963, Bronner moved the company to Escondido, the home of the world's largest avocado packing plant, because he felt that the company's mineral salts made an excellent complement to the food. Advertisements for his "four freedoms" lectures from "Escondido's Own Chemist/Nephew of Einstein" soon appeared in the local paper.[93] He planned to work out a deal—never realized—to sell his salts with avocados on supermarket shelves (he still spoke of this plan to journalists as late as 1990).[94] Beginning in the early 1970s, the soap became a staple of health food stores, evidenced by the advertising that appeared in newspapers. For example, in 1973, Vitamin Village, an Orange County–based health food chain whose name reflected a renewed interest in vitamins and dietary supplements, highlighted the "Coconut, Olive, & Peppermint Oils" of the "non-detergent" soap; in 1977, Food For Thought, a chain in Long Island, New York, included the soap in an advertisement for a 20-percent-off sale.[95]

Bronner's ethos was flexible enough to fit in the emerging ecological consciousness that developed in the 1960s, when consumers began

FIGURE 12. Emanuel Bronner (right), his son Jim (left), and his son Ralph's wife (second from right) prepare a shipment of Dr. Bronner's Soaps in the early 1960s. Photo courtesy of Dr. Bronner's.

to call for a return to natural products that were less toxic to their bodies and the environment. They tended to see themselves holistically, since "the monism of the counterculture projected an underlying totality binding self with a social and natural world whose linkages eluded the categories of traditional knowledge."[96] That is, the individual was connected to, rather than separate from, the natural world; it too could be polluted by chemicals by lathering with soap, applied via cosmetics, or ingested through food. This concept meshed perfectly with Bronner's "All-One" ethos.[97] Nineteenth-century industrialization severed the historic link between medical and beauty knowledge: whereas medical knowledge began to emphasize clinical trials over "craft knowledge" and myth, the beauty industry focused on aspiration.[98] Similarly, the rise of agribusiness and chain supermarkets had alienated Americans from their food sources. These critiques emerged in ideas of "science," "beauty," and "diet" in the sixties: environmental critics pointed to the ecological damage of chemicals used in detergents and personal care products; feminists charged that the beauty industry created unrealistic expectations on and for women; and organic food proponents critiqued the use of pesticides and preservatives that made American diets unhealthy.

Market forces quickly responded to this new ethos, which viewed personal care products as a way of either further alienating consumers from nature or, alternatively, facilitating a returned connection to nature. A soap could now signify a body's investment in "environmental values such as ecological health, planetary unity, and connection with nature."[99] A new interest in "natural" and "green" ingredients emerged in both the beauty and grocery industries. Over the course of the next decade, new regulations required testing and labeling of products, and new brands arose to challenge the personal care products; at the same time, concerns about food safety and the environment led to the 1978 founding of Whole Foods—first known as SaferWay, in contrast to the Safeway chain.[100]

Dr. Bronner's Soaps benefited from this trend by bucking the divergence between "science" and "beauty" and the increased specialization in purpose and ingredients that characterized the industry for much of the twentieth century (the company's organic health food product line gradually faded away). The soap's "18-in-1 uses" motto made it a utilitarian item rather than a luxury good. Even the revelation in magazine profiles that he was a third-generation craftsman, not a "doctor of chemistry," worked to his advantage. And the soap's natural ingredients anticipated the "greening" of the industry in the 1970s and 1980s. For example, Tom and Kate Chappell founded Tom's of Maine in 1970, Anita Roddick opened The Body Shop in England in 1976, and Horst Rechelbacher established Aveda in 1978. Like Dr. Bronner's, each brand adhered to a social, environmental, and—sometimes—religious philosophy: Tom Chappell had a M.Div. degree from Harvard and donated 10 percent of pretax profits to charity; Roddick dedicated her company to natural ingredients and feminist principles; and Aveda, which adhered to Ayurvedic philosophy and aromatherapy, began after Rechelbacher, a hairstylist who disliked the chemicals in salon products, heard Swami Rama—founder of the Himalayan Institute—speak at the University of Minnesota.[101]

People often connect Dr. Bronner to the counterculture because of the soap's popularity with those who identified with its antiestablishment ethos. Although Bronner sought spiritual renewal and felt a general distrust of state intervention, he did not share the progressive commitments of some of the activist businesses established in the 1960s. He nevertheless found customers among young people who sought to challenge dominant norms. The company's enthusiasts included a young Steve Jobs, whose former girlfriend reported that Jobs, following time spent in India, viewed Dr. Bronner's All One Peppermint Soap as "the perfect commercial achievement: its broad usefulness, its ecological foundation; its philosophically monistic aesthetic."[102] Before the late 1960s, however, the soap was not sold in any significant volume. During the 1960s, when American cosmetic companies spent an average of 15 percent of sales on advertisements, Dr. Bronner's expanded via word-of-mouth endorsements among friends and customers of small health food stores.[103] According to a 1976 article in *New Age*, the company went from making about ten gallons of soap per week in 1961 to one hundred fifty thousand gallons per year in 1973.[104] The surge in popularity coincided with a redesign of the soap's label. According to Jim Bronner, in 1968 Dr. Bronner made a deal to give away one hundred thousand bottles of soap in Israel and overhauled the label from a gold and black design to a blue and white scheme to match the Israeli flag. The deal faltered, but the company kept the new design (Bronner also constantly revised the wording of the labels).[105] Jim Bronner estimated that the soap took off in 1968 based on its smell and lack of synthetic ingredients.[106] Ralph Bronner had a fraught relationship with his father for many years until he saw attendees at a Las Vegas health food convention fawning over his father. He later remembered, "People were hugging him, telling him how wonderful his teachings are, how they changed their life."[107] Many of these devoted customers arrived (and stayed) at his house after finding his address and phone number on the label.[108] Although not self-consciously countercultural or bohemian, the label's patched-together layout and stentorian writing style, especially when paired with Dr. Bronner's famous accessibility to customers, diverged from the professional corporate appeals of television and print ads. It had the refreshing aura of authenticity.[109] Bronner in fact had no affinity for hippies who drove the company's approximately $1 million-per-year sales in the late 1960s and 1970s despite having no salesman and no advertising—only "excellent soap, the best soap that can be made."[110]

Emanuel Bronner ran his company as if it were a religious nonprofit. It was not. A 1981 United States Tax Court finding noted his longtime penchant for weekly lectures, first at the Embassy Auditorium in Los Angeles in the 1940s and 1950s and later in Escondido. He received an ordination from the Universal Life Church in in 1971, whereupon he established a church, All-One-Faith in One God State Universal Life Church, which was premised on a mission to do "that which is right."[111] As a consequence of his idiosyncratic business practices, the company endured hard times when it was discovered in the 1980s that they owed $1.3 million in back taxes. In the aftermath of the case, Jim Bronner—an industrial chemist who invented a kind of foam used in fighting structure and forest fires—reluctantly took over in 1988. He converted the company to a for-profit company but died of lung cancer in 1998.[112] After Emanuel Bronner died, his other son, Ralph, took up the mantle of promoting the soap in his role as a product ambassador, a job recorded in the 2006 documentary about Dr. Bronner and his family. Ralph continued in this role until his death in 2015. In this way, Bronner's sons carried on their father's mission.

GREEN CONSUMERISM AND BRANDING

The ascension of Emanuel Bronner's grandsons, David and Michael Bronner, to the leadership of the company in 1998 marked a moment when the company became both more conventionally product oriented but also more intentionally progressive in its mission. In attuning itself to market forces rather than Bronner's spiritual goals, the company faced a potential ethical dilemma. As president of the company, Michael Bronner focused on expanding sales overseas. David Bronner, named CEO (Cosmic Engagement Officer), held a degree in biology from Harvard and credited a post-college period living in squatter communities in Amsterdam with informing his desire to become an activist. Michael Bronner summarized their dual roles by saying, "My brother is mission driven, whereas I'm more product driven. . . . He is looking to pioneer progressive measures that people don't know they want. I am looking at what people want. And the company needs both."[113] Together the grandsons transitioned the company's religious mid-century vision of human solidarity amid the traumas of genocide and nuclear war to one informed by anxieties of environmental limitations and climate change. As they did so, they nevertheless remained consistent to Emanuel Bronner's "All-One" solidarity. They ascended to leadership roles at a moment when other businesses sought to reform business practices along environmental and social justice lines.

In the first two and a half decades of the grandsons' leadership (1998–2022), revenue went from $4 million to $170.3 million/year.[114] During this period, Dr. Bronner's became the top-selling organic liquid and bar soap in North America. The company also began to sell products overseas. Mainstream retailers like Target featured Dr. Bronner's soaps on its shelves; however, while Target accounted for about 5 percent of annual sales, natural grocers accounted for about 65 percent (as of 2012), and continued to be the cornerstone of the company's profits. The company refused to sell its goods at Walmart because the family's disapproval of the retailer's politics and labor practices. Over the years, socially responsible companies like Tom's of Maine and Burt's Bees were acquired by Colgate Palmolive and Clorox and had to struggle to maintain their commitment to natural ingredients and "cruelty-free" practices since the acquiring companies had made no such commitment. The Bronner family resisted selling its business to larger conglomerates despite offers.[115] As one journalist noted in *Mother Jones*, under David's leadership, the company went mainstream by trying "to be as unapologetically counter-cultural as possible."[116]

Dr. Bronner—both the man and the brand—was made for this new context. Given the uniqueness of the soap's labels, no one questioned the sincerity of the founder's beliefs or the urgency described in them. Dr. Bronner's personal story, however tragic or—at times—apocryphal, became part of the charm of the product. At a moment when consumers were searching for natural or unmediated forms of food, clothing, religious practices, or exercise regimes, Dr. Bronner was genuine in his principles.[117] Over the years, Bronner's story was retold in profiles in *Esquire*, *New Age*, the *Wall Street Journal*, *Mother Jones*, and the *Los Angeles Times*. The pieces each tended to describe a bemused journalist's multiday encounter with Dr. Bronner as he narrated a fantastic iteration of his journey. In many respects, Dr. Bronner was perfect fodder for New Journalism's sense of adventure and subjectivity. The stories—and Dr. Bronner's persona—provided the advertising that the company declined to purchase.

Even after Bronner's death in 1997, he remained an eponymous presence within the company. Dr. Bronner's personal story helped the grandsons tell consumers a broader story about their brand. The company's website and annual reports featured photographs and engravings of him. The company's labels continued to invoke his message even as it added changes to reflect its fair-trade, organic, and no-animal-testing certifications. In 2015, the company made *The Moral ABC* available on its company website. The document included a preface by Ralph, an introduction by one grandson, Michael, and an afterward by his other grandson, David Bronner. Each relative explained what the plan had meant to Dr. Bronner before explaining what it had come to mean to them personally and to the company in the present. In addition, the company's website and social media accounts highlighted the historical continuities that connected the contemporary company to its nineteenth-century origins as well as its colorful founder; the 2019 annual report, for example, described the family members' return to Heilbronn, the location of the family's soap factory (seized by the Nazis) and Laupheim, the location of the family's ancestral home. (The current owner sold it back to them at cost, their former housekeeper returned the furniture that had been entrusted to her years before, and the current owner of the factory located the family soap mill machine.)[118]

Although his product became popular with the counterculture, Dr. Bronner obviously had no programmatic dedication to the politics of the Left. Nevertheless, his product's dedication to natural ingredients anticipated eco-conscious consumers' newfound preferences after years of synthetic detergents and chemicals. His sons and grandsons, meanwhile, squared the founder's religious message with the business's for-profit endeavors. The "All One" message provided an orientation: a usable history for reconciling the company's idiosyncratic past with its more self-consciously iconoclastic present. They aligned themselves with their founder's authenticity while doubling down on the natural ingredients. As Dr. Bronner's grandson explained, "Our family consists of many faiths, and in no way do we classify ourselves as a religion" (Bronner's children were baptized as Lutherans).[119] In a 2001 interview, Ralph Bronner reflected on the company and his father's beliefs:

> A few times a month, I'm asked whether we're a New Age religion or a cult. Well, we're not, or if we are, we have no members. Our family is running a soap business based on Dad's teachings. All he did is what any religious person does: he read the great works—the Torah, the Bible, Thomas Paine— and picked what he liked. His theology was a sort of cosmic soup. . . . But it really isn't so much a faith as a collection of ideas. . . . He saw his soap as one way of getting his message across. As he said, "Jew or gentile, everyone needs soap."[120]

In Ralph Bronner's description, Bronner seems like an early advocate of "Sheilaism," a shorthand description created by sociologist Robert Bellah to describe the American move toward individualistic and selective beliefs informed by multiple traditions to create a personal moral code.[121] Yet Bronner also exhorted customers to recognize the need for communal solidarity. To Dr. Bronner's tradition of *tikkun olam*, explained by Roger Chapman, the grandsons added a more explicit commitment to environmental stewardship and social solidarity. The Bronner family stopped short, however, of the radical environmentalism espoused by groups like Earth Liberation Front.

Their belief systems fit better within Bron Taylor's concept of "Dark Green Religion," which connects religion to a "deep sense of belonging to and connectedness in nature, while perceiving the earth and its living systems to be sacred and interconnected."[122] According to Taylor, these beliefs are based in a "felt kinship" with other life forms; a critique of "human moral superiority" that is often linked to a scientific cosmology; and a sense of interdependence based in the sciences.[123] Taylor sees the emergence of a "civic earth religion"—or in the words of political theorist Daniel Deudney, a "terrapolitan earth religion"—that would create a sustainable world based upon a sense of the interdependence and interconnectedness of all the planet's inhabitants.[124] This outlook, which pivots from Dr. Bronner's mid-century body-centric sense of planetary health, views environmentalism as a deeply held spiritual commitment with ethical obligations. Although Taylor views dark green religion as a challenge to nationalism and globalization due to its commitment to biological and cultural diversity, he does not specifically address the challenges of neoliberalism on state and corporate governmentalities.[125] Neoliberalism's policies include the deregulation of national economies, the liberalization of international trade, and efforts to create a global market.[126] The effects of neoliberalism are visible at the level of culture: it has valorized individualism and self-centeredness (or "self-regulation") at the cost of solidarity and has celebrated disruption and innovation in contradiction to reflection or economic reform.[127] It has also proven to be remarkably adept at co-opting efforts—like the environmental movement—to place limitations on markets through regulation.

Some corporations saw potential benefits to the perception of social responsibility in the "market-led environmental management" of the recent past. In sectors like the natural food industry—of which Bonner was once a member—entrepreneurs often continued to consider their work as oppositional even as it became profitable and even corporatized; the emergence of ideas of health, environmentalism, animal protection, and even marijuana legalization allowed founders to see themselves as providing a means to improving society.[128] Moreover, many corporations—especially associated with the Silicon Valley–based economy like Google and Facebook—have sought to embrace "mindfulness" through employee training as a means for establishing an ethos of "ethical sensibility." These programs should not be confused with community-minded business ethics. Instead, as media critic Kevin Healey explains, these corporate programs create "integrity bubbles," which he defines as "limited contexts of work and family life in which a small but satisfied group enjoys an experience of harmony unavailable to others." To avoid this type of insularity, a company needs to be sensitive to the needs of not just its privileged workers but to all workers and the broader community.[129]

Both the rise of "green consumption" and "corporate mindfulness" as a branding strategy therefore require an assessment of Dr. Bronner's "constructive capitalism." And yet Dr. Bronner's Soaps seemed deeply committed to "deep green religion" as demonstrated by its business model and efforts to extend, rather than reduce, government environmental policies. Its principles also adhered to collective justice and a critique of broader systems of power. In a 1970 op-ed entitled "The Social Responsibility of Business Is to Increase Its Profits," Milton Friedman made it plain that the bottom line should dictate corporate decision-making.[130] In contrast, the "All One" philosophy espoused a sense of civic responsibility: an extension of humans' responsibility to both one another and their ecological home. The brand outlined its "cosmic principles" that guide the company's actions "from soapmaking to peacemaking":

1. Ourselves: Work hard! Grow!
2. Our Customers: Do right by customers
3. Our Employees: Treat employees like family
4. Our Suppliers: Be fair to suppliers
5. Our Earth: Treat the earth like home
6. Our Community: Fund & fight for what's right[131]

"All One" was a slogan that sold soap, but it was backed by substantial corporate commitments. At a moment when late capitalism devalued the concept of community and belonging in favor of individual freedom and corporate value, Dr. Bronner's embraced the global public good. Moreover, in the "All One" spirit, they addressed employees, customers, and humanity more generally.

Since becoming involved in the family company, Michael and David Bronner have consistently invoked their grandfather's legacy when discussing business practices. The brand embraced—highlighted, even—the quirks of the brand's founder and label. In 2015, the company updated its labels to include a modern distillation of Dr. Bronner's philosophy: "In all that we do, let us be generous, fair & loving to Spaceship Earth and all Its inhabitants. For we're ALL-ONE OR NONE! ALL-ONE!"[132] From an aesthetic standpoint, of course, idiosyncrasies were now stylish and authentic; its reports had rainbows and bubble fonts that evoked the counterculture. In the company's 2019 annual report, David Bronner summarized the company's goals: "The thousands of my granddad's words written on our soap labels come down to this: We must take responsibility for our own lives while living a life of service to others, for we are all children of the same divine source, sisters and brothers sharing one precious planet."[133] The company published Dr. Bronner's *Moral ABC* treatise on its website with messages from his son Ralph and his grandsons appended as a preface, an introduction, and an afterword. In the preface, Ralph Bronner summarized his father's belief in All-One-God: "the idea that if we could all believe we are children of the same Father, we wouldn't kill each other." His father's beliefs could be summarized in two key sentences: "One is that we're all children of the same eternal ever-loving Father, All-One, All-One. And the other is Constructive Capitalism: Share the profit with the workers and the earth from which you made it."[134] In another appended introduction, grandson Michael Bronner expressed appreciation in the message as well as the fact that his grandfather "had the courage to put it front and center on his labels." From this, he learned, "You live your values and put them out there for the world to see. You don't shrink from controversy if that's what it takes to make this world a better place. At all times be authentic, be genuine, be of service, be of clear purpose, and above all make your actions have positive consequences."[135]

David Bronner went the farthest in repurposing his grandfather's vision toward environmentalism. In an afterword that explained how his appreciation for the philosophy changed over time, especially during his post-college experimentation with drugs in Amsterdam in the mid-1990s, he wrote, "As I became politically and ecologically conscious of the disaster of our unthinking collective consumption on the planet, shredding ecosystems and communities, I also appreciated the simple natural biodegradable soap and lifestyle that my grandfather advocated. . . . We are all children of one transcendent ever-loving-ever-present God and we must realize our transcendent unity or we will destroy ourselves. All-One!"[136] The family managed its brand by invoking its founder's quirky treatise about unifying "spaceship earth," but there was also a genuine effort to invoke the company's religious heritage in the contemporary context of climate change.

Dr. Bronner's Soap resembles corporations like The Body Shop and Patagonia that link progressive causes to consumer capitalism. There is a tradition in American culture of social activists seeking change through small enterprise, most recently among the activist entrepreneurs of the sixties who owned head shops, feminist or Black Panther bookshops, and natural foods stores.[137] As sociologist Laura J. Miller explains, this situation requires an examination of how a movement to reform natural or organic products can be sustained by both individuals and organizations who act "simultaneously as representatives of business and as self-conscious agents of social and cultural change." This trend has accelerated since the 1980s, as activists and entrepreneurs made common cause around social movements.[138] In fact, more recent corporations (and American tax law) have moved this activism to a different scale. Dr. Bronner's is classified as a Certified B (Benefit) Corporation, so its "social enterprise" business model requires that its owners pursue profit as well as social good according to its governing documents and third-party assessment of its practices. David Bronner describes the family business as a "mission-driven" company, which is "half ethical consumer products company and half NGO fighting battles."[139] Tax law scholars suggest that such a model allows businesses to discard the "pursuit of a social mission" as a "mere eccentricity to be indulged" and instead "declare its unconventional approach to business."[140] In its B Corporation documents—and its updated labels—Dr. Bronner's cites its support of "organic integrity," fair trade, fair wage, GMO labeling, animal advocacy, and industrial hemp. The market for environmentally conscious products depends on consumers who signal their status through the knowledge it takes to learn about a product (and the values it signals), rather than the absolute cost of a product. To an environmentally conscious consumer, the B Corporation certification demonstrates that Dr. Bronner's is not "just" a soap on the shelf. It's a soap with a story— and one that can be discussed with other high-information consumers who have time to research staple cleaning products. The transparency offers a broader story about the brand. It allows the company to establish a relationship with engaged customers and to offer information about sourcing, production, treatment of workers, and charitable contributions. It rewards high-information consumers with a sense of belonging to a higher cause.[141]

So how do we assess the company's "constructive capitalism" in an environment where corporate social responsibility also functions as a branding strategy? Scholars of "green consumption" point to the ways that market-led environmental management provides uneven protection and rewards individual choice. The same scholars also show how, in our neoliberal context, the marketplace shapes not just economic transactions but also its opposition.[142] Alternative practices might question the methods of producing, distributing, and consuming goods. They might, for example, support alternative—especially local—distribution networks and call for agricultural policy change. They could also make efforts to alter environmental policy for organic goods or against the domination of agribusiness. And finally, they might call for social justice for oppressed groups, including labor forces. At the same time, the production, packaging, and promotion of these ideals might best appeal to affluent white audiences whose privilege and identity give them access to this type of knowledge.[143]

In interviews and profiles, the Bronners emphasize that the practice of "constructive capitalism" began with the company's policies regarding employee compensation and advertising. Early in their tenure, David and Michael, along with their mother, Trudy, the company's CFO, met to establish company policies on pay and benefits. At a moment when executive pay was 278 times that of an average worker (compared to 20-to-1 in 1965 and 58-to-1 in 1989), the company capped executive pay at five times what the lowest-paid worker made.[144] They also established full health plans for all employees, retirement plan contributions at 15 percent of salary, annual bonuses that were 10 percent of their salary, $7,500/year in childcare costs, and a free vegan lunch served at work. In keeping with its policy that "all profits not needed for business [are] dedicated to progressive causes and charities," in 2022 the company gave $8.7 million—about a third of its net profits—to progressive causes including conservation, drug reform, animal welfare, Black Lives Matter, and LGBTQ+ causes. It also released a midterm voting guide to seventeen state and local ballot measures.[145] In a 2012 interview, David Bronner argued that these practices served as effective recruitment and retention devices for professionals in accounting, inventory control, and sales that, in turn, made the company more efficient.[146]

Despite the decline in state-mandated regulation, many corporations discovered a business model in sustainable or environmentally friendly management and production practices. Many of the practices originated in the natural foods business, including Erewhon Trading Company, an early organic food store established in 1966 and managed by Paul Hawken who became a leader in the sustainability movement; in 1971, Erewhon netted $1.8 million in sales at locations in Boston, Los Angeles, and Seattle and had become part of a $200 million alternative foods retail economy.[147] In the 1980s, efforts such as CERES (Coalition for Environmentally Responsible Economies), a nonprofit founded in 1989, sought to align corporate conduct with environmental practice included; following the *Exxon Valdez* spill, the organization set forth a ten-point code of conduct (the Valdez Principles) that corporations could sign on to follow. In the late 1990s, David Schwerin, a Philadelphia-based investment counselor, published *Conscious Capitalism: Principles of Prosperity*. The concept of "conscious capitalism" became popularized by baby boomer business owners like John Mackey of Whole Foods for its potential to use market solutions to solve social, environmental, and economic problems.[148]

Books such as Hawken's *The Ecology of Commerce: A Declaration of Sustainability* (1993) made the case that even "socially responsible" businesses of the 1990s like Ben & Jerry's, Patagonia, and 3M nevertheless used up resources; going forward, businesses needed "to integrate economic, biologic, and human systems to create a sustainable method of commerce." Hawken notes the need to "design a system . . . where doing good is like falling off a log, where the natural, everyday acts of work and life accumulate into a better world as a matter of course, not a matter of conscious altruism."[149] Hawken's solutions for business called for reductions in energy and natural resource use, but it also embraced "market principles" as opposed to government regulation or moral mandates.[150] The 3M company pioneered "industrial hygiene" (or "industrial ecology")—"making money from preventing waste"—in the mid-1970s when its environmental department sought to save money by phasing out air and wastewater pollution from its manufacturing process. In doing so, the company helped reframe environmentalism as a problem-solving opportunity—one of resource management—rather than one of prohibitive restrictions; it nevertheless also framed the issue as a challenge for business management.[151] Businesses have also enlisted customers in efforts to create sustainability, thus positioning well-informed consumers as important pieces to solving waste. Hawken defined "sustainability" as

> an economic state where the demands placed upon the environment by people and commerce can be met without reducing the capacity of the environment to provide for future generations. . . . Sustainability means that your service or product does not compete in the marketplace in terms of its superior image, power, speed, packaging, etc. Instead, your business must deliver clothing, objects, food, or services to the customer in a way that reduces consumption, energy use, distribution costs, economic concentration, soil erosion, atmospheric pollution, and other forms of environmental damage.[152]

In these early years of "sustainability," the market—not the earth—defined the terms of engagement.

Beyond its in-house policies, Dr. Bronner's sought to examine its growth in the context of its total impact on, in the words of its annual report, "humans, animals, plants, life massive and microscopic, and the multi-layer spheres of the earth that sheath us all."[153] Dr. Bronner's product is soap, not detergent, which means it uses natural rather than synthetic ingredients made of petrochemicals, foaming agents, preservatives, or fragrances. Unlike mass-produced soaps, it also does not use animal fats like tallow or lard; indeed, in keeping with its "deep green" ethos of refusing to favor humans over other species, the company has called for a ban on animal testing and has partnered with the Humane Society of the United States. In an environment where businesses have sought less oversight, Dr. Bronner's sought greater government regulation in the pursuit of transparency and fairness, and—perhaps—leveraging an advantageous market position. In 2003, the USDA certified Dr. Bronner's liquid and hand soaps as organic; the USDA rarely enforced the distinction in personal care and cosmetics brands—in fact, only Whole Foods monitored the status. At the same time, the company proactively defended its definition of "organic" when it sued Kiss My Face and Avalon Organics for advertising products as organic.[154]

Like many corporations in the globalized economy, Dr. Bronner's used a world-wide supply chain to create its products. In 2005, the company decided to require suppliers to follow certified fair-trade suppliers.[155] The company struggled to find certified organic and fair-trade sources for palm, coconut, or olive oil, so it established partnerships in Ghana, Sri Lanka, and the West Bank that provided fair wages, safe working conditions for farmers, and a 10 percent "Fair Trade" premium to fund community development projects.[156] A press release about its efforts tied the initiative to the "social and environmental ideals" of their founder and their current vision. Beyond this "mission-driven initiative," however, David Bronner pointed out in a press release that the company also sought to "raise more awareness and build a movement of conscious consumers dedicated to making all trade fair."[157] This language suggests that the company was not above touting its corporate social responsibility in branding itself to discerning customers.

Organic and fair trade also linked to David Bronner's interest in hemp and marijuana legalization. In 1999, David Bronner decided to use hemp oil rather than caramel coloring, in part because the ingredient made the lather smoother but also because it "was at the nexus of a bunch of hot issues" that included environmentalism and drug policy.[158] In 2001, the Bush administration outlawed most hemp products, which led to a lawsuit against the DEA that was eventually dropped (federal courts struck down the ban in 2004), but not until after Adam Eidinger, the company's director of social activism, staged an intervention at the DEA's Washington, D.C., bureau where he served agents free poppy seed bagels and orange juice as a reminder of other products that include traces of controlled substances. Like his grandfather, David Bronner showed a flair for dramatic demonstrations. In 2009, Bronner was arrested for planting hemp seeds on the lawn of the Drug Enforcement Administration in D.C. to protest ban on domestic cultivation; he was arrested again in 2012 for milling hemp oil in front of the White House.[159] Citing this type of activism as a reason that his family would never sell the company, David Bronner noted, "This is not feel-good sustainability, buying offsets and crap like that. This is taking on the Drug Enforcement Administration" (hemp agriculture became legal through the 2018 Farm Bill).[160] In this sense, Bronner evoked the activist-entrepreneurs of the sixties who condemned law enforcement's policies on illegal substances; he also exemplified the businessmen who aligned themselves with more traditional social movement activists in seeking changes to drug laws.[161] As was often the case for Emanuel Bronner, the publicity generated by the challenge obviated the need for purchased advertising: the brand's target customers could simply read about the challenge in the news, especially in progressive-leaning magazines. Or they could partake in the spectacle through the Magic Foam Experience, a see-through plexiglass container pulled by a renovated fire engine to mud runs, gay pride parades, music festivals, and community events, that allowed a few dozen participants at a time to luxuriate in a foam shower.

Dr. Bronner's stewardship likely appealed to high-information and privileged consumers who viewed themselves as environmentally virtuous. Yet as a social movement, environmentalism has struggled to incorporate broader strategies of common cause beyond conventional ideas of nature and ecology; this short-sightedness has caused the movement to exclude "ecological others" whose existence or practices do not align to its immediate concerns. Potential "estuaries of concern," as critic Sarah Jaquette Roy explains, might include, among others, sex tourism, food culture, genetic modification, and immigration policy.[162] The company's appeals to social solidarity both locally and globally fit this appeal.

The company's activism extended to its opposition to genetically modified organisms (GMOs), which linked to a "right-to-know" for consumers. In 2013, voters in Washington State went to the ballot box to decide the fate of Initiative 522, which would have required the labeling of genetically modified foods. Dr. Bronner's donated $2.2 million to the cause, which was about 25 percent of the $8 million raised to support in comparison to the $5 million spent by Monsanto and the $4 million spent by DuPont. (Dr. Bronner's donated $620,000 to a similar effort in California in 2012.) One *Seattle Times* columnist and skeptic complained that Initiative 522 looked like an "organic-food industry effort to impose a label on its competitors," thus making the issue about market leverage.[163] Perhaps more importantly, in an example of how company leaders aligned their contemporary beliefs to their grandfather's vision, the company issued a special "Yes on 522" version of its iconic label to appear on bottles and in magazines.

The company's activism also encompassed nonenvironmental or product-related progressive causes that addressed inequity. In 2016, the company advocated for fair wage campaigns in support of "all one" social justice by partnering with the Fairness Project and several other companies—including, among others, Maggie's Organics, Seventh Generation, Cambridge Naturals, and MOM's Organic Market—to support ballot initiatives to raise the minimum wage. The members of the Fair Pay Today Campaign also signed a statement that called for a rise in the federal minimum wage to $12 by 2020; wherever possible, they would support ballot initiatives to raise the minimum wage.[164] The company donated over $500,000 to minimum wage ballot measures that year alone.[165] The company website explained the business logic behind the effort, but it also created a special-issue label that invoked the Dr. Bronner's "All One" philosophy to the cause at hand. The special label used the brand's familiar color scheme, layout, and font but included phrases such as "Support thriving community & economy! Back local efforts to raise the minimum wage! It's the right thing to do!" In a larger font, the label read,

> Dr. Bronner's believes that we can only prosper in the long run if we contribute to the prosperity of society as a whole. It's why we compensate all our staff fairly, cap executive compensation at five times the lowest paid position, and dedicate profits to support and advance progressive causes.
> It's also why we've joined the growing movement to raise the minimum wage.
> GOOD FOR BUSINESS! GOOD FOR US ALL![166]

Other blurbs on the label protested the unfairness of the current economic climate: "When a person working 40 hours a week can't cover the basic costs of living, there's something deeply wrong with our economic system." The label also had the original Dr. Bronner's penchant for repetition: "Honest wage for honest work!" "Fair pay—good for communities! Fair pay—good for business big & small!" It also showed

FIGURE 13. In 2016, Dr. Bronner's Soaps partnered with the Fairness Project to support an increase in the minimum wage in several states. The company's support included a $500,000 donation as well as a special label with the brand's signature layout and color scheme as well as the urgent tone of the *Moral ABC*. Photo courtesy of Dr. Bronner's.

the original's fondness for religiously and historically eclectic inspiration, with quotations from I Corinthians 12:21–22, 26, Ralph Waldo Emerson, Adam Smith, George Eliot, Buddha, Franklin D. Roosevelt, Eugene V. Debs, and two passages from Dr. Bronner's original *The Moral ABC*. Each quotation pointed to the importance of social solidarity and the responsibility of individuals or companies to the greater good (figure 13).

"All-One" solidarity extended to the issue of immigration. The company denounced the Trump administration's treatment of immigrants, including asylum seekers at the border, by locating its commonality with employees and suppliers of diverse origins. In a January 2017 press release that followed Trump's initial closing of the borders, the company noted Dr. Bronner's loss during the Holocaust and desire to help people "realize our unity across religious and ethnic divides or perish." The Bronner family's heritage included a mixture of Christian and Jewish ancestors, but it also included "fair trade sister companies around the world" in Ghana (largely Christian workforce), Sri Lanka (largely Buddhist workforce), and Israel/Palestine (Jewish, Christian, and Muslim).

In addition, the company's northern San Diego workforce was largely of Mexican ancestry, many of whom were immigrants, "just as Emanuel Bronner was." In 2017, shortly after Donald J. Trump's inauguration, the company donated $50,000 to the National Immigration Law Center; in 2018, during the family separation crisis, the company donated $10,000 to RAICES and $50,000 to Alliance San Diego.[167] Beyond immediate causes addressing ecological preservation, the company supported causes closely tied to addressing the environment of recent immigrants, including undocumented people.

CONCLUSION

Late modernity occasioned a redefinition of the boundaries of religion that requires an examination of, as one scholar notes, "the interaction of local communities, global networks, representational and technological media, and the active biophysical . . . landscape."[168] The consumer marketplace increasingly provided the framework of these interactions, and this chapter has tried to show how spiritual and religious values work within this context. As social critics like David Harvey explain, neoliberal ideas and rhetoric about freedom, which empower individual decision makers operating in a range of marketplaces, can capably redirect impulses for social solidarity toward "libertarianism, identity politics, multiculturalism, and . . . narcissistic consumerism." When not consciously wed to ideas of social solidarity, consumer citizenship based in notions of cosmopolitan religious experimentation represents a powerful example of the "neoliberalization of culture."[169] In many instances, "ethical" consumerist practices of the post-Fordist era reinscribed privilege and valorized personal choice, but Dr. Bronner's Soaps generally espoused business and consumer practices that fostered notions of "All One" social solidarity.

PART TWO

Religious and Spiritual Belief in Civic and Social Imaginaries

Part 2 examines the long-range impact that alternative spiritualities made on specific Southern California communities. The chapters trace how ideas and practices drawn from around the world came to define the politics of place in two very different Southern California communities: Loma Linda, a town with an observant Seventh-day Adventist community in San Bernardino County; and Encinitas, a surfing community in San Diego County and the site of Yogananda's seaside ashram. Each chapter explores how belief informed the development of concepts of wellness, fitness, and multiculturalism in the early twenty-first century. Both chapters examine how religious inheritances of one era were transformed into civic and social imaginaries that defined the "good life" for residents, who then often turned out to defend their community's civic identity from perceived threats. Concepts such as "religion," "spirituality," and "sacred" were often renegotiated—often through appropriating and redeploying language, icons, and practices—in ways that promoted privilege to the detriment of social equality. In tracing the origins of beliefs and practices from the early twentieth century into their forms in the more recent past, the case studies that follow highlight the ongoing tensions between pursuing a social good and privileging individual choice, especially those of affluent white seekers.

Concepts of wellness and social connectivity are integral to both case studies. Both communities endorsed lifestyles and practices that aligned to emerging scientific research on wellness, happiness, and longevity. Chapter 4 investigates the concept of "wellness" through an analysis of the health-conscious lifestyle practices of Loma Linda. Over time, the long and healthy lives of Loma Linda residents—linked to Adventist-prescribed vegetarian diets, active lifestyles, and community engagement—brought the city increased national and international attention. Outside health experts seized upon long-standing devotional practices as "best practices" that could—regardless of belief—be adapted and deployed by nonbelievers seeking to maximize their longevity. Their collective health consciousness became a checklist for individual wellness. As growth made Adventists' lifestyle less prevalent in the community, some observant residents responded by deepening efforts to preserve their perfected health space.

Chapter 5 uses the city of Encinitas to understand how a cultural pluralism based in religious experimentation came to define the city's overall civic imagination since the early 2000s. Given its proximity to the ocean, Encinitas offered its residents access to "Blue Mind"—access to water features that neuroscience researchers believed lessened stress. Although city residents seemed to celebrate spirituality defined by self-consciously therapeutic lifestyle practices, their civic imaginary tended to harness alternative beliefs and practices to a California dream that was characterized by an exclusionary economy of bourgeois consumption and culturally appropriative branding. It is important to consider the extent to which communities sought to balance communal solidarity and individual choice. Taken together, the case studies in part 2 demonstrate the ways that religious and spiritual beliefs evolved over time to become inherited social imaginaries that broadly informed collective ideas of health, wellness, and therapeutic leisure.

CHAPTER 4

Wellness in the "Blue Zone"

The Cultural Politics of Vegetarianism
in Loma Linda

In November 1911, the Woodland (California) *Daily Democrat* flagged "a very interesting and instructive lecture" by Dr. D. H. Kress of the College of Medical Evangelists in Loma Linda. The article summarized the doctor's lecture titled "Health and Happiness, and How Secured." Kress expounded on the importance of mental wellness on sickness, but he also emphasized that "food and drink also exert a great influence upon health and happiness." The doctor advised against the "free use of sugar and fats"; he also noted that "the prevalent use of tea and coffee" among women and children was a cause of impatience and that the consumption of meats, in addition to producing rheumatism and gout and "irritating the brain and nerve cells," "stimulates the lower nature" and "lessens the power of self-control." Kress concluded, "When the true relation existing between our food and drink and our health and morals is better understood, much more will be said from the pulpit in regard to the need of eating and drinking to the glory of God."[1] Dr. Kress's prescription for health and happiness captured the vision of Ellen G. White, the founder of the Seventh-day Adventist Church, who became known for her pronouncements about diet when she described a vision she had that required her to establish a place where the sick could be taken and "taught how to live so as to preserve health."[2] Shortly thereafter, the church purchased a ninety-room sanitarium—later expanded to include a medical school—about sixty miles east of Los Angeles in Loma Linda. In a letter directing her agent to make the transaction, White expressed her hope that the institution would provide a foothold from which its medical missionaries could bring "spiritual as well as physical advantages to those for whom they labor."[3]

Over a century later, the church's efforts at securing "health and happiness" remained an integral part of Loma Linda's civic imagination. The city was the only American municipality selected as a "Blue Zone," a designation created by a *National Geographic* reporter in 2005 (and revisited in a 2023 Netflix documentary) that used quantitative and qualitative analysis to measure the health and longevity of populations in different parts of the world. The distinction linked area residents' extended life expectancy to the disproportionate number of Adventists in Loma Linda who observed the denomination's traditions for a vegetarian diet and positive, active lifestyle that emphasized community engagement. In the aftermath of the honor, the long and healthy lives of community members brought the city increased attention, which in turn influenced local public health campaigns and, more broadly, the city's social imagination.

This chapter examines the politics of food and wellness as it became associated with community identity in the recent past. Loma Linda provides an opportunity to examine how, over time, dietary prescriptions transformed from religious and sacred practice to a more generalized understanding of civic and individual wellness. The contemporary consumer marketplace provided new justifications for food activism, but the practices were rooted in historical traditions. Although recent aspects of the natural foods movement coalesced around the sixties-era counterculture, the movement had always been diverse. Adventists had advocated for natural foods since the late nineteenth century.[4] These marketplace transformations intersected with the Adventist-informed dietary habits of Loma Linda's residents. In this instance, the "Blue Zone" designation intensified residents' desire to promote healthy lifestyles through policy and planning, yet it also connected the city into a global conversation about indigenous foodways that could be adopted as part of a wellness lifestyle.

Scholars use dietary practices to expose a range of power dynamics in contemporary American society. *Foodways*, according to food scholar Lucy M. Long, "refers to the network of behaviors, traditions, and beliefs concerning food, and involves all the activities surrounding a food item and its consumption, including the procurement, preservation, preparation, presentation, and performance of that food." This understanding of foodways offers insights into historical processes of cultural meaning and social position.[5] Tradition and cultural norms create differences in food consumption, as do economic access and prestige, including disparities and inequalities in diet and health along race and class lines. Food traditions illuminate group attachments to location and time constructed through consumption patterns and lived practices. There is often an imperative to maintain group identity through conservation of food traditions in spite of new situations, while "hybrid" developments reveal the convergence of past and present influences and the migration of ideas, people, or food source. As corporations have come to dominate the American food environment, marginalized or poor communities have struggled to maintain "food sovereignty" based in collective traditions.[6] At the same time, the proliferation of choice created by globalization has empowered Americans to sample other cultures through food consumption. It has also raised concerns about cultural homogenization and a need for a preservation of distinctive foodways (or at least those that are presumed to be distinctive or authentic), a concept captured by the "Slow Food" movement's desire to maintain both regional uniqueness and diversity surrounding food ingredients, preparation techniques, and communal consumption practices.[7] Scholars have further noted the ways that class and racial inequalities emerge within alternative food practices that deploy scientific and ideological arguments for "healthful food and healthy bodies." In particular, alternative food practices in the recent past have appealed to affluent white consumers who were both interested in personal health and environmental conservation and armed with knowledge about how foods are "produced, packaged, promoted, and sold."[8] These choices—often reached as a result of having the time and educational resources to make informed decisions as well as the physical and economic means to purchase certain products—reinforced the hegemonic belief that health is an issue of individual responsibility rather than structural forces.

Although scholars have often associated present-day alternative foodways with educated white consumers, the historical origins of those practices were diverse and included those who used food as a means of religious critique. Food politics offer insights into the tension between religious and scientific belief systems. Like other Western societies, the United States has developed biomedical explanations for the physical condition of bodies, and medical research underlies the modern nutritional science that informs understandings of positive eating habits. Together these practices inform contemporary ideas about health.[9] At the same time, many religious traditions have made the ingestion of certain foods taboo while attaching supernatural significance to the consumption of others. Belief systems influence how people think about and consume food, but debates about food tend to be waged using science because "alternative belief systems cannot be validated by scientific methods."[10] The dietary habits of Loma Linda's Adventists therefore exist within a convergence of contemporary discourses about health, wellness, and happiness; they were, from the start, an expression of both group solidarity and personal regulation that informed how Adventists engaged with nonbelievers. At a moment when the boundaries among governmental, religious, corporate, and scientific authorities blurred, food politics became a contentious political issue as public health officials, government regulators, corporations, and consumer and citizen activists argued what constituted healthy food and to what degree federal, state, or local government might regulate what citizens consume to promote civic wellness.[11] In this moment, fostering a healthy and productive community became a governing logic, a power that "exerts a positive influence on life, that endeavors to administer, optimize, and multiply it, subjecting it to precise controls and comprehensive regulations."[12] In Loma Linda, the governing logic of civic wellness became visible in cultural, economic, and social policy.

Health trends often benefit from a "collective amnesia" of earlier movements that sought better living through food, exercise, or spiritual practices. The opposite was true in Loma Linda.[13] Over time, alternative health traditions came to shape the "social imaginary" of Loma Linda in that food politics had "[endured] through time and so [became] increasingly embedded in all ... institutions," including the community's "founding fictions" and "cultural traditions."[14] This sense of civic inheritance—evident in cultural traditions, educational institutions, city planning, and even public health data—influenced the way that the community governed, conducted, and imagined itself.[15] Community members prided themselves on the origins and purity of the city's food culture and the ways its institutions preserved them over time. Residents viewed their health consciousness—including vegetarianism but also physical exercise and religious faith—as a distinctive part of their civic heritage and, furthermore, compared these practices to other traditions around the world. These comparisons, in turn, brought Adventists into conversations about food politics in the context of public health, personal choice, and government regulation. Civic inheritance also caused conflict in instances when citizen-activists needed to recognize and accommodate difference. Moreover, as American culture became more consumer oriented, health consciousness became an individual asset rather than a community good to an individual asset.

This chapter identifies and explores the tension between community and individual health and wellness practices as practiced by the Adventist community in Loma Linda. Although chapter 5 will also show the connection between the politics of wellness and cultural lifestyle practices, this chapter features a Protestant denomination—though one that has not always been accepted by conservative evangelicals.[16] The cultural politics of vegetarianism in Loma Linda demonstrate how Adventist religious beliefs were reshaped and reimagined within new economic and cultural contexts. In the early twentieth century, Adventists converged on Loma Linda to build a community of belief and practice that might serve as a model for the outside world and the basis for the faith's evangelism. These beliefs became deeply embedded in the fiber of the community. As Adventists sought to convince more Americans to observe their food practices, its citizen-activists frequently invoked the cultural and religious traditions that informed the city's health imaginary as cause for preservation. This chapter reveals how, over time, aspects of their combination of vegetarianism, health, and spirituality intersected with the emergence of "wellness" and longevity as an individualized consumer practice. About 3 percent of American adults are vegetarians compared to approximately 30 percent of Adventists.[17] Adherents practice vegetarianism for a variety of reasons ranging from communal, environmental, and religious commitments to reasons related to health and self-improvement. As American belief systems empowered individual choice over all-encompassing rules, vegetarianism became a consumer lifestyle that one could "opt" into to maximize personal health. Yet ideas of "wellness" were also connected to place in Loma Linda, a city that was founded thanks to its proximity to the Southern Pacific Railway station and that is adjacent to one of the busiest interstate freeways in the nation.

BACKGROUND

Seventh-day Adventism emerged out of the millennial enthusiasm that originated in the Second Great Awakening. William Miller, a farmer and revival preacher in New York, New Hampshire, and Vermont, typified the belief in the imminent Second Coming (or Advent) of Jesus in the 1830s and 1840s. Believers endured a series of predicted arrivals followed by unforeseen setbacks—culminating in what became known as The Great Disappointment of October 22, 1844, when Jesus Christ failed to return to earth as Miller had prophesized—before the movement disintegrated. The date nevertheless became important to members of the movement, who insisted that the judgment of saints and sinners began at that time and that the Second Coming would take place sometime after the judgment was complete.[18]

The original enthusiastic outburst spawned the broader Adventist movement. Since then, the Seventh-day Adventist Church has increased its membership from a handful of marginalized converts expecting the second coming of Jesus to a racially diverse church with 1.2 million members in the United States (.5 percent of the American population) and over 18 million members worldwide. The Pew Research Center estimated the church to be the most racially diverse religious group in the United States, with membership divided among white (37 percent), Black (32 percent), Hispanic (15 percent), and Asian (8 percent) populations.[19] As with many American Protestant sects and denominations, members nurtured an "outsider" status from the dominant culture that originated in the ridicule they received from the mainstream for ill-fated predictions.[20] The church's roots in end-of-world apocalypticism and continued faith in the role of biblical prophecy, combined with their observation of a Saturday sabbath (i.e., the "Seventh Day") based on a reading of the Book of Revelation and belief in creationism, made them easily caricatured within American society. Moments when Adventists entered the news—such as when the Branch Davidians, a radicalized offshoot led by David Koresh, confronted the Bureau of Alcohol, Tobacco, and Firearms in Waco, Texas in 1993—only seemed to confirm the sect's peculiarities in the social imagination.[21] Adventists' sense of alienation sustained their belief in the righteousness of their cause. This was particularly true of their belief in observing a natural diet, which also paradoxically became the basis for their outreach to mainstream culture.

Religious leaders have long asserted that average people were capable of attending to their own physical health. During the First and Second Great Awakening, when religious dissidents chipped away at religious—as well as social and political—hierarchies, physical well-being became another way for common folk to assert their autonomy. Moreover, science, magic, and religion blended in popular culture until (and even after) medical thought emerged as a secular discipline in the late nineteenth century.[22] Concerned that the accrual of human culture gradually alienated believers from biblical law, religious reformers focused not just on institutions and rituals but also health and dietary practices as a means to achieve personal purification and the restoration of an Edenic ideal. In 1747, for example, John Wesley, the founder of Methodism, published a medical advice book entitled *Primitive Physic*, which provided an inventory of simple cures that might help people avoid the clutches of physicians.[23] Wesley consulted the work of his acquaintance George Cheyne, an early eighteenth-century English physician who wrote about eating patterns, especially chronic obesity among the aristocracy (including himself) and counseled abstention from the exotic and rich foods then entering the English diet. Having classified the types of foods available, Cheyne developed an early system of vegetarianism that emphasized simplicity of preparation and treatment.[24] Anxieties that civilization led to over-consumption and over-indulgence continued during the nineteenth century, when the advancement of the market economy—particularly canal and railroad networks that linked midwestern farms to urban centers and altered food processing and availability—created a sense that Americans were estranged from their natural selves.[25] Reformers sought a return to earlier—at least as they remembered them—methods for the preparation and consumption of food. In the 1830s, Sylvester Graham, a Presbyterian minister who espoused a series of hygiene, body, and dietary reforms, created a series of products—including graham bread (made of unbolted wheat flour that sat for twenty-four hours), which evolved into the graham cracker—based on his belief that store-purchased flour made with machines went against the "laws of the Creator."[26] Many Northern religious reformers established utopian communities—including Fruitlands, founded by Louisa May Alcott's father, Bronson—that would live according to communal ideals, including strict dietary practices like vegetarianism, that would serve as models for the outside world.[27] In the following years, Adventists incorporated many of these practices, including many of Graham's ideas. These concerns confirmed the idea that, as Edward Jarvis announced in an 1850 medical primer, "Every human being is responsible for the care of his own health, and the preservation of his own life."[28]

During the Second Great Awakening, religious movements searched for physical as well as moral manifestations of human perfectibility. Drawing upon new readings of religious texts as well as emerging understandings of health and personal cleanliness, reformers provided practices that adherents could take to improve themselves, including not just dietary practices but also fresh air, temperance, and personal hygiene. Over time, these positive steps became understood as methods of prevention aimed at curtailing physical degeneracy.[29] As historian Ronald G.

Walters explains, sects like Seventh-day Adventism provided a bridge between efforts among antebellum evangelical Protestants to change individual behaviors (including legislating morality via temperance) and reformers of the late nineteenth and early twentieth centuries who favored secular methods of reform driven by state action and scientific expertise. Bodily reform groups like the Adventists often linked religious and physical purity. Their holistic regimen provided clear ideas about self-control, restraint, and discipline for believers eager to take responsibility for their own well-being.[30] Indeed, according to Walters, to these groups "physical perfectionism, a belief that salvation was to be found in improvement of the body or the species," was a key element of the health reform movement of the late nineteenth century. These groups helped translate the language of reform from the parlance of Protestantism to science.[31]

When Ellen G. White began to describe her religious visions, she drew upon overlapping currents of religious, cultural, and scientific reform traditions.[32] Born Ellen Gould Harmon in Maine in 1827, she converted in 1842 and began having visions in late 1844, when she was seventeen years old. In 1846, she married James White, an early Adventist elder involved in the Millerite movement. At the invitation of a group of disciples in 1855, the Whites relocated to Battle Creek, Michigan.[33] In 1863, the church was formally established—with approximately 3,500 believers—around an organizational structure with a General Conference and state conferences. White never held a formal office in the church, but the church accepted her interpretations of the Bible and considered her pronouncements to be divinely inspired.[34] Over the course of her life, White experienced an estimated two thousand visions, including teachings on atonement (the path to salvation) and Sabbatarianism (the proper day to observe the Sabbath) as well as health, medicine, and diet.[35] In keeping with the folk traditions of the day, spiritual pronouncements were not divorced from science. Although some health reformers of the period viewed their actions as a method for eradicating disease and hastening the onset of the millennium, White viewed health reform primarily as a requirement to enter heaven. Over time, the church prescribed dietary rules for achieving health as well as therapeutic methods for recovery.

In autumn 1848, White, already a temperance advocate, had her first vision regarding "healthful living" which detailed the need to abstain from tobacco, tea, and coffee.[36] Six years later, she received a message pertaining to the foods consumed by believers. She saw that "rich food destroyed the health of the bodies and was ruining the constitution, was destroying the mind, and was a great waste of means."[37] In 1863, White experienced a revelation that transformed her outlook on food and health. In this vision, she "saw that it was a sacred duty to attend to our health, and arouse others to their duty . . . to come out against intemperance . . . and then point them to God's great medicine. . . . The more perfect our health, the more perfect will be our labor."[38] This insight, known as the "Comprehensive Health Reform Vision," remains the basis of Adventist health teachings. The ten "categories of counsel," compiled in *Spiritual Gifts, Volume 4*, included a religious duty to be mindful of health, that there were "laws of health" that must be maintained, the importance of temperance (including tobacco but also powerful medications of the day such as strychnine, opium, mercury, calomel, and quinine), vegetarianism, a regularity in eating habits, the importance of the mind to remaining healthy, the use of natural remedies for healing, personal and environmental cleanliness, and the role of the church in teaching health education.[39] In brief, health reform meant three things to early Adventists: "a vegetarian diet, two meals a day, and no drugs or stimulants."[40] At the beginning of the twentieth century, White renewed her commitment to abstaining from meat and barred it from the Battle Creek Sanitarium; she herself reportedly consumed no meat from 1894 until her death in 1915. In contrast to her earlier work, in *The Ministry of Healing* (1905), White enumerated her opposition to animal flesh based on its (alleged) cancer- and tuberculosis-causing properties as well as its cruelty to animals. In 1908, she urged the General Conference to circulate an anti-meat pledge. Rebuffed by the president of the conference regarding this initiative, she accepted an alternative for physicians and ministers to carry out educational work that recommended but did not require observance.[41]

White sought ways to treat sickness that led her to institutionalize her health beliefs. She had personal reasons to do so. Her husband, six years her senior, struggled with his health and predeceased her by over thirty years, and she lost two sons to infant and childhood sicknesses. She experimented with hydropathy, or "water cure," a treatment that applied water of varying temperatures and pressures to the body to stimulate natural cures (that, as scholars have noted, had the secondary effect of drawing city dwellers into the countryside to partake of mineral springs for healthful leisure).[42] Following the White family's two visits to the drug-free Our Home on the Hillside, a hydropathy retreat with strict dietary rules run by Dr. James C. Jackson in Dansville, New York, White had a vision in 1866 that led the church to establish the Western Health Reform Institute based on teaching "healthy living and drugless medical cures to the masses." The institute's popularity resulted in the hiring in 1876 of John H. Kellogg, a physician with ties to both Adventism and mainstream medicine, to serve as the superintendent; it became known as the Battle Creek Sanitarium.[43] Kellogg suffused his arguments for vegetarianism with scientific concepts while seeking to commercialize his version of natural foods. At a time when there was no regulation of either medical training or medical practice, Kellogg's education combined vernacular remedies with the latest modern techniques. Kellogg—as well as two of White's sons—first studied with Russell Trall, one of the first American advocates for hydropathy (he ran New York Hygieo-Therapeutic College, one of the first American institutions to admit female candidates for a medical degree) who also experimented with herbal and homeopathic medicine. Kellogg subsequently graduated from Bellevue Hospital Medical School and studied surgery in London and Vienna.[44]

Kellogg's work at Battle Creek largely aligned with the teachings of Seventh-day Adventism. Whereas a "sanitorium" tended to the needs of the chronically ill, Kellogg coined the term *sanitarium* to demonstrate the institution's attention to sanitation and hygiene.[45] The words perhaps also refer to the transformation of hospitals from charitable institutions to care for the sick to medical institutions seeking to provide a cure and, starting in the United States in the late nineteenth century, a basis for medical education and practice.[46] Given his training, Kellogg was attuned to broader trends in religious, medical, and nutritional health. He spread his theories not just through sanitaria but also food manufacturing, publications—such as *The Health Reformer* (later renamed *Good Health*), which he edited in addition to *The New Dietetics* (1921)—as well as international exhibitions. Kellogg sought to prove the effectiveness of natural treatments using modern equipment and resources that combined "technological advancement and efficiency." As a result, widespread folk remedies like hydropathy were deemed "rational" through experimental study, clinical observation, and prescriptive dosage.[47] His fascination with technology, human improvement, and purity later led him into the eugenics movement—an American cultural movement imbued with racialized understandings of "science" and "progress"—particularly after he left the church in 1907.[48]

Kellogg emerged as the American diet became more reliant on regional and global supply chains and as a new subset of reformers, muckrakers, professional experts, and government officials emerged to call for food regulation in the name of purity.[49] Kellogg's work fit within the broader emergence of prescriptive nutritional science, as scientists began to embrace the "New Nutrition" by learning to categorize foods as protein, carbohydrates, fats, minerals, and water.[50] In the same era, social scientists began to wield information about diet in debates about poverty, labor efficiency, and costs of incarceration and institutionalization.[51] In addition, as food became more industrialized and globalized during the Victorian era, fears intensified about food tampering and adulteration, especially if goods were produced by "foreign" hands.[52] During this period, the leading causes of death and disability among Americans were "infectious diseases related in part to inadequate intake of calories and nutrients" even as scientists also learned of the impact of bacteria and germs on food supply. As a result, government officials, nutritionists, and the food industry had a common interest in encouraging Americans "to eat more of all kinds of food."[53]

The work of muckrakers like Upton Sinclair (in *The Jungle*) and Samuel Hopkins Adams (in *The Great American Fraud*) justified concerns about contaminated and dangerous food processing and preparation as well as the dangers of patent medicines. Adams echoed White's concerns about medications when he lamented that Americans would spend $75 million on patent medicines that allowed gullible patients to "swallow huge quantities of alcohol, an appalling amount of opiates and narcotics, a wide assortment of varied drugs" in search of a cure.[54] The 1906 Pure Food and Drug Act prescribed new safety measures. Science, technology, and even branded packaged foods provided another response to concerns about safety.[55] Processed food, in particular, became an engineering marvel of industrialization alongside the Bessemer steel process, Chicago's early skyscrapers, and the Brooklyn Bridge. Kellogg's entrepreneurial genius allowed him to convince customers that manufactured food helped bring diets closer to an Edenic ideal—rather than alienating them from their nature as earlier food reformers had worried. He argued that processing natural substances—resulting in products such as Corn Flakes and peanut butter but also lesser-known health foods like caramel cereal coffee substitute, a combination of bran and molasses, and protose, a vegetable meat—enhanced their nutritional value.[56]

But concerns remained. Indeed, while state-sponsored public sanitation campaigns aimed to ameliorate cholera-inducing conditions in tenements and factories, they did little to address a second set of maladies brought about by industrialization, urbanization, and the emergence of a white-collar workforce. These so-called "desk diseases"—ailments of the nerves and stomach—became a "durable, neurotic regime based on personal hygiene and self-diagnosis."[57] Marketers positioned themselves as confidantes and teachers for young transplants attempting to navigate an urban world of strangers. Using testimonials, celebrity endorsements, and deceptive claims, newspaper advertisements offered cures for rashes, asthma, indigestion, heartburn, dyspepsia (or "sourness"), constipation, consumption, kidney pain, nervousness, foul breath, bronchitis, headaches, backaches, weight gain, and the common cold. Drug companies offered pills, powders, syrups, oils, laxatives, lozenges, balms, creams, and malted milk, among others to relieve these afflictions. These palliatives sought to ease the consequences of a poor diet—whether through overconsumption or contamination—and nervous disposition. They did not provide an alternative.

Experts asserted that Americans, who were no longer eating to subsist, needed guidance on controlling or correcting appetites. Scientific living became the ongoing concern of a new generation of health entrepreneurs. Whereas previous reformers turned to Sylvester Graham's unbolted wheat-meal bread, health seekers of the late twentieth century sought remedies such as Grape Nuts (invented by C. W. Post, a former patient of and competitor to Kellogg), oatmeal brands, and Shredded Wheat. Beyond the emerging products catering to health, Adventists provided a programmatic solution—and, better yet, a needed dose of prevention—for modernity's health and anxiety woes and, in fact, denounced the use of patent medicines and pain killers.[58] Middle- and upper-class Americans, whether believers or nonbelievers, arrived at Battle Creek to correct "lifestyle errors" connected to the emerging American consumer society by instructing visitors in diet, exercise, and temperance that were intended to become daily habits to promote individual health. All visitors were required to practice vegetarianism, and the sanitarium's kitchen experimented with "scientific" recipes—including meat substitutes—that aligned with these practices.[59] As visitors learned to control their appetites and exercise discipline, the path from sickness to wellness became a lifestyle.

THE CALIFORNIA HEALTH ECONOMY

When Adventists arrived in California in the late nineteenth century, they encountered a culture that already had a developed sense of its place in the

American therapeutic imagination as a place that featured both health-inducing weather and a scenic landscape. Books like Charles Nordhoff's *California: For Health, Pleasure, and Residence* (1873) hailed the state's salutary climate and the plethora of Chinese, Native American, and Mexican workers ready to support Anglo settlement and leisure. Anglo transplants built infrastructure to support an enormous citrus industry, which in turn was used to envision California as a garden of Eden—an idea that justified the reality of broader patterns of colonial conquest as well as modern industrial exploitation and forced relocation.[60] Whereas Puritans might have seen nature as depraved, the romanticism of the nineteenth century imbued the countryside with a "grandeur and sublimity" that could instill physical health as well as peace of mind.[61] As historian Shana Klein has explained, fruit cultivation (and renderings of these activities) came to symbolize national expansion because "the establishment of orchards, vineyards, and orange groves would advance the American empire by converting wild frontiers into refined gardens."[62] The sanitarium at Loma Linda fit within these historically constructed views of the region's landscape; it also sought to serve the influx of health tourists.

As Southern California attracted more wealthy white tourists, resort hotels like the Hotel Del Coronado (1888) in San Diego and The Raymond (1886) in Pasadena sprung up to cater to their needs. Other upper- and middle-class visitors arrived seeking cures to disease and, perhaps, ennui, patronized the segment of the resort industry offering "naturopathy"—a medical philosophy offering "a holistic approach that focused on preventive care" organized around plant-based medicines as well as "a healthy diet, sunlight, fresh air, and water"—following the popularity of such places in European mountain towns like Davos and Badenweiler. Health entrepreneurs imported these practices to American locations in the Adirondacks and Southern California, creating what became known as the "Sanitorium Belt."[63] Architectural design, exercise regimens, and food practices became as important to California's resorts as the region's climate, geography, and flora.[64]

The emphasis on health coincided with a politics of exclusion. In an early indication of the politics of health responsibility, the possibility of recovery meant that people with persistent health issues were blamed for their own sickness. Redemptive health required positive lifestyle guidance but also restrictive action. Indigent consumptives without the means to afford treatment were carefully monitored and barred from recuperative spaces. After the failure of an effort by the State Board of Health in 1900 to exclude all people with tuberculosis from entering the state, public health officials discouraged migration via flyers, letter-writing, and pleas to charitable organizations. At this time, there was a "right" kind of health seeker in Southern California, and "the ill represented everything Angelenos were supposed to be able to avoid—dependence, uncertainty, deterioration, and premature death."[65]

The health economy isolated and excluded entire groups. For example, during a 1924 outbreak of the bubonic plague, the Los Angeles health department quarantined the "Mexican district" and, in pursuit of disease-spreading rats, initiated a "plague eradication" effort that laid waste to over twenty-five hundred structures, much of it housing for ethnic Mexicans.[66] Although African American migrants moved to Southern California to pursue economic opportunity and partake in its warm climate, they were most often excluded from its health economy.[67] The NAACP fought for nearly a decade for African Americans to be admitted to the county hospital's nursing school (finally prevailing in 1919). Yet health care facilities remained segregated. In fact, in the mid-1920s a consortium of African American businesspeople met with an array of elected officials from northern Mexico to discuss the feasibility of building a health resort near sulfur springs that had been hailed by Mexicans for years "for their medicinal quality." The institute would be open to African Americans as well as Mexicans. Although fundraising occurred, the sanitarium was never built.[68] A few Adventist-led tuberculosis facilities seemed to be an early exception to providing care to tuberculosis patients. Neither the Glendale Sanitarium (also Seventh-day Adventist-affiliated) nor the Loma Linda sanitarium advertised in the *California Eagle* (they focused on health regimens, not tuberculosis care), although the Glendale organization held trainings with the African American community. There were two Adventist-affiliated sanitariums that appeared to accept African American patients, including for tuberculosis: the Los Angeles Sanitarium, founded by German-born doctor John F. Gernhardt, who performed at the Loma Linda sanitarium (and whose daughter attended the nursing school) and who advertised in the *California Eagle*; and the South Los Angeles Sanitarium, established by Anna Stokes, Ludy Albans, and the Reverend T. F. Jones. The Los Angeles Sanitarium trained at least one African American graduate who opened a massage and bath center. The Los Angeles Sanitarium and South Los Angeles Sanatarium offered health lectures and promised "Battle Creek Methods" as well as a specialization in diets, electric and sun baths and hydropathy treatments. When the sanitarium reopened in 1933, an article hinted at its Adventist connections by stating, "the healing of the body is good for the soul."[69] In 1942, a more extensive tuberculosis care center that accepted African Americans—but that served all races—was built in Duarte. The founding association, The Outdoor Life and Health Association—was established in 1935 by Dr. Leonard Stovall to teach disease prevention and the appreciation of outdoor activities.[70]

From its inception, the city of Loma Linda was a perfected health space. Like many cities of the Inland Empire—including Riverside, Redlands, and Pomona—Loma Linda was built on a bedrock of agriculture— especially citrus—and health resorts.[71] In October 1900, the *Los Angeles Herald* reported that investors, including eighty physicians, intended to open a sanitarium in "Mound City" at a "very picturesque" hotel site five miles south of San Bernardino at a former railroad tourist hotel.[72] Within three years, an ad for the sanitarium, now run by the Loma Linda Association, touted the city—"The Switzerland of America"—as "an ideal hotel for the health and pleasure seeker":

> Among groves of blooming oranges, surrounded by snow-capped mountains.
>
> No consumptives or persons with infectious diseases admitted.
>
> A place to rest, a place to enjoy life.
>
> Amusement pavilion, bowling, billiards, pool, ping-pong, out-door games and sports; charming drives; delightful rides.[73]

Like much of the era's promotional literature, the advertisement heralded the area's "natural" landscape, only recently transformed by Anglo transplants intent on creating a commercial garden.[74] A review in *Sunset* magazine, known for its veneration of Southern California's climate, wistfully observed,

> Green fields and greener orange groves dotted with pretty white cottages are all about us. This place is not, in a sense, a sanitarium. It is a home-like hotel with all appliances of a modern sanitarium, but no consumptives or sufferers from other infectious diseases are admitted.
>
> The guests here drive about among orange groves, climb the near-by hills, scale the heights, take light exercise in the "gym" and amusement hall, eat moderately of well-prepared food and sleep much under conditions which make sleep a luxury.[75]

The sanitarium balanced yearning for a "home-like" world with modern advances. As the article took pains to explain, the therapeutic imagination hinged on an exclusionary politics with idealized visions of the restorative properties of nature. Economic reality intruded on the idyllic setting when the sanitarium went up for sale.

The success of the Battle Creek sanitarium led the Adventist church into more systematic medical work, as White found these efforts an effective means for evangelism. The proselytizing tendency represented a central contradiction in the relationship of Adventists and American society. Accounts of Adventists may have represented those in the natural foods movements as eccentrics, but vegetarianism provided both a "social glue" for believers and, for much of the religion's existence, a firm sense of identity in a hostile world.[76] The "moralistic stance" taken by Adventists not only provided them with a material sense of the boundary between "the virtuous and the corrupt," but it also "gave advocates the moral conviction to endure their marginal cultural status."[77] Even as their sense of outsiderdom—nurtured by their food practices—provided them with stamina for critiques from the mainstream, Adventists sought to bring these habits to nonbelievers. Adventists began evangelizing in the northeast in 1848 and by the 1870s began to expand their mission work across the country and overseas. They also sought vindicating evidence—a kind of scientifically produced proof text—that supported their beliefs; over time, these studies were offered as lifestyle habits to nonbelievers. They pursued these objectives through institution building and civic involvement.

With Kellogg's guidance, the denomination's medical education programs came to include medicine and nursing as well as training for hygienic cooking and "health missionaries." Sanitariums tended to be in rural areas just outside the perimeter of large cities to ensure fresh air but also avoid problems that beset large urban areas. As White wrote, "Out of the cities! Out of the cities! . . . We can not expect the sick to recover rapidly when they are shut in within four walls."[78] After 1899, the church opened medical centers in St. Helena, California; Portland, Oregon; Boulder, Colorado; Copenhagen, Denmark, and Sydney, Australia; from 1900 to 1910, the institution building intensified and reached Paradise Valley (San Diego), Glendale, Takoma Park (Washington, D.C.), Chicago, Boston, and Nashville.[79] The institution building reached Loma Linda in June 1905, when White purchased the sanitarium for $50,000. In explaining her investment in California, she echoed the rhetoric of the region's most enthusiastic boosters. Reflecting on a drive through Redlands and Riverside that precipitated the purchase, White recalled,

As I looked from the car window, and saw the trees laden with fruit, I thought, Would not earnest, Christlike efforts have brought just as abundant a harvest in spiritual lines? ... Every year thousands of people visit Southern California in search of health, and by various methods we should seek to reach them with the truth.[80]

Southern California, a destination for migrants and tourists, represented an opportunity. In November 1905, the Loma Linda Sanitarium and School of Nursing opened with thirty-five employees.[81] A few years after its founding, the Loma Linda College of Medical Evangelists, founded in 1909, was one of six medical schools in the state of California.[82] Although its programs were not overseen by J. H. Kellogg, the sanitarium thrived within the flourishing health resort economy in Southern California. Its patients and employees usually numbered around three hundred people—including physicians, students, and support staff as well as between seventy-five and ninety-five guests—at any given time.[83] Marketing campaigns extended earlier claims that offered a scientifically mediated—and thus more perfect—version of nature. A 1910 advertisement for the sanitarium continued to highlight its elevated location overlooking "the fertile, fruitful valley" below as well as the "sun-kissed, snow-capped mountains shimmering in the distance." It also touted the "comfort and convenience" of the medical attention to be accessed. But most of all, advertisements accentuated access to pure and local foods prepared via scientific methods:

> The Sanitarium has its own dairy, orchard, vegetable gardens and Bakery, from which the dining room is supplied with an abundance of the purest foods.
> The Loma Linda Bakery is a part of the Sanitarium idea or system of healthy living and rational cure of disease carried on at Loma Linda. Pure food carefully prepared and well digested is one of the first requisites for continuous good health.
> A special claim for these foods is the purity and carefulness with which they are prepared, according to the most approved and scientific formulas.[84]

By emphasizing the "abundance" of the "purest foods" prepared using "scientific formulas," the advertisement echoed the message of boosters in extolling the "civilizing work" of Anglo migrants who had brought land under cultivation. It also promised to deliver "pure food" at a moment in the Progressive era when the American public feared contamination of its food sources. It mimicked advertisements that heralded the curative powers of California's agricultural abundance. Given access to

Loma Linda (California) Sanitarium,
Hospital and Laboratory in foreground.

FIGURE 14. This 1920s postcard depicts the Loma Linda Sanitarium nestled beside orange groves in front of the snow-topped San Bernardino Mountains. From the beginning, advertisements and souvenirs like postcards projected the sanitarium as existing in a perfected health space. Photo courtesy of the Mrs. Arthur Smith Photograph Album, Department of Archives and Special Collections, Loma Linda University, Loma Linda, California.

the restorative properties of nature—produced by an expanding citrus industry—visitors might restore their health (figure 14). Another advertisement hailed the Loma Linda Sanitarium as "The Great Health Station of the Pacific Southwest" and praised how the resort's "gardens, orchards, vineyards, dairy, and bakery furnished its tables with nature's purest and best produce." In contemporary parlance, the resort offered "farm-to-table" menus.[85] A 1913 advertisement in *Life and Health: the National Health Magazine*, an Adventist-sponsored magazine, touted three of Southern California's Adventist sanitaria—in Loma Linda, Glendale, and National City—for their "ethical," "scientific," and "progressive" approach to medicine and surgery. The principles included "every modern curative measure known" in addition to having staff who provided "special attention to classified dietetics," including bills of fare ordered by "nature's first principles" yet fulfilled locally by the sanitaria's "own food factories."[86]

The sanitarium aimed to capture a piece of the emerging Southern California leisure market. A 1910 advertisement boasted of the sanitarium's "large staff of experienced physicians, both ladies and gentlemen, and well trained attendants" who could administer to "the convalescent, the invalid, or the modest pleasure seeker" thanks to the institution's "garden, orchard, dairy, and poultry farm."[87] The Loma Linda sanitarium, like its predecessor in Battle Creek, catered to an emerging middle class that used leisure time and money to cure maladies by traveling to bucolic settings to have medical professionals administer diets that were at once "natural" and "rational." At the same time, even as the medical profession became more professionalized and inclined to use drugs and surgical procedures as a means to cure, Adventist physicians deemphasized drugs and instead advocated more instruction in wholesome foods and physical exercise.[88] The methods provided not just a cure but a dose of prevention. A small ad for the sanitarium that appeared in the *San Bernardino Daily Sun* promised that "a pleasant, smiling, happy disposition always comes after a good meal of well cooked food, to be had at the Loma Linda Sanitarium."[89] The availability of fresh produce allowed advocates for vegetarianism to establish themselves in Southern California, but Adventists in Loma Linda believed they had perfected it into a lifestyle.[90]

Sanitarium menus offer insight into the curated minimalism served to guests (figure 15). European visitors frequently remarked upon the abundance of food available to and consumed by Americans, but the sanitarium fare was different.[91] A dinner menu (served from 1 to 2 p.m.) from the sanitarium's early years listed two simple soups (vegetable broth and cream of barley), a few relishes (olives, green onions, plain lettuce, and cold [sic] slaw), two entrees (timbales of corn and nut cero cutlets—jardinere [sic]), a host of vegetables (baked potatoes, roasted new potatoes, cauliflower au gratin, mashed potatoes—gravy, asparagus hollandaise, string beans, and stewed turnips), breads (white, graham crackers, zwieback, no-soda crackers, graham, roman meal), desserts and fruits (mixed nuts and raisins, oranges, strawberries, canned peaches, canned pears, cream rice pudding, and dewberries), and beverages (milk, cereal coffee, fresh buttermilk, and yogurt). Guests could also request "specials" (cream, butter, olive oil, farina and dates) as a side. Holiday menus were not much more elaborate. The sanitarium's 1913 Christmas menu shows similar combinations of soups, relishes (now including nut loaf salad, celery hearts, and sliced fresh tomatoes), and vegetables with entrees that included cereal nut roast with cranberry sauce and pecan nut croquettes with parsley sauce.[92] The sparsity of these offerings becomes more striking when compared to the items available at the Hotel Alexandria, a luxury hotel in downtown Los Angeles that offered as many as

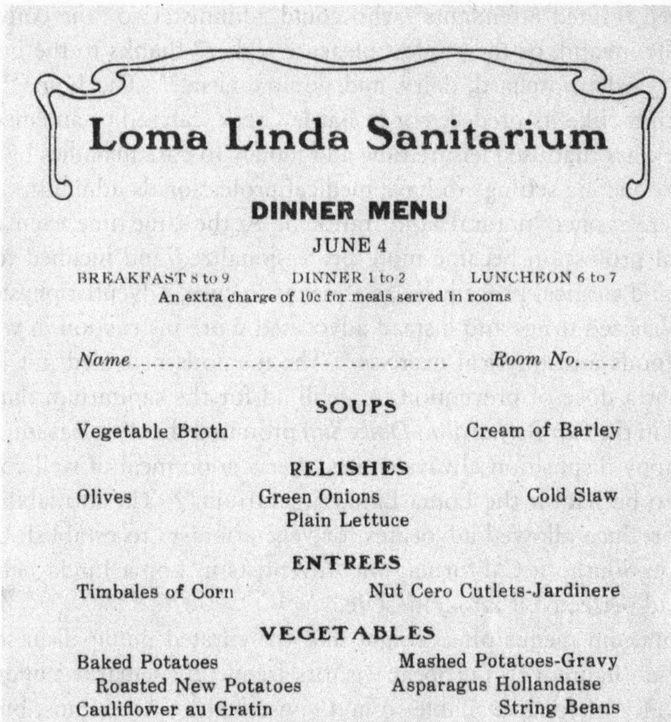

Loma Linda Sanitarium

DINNER MENU

JUNE 4

BREAKFAST 8 to 9   DINNER 1 to 2   LUNCHEON 6 to 7
An extra charge of 10c for meals served in rooms

Name ....   Room No. .....

SOUPS

Vegetable Broth   Cream of Barley

RELISHES

Olives   Green Onions   Cold Slaw
Plain Lettuce

ENTREES

Timbales of Corn   Nut Cero Cutlets-Jardinere

VEGETABLES

Baked Potatoes   Mashed Potatoes-Gravy
Roasted New Potatoes   Asparagus Hollandaise
Cauliflower au Gratin   String Beans
Stewed Turnips

SPECIALS

Cream   Butter   Farina-Dates
Olive Oil

BREADS

White   Zwieback   Graham
Graham Crackers   Nosoda Crackers   Roman Meal

DESSERTS and FRUITS

Mixed Nuts and Raisins   Oranges   Strawberries
Canned Peaches   Canned Pears
Cream Rice Pudding   Dewberries

BEVERAGES

Milk   Cereal Coffee   Fresh Buttermilk   Yogurt

An extra charge is made for all articles served not on menu

FIGURE 15. An undated menu from the Loma Linda Sanitarium's early years lists the simple meals available to guests. The kitchen served only vegetarian fare. The menu included meat substitutes such as nut cero, a kind of "nut meat" made from ground nuts. Photo courtesy of the Loma Linda Sanitarium and Hospital Menu Collection, Department of Archives and Special Collections, Loma Linda University, Loma Linda, California.

75 items for breakfast and 145 items for dinner.[93] In contrast to the sanitarium's light fare, guests dining at the Mission Indian Grill in March 1911 could choose from nine types of oysters, hors d'oeuvres that included Lyon sausage, caviar, anchovies in oil, two types of olives, pâté de foie-gras, ten types of hot and cold soups, fish (including but not limited to sand dabs, broiled shad, shad roe with bacon, fried scallops with bacon, Bordelaise-style mussels, broiled barracuda, broiled live lobster, broiled salmon steak), hot entrees (vol-au-vent of shrimp, salmi of domestic duck, sweetbread en cocotte, tenderloin steak, or rack of lamb) other meats that were broiled (corn-fed turkey), roasted (beef, lamb, turkey, veal), or cold (pâté de foie-gras, boned squab en aspic, galantine of guinea chicken, pickled lambs' tongue or pigs' feet, eel in jelly, chicken, or turkey), a robust selection of vegetables prepared in thirty different styles (including spinach in cream, artichokes, cauliflower, fried eggplant, lima beans, and fried or stewed parsnips), nineteen types of salads (many including fish or meat), custards, fresh fruits, ice cream, pies, a range of imported and domestic cheeses, tea and coffee, and domestic and imported beers.[94] For the visitors in Loma Linda, to eat less was to choose less.

From its founding, the Loma Linda sanitarium and medical school became part of a broader regional conversation about health, medicine, and productive leisure. These contributions informed the area's social imaginary. Around this time, "the new public health" began to emphasize education in personal hygiene as well as the role of physicians in helping the cause of prevention by communicating the latest advancements in medical research, organizing the general population, and setting an example in the community.[95] Home economics—founded at MIT by the institution's first female professor, Ellen Swallow Richards—assigned respectability to women seeking careers in academia, and many women sought to educate upper- and middle-class Americans into the science of keeping a home.[96] Personal moral standards were tied to Adventists' medical judgments and training in domestic science. Adventist health professionals entered the community not just as those who cared for the sick but as educators who encouraged "right habits of living" and spread "knowledge of right principles," which included guidance on how to improve the quality of consumed food.[97] Students, nurses, doctors, and spouses soon appeared in the social notes and program schedules of local civic groups.

As was the case in many Progressive-era initiatives, female Adventists took the lead, often by expanding the scope and recasting the rhetorical framework of both women's church and community activities. These endeavors, aimed at improving maternal care or housekeeping skills, provided an air of moral authority and made the domestic sphere a site for promoting positive health. For example, Dr. Julia White, the sanitarium's first female physician, took an active role and added an air of expertise to domestic science demonstrations. She was the featured speaker at an afternoon women's event at a local residence on treating colds, including foot baths, chest packs, and other remedies.[98] In nearby Colton, Dr. White provided a lecture on "the care of the body along hygienic lines" to the woman's club; this included taking time to eat and having a "happy state of mind" to promote digestion. Keeping with the later Adventist practice, she advised listeners that they did not need large amounts of food and that Americans should "consider quality and not quantity" in their diets.[99] When the Household Economics section of the local woman's club held a "salad demonstration" for aspiring hostesses looking for luncheon dishes, Mrs. J. R. Leadsworth, the wife of a physician at the sanitarium, prepared an asparagus salad and a Nuttolene (a meat substitute invented by J. H. Kellogg) salad, which were described as "very attractive" and "palatable" and were served with heart-shaped crackers and wafers baked using the sanitarium's recipe. At the conclusion of the demonstration, one of the sanitarium's nurses, Miss Jennings, gave a presentation entitled "Foods and Their Relation to Disease" that explained Adventism's teachings about the uses of tea and coffee, baking soda, and vinegar.[100] The sanitarium's male physicians framed their practices around scientific advances in Progressive-era domesticity. When Dr. D. H. Kress addressed the local woman's club, the title of his talk was "Food and Drink as Related to Health and Efficiency"; the lecture highlighted the growth in Americans' consumption of meat over the course of the nineteenth century and suggested the number of nervous breakdowns and early deaths in the United States was related to "inferior nerve and brain structure" associated with this consumption of protein from meat.[101]

Alcohol and tobacco also threatened physical and moral wellness, and officials from the sanitarium acted against the vices. Eighteenth-century critics viewed nicotine as a "poison," but the new interest in hygiene in the early twentieth century produced arguments criticizing tobacco for its negative impact on "mental and physical efficiency."[102] White denounced tobacco as "a slow, insidious, but most malignant poison" that adversely affected an individual's constitution.[103] Most physicians accepted cigarette smoking as a cultural norm well into the 1920s, and the first scientifically definitive evidence of smoking's connection to disease did not emerge until the 1950s.[104] Adventist medical professionals were a notable exception to the conventional wisdom about tobacco. In 1904, White wondered if physicians were themselves users of tobacco or intoxicants: "What weight will be given to their words? . . . How can physicians stand in the community as examples of purity and self-control, how can they be effectual workers in the temperance cause, while they themselves are indulging a vile habit?"[105]

Along with other proponents of "tobacco temperance," Adventist medical workers condemned tobacco for its moral and medical side effects and voiced support for temperance work.[106] In 1907, White and the sanitarium's student nurses took part in a WCTU program at St. Paul's M.E. (Methodist Episcopal) church in San Bernardino that featured a devotional service and songs (including one entitled "Chewing," likely a reference to proper mastication for digestion, pioneered by Horace B. Fletcher) as well as short lectures on "Alcohol as a Food" (Dr. G. K. Abbott), "Cigarettes" (Dr. Cunning), "Other Narcotics" (Dr. Julia White), and "Things That Cause Thirst" (Miss C. Hoffman). A week after speaking on health and efficiency, Dr. Kress gave a stereopticon lecture entitled "That Boy and the Cigarett [sic]" for boys and young men; at the time, the "boy smoker" was a favorite archetype of reformers who railed against the vice.[107] Dr. Kress's colleague, Dr. D. K. Abbott, spoke in 1913 on the impact of alcohol and tobacco on health.[108] At the national level, Adventists' efforts to urge the national government to eliminate tobacco use had some effect. In 1922, J. H. Kellogg, although no longer officially affiliated with the Adventist Church, published a tract, *Tobaccoism, or How Tobacco Kills*, that combined the medical and reformist elements of the tobacco temperance crusade alongside calls for "race betterment." The result of Kellogg's and others' temperance advocacy was the Surgeon General's first warning against tobacco (a statement one historian has characterized as "at best half-hearted") in 1929 and unsuccessful efforts to bring tobacco under the regulation of the Pure Food and Drug Act.[109]

For much of the twentieth century, dietary habits were one of several ways that Adventists' faith placed them outside the mainstream of American society. In the middle of the twentieth century, mainstream health professionals and government regulators—not to mention agribusiness interests—became more hostile toward health food. This opposition occurred even as there was a growing market in the United States for natural foods, which meant more people had dietary habits resembling those of Adventists. Beginning in the late twentieth century, retail sales of health food boomed, with sales rising from $100 million in 1972 to $1.7 billion in 1979 to $73 billion in 2011.[110] As a consequence, many members of the natural foods movement came to question medical and scientific expertise (even if they mimicked the language and claims) in favor of popular medicine and health.[111] The medical and public health schools at Loma Linda, however, allowed Seventh-day Adventists to develop their own infrastructure of expertise committed to researching, legitimizing, and, when deemed necessary, defending their way of life.

Although medical professionals scoffed at eccentrics in the health food industry, Adventists—given their distinctive and systematic abstention from alcohol and tobacco—became profoundly useful to scientists as they began to research the environmental and etiological impact of tobacco on long-term health. Since allegations about the health and moral impact of tobacco were met with skepticism in the 1930s, scientists began to establish etiological factors linking tobacco to certain diseases.[112] Interested in proving the correctness of their practices, in the 1950s Adventist researchers—many of them based at the Loma Linda Medical School—spearheaded efforts to assess the impact of the denomination's dietary and lifestyle practices on disease and mortality.[113] They aligned themselves with members of the medical profession who were seeking to establish a causal connection between cancer and tobacco. Ernst Wynder, a scientist at the Sloan Kettering Institute, was one of the pioneers of establishing the harms associated with tobacco through his use of epidemiological studies, which sought to link data obtained via "demography, statistics, physiology, pharmacology, chemistry, biology, pathology, and clinical medicine."[114] Lifestyle choices that included abstention from tobacco, alcohol, and caffeine, as well as dietary habits like consumption of dairy and meat, thus made Seventh-day Adventists useful subjects when compared to control groups who smoked, drank, and consumed meat and caffeine at much higher rates. These issues became the basis of the Adventist Mortality Study (1958), which examined heart disease and smoking-related cancer.[115] Wydner coauthored a study with Frank M. Lemon, a physician at Loma Linda University, based on records of admissions to Adventist hospitals (including Loma Linda and seven other Adventist hospitals in California and the rest of the country) between 1952 and 1956. They found that epidermoid cancer of the lung was ten times less likely in Seventh-day Adventists living in the Los Angeles area; the same study also found cancers of the mouth, larynx, and esophagus associated with smokers and drinkers to be less common among Adventist men.[116] Their findings were reported in outlets like the New York Times and Time, which noted its importance to providing the causal connection between heavy smoking and lung cancer through its comparison of smokers and nonsmokers (half of whom had been exposed to the "industrial air pollution," or smog, in the Los Angeles area).[117] A representative of the tobacco industry trade group used the dietary habits of Adventists to cast doubt on the causality of the study's findings.[118] In a follow-up study, the researchers reasserted their findings that there were lower levels of coronary artery disease among Adventist men in comparison to men in the general population (the incidents were similar in Adventist and non-Adventist women).[119] The US Surgeon General finally acknowledged the connection between cigarette smoking and deadly diseases in 1964.

Adventists continued to seek empirical vindication for the validity of their beliefs. Adventist Health Study-1 (AHS-1), started in 1974, examined the effects of foods on cancer and heart disease risks (and included research comparing thirty-four thousand white non-Hispanic vegetarian and non-vegetarian Adventists in California). Another more recent study, undertaken from 2002 to 2007, included ninety-six thousand Adventists from every state of the United States and Canada to understand the relationship between diet and cancer.[120] This study, known as AHS-2, expanded research to include minority groups, including twenty-six thousand Black Adventists, to test for the impact of diet, lifestyle, and spirituality on health.[121]

Contemporary research suggests that Adventists lead longer and healthier lives than the average American. As of 2013, Adventists in Loma Linda led the country in longevity: vegetarian Adventist women in Loma Linda had a life expectancy of eighty-six compared to age eighty-one for the average American woman; for vegetarian Adventist men in Loma Linda, life expectancy was eighty-three compared to seventy-six for the average American man. Studies also showed lower rates of cancer and heart disease for Adventist men in comparison to other Californians.[122] Loma Linda's purified health space was all the more remarkable when placed in contrast to places like Watts, a Los Angeles neighborhood where a combination of redlining, deindustrialization, and structural disinvestment created what became known as a "food desert" that limited restaurant and grocery store options. Between 2006 and 2008 (the period measured for the 2013 Los Angeles County health index), life expectancy in Watts, where the population was largely African American and Latinx, was 72.8, a rate that was the lowest in the state (which had a life expectancy of 80.1) and that had not improved in forty years. San Bernardino, a Latinx-dominant city neighboring Loma Linda, had a life expectancy of 76 in 2015.[123]

A PERFECTED HEALTH SPACE

Over the course of the twentieth century, Loma Linda University drew adherents to the area so that the city had one of the highest concentrations of Adventists in the world. In the middle of the twentieth century, Adventists made up about 80 percent of the city's population; in 2011, they made up about half of the city's twenty-three thousand residents.[124] Although the area's health care industry had expanded to include a Veterans Administration hospital in the early 1970s, Adventist practices still informed the lifestyle practices and foodways in the city. News articles about the area inevitably mentioned that, out of respect for Adventist community members' belief in a Saturday Sabbath, the US Postal Service did not deliver mail in Loma Linda on Saturdays (mail was instead delivered on Sundays) for eighty-one years, ending the practice only after budget cuts in 2011.[125] For years, it was difficult to find meat in grocery stores in the city, especially in the old downtown core dominated by the university. In fact, the university owned one of the grocery stores, Loma Linda Market (established 1936), which catered to vegetarians and vegans and did not stock meat. And, finally, only large restaurants had licenses for alcohol sales.[126]

Over the course of the twentieth century, biblical prophecy (especially relating to the Book of Daniel and Revelations), judgment day and the end of the world, and the path to salvation remained at the core of the Adventist religious faith. Adventist foodways remained a key element in the denomination's outreach efforts. Even as the mainstream medical and scientific communities continued to challenge the truth claims of natural foods advocates, Adventists funded schools of medicine and public health that researched the benefits of believers' practices; members also supported business ventures like Loma Linda Foods and a variety of health food stores and restaurants opened by members.[127] Moreover, health care institutions remained a cornerstone of the church. In the United States in 2001, the church ran 62 hospitals with 12,311 beds with hospital admissions of over a half a million patients. The church also owned 37 nursing homes and retirement centers. The church's network of schools included thirteen American colleges and universities.

Furthermore, the church supported two publishing houses that printed books by White and other theological titles, as well as a range of self-help and spiritual works. The organization also published over one hundred periodicals. Worldwide, the church supported 169 hospitals and sanitaria, 128 nursing or retirement homes, and 57 publishing houses.[128]

For Adventists, dietary practices had historically served simultaneously as a source of alienation from as well as a basis for proselytizing to mainstream culture. Adventist health studies were well known in medical circles (their most famous adherent in recent history was Dr. Ben Carson), but lay audiences might have best known about the food products by way of J. H. Kellogg's test kitchen or, perhaps, T. C. Boyle's 1993 novel *The Road to Wellville*. They were less likely to have come across *How You Can Live Six Extra Years*, a book about Adventist health practices published by Lewis R. Walton in 1981, or to have noticed (much less purchased) the vegetarian products manufactured by Loma Linda Foods stocked on a grocery store shelf. As Americans began to recognize the connection between longevity and health and dietary practices, however, Adventist health reform became self-help fodder for general audiences. In fact, thousands of dieters in the 1980s passed time at the Pritikin Longevity Center, whose founder, Nathan Pritikin, acknowledged that he had read Ellen G. White's writing and worked as an adjunct professor at Loma Linda University. As health habits focused more on lifestyle rather than vitamins and additives, Adventist practices that favored holistic approaches to health seemed to counter the "Negative Nutrition" that offered only prohibitions.[129]

Loma Linda's commitment to healthy lifestyles became national and international news in 2005 when journalist Dan Buettner published an article in *National Geographic* that designated Loma Linda as one of three global "Blue Zones" where residents "live longer and have healthier lives than anyone else on Earth."[130] True to the magazine's long-standing interests in science, history, and geography, Buettner's article sorted broad demographic information to produce self-help advice. Using data from the United States National Institute on Aging that studied communities with a disproportionate number of centenarians, Buettner put Adventist practices into global context. The article featured locations where residents suffered fewer diseases and lived healthier lives. The main text featured personal interest stories about feisty centenarians going about their daily lives in Loma Linda, Okinawa Japan, and Sardinia, Italy, and asked them about their "keys to success"; the sidebars summarized vernacular "best practices" like "honor family," "stay active," "eat vegetables," "have faith," and "celebrate life" that readers could emulate.[131] The language focused on affirmative, positive steps for self-regulation; of course, any application of these practices would be decontextualized. The article warned of the impact of "globalization and modernization" on "traditional" habits such as walking and diet; J. H. Kellogg might have been surprised by this characterization of the "scientific eating" he had considered to be on the cutting edge of modernity.

In 2008, Buettner published a book-length study of "Blue Zones," adding a section on Costa Rica. This longer study featured a conclusion entitled "Your Personal Blue Zone" that presented a "Power Nine" list of lessons gleaned from the communities: "a cross-cultural distillation of the world's best practices in health and longevity." Each lesson came with a list of strategies that, while not guaranteeing a long life, might help practitioners "stack the deck in [their] favor."[132] As Buettner explained years later, the people in the "zones" were living longer "not because of one special diet or one other thing; they're living longer because of a cluster of mutually supporting factors that enable [residents] to do the right things long enough and avoid doing the wrong things long enough so as to [lower risk] of developing a chronic disease."[133] This remark demonstrates an awareness of structural factors that contribute to illness, yet the "lessons" presented in the book focused on individual decisions. These choices, known as prevention, were shaped by social, economic, and cultural forces; "lessons" had to be learned by a self-auditing individual with access to knowledge and the ability to act upon that information. Environmental factors such as water and air pollution were not mentioned.

Late capitalism empowered individuals to feast on a surfeit of choice. In the late twentieth century there was mounting evidence that individual behavior played an important role in health outcomes; Adventist studies on adherents' diet and abstinence from alcohol contributed to this literature.[134] The idea of a "personal Blue Zone" made diet and health into an arena of consumer choice at the expense of social context. Empowered with wisdom from the global marketplace, discerning consumers had the opportunity to pick and choose from a range of world traditions to design their own personal health "zone." As globalization provided the opportunity to consume a range of cultures via "kitchen table tourism," the ability to take on best practices became a mark of distinction. Taken out of their cultural and socioeconomic contexts, these methods of food preparation became self-help tips that ignored broad structural and environmental factors that influenced health. But beyond that, the concept of the "zone" repositioned consumption as an enterprise that held the potential for creating a new kind of subject. The site of perfection moved to the body in ways that Ellen G. White might never have imagined. Choice became a way for the individual to reposition themselves in the market to maximize their life span.[135] Nevertheless, the contemporary celebration of longevity echoed Victorian notions of old age as a reward for "right living," a concept that White herself advanced.[136]

The way the "Blue Zone" designation helped transition Adventist practice from belief to lifestyle became clearer in 2018 when John Howard Weeks—White's great grandson and a long-time journalist—published a book entitled *The Healthiest People on Earth: Your Guide to Living 10 Years Longer with Adventist Family Secrets and Plant-Based Recipes*. The front matter of the book contained an assurance for readers, "This is not a book about religion. It's a book about health and happiness." The book hailed White for her "whole person" approach of wellness that "emphasizes health of body, mind, and spirit." Weeks explained how White's descendants had carried the family business forward into medicine, health food stores (including Burbank's Full O'Life Natural Foods, an early purveyor of Dr. Bronner's products), and publishing. Weeks presented himself as a fallen-but-redeemed slacker who had lapsed from the Adventist faith of his childhood, allowing him to claim both outsider and insider status for providing advice as well as old family recipes. Far from being a "health nut," the author claimed to have "rebelled against my family, my genes, my heritage, my destiny." Few industries escaped Weeks's indignant tone: not doctors, who concentrated "almost of their attention on disease and damage" without bothering to address "nutrition and fitness"; not the food industry, with its additives, or USDA, which flogged them; not health insurance companies (who made "money by betting that you'll bet against yourself") or drug companies (who made "enormous fortunes selling their dope" to the sick). The answer, according to Weeks, was "We stop being sick and scared."[137] The book echoed the anti-expert tone that characterized his ancestor's desire for autonomy in health decisions but failed to critique structural factors that impeded preventative health. Instead, Weeks focused on empowerment as a metaphorical place, "a space for yourself, a zone of your own . . . that will help you reach your highest potential."[138] In a column in the local paper, Weeks assured readers, "Anyone has the power . . . to create a Blue Zone of your own, no matter where you live . . . and you can turn it as many deeper shades of blue as you like."[139] This language further cast readers as entrepreneurs building human capital in their bodies—their personal empowerment zone.

Mainstream news articles minimized the spiritual element of the Loma Linda formula, even as belief was paramount in the institution's understanding of and research about the longevity phenomenon. Furthermore, a casual reader of articles about the "Blue Zone" might overlook the emphasis on "civic engagement"—an element of Adventist lifestyle focused on community and church life—that accompanied the rigorous adherence to diet. White's vision of spirituality and health remained a key mission of the university, whose motto was "To Make Man Whole." Investigators for the institution's Adventist Mortality Study, for example, hosted a health symposium where the school of public health's experts "translate[d] the health secrets of the Loma Linda Blue Zone for the people in the community."[140] In 2019, Loma Linda University organized the Third Global Conference on Lifestyle and Health, which examined the "interaction of mental, spiritual and physical health and well-being" and the "pivotal role of lifestyle and wholistic living in a broken world."[141] From their origins in the Second Great Awakening, Adventists saw themselves as onlookers to a damaged world nearing its earthly end; spiritual and civic elements of Adventist beliefs were fundamental. They participated in community life as a method of intervention, yet "Blue Zone" logic translated civic action into a kind of positive thinking. Vegetarianism provided both a method of sharing their faith and creating communal solidarity. For many members, it acquired ethical (e.g., animal rights) and environmental components. Community members in Loma Linda retained an attachment to the routines and the collective identity it represented even as the beliefs became a kind of check-the-box lifestyle. Cast in lifestyle terms, social and civic engagement became utilitarian rather than moral or ethical.[142]

Although the city of Loma Linda had long considered itself a site for wellness, the "Blue Zone" title provided a shorthand for its therapeutic social imagination. The designation relocated the concepts from a civic platitude born out of religious prescriptivism to a prevailing governing logic that sought to ensure the physical and economic health of its population. In these formulations, civic policy and planning suggested that *healthy* individuals simultaneously making *healthy* decisions created *healthy* communities. In the 2006 General Plan, city managers envisioned the municipality's future: in 2025, it aspired to continue to be "a small, friendly, beautiful community with natural assets, a unique economy, and healthy lifestyle." The plan anticipated itself as having avoided the "large-scale, high-density development" that characterized large cities. Instead, it would have "diverse housing opportunities where the natural environment is protected and enhanced to enrich the body, mind, and human spirit; where ethnic diversity and religious orientations are celebrated; and where citizens play an active role in government"; in comparison, a similar document for the neighboring city of San Bernardino mentioned "community health" amid a list of sustainable resources including education, public safety, housing, retail, and arts and culture.[143] The plan hoped to carry the city's roots into the future. In mid-2013, the city redesigned its website; a town that had sought to attract tourists seeking "health and pleasure" now presented itself to prospective visitors (or, more likely, residents and businesses) as "A city focused on health and prosperity."[144] The Chamber of Commerce site, which had the slogan "Building Healthy Businesses!" in 2017 and 2018, changed its motto to "Promoting Healthy Business in the Zone" in early 2019.[145] The Chamber of Commerce had a mission statement for development achieved by "modeling ethical business practices, including diverse cultural and generation influences, fostering healthy lifestyle [sic], promoting the community," and "providing networking opportunities."[146] Yet the community also struggled to strike a balance between individual choice and communal traditions of healthy lifestyles.

PROTECTING CIVIC HEALTH LEGACIES

In January 2012, the *Los Angeles Times* took note of a Loma Linda city council meeting where medical professionals affiliated with Loma Linda University had protested the board's recent approval to construct a McDonald's within city limits. The article quoted a specialist in preventive medicine, Wayne Dysinger, who lamented, "McDonald's does not fit the Loma Linda brand of health and wellness."[147] The battle pitted one of the most visible consumer brands against religious practices that, over time, had become synonymous with the city's reputation. Residents of Loma Linda—especially some of those affiliated with the university—viewed the designation as an affirmation of their heritage and sought to protect it in planning and civic ordinances. These actions continued the church's tradition of civic involvement that started a century before with public speeches and cooking demonstrations.

Much had changed in the years since Ellen G. White authorized her agents in California to purchase the sanitarium. In the early years after its founding in the late nineteenth century, the USDA's responsibility was to urge Americans to "eat more" of a range of agricultural products in order to stave off nutritional deficiencies. At that time, the leading causes of death among Americans included tuberculosis and diphtheria, which were worsened by nutritional deficiencies and malnutrition.[148] A century later, the federal government had assembled a stronger regulatory apparatus for food safety, and advances in medical science, public health, and food safety had extended life expectancy from 46.3 years for men and 48.3 years for women in 1900 to 75.4 years for men and 80.4 years for women.[149] However, although access to and knowledge about nutrition and medicine had changed, many Americans nevertheless struggled to maintain healthy diets. Moreover, regulatory agencies of the early twenty-first century had to balance the pressures of corporations, scientists, public health officials, and citizens as they advocated far less popular efforts to "eat less"—including "calories, fat, sugar, and salt"—to prevent the chronic diseases related to diet like coronary heart disease, diabetes, stroke, and liver cirrhosis that had become the primary causes of death in the United States of the late twentieth century.[150] White had counseled an abstemious—even bland—diet in addition to a religiously observant and active lifestyle. Over time, her instincts about "eating less" and abstaining from meat, fatty foods, alcohol, and tobacco came to reflect the consensus opinion of food scientists, public health officials, and environmentalists concerned about obesity and heart disease as well as climate change. The science about nutrition had migrated toward Adventist dietary practices. However, when government officials attempted to enact new guidelines, as they did in 1977 and 2000, advocacy groups and lobbyists from the meat, dairy, and egg industries managed to weaken the recommendations.[151] Social and economic policy preferred to assign diet and health to market-based lifestyle habits practiced by autonomous individuals.

Although citizens of Loma Linda embraced the "Blue Zone" designation, the label also exacerbated tensions that had always been embedded within Adventism and its members' position in American society. As corporations found vegetarianism to be viable in the marketplace, there was a move to make vegetarian lifestyles more flexible: diet became about personal preference rather than regimentation.[152] Yet some Adventists maintained the need for purity in keeping with White's belief that health reform was a condition for hastening the return of Jesus and for living a Christian life. Even as they were excited that the marketplace and government agencies had lauded their practices, Adventists worried about maintaining the integrity of their food culture. Religious certainty that these practices helped to restore God's order helped sustain their faith despite marginalization in American society. Over time, the belief in hygienic living shaped the organization's institutional apparatus and outreach efforts as food reform provided an opportunity for proselytizing. On the other hand, even as it made concessions to consumerism, some did not have complete faith that the market would deliver victory to proponents of vegetarianism. They continued to organize around collective action to protect their community's "healthy" civic heritage.

The question whether vegetarianism was an expression of religious devotion, an individual lifestyle choice, or a civic health concern came to a head in mid-2011, when Terra Linda Commercial LLC unveiled plans to build a business center at the corner of Barton Road and Mountain View Avenue, less than a half mile from the Loma Linda University Medical Center. The plans included a McDonald's with a drive-through as a prospective tenant. In the wake of this announcement, ten people attended the mid-June city council meeting to voice opposition to the plans. News reports from the meeting suggest that while a few citizens complained about the potential increase in traffic (and the detriment to pedestrian access), many others highlighted the impact the restaurant could have on the city's reputation as an international "Blue Zone" city.[153] After being told the council could not yet act because the planning commission had to consider the proposal, the protesters—now numbering over thirty concerned citizens—reconvened a few days later at the monthly planning meeting. It hardly mattered that nine other fast-food restaurants already dotted the city's landscape—the Wienerschnitzel franchise, in fact, was the first location in the nation to offer a vegetarian hot dog—or that the original McDonald's had opened in 1948 in nearby San Bernardino. To its detractors, McDonald's exemplified unhealthy living in both its food options and its connection to car culture. To protestors' disappointment, members of the planning commission explained that they could only prescribe issues related to land use and architecture.[154] The commission ultimately supported the plans at its November meeting with minor adjustments to the outdoor seating areas and a stone façade. In its report, the commission noted the proposal's alignment to the city's general plan, which sought to increase the amount of commercial development in order to retain tax money in Loma Linda rather than sending it to neighboring cities.[155]

By the time the city council approved the project in December 2011, the national media had taken notice. *Nightline* featured a segment on the issue, during which a university employee explained his opposition,

"Loma Linda is sort of a symbolic city for healthiness, and McDonald's is sort of a symbolism of unhealthiness." And while he did not want to "legislate health," he argued, "We have to do everything we can to create a healthy environment."[156] In an interview with the *Los Angeles Times*, he compared the group's efforts to enacting smoking laws: just as smoking is harmful to health, "Exposing people to fast food also is harmful to their health."[157] Dysinger's ally and colleague Sylvie Wellhausen, a clinical nutritionist at the university, defended accusations leveled against the group that they were trying to legislate vegetarianism and limiting the "freedom" of consumers to eat as they wished. Wellhausen argued, "Freedom of choice is different than the freedom of unknowingly harming ourselves. . . . [Freedom] comes with the knowledge that you are informed about what you are doing to yourself. At least cigarettes are labeled. Fast food is not labeled."[158]

In Wellhausen's view, market freedom placed the burden of knowledge on informed consumerism and limited the action that local governments could take. At the same time, freedom depended on knowledge and rational decision-making—including access to choose. Cigarettes, in contrast, had become an issue of public health, as public interest groups in the 1960s and 1970s had established the nonsmoker as a "right-bearing political subject" as part of a broader movement that drew attention to the "negative externalities of modern American life." Activists tried to articulate a public interest around the dangers of fast food, yet they struggled to identify how the restaurant's presence endangered their health and safety.[159]

They did, however, link their cause to the integrity of the city's social and cultural environment and history, which fit within broader notions of "quality of life." At times, coverage framed the confrontation as a kind of historic preservation—except the artifact in question was a set of religious practices, not an architectural relic. The "real" Loma Linda had coalesced around food practices of the late nineteenth and early twentieth centuries, and activists sought to protect this tradition.[160] The *New York Times* quoted Buettner, the author of the *National Geographic* article, who emphasized the ease with which residents could remain healthy in Loma Linda because "it's the default choice. . . . Your social network is all concerned about the same thing." Opponents, he added, "are really trying to preserve the culture that has been established for a really long time."[161] Other believers failed to see the arrival of McDonald's within the city limits as a threat to the Adventist lifestyle. The vice mayor, who was also an assistant dean at the Loma Linda Medical

FIGURE 16. In 2011, Adventist activists in Loma Linda protested the proposed opening of this McDonald's, believing it would affect the city's healthy image. The restaurant opened in 2013. Photo courtesy of Regan Cameron.

Center, argued that the city should not get "into the business of legislating vegetarianism," although he was willing to support a citywide vote on banning fast-food restaurants. Ellsworth Wareham—a ninety-five-year-old recently retired heart surgeon, Adventist, and star informant in Buettner's *Blue Zone* volume—noted that McDonald's was hardly different from the average American restaurant:

> I don't subscribe to the menu that these dear people put out, but let's face it, the average eating place serves food that is, let us say, a little bit of a higher quality, but the end result is the same—it's unhealthy, . . . They can put [McDonald's] right next to the church as far as I am concerned. . . . If they choose to eat that way, I'm not going to stop them. That's the great American system.[162]

The plans for McDonald's ultimately prevailed, and the restaurant opened in fall 2013 (figure 16). Wellhausen, a member of the Loma Linda Health Coalition, confessed, "I get a little chest pain every time I see it."[163] An article in an Adventist online site lamented that members of the denomination were no longer the majority in the city and concluded, "It remains for the Adventists who came here with a vision for healthy living and careers of compassion to demonstrate how to live in a 21st-century, secular context without losing their passion."[164] The city's economic development director, however, suggested that the denomination had bestowed another identity on the city: health care. The city needed to accept and accommodate that change. "This is the Disneyland of health care," explained Konrad Bolowich. "People come here for a reason. They come to town and we have to take care of them and offer them hospitality." Bolowich hoped that the city's drive-through restaurants would incorporate vegetarian options to "capture that part of the market."[165]

The opposition in Loma Linda to "formula-based fast-food restaurants" generally and McDonald's more particularly offers an interesting case study in the evolution of consumer lifestyles for the ways it both contradicted and affirmed aspects of ethical consumption in the neoliberal era. In calling for the city council to veto plans for the restaurant, opponents flouted the usual "market-led" mentality of the ethical consumer movement wherein consumers—rather than government—called on corporations to embrace "responsible" manufacturing or business practices (for example, fair trade or anti-sweatshop practices). These practices tended to rely on a shrinking government role in regulating corporations, instead relying on high-information, "self-auditing" consumers to force market change through the impact of their individual choices. These changes placed the brunt of responsibility on private standards rather than government regulation.[166] Several city council members, including Adventists who ultimately voted for the project, highlighted their opposition to government regulation.

Public health experts distinguish between health promotion, which focuses on behavior and lifestyle issues—and health protection, which focuses on the physical environment. The emphasis on "individual responsibility" in the United States" comes at the cost of considering "physical and social environmental factors," as many European nations do.[167] The opponents in Loma Linda called for an expanded role for government in protecting and promoting public health to include more environmental factors.[168] Those opposing the fast-food restaurant reasoned that if a project could be assessed for impact on traffic as well as air, noise, and water pollution, it should also assess public health in terms of nutrition. The city government had indeed already signaled a willingness to pursue policies that would optimize health practices. In particular, many opponents pointed to the impact of fast-food restaurants on children, a common tactic of conservative campaigns against literature, music, and film. At the same time, the "Blue Zone" relied on a particular kind of "ethical consumption" associated with Loma Linda in particular: the religious beliefs associated with Adventism. As many opponents of the restaurant pointed out, the McDonald's "brand" conflicted with the "brand" that the "Blue Zone" had created around the community of Loma Linda. The "Blue Zone" designations filtered Adventism through self-help tips that could be applied to individual lifestyles. Indeed, in the wake of the restaurant's opening, the city hired an intern from the school of public health to create "healthy city programs," an option more in line with using the marketplace to foster wellness rather than specifically prohibit certain practices.

The criticism of McDonald's menu for unhealthiness was nothing new. The corporation had become a stand-in for capitalism as well as unhealthy food practices that emerged in the postwar period where restaurants and manufacturers pitched "convenience" foods and meals.[169] For example, in Rome in 1986, Italian activist Carlo Petrini and a band of pasta-bearing protestors demonstrated against the opening of a McDonald's on the Piazza di Spagna in Rome in what was the opening salvo of the "Slow Food" movement, which promotes community-based food practices around the world.[170] Eric Schlosser framed *Fast Food Nation* (2001), his history of the American fast-food industry, around the impact of the postwar expansion of fast-food restaurants on public health.[171] He took particular note of the ways that the fast-food restaurant homogenized regional differences in foodways, just as opponents in Loma Linda feared. Morgan Spurlock premised his 2004 documentary *Supersize Me* around the health and weight consequences of eating too much fast food. These earlier battles no doubt prepared the company for this type of public relations issue. As the events in Loma Linda unfolded, McDonald's affirmed its community-mindedness and its commitment to health consciousness. In a press release that highlighted the restaurant's healthy menu choices, the company explained, "McDonald's wants to be a good neighbor in the communities we serve. We have been working hard over the past several years to ensure we have options on our menu to meet a variety of dietary needs."[172] Scholars of branding have argued that corporations see profitability in marking their virtuousness in community, humanitarian, and environmental affairs, so the statement typified efforts to highlight social responsibility and sensitivity to local foodways.[173]

Even after McDonald's opened in September 2013, public health advocates continued to organize against fast-food restaurants. In this instance, however, advocates adhered more closely to an element frequently referenced in the 2006 General Plan: the pedestrian-friendly quality of the community. As part of its "healthy community program," the city held workshops, community meetings, and hired an intern from the university's school of public health to work with the council. In the wake of these events, the community developed an ordinance to regulate drive-throughs at "formula-based fast-food restaurants."[174] The city based its decision on the ways that the nine drive-through restaurants already in existence changed "the character of the community" by encouraging consumers to drive rather than walk.[175] The city manager's official report noted the financial impact, in that fast-food restaurants with drive-through options tended to generate $20,000 in tax revenues compared to restaurants without drive-throughs, which generated about $5,000.[176] The ordinance based the council's action—which banned future drive-through options—on its responsibility to protect the "public health, safety, and welfare." Furthermore, the ordinance cited the "vital and active" city with a "small town professional atmosphere and a strong sense of community and community character" as well as its claim on the "Blue Zone" designation for "health and longevity" and that it wanted to "retain and improve the conditions that led to this designation, including independent restaurants compatible with healthy food selections that are an amenity of neighborhood streets and promote health through physical activity and community engagement." Finally, the ordinance pointed to issues relating to traffic congestion and pollution, standardization, over development, and the use of outside—rather than local—vendors.[177] These steps demonstrate the ways that often affluent, well-organized municipalities have used zoning laws to protect community character in ways that would prove more difficult in urban areas that are characterized by food deserts and the absence of local control.

CONCLUSION

In 1911, Dr. D. H. Kress promised to help unlock the promises of "health and happiness" in a lecture that explained the connection between dietary habits and morality. A century later, these same ideas—now practiced by a much wider cross-section of the population—were firmly entrenched in discussions about wellness. Adventists felt vindicated by the "Blue Zone" label. A denomination whose beliefs and routines had long seemed peculiar found itself at the center of debates about healthful living and the tension between individual and collective choices about wellness.

In the wake of the article's success, Dan Buettner established "Blue Zones," a company that described itself as a "lifestyle brand" that sought to "help people live longer, better lives by improving their environment." The website in 2020 states, "We have now applied the tenets of the Blue Zones in over 40 cities throughout the U.S., significantly improving health and lowering healthcare costs. We use an innovative, systematic, environmental approach to well-being that optimizes policy, urban and building design and social networks." As a brand, "Blue Zone" sought to "optimize" health as a consumer choice at a civic level. The site suggested that by accessing "secrets" from original "Blue Zones" the company helped "people live longer, better through community transformation programs that lower healthcare costs, improve productivity, and boost national recognition as great places to live, work, and play." The solutions reflected technocratic innovation rather than the moral commitments to health articulated by White. "Blue Zone" aligned to the so-called "Health 2.0" technologies that monitored well-being. This consultancy sector of the economy drew upon several realms of expertise— psychology, physiology, neuroscience, and the humanities—to create an ideal form of human existence.[178] The "data-driven" methodology, softened by humanistic "anthropological" inputs, demonstrated the health care field's focus on the measurable impact on bottom-line issues like "productivity" and health care costs. Its endlessly positive website described how American cities had enlisted the company's support for help addressing health issues such as obesity and smoking. Beyond these immediate health concerns, however, the company had also helped redesign streetscapes and parks, grocery and restaurant choices, and school health policies and programs to help residents make the "easiest" or default choice a "healthy" choice.[179] "Health," however, had become a concept governed by market logic that focused on individual choice rather than democratic or collective outcomes. The "Blue Zone" became a means for achieving community order via social health.

Yet the search for healthful tips also revealed disparities in access to care. When *National Geographic* published the original article about "Blue Zones" in 2005, 46.6 million Americans (about 15.9 percent) lacked access to even basic health insurance coverage.[180] Although Americans often associate health care with acute or chronic illness, those without health insurance (or with inadequate coverage) also lack access to preventive care. Disparities in access to care were particularly pronounced within communities of color. Even after the Affordable Care Act was passed in 2010, people of color were almost twice as likely to be uninsured as adults (20% vs. 11%); Hispanic adults were particularly vulnerable (27%).[181] Because health had become a commodity, the market was the arbiter of who had and deserved health. Rather than seeing health care—even preventive care—as a human right or an ethical issue of social justice, however, market logic commodified happiness and health into personal and civic attributes that saved money or attracted businesses. "Blue Zone" offered no information suggesting more people had access to health care, but there was proof that people were induced, whether consciously or unconsciously, to make healthier choices. In the neoliberal era, "Blue Zones" therefore provided a profound example of the infiltration of market logic into every aspect of political and cultural life.

In the nineteenth century, Ellen G. White's initial health visions reflected the creation of the self-auditing individual responsible for their own wellness, but it also created a means for solidifying group identity through both adherence to diet and civic engagement about health. The neoliberal era found additional ways to commodify the health sphere through an "economization" of political life in which market-based language became pervasive in public dialogue at the same time that the rhetoric of management and "governance" replaced democratic political language.[182] The "Blue Zone" logic showed how Loma Linda's inherited social imaginary—where shared religious commitments combined to form a collective health movement—transformed into a checklist for individual wellness. The perfected health space of the "Blue Zone" thus created a form of "self-managed care," rather than collective well-being.

CHAPTER 5

Seeker, Surfer, Yogi

The Progressive Religious Imagination
and the Politics of Place

On Earth Day 2011, which coincided with Good Friday, two men disguised in construction helmets and neon vests erected a ten-by-ten-foot glass mosaic of the Virgin of Guadalupe on a train bridge in downtown Encinitas, California (figure 17). The mosaic depicted the Surfing Madonna, as she came to be known, in glorious greens, blues, and reds surfing a wave with her hands clasped in prayer and her feet cloaked in surfing booties, with a graphic of Juan Diego, the first indigenous American saint, decorating the tip of the surfboard. A message, "Save the Oceans," adorned the side of the piece. The Virgin first appeared to Juan Diego in 1531, but her interlocutor in 2011 was Mark Patterson, a "free-ranging spiritual thinker" and former business developer for Microsoft. Patterson, while not a Catholic, was a member of the Encinitas surf community who quit his job to pursue his vision of the Madonna after she appeared in his sketchbook.[1] Locals flocked to the piece and treated it with a reverence reserved for a religious relic—by touching it, taking pictures, and leaving votive candles and flowers at the site.

This chapter focuses on the religious and civic imagination of contemporary Encinitas, a wealthy suburb of San Diego known to locals as a "holy land" for yoga enthusiasts and surfers.[2] It shows how this affluent and hippie-rich beach community in northern San Diego County came to acquire both locally and in the popular regional imagination an aura of religious sanctity, diversity, and tolerance in the recent past that embraced a self-consciously expansive, ecumenical, and safely eccentric

FIGURE 17. In 2011 two men installed the Surfing Madonna mosaic on a public railroad bridge by a busy street in Encinitas. The mosaic became a popular landmark, but state officials refused to allow it to remain there or at a nearby state beach. The mosaic is now displayed on an outside wall of a nearby restaurant. Photo courtesy of the Surfing Madonna Oceans Project.

"new ageism" while simultaneously reinforcing an exclusionary neoliberal economy of privileged bourgeois consumption and culturally appropriative branding. Yoga and surfing, along with other seemingly nonmaterial activities that reflected a regional culture of nature, spirituality, and transcendence, came to serve in Encinitas as signifiers of a progressive pluralism in the name of conscious living and good vibes that nonetheless supported possessive investment in real estate, innovative schools, and an exclusionary brand of citizenship.[3]

Given the shifting nature of religious and cultural authority in this period, case studies grounded in a specific location offer an opportunity to see how the "generically cultural" becomes "specifically sacred" and "religious" as well as how the "specifically sacred" or "religious" becomes "generically cultural" within a particular socioeconomic moment.[4] Grounded in American religious history and scholarship on the emergence of consumer citizenship, this analysis of Encinitas—a community whose civic imaginary encompassed popular environmentalism and new age spirituality as well as a dedication to lifestyle practices like surfing and yoga—both historicizes and explores how religious beliefs informed the cultural politics of place under late capitalism in a neoliberal era.

The religious and civic imagination of Encinitas celebrated a diverse heritage not reflected in its population. Immigration patterns—especially those of Asians and Latinx—during the 1980s and 1990s made California a more ethnically and racially diverse state. Yet while a 2002 Public Policy Institute study showed a general decline in residential segregation statewide, its "diversity index" found Encinitas, with a population of 81 percent white and 13 percent Latinx residents at the time, to be, along with several other wealthy coastal cities, one of the least diverse cities in the state.[5] In 2019, the city was among forty-seven California cities—and the only one in San Diego County—to be threatened with a lawsuit by Governor Gavin Newsom for having failed to meet state-mandated affordable housing benchmarks. The issue arose when in 2013 slow-growth forces in the city passed an ordinance, Proposition A, that required developers to seek voter approval before making land-use changes (the city subsequently reached an agreement to avoid a lawsuit). Some residents also opposed efforts in late 2019 by the Jewish Family Service to locate an overnight parking shelter for homeless people in a residential area owned by the Leichtag Foundation.[6] Nevertheless, Encinitas constructed a multicultural civic pluralism that expropriated global religious imagery and practices in conflicting ways.

This chapter explores those cultural fault lines by examining three contemporary controversies where Southern California spirituality, including self-consciously therapeutic lifestyle practices, occupied the foreground in community debates about the proper relationship between religion, identity, and public space: first, in objections in 2010 over access to, and the commercialization of, Swami's, a regional surf spot that was adjacent to a Self-Realization Fellowship (SRF) ashram and had acquired an aura of religious sanctity; second, in a 2011 debate over the meaning and legality of a public artwork, the Virgin of Guadalupe on a surfboard, which signified locals' environmental commitment to the beaches; and, third, in a heated debate over whether the introduction of a yoga curriculum into K–6 Encinitas schools in 2012 undermined the religious neutrality of the public school system. These examples reveal how the community drew on global religious signifiers both to inform civic identity in Encinitas and to protect local resources in ways that reinforced class and racial prerogatives. Beyond showing how community members negotiated the shifting boundaries of belief in the late modern era, these incidents convey the public promise of a progressive California dream that was at once self-consciously tolerant and professedly open while increasingly available in practice to only the privileged few.

The religious imagination of Encinitas took root amid an economic landscape shaped by the rise and fall of the Cold War defense industry, the rise of the technology sector, and the housing boom. Traditionally a conservative stronghold, San Diego had based its economy on a vision of "patriotism and free enterprise" that blended militarization, tourism, and boosterism and obscured the contributions of service workers, trade unions, and recent immigrants.[7] The late Cold War economy proved a boon to north county communities like La Jolla, where UCSD formed public-private partnerships with venture capitalists to create technology firms in software, biotech and life sciences, and green technology.[8] Over time, the growing high-tech economy attracted well-educated and socially progressive professionals—members of what Barbara and John Ehrenreich referred to as the "professional-managerial class"—characteristic of liberal bastions like San Francisco and Boston. During the late twentieth century, residents of these types of communities became outwardly progressive on environmental, gender, and racial issues. Although prizing diversity and education, they nevertheless invoked meritocratic values that validated their own position and obscured, as historian Lily Geismer suggests, the "structures and forms of privileges and entitlements"— including "power, property, and the politics of race"—that organized their relationships with other social groups.[9]

As a meritocratic individualist outlook characterized political liberalism, market-based consumption practices mediated attitudes about cultural identities, beliefs, and practices. Lifestyle consumerism—including practices like surfing and yoga—allowed high achievers to express their individualist ethos through leisure and spiritual practices. Scholars have shown that the emergence of multiculturalism among postwar liberals included borrowing religious wisdom from a multitude of traditions.[10] In the late twentieth century, Southern California developed a reputation as a site where global migration and encounter nurtured heterogeneous religious movements.[11] The fluid identities were foundational aspects of the emerging cosmopolitanism of neoliberalism, which privileged individual "freedoms" while concealing uneven global economic structures and often deepening histories of expropriation, colonialism, and conquest.

If chapter 2 and chapter 3 of this work examined the ways that the "professional-managerial class" drew from countercultural and spiritual beliefs to inform business and consumer practices, this chapter explores recuperative recreational and spiritual practices that were components of California's "brand" in the new economy. In its civic imagination, Encinitas was a community offering therapeutic leisure informed by spiritual practices, many of them drawn from non-Western traditions. As the case studies will show, community members had to navigate between individual and collective understandings of "right" living and to determine how (or if) to alter or expand access to the "good life" along racial and economic lines. The global exchanges that informed the American religious imagination and its critiques of materialism did little to disrupt the consumer-based individualism that took root in this period. In keeping with values of diversity and open-mindedness, progressives looked outward for alternative beliefs and practices. As Stuart Hall explains, the progressive adoption of multiculturalism after the war paradoxically helped create a globalized sense of "difference" that appropriated "new exotics" in the production and sale of postwar mass culture.[12] The new consumer economy produced and capitalized on, so to speak, a "global multiculturalism" that disarmed difference even as its advocates imagined they were critiquing the materialism and individualism of the consumer society of which they were a part.[13] Although practices like surfing and yoga both had connections to sixties-era critiques of Western materialism, the examples in this chapter show how both practices risked being subsumed by the evolution of a "consumer citizenship" that reveled in a pluralistic politics of consumption reinforced by the logic of a neoliberal economy that delimited the range of political, social, and civic debate to a type of consumers' freedom and lifestyle branding.[14] Based in religious experimentation and expressed through often-commercialized leisure, the area's religious imagination, while nominally tolerant, nevertheless generated questions about "feel-good" pluralism in collective practice.[15] In "Omcinitas," as the city was occasionally known, an American vocabulary of personal therapy, liberal commitments to self-transformation, and a market-driven economy allowed consumers to adopt, modify, and appropriate an array of global religious values for the bourgeois individual without seriously interrogating his or her subject position.[16]

SWAMI'S BEACH: SPIRITUAL REALIZATION
AND THE SACRALIZATION OF SPACE

Encinitas's expansive religious imagination traces to Paramahansa Yogananda, the founder of the Self-Realization Fellowship, who arrived in the United States in 1920 for the International Congress of Religious Liberals to deliver a speech titled "The Science of Religion" and then embarked on a three-decade-long missionary career in the United States. In 1935 Yogananda's followers built an ocean-side hermitage and ashram in Encinitas while their leader traveled in England and India. Possessing a keen aptitude for spiritual entrepreneurship, Yogananda valued "the art of spiritual living" and made the temple in Encinitas the original colony in his quest to establish "world brotherhood" by helping man "enlarge his sympathies."[17] The center's public gardens provided spectacular vistas for quiet contemplation (figure 18). By the 1980s, the seventeen-acre SRF was a community landmark with an estimated property value of $150 million.[18] A redevelopment project along the city's "historic downtown corridor" honoring the city's "agriculture, floriculture, surfing culture, Highway 101 culture and art" included a tribute to Swami's beach and the SRF buildings.[19] More than just memories, these landmarks were part of Encinitas's "brand" of offbeat spiritualism and naturalism.

Envisioning Encinitas as a locus for world citizenship, Yogananda imagined a practice based in reverence for conscious living and a commitment to transcendental outdoor leisure. His vision fit within a longer historical trajectory about the physical and mental benefits of the beach. The modern appreciation of the beach emerged in the West in the eighteenth century, as English physicians—not yet aware of germ theory of disease—prescribed palliative visits to the seaside to their elite patients so they could bathe in the cold water, drink seawater, and inhale the sea air. In the Victorian era, leisurely seaside visits became therapeutic interludes for bourgeois men and women seeking relief from the "overcivilization" caused by urbanization and industrialization. By the 1930s, with more paid holidays for workers, greater access via roads and rail lines, and—despite efforts to transfer beaches into private hands—an undertaking by governments to create more public access to oceans (Doheny Beach, California's first state beach, was established in 1931), the beach had become a site for recreational activities like swimming and sunbathing.[20] San Diego County's beaches became a destination for outings and Anglo settlement. Oceanside, in northernmost San Diego County, was perhaps the larger resort city, but an 1896 piece about Encinitas in the *San Diego*

FIGURE 18. The Golden Lotus Temple in Encinitas. Photo courtesy of *Herald Examiner* Collection/Los Angeles Public Library.

Union entitled "Here's Contentment" characterized the town as a "summer resort and home of happy people." A 1921 feature in the *Imperial Valley Press* reviewed the region's "ideal spots," including Encinitas, for inland readers looking for respites from the hot weather; similarly, a 1939 ad in the same paper promised that San Diego was "where COOL sea breezes blow."[21] After World War II, the beach lifestyle—including surfing, a signature activity—prevailed in San Diego County after struggles over coastal access among property owners, industrial interests, and leisure enthusiasts. By 2003, San Diego County featured sixty surf shops and two hundred thousand surfers.[22]

Swami's was the best known of Encinitas's many surf breaks. Originally named "Sea Cliff Roadside Park," locals at some point began referring to the public park as "Swami's" because of its location next to the SRF. A founding member of Swami's Surfing Association, a club established by teenagers in the 1960s, later reflected, "Swami's is a center of surf culture. It has seen generations of surfers grow up, and yet keep coming back. . . . [Swami's] is like an anchor of the past."[23] In 1987 the newly incorporated city officially adopted the locals' name for the park after seeking approval from the SRF. The city constructed golden domes for the pillars leading to the stairway and a commemorative plaque noting the local history of surfing.[24]

As surfing became more commodified over time, many surfers sought to cordon off their activities by endowing them with sacred qualities. Their sentiments aligned to paradoxical impulses within surfing: as the sport became mainstream, surfers nevertheless invoked its "individualistic, natural roots."[25] These characteristics typify "soul surfing," which the religious studies scholar Bron Taylor describes as one of several types of "dark green religion" that redefined traditional understandings of belief in the 1960s. This view positions surfing as more than a consumer lifestyle: it is an ecstatic or mystical experience that fosters "self-realization" and a deeper understanding of and connection to nature and other living beings.[26] These beliefs suffused descriptions of the area's surf culture—especially among longboarders, whom the historian Matt Warshaw has characterized as "older, slower, balder, and heavier" but also "more settled" and "better grounded" than their shortboarding counterparts.[27] A photo spread in the local paper captured these sentiments among the longboarders at Swami's, who made statements that the feeling of "riding a wave . . . takes you into a better level of life" and emphasized the connection "of being out in nature that is God's creation, enjoying the waves he made."[28] Over time, Swami's acquired ritualistic importance that connoted an authentic experience untouched by market forces. Tom English explained why Swami's Surf Club held its annual surf contest at a different beach: Swami's had an aura of "sacredness" that the club sought "to preserve" and keep "for 'soul surfing.'"[29] Charged with explaining what made Encinitas—and especially Swami's—a top-ten surf destination in *Surfer* magazine, the writer Scott Bass noted the "spiritual power that definitely pervades the area . . . there's a special allure about Swami's."[30] Such language, which dated to the backlash against the sport's commercial growth, suggested that surfers equated competition with a commercialism that did not befit the site.[31]

During the same period, a new line of scientific research combining neuroscience and marine biology advanced the theory that there was something uniquely important about humans' relationship to water. This belief had a rich history. In the eighteenth century, physicians prescribed the natural environment to bring back into balance bodily constitutions disrupted by civilization. In the twenty-first century, researchers used neuroscience to measure the impact of "blue spaces"—including the sea and coast but also rivers, lakes, canals, and urban water features—for mental and physical well-being, bringing to mind the "Blue Zones" that identified healthful lifestyle choices in food practices and community life (chapter 4).[32] This research was part of a new genre of nonfiction that used the "hard science" of the brain to make a broader case about managing stress in the neoliberal era.[33] For example, *Blue Mind*, a general audience book by marine biologist Wallace J. Nichols, used neuroscience to identify sources of happiness and fulfillment. The author argued that evolution allowed humans to develop an attachment to landscapes with water; humans are therefore hard-wired to seek out water to restore energy. The author characterized this attachment as the "Blue Mind":

> a mildly meditative state characterized by calm, peacefulness, unity, and a sense of general happiness and satisfaction with life in the moment. It is inspired by water and elements associated with water, from the color blue to the words we use to describe the sensations associated with immersion. It takes advantage of neurological connections formed over millennia.[34]

According to Nichols, both overstimulated and overstressed "red" minds and depressed "gray" minds could, through a trick of brain chemistry, be washed by "blue" environments; proximity to a coast or estuary improved general health and mental wellness. Wallace advocated "Blue Mind" as an antidepressant therapy for "the stresses of modern life."[35] Water thus provided a natural therapy for the overstimulated and overstressed modern mind and body—in a sense echoing the logic of earlier "hydropathy" cures taken at spas and the cold saltwater baths at beach retreats.

Real estate and surfing were key access points to water. Nichols did not single out Encinitas for mention, but he discussed an exorbitantly priced eight-hundred-foot ocean-front bungalow for sale in 2003 in nearby Del Mar as evidence of the human imperative to live near the water. Surfers "exhibit more Blue Mind than anyone" because they were attuned to water's patterns and power and stimulated by the combination of dopamine, endorphins, and adrenaline released through the activity. When Nichols asked surfers to describe the feeling they got from surfing, words often failed them. Instead, they made statements like, "This feeling, right now, makes it [surfing in cold water] . . . worth it" or "Surfing isn't the solution to all one's woes or social problems; . . . it's not a cure per se, but there is definitely something there . . . something that it gives us."[36] In the absence of words to describe exhilaration (or perhaps as a result of their understandable ignorance of the science of dopamine), proponents often substituted the language of the sacred. Nichols preferred the word "flow," but he also used the word "mystical."[37] Even with its in-depth justification via neuroscience, the book at its core made a back-to-nature argument: humans might feel the "interconnectedness" of things by connecting to water, which Nichols characterized as a "Blue Mindfulness" that provided a "biocentric" approach for understanding the interdependency between humans and nature.[38]

While providing a path for recentering the individual, the argument lacked a broader social critique. As critic Ronald E. Purser has observed, "mindfulness" by itself only provides a private coping mechanism; it does not reorient action toward collective or civic action.[39] Modern conditions had alienated humans from their "natural" connection to water, and they needed to readjust their lifestyles to reconnect to the blue world. But there was no collective solution. "Blue Mind" created a convincing case for conservation. Yet, if the science of the "Blue Mind" showed a universally accessible mindset, it did not question how to address the structural inequalities of access points to water (and waves). The work of the California Coastal Commission in the 1970s made some inroads into improving public access to the beach (there are now 420 public beaches in California), but access has historically depended on race and class. In the early twentieth century, boosters used exotic ethnic signifiers to sell the region to potential tourists, but the culture of exclusion most frequently barred African Americans from recreational spaces including beach clubs, bathhouses, amusement centers, and dance halls; municipal swimming pools in Los Angeles only allowed African Americans to swim at specified times, usually the day before cleanings. Although a vibrant African American leisure culture existed in Southern California in the 1910s, Anglos gradually expropriated nearly every access point to the coastline—via eminent domain, ordinances, harassment, vandalism, and arson—in places like Manhattan Beach, El Segundo, Santa Monica, and Huntington Beach. As Anglo housing stretched toward the coast, African Americans were hemmed in by residential segregation, a process enabled by the courts beginning in 1919. Beachfront property owners adopted racial covenants to prevent purchase or occupancy by African Americans. The NAACP spearheaded the protests of Black Californians, but historians have noted the ways that the removal negatively affected generational wealth and erased African Americans from regional history, creating an Anglo-dominated memory of recreational and leisure space.[40] In the recent past, wealth disparities persisted, limiting easy access to beach recreation even as coastal enclaves like Encinitas continued to be contested sites for individual paths to self-optimization and surfing became a commodifiable unit in the "happiness economy" where lifestyle pursuits were equated with mental well-being.[41]

The SRF and local surf culture—each endorsing the pursuit of "self-realization"—became intertwined at Swami's as the cultural practice of surfing acquired the religious sanctity of the local ashram. As early as the 1950s, the trope of the "search for the perfect wave" encouraged local surf protectionism and an individual quest over a communal experience.[42] By the 1960s, surf enthusiasts also drew inspiration from Asian religions.[43] These rhetorical and visual traditions fit within a larger debate about whether surfing was a sport with a countercultural or competitive spirit and—relatedly—whether the sport should celebrate commercialization and possessive individualism that arrived with its growing popularity. The SRF's presence seemed to grant locals license to invoke the language of authentic sacredness as a shield from defiling competitive and market forces. When, within the span of a week in 2015, two local surfers died—one from drowning and one from a heart attack—mourners at the site paid tribute to the spot, explaining that "People come to Swami's as part of their journey, to enjoy the goodness, the spiritual feeling."[44] Given that so much of the experience of surfing had been given over to the market, the desire to establish a sanctuary provided a way for practitioners to connect the practice back to a different, less commercialized (in their minds) moment in time.

The site's marketability was such an irresistible marker to businesses that when another civic tradition, craft breweries, emerged in the 1980s, brewers paid homage to the site. In 1987, Pizza Port, one of the first craft breweries in San Diego, named its first IPA Swami's IPA. Pizza Port's cans, designed by local artist Sean Dominguez, often depicted northern San Diego County sites and communities, and Swami's IPA was no exception. Until it was redesigned in 2021, the sixteen-ounce IPA can advertised "Swami's" in a stylized font. In the foreground, a shirtless and racialized snake charmer on a mat plays a pungi (a woodwind instrument popular in India); a keg tap emerging from the basket before him pours beer into a pint glass. The flower of a hop plant festoons the snake charmer's turban and indicates the West Coast IPA's signature flavor. The background shows a large crowd of surfers riding the curling waves and, atop the bluff, the Self-Realization Fellowship and a mo'ai head that was carved out of a dead Torrey pine in 2011. On a redesigned can, debuted in 2021, a shirtless blonde yoga practitioner sitting in lotus position replaced the snake charmer as male and female surfers gazed toward their brethren already in the water.

As the spot became more famous, the SRF—once merely a landmark—became integral to maintaining the beach as a sanctuary for the community, even as it had clearly been commodified. The suggestions that Swami's existed as a "sanctuary" for a portion of the population fit within historical understandings of the "wilderness"—albeit in this case, the ocean—as a restorative space of refuge from civilization. A debate over a potential women's longboard competition exemplified how Yogananda's ashram, which sought to promote the universal availability of spiritual enlightenment, came to be identified with the local exclusivity of surfer bliss. Citizens agreed about the hallowed nature of the site but disagreed about how best to honor and preserve its sanctity. In 2010 Linda Benson, an Encinitas native and surfer at Swami's since the 1950s, sought a permit to hold the Women's World Longboard Championship at Swami's. Logan Jenkins, a local columnist, noted that Encinitas was the "Jerusalem of the surfing world" and opined that "no mere mortal could even dream of holding a surf contest at Swami's. . . . It would take a surfer of divine stature" to obtain a permit that might endanger the "sanctity" of the break. Benson was perhaps that ideal figure: "a goddess of her sport, the most admirable applicant in the universe."[45] On the other hand, opponents focused on keeping the site as a preserve for locals. An online petition advertised on local surf websites argued, "A pro surfing contest does nothing for community surfers, does not benefit the city of Encinitas local surfers or make sense for the aesthetic and vibe of the wonderfully peaceful Self Realization Fellowship. . . . STOP SURFING CONTESTS AT SWAMIS—FOR GODS SAKE—IS NOTHING SACRED?"[46] The opposition noted the position of community stakeholders while mobilizing religious language to protect the surf break. As both the opposition and Benson agonized about protecting the "sanctuary-type vibe at Swami's," one prospective contestant speculated that the opposition was a turf battle. After all, she suggested, "anyone who's paddled out to Swami's knows it is one of the more localized, ego-filled areas to surf on our coast."[47]

Locals argued their case at a four-hour city council meeting to determine whether to proceed with the permitting process. Credible arguments—logistics, environmental impact, liability concerns, and, given the 142-step descent to the beach, a lack of disabled access—existed for refusing a permit to a private entity to hold a large-scale event at a public park designated for medium-intensity usage. Regardless of their position, speakers framed their arguments in terms of whether the event might befit the break's special atmosphere. Benson vowed to adhere to the "spirit of the location"; likewise, potential competitors promised that women's longboarding exuded an "element of positivity"—values such as "friendship, respect, togetherness, and encouragement"—that suited the site. Not everyone spoke of Swami's in reverent terms: one potential contestant characterized the break as "a zoo" when the surf was good and noted that it might benefit from a firm organizing hand.[48]

Locals who opposed the event suggested that competition and commercialization violated the site's reputation and proposed that organizers hold the competition at another beach. One speaker emphasized the importance of "being an honorable and respectful neighbor" to the SRF, but others transferred the sacredness of the ashram to the wave. Chris Aarons, a Swami's surfer since 1962, said,

> I am not a member of SRF, so I do not see Swami's as sacred in the traditional sense. But maybe it is sacred to those who walk the sand, do tai-chi, meditate, or pray.... Swami's has been a quiet place ... something we are running out of in this area. It is a place where kids ride their first waves and where longtime friends of the city ... rode their last waves. It is the place where ashes of friends ... have been scattered. It is a place where we flee the competitive world of our jobs to find something that is not commercial in any way. To me, it belongs to all of us and none of us exclusively.

To Aarons, "sacred" connoted the preservation of a fleeting way of life. A former member of Swami's Surf Association described the location as a "mystical place" to surfers around the world that should be kept "sacred." Still other speakers described the site as "a great sanctuary; it's very soulful" and the spot where residents experienced "those sweet moments we all live for."[49]

Representatives of the SRF maintained an open attitude toward the application that reflected a concern for building solidarities. Brother Anilananda, whose organization had previously raised concerns to the subcommittee charged with investigating the case, offered to work with Benson. He cautioned that future events, if too numerous, might disrupt the SRF's slate of activities, something the SRF had objected to during the 1970s when the organization publicly opposed the authorization of a nude beach north of its beachfront.[50] In 2010 the SRF was willing to negotiate, although it had already scheduled a silent women's retreat during the dates under consideration. In his remarks at the meeting, Anilananda concluded,

> This is *maybe* our contribution to world peace ... there's conflict in so many parts of the world and ... here in Encinitas ... we've talked about the

sanctity of Swami's—but I hear of some pretty unholy stories of what takes place down there. [If] SRF is willing to bend a little bit . . . maybe [Benson] is willing and maybe everyone can bend a little bit . . . and do something that would increase the holiness of the place.

Anilananda articulated a perspective that linked religious behavior to tolerance and empathy for other viewpoints. Unlike many surfers, Anilananda did not contend that the event would desecrate Swami's; he suggested that cooperation achieved through mutual goodwill might best honor the location. Nevertheless, while admitting, "We're trying to be good neighbors," he cautioned the council against changing the historic use of the beach.[51]

Benson received the go-ahead to apply for the permit but, after conversing with Anilananda, decided not to proceed. She explained, "I do not want to risk the future serenity of the Self-Realization Fellowship by others who might take advantage of the precedent set by my contest." In the end, Benson agreed with locals who sought to protect Swami's by protecting it from market forces. Anilananda praised Benson's decision, adding, "Your story will inspire people around the world. This process contributes to world peace: the changing from a desire to a higher purpose." While Anilananda suggested that "world peace" existed in process rather than place, locals remained focused on the site's sacredness. Jenkins hailed the victory for the "culture of localism" by proclaiming, "If a goddess . . . said no, no mortal would ever dream of holding a contest at Swami's."[52]

The public debate about whether to allow a competition at Swami's shows the culmination of a process of sacralization in which a location that is "generically cultural" becomes "specifically sacred and (even more specifically) religious." In their efforts to protect the purity of experience available in their pastime, local surfers framed their appeals in religious and natural terms that also aligned with the area's civic identity of openness to therapeutic living. Yet the sacralization of a kind of lifestyle consumerism reveals questions about the cultural politics of access in the neoliberal era. The SRF's importance to the civic culture of Encinitas might have signaled an inclusive religious imaginary. Even in a surf spot noted for "soul surfing," locals used language that reinforced the sport's tendencies toward territorial and arguably sexist behavior to protect the interests of a wealthy beach community. At Swami's beach, the city's cosmopolitan religious imagination provided a vocabulary for restrictive access.

OUR LADY OF PERPETUAL SURF: THE APPROPRIATION OF A RELIGIOUS ICON

If Swami's represented an instance of the sacralization of a landscape based on religious and natural associations of the surfing lifestyle, the Surfing Madonna represents an example of the appropriation of a religious icon into a more generally cultural context. Bron Taylor approvingly notes the "bricolage" involved in surfing's ability to "foster understandings of nature as powerful, transformative, healing, and sacred."[53] Placing a premium on stylistic innovation, surfers have historically scoured the cultural marketplace for icons and language that captured their transcendent experience and spiritual commitment to nature. Since at least the 1970s, Southern California surf iconography had included religious figures—including Jesus as well as Swami Yogananda, who after all had a beach named after him. Although some viewed her as a nod to surfing's multicultural mixture, the transformation of the Virgin of Guadalupe from a Latinx religious icon to a harbinger of Anglo environmentalism reveals how a deeply felt reverence for bourgeois lifestyle pursuits can nevertheless continue or deepen histories of expropriation, colonialism, and conquest.

Discussions in the following months revealed conflicting understandings of the Surfing Madonna and the Virgin of Guadalupe. Mindful of the California constitution's disestablishment clause, officials feared the religious figure's presence on a public bridge might violate the separation of church and state. Officials responded to public outcry about the installation's removal by agreeing to display it at Moonlight State Beach provided Patterson secured the cooperation of the state's Department of Parks and Recreation. In presenting their case to the state, Patterson and his representatives argued that the mosaic was "art" whose purpose was "secular" and whose message was clear: "save the ocean."[54] Patterson associated his work, and the Surfing Madonna foundation he established to fund community projects, with another secular movement—environmentalism—that had become suffused with sacred language and symbolism. His sentiment aligned to a broader sense of "ocean stewardship" that developed in Southern California surf culture in the early 1970s and continued through the establishment of organizations such as Surfrider in the 1980s.[55] Surfers frequently highlighted their sport's naturalistic roots through references to an Edenic past or by referring to the sea as "Mother Ocean."[56] Patterson's mosaic wedded this naturalistic trope to a revered figure, particularly among Mexican American Catholics.

Given the ubiquity of the Virgin of Guadalupe in Southern California— on United Farm Workers and immigrant rights protest signs, murals adorning the outside walls of bodegas, elaborate tattoos on hipster baristas, and votive candles, dashboard ornaments, and air fresheners for sale in supermarket aisles—one could perhaps forgive Patterson for mistaking her for a cultural, rather than a religious, figure. In vetoing the installation based on the state constitution's no-preference clause, the state's attorney stated, "Because the image of the Virgin of Guadalupe is central to the mosaic, an objective observer would conclude that Parks wished to convey a message related to that potent symbol of Catholicism. And even if the message is one protecting the oceans, it is the Virgin who is stating the message."[57] Charged with monitoring the boundary between church and state, the official suggested the Virgin of Guadalupe could never be deployed as a cultural or environmental figure: regardless of context, her aura remained exclusively religious. Spurned by the state attorney's office, the mosaic found an outdoor home at a restaurant just a few feet from the original installation.

The Surfing Madonna exemplified the city's desire to incorporate difference as a part of its civic pluralism, yet it also masked the role of race and class privilege in market-driven cultural appropriation. The surf scholar Krista Comer argues that surfing's affinities for non-white symbols and spaces should not be dismissed as "mere appropriation, cultural primitivism, or racial masquerade." Instead, she suggests that the impulse initially arose from a genuine disaffection with Cold War–era racial ideologies that spurred the impulse for better—or "alternative"— ways of living.[58] Yet negotiations over the meaning of surfing fit within broader historical debates that reposition the sport as a "cultural force" that grew alongside the twentieth century's "empire in waves."[59] Despite the celebration of surfing's Hawaiian roots, enthusiasts seldom acknowledged the colonial encounter and annexation that accompanied its modern revival and popularization. This historical blind spot, in turn, allowed white surfers to claim surfing and its signifiers as part of their cultural patrimony.[60] The Surfing Madonna continued this practice, recalling an earlier generation of Anglos who created a regional identity around a Catholic Spanish fantasy past.[61] Informed in part by surfing's multicultural influences, the area's religious imagination allowed the creation of an expansive racial diversity not reflected in its demographics.

Encinitas encompassed some of the whitest pockets of San Diego County: according to the 2010 US Census, white residents (not Hispanic/Latinx) constitute nearly 79 percent of the population (versus 40 percent statewide), with Latinx residents the next largest population group at 13.7 percent (versus 37.6 percent statewide). Officials initially fretted that Patterson had committed sacrilege by depicting the patron saint of the Americas and the national icon of Mexico in a secular posture. A story surveying Latinx residents' opinion about the installation suggested divided opinion between those who found the piece "disrespectful" and those excited by the representation of an "iconic Latino figure"; the priests at the two local Catholic parishes also disagreed about the meaning of the figure.[62]

The question of sacrilege—never mind mention of the history of encounter and conquest—gradually faded from news stories; instead, the bulk of public discussion centered on what benefits the new civic landmark might yield for Anglo beach culture. In 2013 the artist created a nonprofit, the Surfing Madonna Oceans Project, that organized community events including educational workshops, surf clinics, and fun runs for charity.[63] The city sought to sever the symbol from her roots in Catholic iconography—and indigenous resistance—and recast her as a harbinger of ethical beach living. Although the local surf culture was capable of banding together for a cause—in 2008 they rallied to oppose a toll road expansion at nearby Trestles—the desire to make the Surfing Madonna a local icon arose from civic interests. Officials hoped the reimagined holy surfer girl could reinforce the city's identity as a surf destination. In 2002 *Surfer* magazine named Encinitas one of the nation's "best surf towns"; a 2009 edition of the same list noted approvingly, "If you're looking for 'real' culture, move to Paris. If you're looking for surf culture, Encinitas is your place."[64] Even as the area became one of the wealthiest cities in the nation, citizens and real estate brokers alike steadfastly clung to the notion that its connection to surfing made it a laid-back place. In a *New York Times* real estate feature highlighting homes for sale—the 430 single-family homes for sale in 2019 had a median price of $1.4 million—a broker raised in Encinitas boasted, "Encinitas has maintained its surf culture and laid-back heritage while its real estate market and retail space has showed gentrification."[65]

Unlike the controversy over the surf competition at Swami's, where locals used the language of the sacred to restrict access, discussions about the Surfing Madonna centered on her ability to attract visitors.

Actions surrounding the Madonna align to the type of "commodity activism" used by lifestyle brands—especially those endorsing progressive causes—to urge "ethical consumption" as environmentally responsible behavior for individuals. The Surfing Madonna demonstrates how this logic extends to civic identity: the Madonna appeared in the mosaic as an environmental steward urging passersby to "save the ocean" rather than as a religious icon or even as an acknowledgment of Latinx in the local community.[66]

As in the case of Swami's, the Madonna's presence cemented the community's self-image as a surfing destination. Officials believed that the Surfing Madonna—a religious icon—could take a place next to nearby Swami's and become another iconic talisman for devotees of the Golden State's casual beach lifestyle. The City Arts Commission said as much in its report recommending the piece to the state board: "The depiction of the cultural figure surfing fits in with the character of the City. Encinitas is known as a 'classic California beach town' where surfing is a major attraction. A concern for the environment and in preserving natural resources is a high priority of the community." The piece was not religious in nature; rather, it provided "a secular interpretation of the cultural figure Our Lady of Guadalupe." Jenkins, the local columnist, praised Patterson for identifying a "worldly sweet spot between the mystical allure of the ocean and the instinctive reverence many feel for religious imagery rooted in the region's Latino heritage." A local pundit, identified as "Swami Bruce," praised the piece for its "transcultural" embrace of surfing, religion, and ecology.[67] Patterson further embraced spiritual iconography when he unveiled the "Boogie Boarding Buddha," a companion glass mosaic depicting a robed Buddha riding a wave on a boogie board in namaskara mudra, at the 2014 Surfing Madonna fun run; this mosaic never found a permanent public home. To local surfers, the Surfing Madonna represented the transformation of a religious icon from narrowly sectarian and religious to broadly cultural and popular—one that, it should be noted, erased her Mexican origins in favor of a trendier consumer lifestyle. The transformation positioned the Madonna as an icon of a branded regional identity based on notions of an ethical consumer lifestyle.

The Surfing Madonna was not the last piece of public art that caused a controversy. In 2015, Miciah Hardison, a local white artist, painted a mural on the side of a 7-Eleven on the Coast Highway. The forty-foot triptych mural, titled "Encinitas Harmony" and sponsored by a local arts organization, depicted three scenes: two hippies watching a sunset on a bluff outside the gates of luxury ocean-front houses in Leucadia; the Self-Realization Fellowship at sunset; and Latinx immigrants landing at Cardiff beach in a panga boat. A local Latinx barber, Raul Villamar, disagreed. After his questions to the business owner and city were ignored, Villamar contacted local media to express his outrage. He questioned the representation of immigrants, which he thought associated them with the drug trade and undocumented status. The artist believed he had created an accurate depiction of contemporary Encinitas. In a public statement, Hardison explained that the vignette of the hippies showed the consequences of the gentrified countercultural surf community. In describing the boat landing, Hardison wrote,

> I have always been inspired by the bravery, humility, honesty and work ethic of this segment of our community. For the models, I chose a few friends who had themselves crossed the border illegally and are now productive locals with growing families and businesses. I even built a faux panga in my yard and lured my friends over with Tecate and pizza.

The owner of 7-Eleven, public officials, and Paint Encinitas, the organization that arranged the installation, ducked questions about the mural by noting that art evokes conversation and dialogue.[68] Beyond its obvious stereotyping, "Encinitas Harmony" underlined the lack of opportunities for self-representation among Latinx citizens in the community. They were objects within a story that white citizens in the city told about their home.

The Surfing Madonna exposed the limits of infusing California's cultural conversation with appropriated Latinx symbols. It also demonstrates how concepts such as the "marketplace of religion" or the "consumer marketplace" privilege individual choice in the construction of cultural and religious identities while obscuring the power dynamic involved in these transformations. In its decontextualized appropriation of the symbol as well as the general failure to acknowledge Latinx in the community, the piece represented an example of the "festive deployment of race and ethnicity" in California culture for the purpose of commercial boosterism.[69] The Virgin of Guadalupe—itself a syncretic tradition that had translated Mexican symbols into Catholic iconography at a moment of reinvention for indigenous peasants—had undergone another transformation from a Latinx and Catholic icon to a symbol of Anglo beach culture.

YOGA IN ENCINITAS SCHOOLS:
A FLEXIBLE CULTURAL PHENOMENON

In fall 2012 the Encinitas Unified School District (EUSD), a K–6 district with approximately fifty-six hundred students, received a $533,000 grant from the PK Jois Foundation (later renamed the Sonima Foundation), an organization established by the founder of Ashtanga yoga, to implement the first school-district-wide yoga curriculum in the nation. In February 2013, the National Center for Law and Policy, a nonprofit legal defense organization aligned to conservative Christian causes that advance the "protection and promotion of religious freedom," filed a lawsuit on behalf of the parents of two school-aged children among the thirty who reportedly opted out of the program.[70] Expert witnesses at the trial, held in May 2013, differed in their views of yoga. Testifying for the defense, Mark Singleton, author of *Yoga Body*, suggested that yoga "is a distinctly American cultural phenomenon . . . rooted in American culture as much and sometimes more than in Indian culture" (a comment that surprised observers in India).[71] On the other hand, Candy Gunther Brown, a religious studies expert called by the plaintiffs, testified to the religiosity of Ashtanga yoga as well as practices such as karate, Tai Chi, acupuncture, and chiropractic. Although Judge John S. Meyer agreed with aspects of Brown's testimony, he cited the 1971 religious test case *Lemon v. Kurtzman* as well as *Alvarado v. City of San Jose* and *Brown v. Woodland School District* and determined that the purpose of the curriculum was secular and that a reasonable hypothetical student would not see religious overtones in EUSD yoga.[72] Although EUSD prevailed in its case to keep the curriculum, outcry against the program arose once again when the Sonima Foundation cut grant funding in 2016, leaving yoga to compete for district and parent-initiated funds with other enrichment activities.[73]

Whereas debates over Swami's and the Surfing Madonna showed conflicting understandings of a location and a religious icon, the yoga curriculum offers insights into disagreements about a specific practice within a neoliberal marketplace that offers affluent white consumers paths to self-improvement through non-Western therapeutics. The controversy revealed fears about the blurred line between cultural, religious, and wellness practices and efforts to navigate concepts of religious disestablishment in a world with overlapping sources of authority. On the one hand, proponents viewed yoga as an "Americanized," health-inducing modern practice that prepared kids to thrive in a competitive marketplace. Given the significance of education as a marker of identity and status for the professional class, the curriculum fit perfectly within the creation of a bourgeois consumer citizenship that drew on natural, scientific, and civic discourses while potentially reifying certain kinds of privilege.[74] On the other hand, yoga opponents believed the program was a state-mandated spirituality curriculum based in ancient religious tenets that located self-transformation in the self rather than in an external savior.

With its affluent citizenry and early and sustained access to global therapeutic practices, Encinitas provides an excellent opportunity to explore how "alternative" lifestyle practices informed the cultural politics of place. Encinitas was an exclusive preserve: although not as wealthy as nearby Rancho Santa Fe, estimates placed the 2008–12 median value of owner-occupied housing units at over $700,000 (versus $419,000 countywide and about $383,000 statewide) and median household income at nearly $91,000 (versus $61,000 statewide).[75] In addition, the city's position as a hub in the global yoga circuit informed the city's reverence for authentic and natural lifestyles. The Self-Realization Fellowship characterized the city as "the healthiest place in America" in 1937 and shortly thereafter opened a roadside restaurant that served "cleansitarian" mushroom burgers and fresh vegetable juices.[76] But Yogananda's most important contribution to the city's therapeutic imagination may have been the mail-order courses that introduced thousands of Americans to spiritual and scientific meditation. The city's connection to global spiritual markets continued in the mid-1970s when Krishna Pattabhi Jois arrived in Encinitas to teach Ashtanga yoga to enthusiasts in an abandoned Episcopal church. Born in Karnataka, Jois created a yoga that linked a series of six postures to breathing exercises that resembles "some sort of slowed-down, slightly repetitive, possibly exhausting gymnastic routine." Jois described the purpose of his yoga as an "internal cleaning," which one scholar describes as an effort "to fix the mind in the Self" and "realize one's true nature."[77] The visit—along with subsequent journeys by local instructors to Jois's Mysore headquarters—cemented the community's reputation as a "ground zero" for yoga in the United States.[78] Both Yogananda and Jois presented their practice as an antidote for individual betterment rather than as an avenue to collective experience.[79] Residents, in turn, considered yoga an indigenous health practice that, like surfing, characterized their brand of Southern Californian recuperative practice.

As several scholars note, "yoga" refers to a spectrum of mental and physical regimens that have evolved over time and space as different cultures have adapted them to their needs.[80] Religious studies scholar

Andrea Jain has explained that yoga has no single essence or origin, but it "functions as a source of a wide range of meanings and functions." Members of numerous religions, "including Hindu, Jain, Buddhist, Christian, and New Age traditions, have constructed, deconstructed, and reconstructed it anew." In this respect, there was evidence to support Christian parents' concerns about the spiritual and religious influences. But yoga's influences were not monolithic. Yet some groups—including those espousing a "Christian yogaphobic position" as well as those advancing a "Hindu origins position"—have represented yoga as a "homogenous, static Hindu system" to advance their perspectives.[81] In the United States, yoga's meaning evolved from countercultural technique to mainstream lifestyle practice within understandings of consumer culture. The notion of its Indian spirituality fit within the countercultural critique of American society and materialism in the 1960s. American anxieties about yoga dated to at least the early twentieth century, when pundits fretted about its impact on affluent white women, but there were also fears about its impact on children: in a 1979 case, *Malnak v. Yogi*, the US Third Circuit court determined that an elective course offered at several New Jersey high schools, "The Science of Creative Intelligence-Transcendental Meditation," violated the First Amendment; and in 1993, the Alabama Board of Education voted to prohibit yoga, hypnosis, and meditation in public schools.[82]

Yet as scholars like David Harvey argue, in recent years much of the "revolutionary" rhetoric of the sixties found a comfortable home in the neoliberal consumer marketplace that valorized individual, rather than structural, transformation and freedom: in 2012 an estimated 20.4 million American practitioners spent $10.3 billion on yoga classes and accessories.[83] By adapting yoga to scientific and medical discourses about healthy living, in the long term, religious entrepreneurs like Yogananda positioned it as a therapeutic practice that empowered consumers seeking to adjust to their circumstances. Indeed, according to scholar Kimberly Lau, yoga represents an "exoticized means of spirituality, mind-body integration, relaxation and stress release, as well as staying well, building strength, and transforming the body's shape."[84] Its popularity exploded at a moment when health emerged as a "supervalue" in the neoliberal economy in which, according to Robert Crawford, "personal responsibility for health is widely considered the *sine qua non* of individual autonomy and good citizenship."[85] Individuals could turn to yoga as a means for honing self-control, discipline, and overall mental fitness in a competitive (and atomized) world.[86] Indeed, one observer noted the irony in the way in which the labor movement's notion of social solidarity through "union" declined at the same moment that yoga—also meaning "union"—emerged as a balm for the individual soul.[87] By the turn of the millennium, yoga—which among some practitioners was associated with a life of "privation and discipline"—had come to connote "leisure and control" among a wealthy, youthful, and beautiful subset of the population.[88]

Undertaken by a government entity but underwritten by a private foundation, the yoga curriculum in Encinitas reflected the pervasiveness of health as a lifestyle choice: the district sought to inculcate children with an understanding of how to take personal responsibility for their health, which aligned with the city's virtuous ethos. Through the curriculum, the district might—from early years of childhood—instruct students on self-care, a relatively privileged thing to do considering the narrowed educational curriculum after No Child Left Behind focused on testing. The effort might be characterized as being part of a broader effort among practitioners to form a social movement built around wellness as it aligns to California's physical education curriculum.[89] The California curriculum requires physical activity as well as a broader program of mental well-being that includes "health education, nutrition services, health services, healthy school environment, counseling services, psychological and social services, health promotion for staff, and family and community involvement" in the pursuit of health and "positive social skills."[90] The Encinitas district introduced yoga to help students "cope" with daily stress through "self-mastery"—a means of mental conditioning—learned through yoga as well as gardening, cooking, and character development. The district's website included an endorsement from a local doctor, who cited a 2003 CSULA study linking yoga to improved behavior, physical health, and academic performance.[91] The Jois Foundation envisioned a curriculum that addressed health and stress through a "whole concept" that was "not the preaching of Hinduism."[92]

Both the district and the foundation positioned the curriculum in secular medical discourses about physical and mental self-mastery rather than institutionalized and transnational yoga currents. In doing so, the district's practice aligned to many contemporary uses of yoga and meditation. There is no intrinsic conservatism to yogic practices, which can involve spiritual pursuits as well as ethical action within the world. When exercised as a method to adjust inward thoughts and behaviors rather than outward attitudes or actions toward systemic problems, however, the practice has the potential to encourage the notion that individuals have the "freedom" to create their reality, potentially directing them away from expressions of "collective wellbeing."[93]

The notion that other citizens might object to yoga defied the city's prevailing sense of benevolent pluralism. Nevertheless, members of the school district, which included sections of more conservative and less upscale inland communities like Escondido, were not unanimous in their view of yoga. News accounts referred to yoga curriculum opponents as "Christians," and their specific objections positioned them as conservative evangelicals.[94] The curriculum challenged Christians' understanding of non-Western cultural practices as well as their understanding of sacred texts and religious ritual. Many Christians situated the yoga curriculum within a "literal" or "original" connotation to the exclusion of figurative or historically contingent meanings.

Whereas progressives placed the wellness curriculum within discourses of "self-transformation," religious fundamentalists saw a curriculum that sought to supplant parental and scriptural authority.[95] Evangelical activists have often emphasized the importance of the home and parents for moral instruction, especially after the end of school prayer; several anti-yoga parents who offered testimony during the trial underscored the importance of parental—not government—guidance for religious moral instruction.[96] Anti-yoga parents objected to a district-sanctioned practice that seemed entirely man-centered in its prescription for discipline and problem solving. For example, one mother complained that more than physical poses, yoga taught "children how to think and how to make decisions . . . how to meditate and how to look within for peace and comfort."[97] Anti-yoga parents saw a connection between "religion" and "health and wellness," which aligned to long-term efforts among evangelicals to equate physical and religious prowess through calisthenics, boxing, and general physical fitness.[98]

The school district accepted the neutrality of cultural practices and argued that even if yoga had origins in a religion, it had been thoroughly Americanized. District officials chose to focus on the "usable past" of yoga as a physical regimen with mental side benefits and decoupled its curriculum from Ashtanga practice more generally by selecting the instructors and designing the curriculum.[99] Administrators insisted that the yoga program did not include religious elements. Their logic was simple: teaching religion would be a violation of the Constitution. Students performed the movements (renamed with terms like *Gorilla* or *Mountain*) and breathing of yoga but did not discuss "spiritualism, mysticism, or religion in any context." The district closed a Q&A about the program by noting, "Yoga is a physical exercise regime practiced by millions of people all over the world, representing many different religious beliefs."[100] Indeed, in the wake of the case, one scholar of yoga lamented that, in accepting the position that yoga is "just exercise," the *Sedlock* decision failed to challenge the "Western tradition of seeing mind and body as separate parts" of human existence, as yoga is often described as a "'mind-body-spirit' practice." The decision—and the district's defense, which advanced the position—therefore missed an opportunity to return to an integrated view of educating the "whole child" that once defined progressive education.[101]

Pro-curriculum parents were unfazed about whether yoga occupied a culturally or religiously neutral position. They viewed yoga as a familiar lifestyle practice and—empowered by the "consumer marketplace"—felt entitled to pick and choose among different beliefs and practices without either religious intent or effect.[102] They had an instrumental view of the practice: it provided a path to self-betterment for a largely white student population. Yoga thus demonstrated the ways that affluent whites embraced "best practices" from around the world—increasingly shaped by and through consumer practices—for achieving healthy living.[103] After a school board meeting, one parent suggested, "A lot of things we take on from the eastern world come with religious overtones, but we take what we want from it."[104] The neoliberal marketplace thus empowered bourgeois citizens to assign meaning to practices as individuals saw fit. A representative from the Jois Foundation echoed these claims when he argued that parents need not worry that the yoga curriculum put one god before another in a "competition." On the contrary, practitioners were "good Christians" who do yoga "because it helps us to be better people."[105] Unable to fathom how yoga might challenge core religious beliefs, a local columnist scoffed, "It's as religiously seductive as gymnastics."[106] Yoga advocates related to the practice as a branded regional lifestyle within a consumer marketplace.[107]

The yoga curriculum incited a crisis for conservative Christians as economic and cultural globalization created an encounter between competing understandings of the world.[108] Many evangelical Christians successfully reimagined their beliefs within a consumer framework—indeed, a Christian entrepreneur and former yoga instructor invented "PraiseMoves," a stretching and strengthening regimen offered as a faith-directed "spiritual wellness" ministry. However, opponents struggled with the elasticity of cultural meanings for yoga.[109] In this instance, opponents offered a literalist interpretation of yoga that relegated it to a fixed "original" meaning and failed to contextualize its practice.[110] Concerned parents argued that the physical practice of Ashtanga yoga could not be untangled from its claimed spiritual underpinning or its institutional affiliation with the Jois Foundation; they maintained that yoga practice and poses were "religious practices."[111] The parents' attorney concluded, "There simply . . . cannot be any honest debate among informed and reasonable people as to whether Ashtanga yoga involves Hindu religious beliefs and practices."[112] Rather than view yoga as a modern practice forged through encounter, these comments assert an essentialized view that yoga was ancient and spiritual.

The community's expansive civic imaginary allows us to see how the global marketplace of exotic goods and practices shifted the grounds of concepts like secular and spiritual. The episode demonstrates how Americans invested in maintaining the nation's "Judeo-Christian" heritage confronted overlapping—and sometimes multicultural—sources of authority. As a teacher-led and district-sanctioned practice that opened the day, yoga angered conservatives worried about their perceived marginalization within American culture. Sociological studies suggest that evangelical Christians at times expressed tolerance toward pluralism, but perhaps only when their beliefs were represented as the exemplars. Curriculum opponents sensed that they had been denied the opportunity to represent their beliefs within the diverse perspectives available in the pluralistic school.[113] They wanted "equal time" for their beliefs, a "marketplace" approach that had been a cornerstone of Christians' successful lawsuits against public school textbooks in the 1980s.[114] They believed that tolerance toward other belief systems—especially those potentially framed as "multicultural" or "spiritual" had increased—but intolerance prevailed when it came to representing institutional Christianity in schools. Whereas "religion" was identified with institutions, "spirituality"—associated with and acquired by individuals—nimbly navigated the unstable categories of late capitalism.

The controversy points to broader class divisions in the multiculturalism versus Judeo-Christian values debate, at least within the confines of an affluent Anglo school district. On the one hand, conservative Christians were determined to protect a certain worldview and its interpretation that fixed understandings of the sacred in place. On the other, especially in areas like Encinitas, we see the emergence of a cosmopolitanism in which a class of white elites have the ability and means to adapt, borrow, and redeploy cultural practices, even as it obscures the cultural contexts and encounters that produced those practices. Amid global cultural flows, multiculturalism thrived as neoliberal practice. Although American religious conservatives responded to globalization by waging "culture wars" that sought to reinscribe nationalism and "American" cultural identity, their progressive counterparts constructed expansive identities that embraced pluralism albeit in ways that often reinforced race and economic privilege.

CONCLUSION

Late modernity occasioned a redefinition of the boundaries of religion that requires an examination of, as one scholar notes, "the interaction of local communities, global networks, representational and technological media, and the active biophysical . . . landscape."[115] The consumer marketplace increasingly provided the framework of these interactions. With its long-standing connection to the global cultural networks of surfing and yoga, active sense of civic promotion and identity, and geographic location on the ocean, Encinitas provides a lens for understanding how progressive communities deployed concepts such as pluralism, spirituality, and the sacred in a neoliberal context of global information exchange and local protectionism. The community's civic imaginary also surfaces broader themes addressed throughout this book: the ongoing tension between individual and collective practices that defined understandings of the California "good life" and too often rationed them along racial and economic lines. As social critics like David Harvey explain, neoliberal ideas and rhetoric about freedom, which empower individual decision makers operating in a range of marketplaces, can capably redirect impulses for social solidarity toward "libertarianism, identity politics, multiculturalism, and . . . narcissistic consumerism." When not consciously wed to ideas of social solidarity, consumer citizenship based in notions of cosmopolitan religious experimentation represents a powerful example of the "neoliberalization of culture."[116]

We must therefore consider the limits of the civic religious imagination based in consumer citizenship prevalent in affluent coastal towns like Encinitas. The renegotiation of concepts such as "religion," "spirituality," and "sacred"—often achieved by appropriating and redeploying language, icons, and practices—allows for the reinscription of racial and economic privileges and the extinction of efforts to restructure the economy toward social equality. In some contexts, the practice of yoga and surfing might perhaps have encouraged alternative domestic social movements or a new global community.[117] In Encinitas, however, lifestyle practices acquired monetary value and became the basis for protective localism that reified individualistic achievement and racial privilege and, in turn, inhibited collective consciousness.

Epilogue

Having started this work with one kind of cautionary tale, this epilogue will conclude with another. In 2014, the incident rate of measles—characterized as "eradicated" in 2000 by American officials thanks to aggressive public health campaigns since the introduction of the vaccine in 1963—reached a twenty-year high in the United States. In the period leading up to the spike in cases, California legislators had acted to improve vaccination rates among school-aged children. In 2010, the state had also witnessed a spike in cases of pertussis (whooping cough)—9,120, including ten deaths—more than any year since 1947.[1] Governor Jerry Brown, however, diluted the impact of the law by ordering regulators to create a religious exemption. Moreover, to qualify for a "personal belief exemption," parents need only accept information regarding vaccines from a health professional.[2] As students returned to school in September 2014, the *Los Angeles Times* published a troubling front-page story. Parents in California had, at twice the rate of seven years prior (from 1.5% to 3.1%), decided not to vaccinate their kindergarteners for measles, pertussis, polio, mumps, rubella, hepatitis B, chicken pox, diphtheria, and tetanus, as state law required. Public health officials considered a 92 percent vaccination rate to be the threshold for herd immunity (later articles suggested the rate should be 95%), yet, based on state data, the percentage of kindergartens in which at least 8 percent of students were not fully vaccinated due to personal beliefs had more than doubled in the same period. Nearly 25 percent of private-school kindergartens and 11 percent of public-school kindergartens reported exemption rates of 8 percent or more for at least one vaccine—in other words, groups of unvaccinated children were clustered together in particular neighborhoods and communities, increasing the potential for outbreaks.[3]

Within months, a measles outbreak at Disney during the winter holidays caused state lawmakers to further modify their approach to vaccine mandates. In July 2015, state lawmakers passed additional legislation (SB 277) barring religious and other personal-belief waivers for vaccinating school-aged children; this made California one of three states to disallow personal and religious exemptions for school vaccinations. In 2019, with pockets of medical exemptions once again edging up in certain communities, Gavin Newsom signed yet another law intended to increase vaccination rates, this time by mandating reviews of doctors who granted too many medical exemptions after complaints surfaced about efforts to skirt the requirement—for example, one 2018 study included mention of a public health officer who explained that their jurisdiction had received a medical waiver from a "primary care physician" at a medical marijuana dispensary.[4] Public health officials applauded each measure aimed at protecting the greater good against preventable illness through actions that framed health as a collective concern. On the other hand, opponents decried the loss of "parental choice" when they were best experts regarding their children's health, having researched their options and attuned themselves to their child's needs.[5]

For nearly two centuries, American municipalities and states have implemented vaccine mandates on schoolchildren. Scientists have credited the advancements in vaccines, alongside improved sanitation and nutrition and the discovery of antibiotics, with higher life expectancy and a steep decline in infant mortality in the United States and Western Europe.[6] Yet even before the onset of the COVID-19 pandemic, the World Health Organization named vaccine hesitancy and vaccine-related conspiracy beliefs one of the top global health threats.[7] Massachusetts, having become the first state to provide free public education and to make attendance compulsory, passed the first state vaccine mandate in the United States in 1855 when it required children to be inoculated against smallpox (Boston first required smallpox vaccinations for schoolchildren in 1827). California enacted its first law requiring smallpox vaccination for school enrollment in 1889, drawing condemnations of the "tyrannic law."[8] In a 1905 ruling, *Jacobson v. Massachusetts*, the Supreme Court affirmed local and state requirements for vaccinations. A few years later, California lawmakers replaced the state's 1889 mandate with one that waived the requirement for anyone "conscientiously opposed"; in 1929, the state repealed its requirement altogether, only to reinstate one in 1961 in the wake of the availability of the first polio vaccines in 1955. The 1961 law initially allowed exemptions based on "religious beliefs," but the word *religious* was stricken from the law. The belief exemption remained in California for over five decades until its repeal following the measles outbreak at Disney.[9]

In the wake of the rollout of the COVID vaccine and boosters, Americans overall remained positive about vaccines, especially for children, yet the pandemic served to intensify the politicization of vaccines and the spread of misinformation, especially online. A March 2023 Pew Center Research survey found that 88 percent of Americans believed that the benefits of childhood vaccines outweighed the risks (a number that matches the pre-COVID numbers), with only 10 percent seeing the risks outweighing the benefits. Yet following the charged debates over public mandates for the COVID vaccines, Americans were more divided on where—or by whom—the decision making on vaccines should rest and whether vaccines should be required for schoolchildren. The percentages of Americans who believed that healthy children should be required to be vaccinated declined to 70 percent, a substantial decline from the 82 percent who expressed this view in 2016 and 2019. Twenty-eight percent of Americans—including 42 percent of those identifying as Republican/lean Republican (compared to 14 percent of Democrats)—agreed that "parents should be able to decide not to vaccinate their children, even if that may create health risks for others." Three-quarters of adults who chose not to receive COVID vaccines nevertheless expressed support for the benefits of childhood measles, mumps, and rubella (MMR) vaccines; among parents who had not received the COVID vaccine, 70 percent reported that their child had received the MMR vaccine, even as they expressed skepticism about the necessity of childhood vaccines in higher numbers.[10] As school districts returned to in-person instruction, officials worried that creeping vaccine hesitancy contributed to the downtick in vaccination rates among kindergartners nationally, as rates dropped below 94 percent in 2020–2021 and again to 93 percent in 2021–2022.[11]

In the wake of the COVID pandemic, California faced challenges to its brand of the therapeutic good life, including population decline due to lower birth rates and limitations on immigration, climate change, a shrinking middle class, and lack of affordable housing, particularly in coastal communities.[12] Although some of the problems stemmed from issues related to the federal government, the state also faced NIMBYism on matters like housing that arose from the struggle to balance individual and collective interests. The recent struggle over vaccinations—particularly for school-aged children—offers one final opportunity to assess the ongoing tensions between individualism and community in Southern California. The previous five chapters have sought to show the intersection of therapeutic and spiritual practices, especially as they overlapped with concepts of "progress" that came to define the search for individual fulfillment. But what happens when ideas of progress differ in a community, when one understanding of "progress" asks all members of a community to avail themselves of recent scientific advancements in health measures while another understanding defines "progress" as the absolute freedom of personal choice at the potential loss of life in a community? The shifting attitudes toward public vaccination efforts both reflected and reinforced understandings of health as a sign of individual morality and discipline and, perhaps, the continued effort to balance the emerging vocabulary of emancipation and self-transformation against efforts to unite social collectivities. Vaccination rates illuminate some of the problems inherent in what Andrea Jain calls "neoliberal spirituality," which was centered on individualistic lifestyles based in "balance, wellness, success, freedom, and self-care."[13] The "consumer marketplace" ethos based on autonomy obscured the goals of broader social projects premised on cooperation, as many confined their sense of risk to themselves or their nuclear family without considering a broader social impact. Moreover, the for-profit nature of vaccination research in some respects obscures the importance of vaccines as common good rather than a product for individual benefit. Nevertheless, alternative health treatments also undermined the collective endeavor of vaccinations by catering to individual consumer demands.[14] The high percentages needed to achieve herd immunity made holdouts into objects of curiosity as well as the subjects of a large body of medical and ethnographic research. Those who question the effectiveness of vaccinations based on beliefs about alternative health treatments represent only one part of a broader, diverse movement against vaccines, but it is nevertheless worth understanding how health, wellness, and spiritual practices contributed to a health crisis.

Public health officials have historically tried to steer between individual and social responsibility for health behaviors. At times, environmental approaches to public health created opportunities for scapegoating, as when officials in California used health policy and sanitary reform to attack arriving Chinese immigrants and their communities even as certain locales across Southern California sought to attract recovering Anglo tuberculosis patients to their budding sanitorium economy.[15] Although the preceding chapters in this work have shown the shifting logic of health and wellness, historians and public health experts researching the history of vaccine hesitancy have found resistance to be "historically recurrent."[16] Researchers have suggested that hesitancy is "long standing, locally situated, and linked to the sociocultural contexts in which vaccination occurs and is mandated for particular segments of the population."[17] Over time, heterogeneous groups have expressed scientific, political, and philosophical objections to vaccines, all of which center, as historian James Colgrove argues, on the role that "elite knowledge and scientific expertise" should play "in a rapidly changing liberal democratic society."[18] As scientists began to develop new vaccines in laboratories, citizens and practitioners debated the degree to which a democratic government might empower the medical profession to establish standards for public health.[19] Fears of contamination, distrust of expertise, and resistance to compulsory vaccination have historically driven concerns, which tend to arise within localized contexts.[20]

While the Progressive Era heralded the benefits of scientific advancement—there were human vaccines available for smallpox, rabies, and typhoid, although only the smallpox vaccine was widespread—the technological and social changes also provoked fears about new compulsory regulations by an expanding administrative state as well as greed for profits by the growing pharmaceutical industry. In seeking to introduce preventive care to the American population, medical and public health doctors confronted long-standing beliefs (discussed in chapter 4) about "medical freedom" or "medical liberty," which asserted that average people could attend to their personal health as well as to the well-being of their children. Objections also stemmed from groups like Christian Scientists, who preferred to focus on the mental aspects of health and healing, chiropractors, who sought to combat disease through "drugless healing" and skeletal adjustments, and proponents of physical culture like Bernarr Macfadden, who rejected germ theory and asserted that those who lived a "clean, natural life" with regular exercise and a diet of natural foods and exposure to the outdoors were invulnerable to disease.[21]

The development of atomic weaponry often defines World War II–era collaboration between academic scientists, industry, and the federal government related to national security, but the war witnessed the development of new or significantly improved vaccines for ten of twenty-eight vaccine-preventable diseases.[22] During the postwar baby boom, federally sponsored vaccination campaigns raised awareness about outbreaks of polio, rubella, and measles. Vaccinations for these contagious diseases represented the promise of scientific, medical, and industrial "progress" with top-down efficiency; these programs align to the achievements of the bureaucratic state that also gave rise to the critiques described in the latter half of chapter 2. Wedded to Cold War notions of patriotism, vaccination campaigns sought to protect the national body from weakness or biological attack.[23] These Cold War-era programs that came to represent the promise of modernity, however, also included state- and pharmaceutical-industry sponsored abuses of marginalized people undertaken during the same era, which included the Tuskegee syphilis study, forced sterilization of an estimated twenty thousand women of color under California eugenics law, and the harvesting (and subsequent use in medical research, including for a polio vaccine), without consent, of the cervical cells of Henrietta Lacks.[24] Such experimentation caused long-term suspicion of the medical profession.

The Great Society introduced a measure of collective responsibility for health care through Medicare and Medicaid as well as providing community health clinics to democratize health care. Yet resentment persisted that medical institutions and pharmaceutical companies dehumanized patients and failed to see the whole person. Informed by the sixties-era liberation movements, the ground soon shifted toward empowering the individual. In a critique of the tendency of Western modernity to value clinical interventions to health risks, German theologian Ivan Illich called on the average person to become a health activist who would "reclaim his own control over medical perception, classification, and decision-making."[25] The Patients' Rights movement of the 1960s and 1970s—which gave voice to a disillusionment with the medical establishment, a growing interest in self-help, and a suspicion of the hazards posed by for-profit pharmaceutical companies that manufacture medications and vaccinations—further underscored this trend toward "personalization." Medical consumerism, as it came to be known, empowered patients to question medical authority by using, for example, the *Physicians' Desk Reference*, *Merck Manual of Diagnosis and Therapy*, or any number of counterculture-informed columns that popped up in alternative weeklies; among second-wave feminists, *Our Bodies, Our Selves* (first published in 1970 as *Women and Their Bodies*) became an important advice manual for issues pertaining to contraception, childbirth, and menopause.[26]

As historian Elena Conis has shown, postwar efforts to appeal to parents—especially mothers—to get their children vaccinated had succeeded in making vaccination a widespread bureaucratic success. Indeed, many of these efforts reminded working mothers of the potential impact a sick child might have on her productive hours or career. But the effort to appeal to women cut the other way as well, as mothers were held culpable when their children went unvaccinated. By the late 1970s, top-down efforts at vaccination began to conflict with mothers' insistence that they conduct their own research or follow their instinct and experience as it related to their children's health. Mothers—particularly white women empowered by access to resources—questioned the vaccination campaigns advocated by the male-dominated medical profession.[27] In a moment that encapsulated the convergence of consumer movement and the new scrutiny on medical expertise, a 1982 NBC investigative report, *DPT: Vaccine Roulette,* sparked public outcry and a series of investigations by suggesting that the childhood vaccine against pertussis carried significant risk including encephalitis and brain damage.[28] These concerns combined with growing awareness of the dangers of environmental toxins. An article published in 1998 (and later retracted) by *The Lancet* that suggested a link between the MMR vaccine and autism further undermined trust in childhood vaccinations. The research became conflated with reports about the FDA's request to manufacturers to remove Thimerosal, a preservative that contains mercury, from vaccines. At about the same time, some vaccines that became available—for chickenpox, hepatitis A, and rotavirus—were perceived by some parents as less significant, making them suspicious of the pharmaceutical industry's drive for profits.[29]

A series of broad historical transformations in the recent past have thus altered how Americans understand their relation to society, including their perceptions of where they stand in relation to public health. In addition, as market logic saturated American society, the issue of "choice" took on added weight when combined with notions of individual health, wellness, and purity. As Southern California emerged as a site for new understandings of self-fulfillment and belief based in a consumer ethic, the promise of personal liberation—whether achieved through a cultivated lifestyle practice or an assertion of autonomy and self-improvement—accrued sacred connotations, at times lapsing into neoliberal ideas and rhetoric about freedom and choice and away from social solidarities. The promises of "fulfilling participation in the life of the community" made to consumers have favored marketplace exchange in pursuit of self-improvement over democratic participation and inter-dependence.[30] For many, the individual body became the site for realizing a perfected health space or achieving personal enlightenment. Conservative white evangelicals—a group not fully addressed in this work but an important subgroup in Southern California—engaged in "neoliberalism" by seeking "self-reliance, strong families, and disciplined attitudes toward work, sexuality, and consumption" through abortion bans and an extension of "parents' rights" into public realms like school curriculum as well as vaccine and mask mandates.[31] Each of these paths provide "individualist answers to social problems."[32]

In contextualizing the ways that neoliberalism and consumptive spirituality favor individualism at the expense of the community, I have sought to show an atomized society's struggles to envision or enact collective projects. We can see this transformation in some of the rhetoric surrounding resistance to childhood vaccines, a process that requires collective action (and trust) from individuals, communities, and the state to define social good beyond individual or family metrics. Although parents who chose not to vaccinate their children were not monolithic, research shows that they tended to cluster together in certain communities and schools. Here it is important to note the difference between undervaccinated children and those who have received no vaccinations. In a 2004 study for *Pediatrics*, researchers for the Centers for Disease Control and Prevention noted that "undervaccinated" children tended to be Black, live closer to the poverty level in urban centers, and have mothers who did not have a college degree and were not married. Conversely, "unvaccinated" children tended to be "white, to have a mother who was married and had a college degree, to live in a household with an annual income exceeding $75,000, and to have parents who expressed concerns regarding the vaccines." The largest number of unvaccinated children during the study's period under review (1995–2001) lived in Los Angeles, and the study found that states that allowed "philosophical exemptions" to vaccines for schoolchildren had "significantly higher" estimated rates of unvaccinated children. Among parents of unvaccinated children, nearly half questioned the safety of vaccines, and over 70 percent said that doctors were not influential in making their decisions about having their child vaccinated.[33] These results suggested that individual choice—not access—played an important role in decision making. Similarly, a 2013 study about the 2010 pertussis outbreak in California found that nonmedical exemptions and pertussis clusters "were associated with characteristics of high socioeconomic status" including lower population density, lower average family size, lower percentage of racial or ethnic minorities, and higher education levels and median income.[34]

When they were still available, the personal exemption rates for kindergarteners were particularly high in Southern California's wealthier (and whiter) mountain and coastal school districts like Santa Monica–Malibu Unified (14.8%), Capistrano Unified in Orange County (9.5%), and Montecito Union District in Santa Barbara (27.5%), especially when compared to less affluent and Latinx-dominated districts like Santa Ana Unified (.2%). Private schools also lagged behind in vaccination rates, as one in four private kindergartens reported a vaccination rate that failed to meet the herd immunity threshold.[35] The pattern held in San Diego County as well, where a *U-T San Diego* investigation showed that the county's private and charter schools—as well as public school campuses along the coast in communities like Encinitas—had the highest rates of personal belief exemptions. In this sense, the luxury of "choice"—demonstrated in the ability to battle a bureaucracy or circumvent it altogether through exemptions—fell to affluent white parents. As sociologist Chris Bobel argues, claims of "natural mothering" allow affluent white women—and families more generally—to lay claim to notions of instinctual mothering but rely on their privilege to do so. The extent of their interest rests only in managing risk by making the best choice for family and child while potentially passing on risk to those with fewer resources.[36] "Progress" allowed them to deny the science that underwrote the safety of herd immunity. A charter school official whose sites had low vaccination rates highlighted this by noting that parents who believe in "school choice" had "strong opinions one way or another, and they do their homework."[37] In other words, these parents had the self-efficacy both to navigate and thwart bureaucracy. Similarly, a principal at a private Montessori school with a particularly alarming personal exemption rate—40 percent—seemed resigned that parents drawn to alternative education also had "different views about health."[38] This trend continued when parents debated mask and COVID vaccine mandates in schools, as when one parent in Encinitas argued, "My children's social, emotional and academic needs have been harmed by forced masking imposed by the state of California."[39] These arguments highlighted the way that public goods—including health and education—had been placed at the mercy of individualist arguments, especially by affluent consumers accustomed to prioritizing self-interest over community or collective social good.

Issues of purity and medical autonomy also surfaced when parents objected to vaccinations. For example, in response to the lagging childhood vaccination rates in California, a spokesperson for a national antivaccine organization told the *Los Angeles Times*, "It's only ethical for a person to decide what risk they are willing to take with their body."[40] This line of argument resonated with broader ideas about wellness and individual choice documented in this work, especially chapters 4 and 5; these chapters highlight how communities sought to balance what "right living" might mean for both individuals and the broader community. In many instances, those who expressed skepticism of the benefits of vaccines might have trusted some elements of scientific method but not medical or pharmaceutical authorities; historian Olav Hammer has labeled this desire for truth claims for spirituality as "scientism."[41] The other side of "choice" was comprised of the endangered members of the broader society who were not empowered to choose or lacked access to resources. When wedded to the language of environmentalism, however, this line of argumentation about autonomy and choice also reflected a hyper-individualized ethic that reflected a desire for bodily purity through living a "natural," chemical-free existence. Spiritual challenges to sanctioned authorities around issues like vaccination often emphasize the environment, technology, and health in their objections and deploy amateur research techniques, revelation, and personal testimony to construct their counternarratives.[42] Objectors raised questions about elite forces and government compulsion—the pharmaceutical industry or public health officials. They sought to return authority and decision-making to the individual, especially as it related to a concept of bodily autonomy. Although these objections take issue with institutions and the experts that occupy positions of power, the solutions often lose sight of a sense of social collectivity. Misinformation on social media, combined with long-term distrust of medical expertise based on a history of medical experimentation, exploitation, and exclusion slowed progress on COVID vaccinations among Latinx and African American populations. In April 2022, data showed that 58 percent of Latinx were vaccinated, and 55 percent of Black Californians were fully vaccinated—leading community groups to focus on outreach programs offering information and easier access.[43]

The distrust of the medical establishment among people of color presented a different problem compared to populations for whom health care represented a matter of personal choice and autonomy. As critic Robert Crawford explained in 1980, "healthism" elevates health above other values and repeats the individualizing ethic that critics have made about medicine.[44] Wary of the dangers of consumer products and everyday pollutants introduced into the air, water, and land by manufacturers, skeptics rejected vaccinations, which they compared to chemical-laden products like cigarettes and pesticides, and advocated for natural cures (and, in so doing, recalled nineteenth-century homeopaths).[45] These issues concerning the COVID-19 vaccination surfaced in Southern California's New Age community in 2021; faced with vaccinations developed by government and pharmaceutical companies, communities that had coalesced around alternative, sometimes radical ways of organizing society and achieving social change became divided by some of the same rationales that had informed their development.[46] As historian Jennifer Thomson explains, the focus on individual Western-style health (as opposed to, for example, concerns for the nonhuman world) allowed a "cultural turn away from holistic, collective claims and toward the fetishization of individual consumption practices and the protection of individual rights."[47] These concerns underscored a modern desire for bodily purity that emphasized personal choice. For example, according to sociologist Jennifer A. Reich, vaccine-hesitant mothers often characterize their "intensive mothering"—including feeding and nutrition practices and natural living—as "alternate and superior means of supporting immunity." In prioritizing their perception of risk as it pertains to their children, they also believe that disease exists outside their social networks.[48] The *Times* quoted an Orange County–based mother of three unvaccinated children, two of whom attended public school, as saying that her family believed in staying healthy "from the inside out," which meant taking vitamin supplements, avoiding genetically modified foods, and maintaining an "active lifestyle." According to the *Times*, the mother asserted that parents wanted "the healthiest thing for their child," and therefore "It should be their choice."[49] Waldorf Schools—a network of private schools associated with Austrian philosopher Rudolph Steiner, who experimented with Theosophy before branching off into his own society, the Anthroposophical Society—emerged as a location of persistent vaccine refusal. One principal of a Waldorf-affiliated school in San Diego defended their 56 percent exemption rate by explaining that the school was not "a doctor's office" and made "no claim to being qualified in the realm of medicine" while also noting that they "promote healthy living" through, for example, cooking and gardening classes, which appealed to well-educated parents who wanted to do their own research on vaccinations.[50] This approach to belief grounded in healthy lifestyle practices shifted the concept of health to personal responsibility and autonomy as exercised by a collection of individuals, not as a society.

Golden States has shown how, over the course of the twentieth century, overlapping cultural forms of religion, spirituality, and lifestyle consumption reflected an individualized cultural ethos that came to define California's brand of better living. The case studies in this book have sought to show the ongoing tension between individualism and community in Southern California in the long twentieth century. Vernacular religiosity intersected with other cultural formations like positive psychology, self-help literature, and lifestyle consumer practices.[51] American understandings of authority, including religion but also science, nature, and the state, have competed for primacy as understandings of authority have shifted from "without" to "within" and from external institutions of doctrine or creed to personal instinct and feeling.[52] The sense of collective obligation—concepts of social relationships, institutions, systems, and structures—that had defined the United States earlier in the twentieth century were "dismantled and reconstituted" in favor of individualism and market choices.[53] As anthropologist Susannah Crockford has noted, "A shared consensus on reality is losing ground in America, a problem that goes far beyond spirituality." This is, of course, true, but spirituality also provides insight into social and cultural fragmentation.[54] In some instances—like resistance to childhood vaccinations—understandings of religion and spiritual, personal belief, and alternative consumer lifestyle practices converged in illuminating ways. When parents discussed their opposition to vaccines, they revealed the dilemma of how to balance a culture that valued individual choice with a collective responsibility to act to protect one another. For some, health and wellness had become so deeply engrained in practices that it could only exist as a personal action; in connecting their cause to nature and the environment, moreover, parents invoked a spiritual obligation worthy of protection from state-mandated public health precautions. For late-modern seekers, too often the "Golden State" was an individualistic pursuit.

Notes

INTRODUCTION

1. "Cuckooland: Screwy California May Be the Future Athens of America," *Life*, 21 November 1938, 54; "Speaking of Pictures," *Life*, 21 November 1938, 8.

2. Critics made similar statements in the early nineteenth century about the "burned-over district," which was also referred to as the "infected district." See Whitney Cross, *The Burned-Over District: The Social and Intellectual History of Enthusiastic Religion in Western New York, 1800–1850* (New York: Harper & Row, 1950), chap. 1.

3. John Bunyan, *The Pilgrim's Progress: From This World to That Which Is to Come*, https://www.gutenberg.org/files/131/131-h/131-h.htm (accessed 20 August 2020).

4. See, for example, "A Brief History of L.A.'s Most Notorious New Religions and Cults," *Los Angeles Magazine*, 23 April 2018, https://www.lamag.com/citythinkblog/cults-los-angeles/.

5. Lizabeth Cohen, *A Consumers' Republic: The Politics of Mass Consumption in Postwar America* (New York: Knopf, 2003).

6. William Leach, *Land of Desire: Merchants, Power, and the Rise of a New American Culture* (New York: Vintage Books, 1993); Alan Trachtenberg, *The Incorporation of America* (New York: Hill and Wang, 1982), 130–31.

7. Bunyan, *The Pilgrim's Progress*. This section of *The Pilgrim's Progress* references Matthew 7:13–14.

8. Eva Illouz, *Cold Intimacies: The Making of Emotional Capitalism* (Malden, MA: Polity Press, 2007), chap. 1.

9. For an exploration of a contemporary scholar examining the therapeutic effects of spiritual experience, see Michael Scott Alexander, *Making Peace with the Universe: Personal Crisis and Spiritual Healing* (New York: Columbia University Press, 2020).

10. Barbara Ehrenreich, *Bright Sided: How Positive Thinking is Undermining America* (New York: Metropolitan Books, 2009), 8.

11. Illouz, *Cold Intimacies*, 5, 65.

12. Amanda J. Lucia, *White Utopias: The Religious Exoticism of Transformational Festivals* (Oakland: University of California Press, 2020), 4.

13. Catherine L. Albanese, *America: Religions and Religion*, 3rd ed. (Belmont, CA: Wadsworth Publishing Company, 1999), 4–14.

14. Paul Heelas, "Introduction: Detraditionalization and Its Rivals," in *Detraditionalizations: Critical Reflections on Authority and Identity*, ed. P. Heelas, S. Laash, and P. Morris (Cambridge: Blackwell, 1996), quoted in James Proctor, "Religion as Trust in Authority: Theocracy and Ecology in the United States," *Annals of the Association of American Geographers* 96, no. 1 (2006): 189. For examples of the "marketplace of religion," see Roger Finke and Rodney Stark, *The Churching of America, 1776–1990: Winners and Losers in Our Religious Economy* (New Brunswick, NJ: Rutgers University Press, 1992); Wade Clark Roof, *Spiritual Marketplace: Baby Boomers and the Remaking of American Religion* (Princeton, NJ: Princeton University Press, 1999); Frank Lambert, *The Founding Fathers and the Place of Religion in America* (Princeton, NJ: Princeton University Press, 2006); R. Laurence Moore, *Selling God: American Religion in the Marketplace of Culture* (New York: Oxford University Press, 1994).

15. Bron Taylor, *Dark Green Religion: Nature Spirituality and the Planetary Future* (Berkeley: University of California Press, 2010), 3; Leigh Eric Schmidt, *Restless Souls: The Making of American Spirituality* (New York: HarperCollins, 2005), 5–6.

16. Anna S. King, "Spirituality: Transformation and Metamorphosis," *Religion* 26 (1996): 345.

17. Andrea Jain, *Selling Yoga: From Counterculture to Pop Culture* (New York: Oxford University Press, 2015), 43–46.

18. Andrea R. Jain, *Peace Love Yoga: The Politics of Global Spirituality* (New York: Oxford University Press, 2020), 4–5.

19. Sarah Banet-Weiser, *Authentic™: The Politics of Ambivalence in a Brand Culture* (New York: New York University Press, 2012), 176.

20. Akira Iriye, *Global and Transnational History: The Past, Present, and Future* (New York: Palgrave Macmillan, 2013).

21. Jain, *Peace Love Yoga*, 31, 62–64.

22. Kimberly Lau, *New Age Capitalism: Making Money East of Eden* (Philadelphia: University of Pennsylvania Press, 2000). Kenneth Pomeranz and J. R. McNeill, "Production, Destruction, and Connection, 1750–Present: Introduction," in *The Cambridge World History*, ed. J. R. McNeill and Kenneth Pomeranz (Cambridge: Cambridge University Press, 2015): 31.

23. Moore, *Selling God*.

24. Kathryn Lofton, *Consuming Religion* (Chicago: University of Chicago Press, 2017), 2.

25. Kim Knibbe and Helena Kupari, "Theorizing Lived Religion: Introduction," *Journal of Contemporary Religion* 35, no. 2 (2020): 167.

26. David D. Hall, "Introduction," in David D. Hall, ed., *Lived Religion in America: Toward a History of Practice* (Princeton, NJ: Princeton University Press, 1997), viii; Robert Orsi, "Everyday Miracles: The Study of Lived Religion," in Hall, *Lived Religion in America*, 7; Véronique Altglas, *From Yoga to Kabbalah: Religious Exoticism and the Logics of Bricolage* (New York: Oxford University Press, 2014), 6–7.

27. Knibbe and Kupari, "Theorizing Lived Religion," 159, 166.

28. Catherine L. Albanese, *A Republic of Mind and Spirit: A Cultural History of American Metaphysical Religion* (New Haven, CT: Yale University Press, 2007), 12–18.

29. Schmidt, *Restless Souls*.

30. Catherine L. Albanese, *A Republic of Mind and Spirit*, 12–18.

31. Susannah Crockford, *Ripples of the Universe: Spirituality in Sedona, Arizona* (Chicago: University of Chicago Press, 2021), 11, 17, 20–21, 157.

32. Joel Best, *Flavor of the Month: Why Smart People Fall for Fads* (Berkeley: University of California Press, 2006), 27.

33. Edmund Morgan, *Visible Saints: The History of a Puritan Idea* (Ithaca, NY: Cornell University Press, 1965).

34. Max Weber, *The Protestant Ethic and the Spirit of Capitalism*, translated by Talcott Parsons (New York: Charles Scribner's Sons, 1958).

35. Sydney E. Ahlstrom, *A Religious History of the American People*, 2nd ed. (New Haven, CT: Yale University Press, 2004), 288, 374, 391

36. T. J. Jackson Lears, "From Salvation to Self-Realization: Advertising and the Therapeutic Roots of the Consumer Culture, 1880–1930," in *The Culture of Consumption: Critical Essays in American History, 1880–1980*, ed. T. J. Jackson Lears and Richard Wrightman Fox (New York: Pantheon Books, 1983), 3. See also Paul E. Johnson, *A Shopkeeper's Millennium: Society and Revivals in Rochester, New York 1815–1837* (New York: Hill and Wang, 1978).

37. Ronald G. Walters, *American Reformers 1815–1860* (New York: Hill and Wang, 1978), 16–18, 41.

38. Trachtenberg, *The Incorporation of America*, 5–6.

39. Trachtenberg, *The Incorporation of America*, 45.

40. T. J. Jackson Lears, *No Place of Grace: Antimodernism and the Transformation of American Culture, 1880–1920* (Chicago: University of Chicago Press, 1981), 47.

41. Lears, *No Place of Grace*, 49.

42. Albanese, *A Republic of Mind and Spirit*, 6, 15, 228, 258; Schmidt, *Restless Souls*, 9–13.

43. Lears, "From Salvation to Self-Realization."

44. Leach, *Land of Desire*, chaps. 7–8; William James, *The Varieties of Religious Experience: A Study in Human Nature* (Auckland: The Floating Press, 1994), 133, 163; Wakoh Shannon Hickey, *Mind Cure: How Meditation Became Medicine* (New York: Oxford University Press, 2019), 101–2.

45. Kim Phillips-Fein, "The History of Neoliberalism," in *Shaped by the State: Toward a New Political History of the Twentieth Century*, ed. Brent

Cebul, Lily Geismer, and Mason B. Williams (Chicago: University of Chicago Press, 2018), 347; Lily Geismer, *Left Behind: The Democrats' Failed Attempt to Solve Inequality* (New York: Public Affairs, 2022), 6; Gary Gerstle, *The Rise and Fall of the Neoliberal Order: America and the World in the Free Market Era* (New York: Oxford University Press, 2022), 5.

46. Geismer, *Left Behind*, 7; Daniel T. Rodgers, *Age of Fracture* (Cambridge: Belknap Press of Harvard University Press, 2011), 2–3, 5–10.

47. Gerstle, *The Rise and Fall of the Neoliberal Order*, 77, 90–91.

48. Gerstle, *The Rise and Fall of the Neoliberal Order*, 9, 12–15.

49. David Harvey, *A Brief History of Neoliberalism* (New York: Oxford University Press, 2005), 47; Sarah Banet-Weiser, *Authentic™*.

50. Wendy Brown, interview with Timothy Shenk, *Dissent*, 2 April 2015, as cited in Phillips-Fein, "The History of Neoliberalism," 354.

51. Rodgers, *Age of Fracture*, 2–3, 5–10; Reuel Schiller, "Regulation and the Collapse of the New Deal Order, or How I Learned to Stop Worrying and Love the Market," in *Beyond the New Deal Order: U.S. Politics from the Great Depression to the Great Recession*, ed. Gary Gerstle, Nelson Lichtenstein, and Alice O'Connor (Philadelphia: University of Pennsylvania Press, 2019), 184.

52. Gerstle, *The Rise and Fall of the Neoliberal Order*, 8–9, 12.

53. James Manyika, Susan Lund, Jacques Bughin, Kelsey Robinson, Jan Mischke, and Deepa Mahajan, "Independent Work: Choice, Necessity, and the Gig Economy," McKinsey Global Institute, October 2016 and General Accounting Office, "Contingent Workforce: Size, Characteristics, Earnings, and Benefits," GAO-15-168R (April 2015), as cited in Sarah Kessler, *Gigged: The End of the Job and the Future of Work* (New York: St. Martin's Press, 2018), 9.

54. Illouz, *Cold Intimacies*, 64–65.

55. William Davies, *The Happiness Industry: How the Government and Big Business Sold Us Well-Being* (Brooklyn: Verso Books, 2015), 146–47, 166.

56. Carol S. Dweck, *Mindset: The New Psychology of Success* (NY: Ballantine Books, 2007).

57. Angela Duckworth, *Grit: The Power of Passion and Perseverance* (NY: Simon and Schuster, 2016).

58. Davies, *The Happiness Industry*, chap. 4.

59. Lears, "From Salvation to Self-Realization," 17.

60. Trachtenberg, *The Incorporation of America*, 14–16.

61. William Deverell, "Privileging the Mission over the Mexican," in *Many Wests: Place, Culture, and Regional Identity*, ed. David W. Wrobel and Michael C. Steiner (Lawrence: University Press of Kansas, 1997), 236–39.

62. Rober M. Fogelson, *The Fragmented Metropolis: Los Angeles, 1850–1930* (Cambridge, MA: Harvard University Press, 1967), chap. 9; William Deverell, *Whitewashed Adobe: The Rise of Los Angeles and the Remaking of Its Mexican Past* (Berkeley: University of California Press, 2004); Eric Avila, *Popular Culture in the Age of White Flight: Fear and Fantasy in Suburban Los Angeles* (Berkeley: University of California Press, 2004), 22–24.

63. Lawrence B. De Graaf and Quintard Taylor, "Introduction: African Americans in California History, California in African American History," in *Seeking El*

Dorado: African Americans in California, ed. Lawrence B. De Graaf, Kevin Mulroy, and Quintard Taylor (Seattle: University of Washington Press, 2001), 15, 22; Lawrence B. De Graaf, "The City of Black Angels: Emergence of the Los Angeles Ghetto, 1890–1930," *Pacific Historical Review* 39, no. 3 (August 1970): 345; Lawrence Culver, *The Frontier of Leisure: Southern California and the Shaping of Modern America* (New York: Oxford University Press, 2010), 66–74.

64. Kelly Lytle Hernandez, *Bad Mexicans: Race, Empire, and Revolution in the Borderlands* (New York: W.W. Norton, 2022), 7; George Sanchez, *Becoming Mexican American: Ethnicity, Culture and Identity in Chicano Los Angeles, 1900–1945* (New York: Oxford University Press, 1993), chap. 3.

65. Culver, *The Frontier of Leisure*, 2–3, 6.

66. Culver, 10–11.

67. Laura J. Miller, *Building Nature's Market* (Chicago: University of Chicago Press, 2017), 15–16; Adam D. Shprintzen, *The Vegetarian Crusade: The Rise of an American Reform Movement, 1817–1921* (Chapel Hill: University of North Carolina Press, 2013).

68. Sam Binkley, *Getting Loose: American Lifestyle Consumption in the 1970s* (Durham, NC: Duke University Press, 2007); Lucia, *White Utopias*, 7.

69. Culver, *Frontier of Leisure*, 71–75.

70. Allison Rose Jefferson, *Living the California Dream: African American Leisure Sites during the Jim Crow Era* (Lincoln: University of Nebraska Press, 2020), chap. 2; "'Disregarded as Human Beings': Survivors of Palm Springs Demolition Demand Justice 60 Years On," *Guardian*, 15 January 2023, https://www.theguardian.com/us-news/2023/jan/15/california-palm-springs-section-14-homes-burned-survivors-justice; City of Palm Springs, "Human Rights Commission Agenda," 8 March 2021, https://www.palmspringsca.gov/home/show publisheddocument/78114/637504756494600000.

71. Ahlstrom, *A Religious History of the American People*, 1115–17; Schmidt, *Restless Souls*, chap. 3. For more on spiritual assemblage and *bricolage* as it relates to "religious exoticism" and social practice, see Altglas, *From Yoga to Kabbalah*, introduction.

72. Kristin L. Hoganson and Jay Sexton, "Introduction," in *Crossing Empires: Taking U.S. History into Transimperial Terrain*, ed. Kristin Hoganson and Jay Sexton (Durham, NC: Duke University Press, 2020), 2–10.

73. Emily Rosenberg, "Transnational Currents in a Shrinking World," in *A World Connecting, 1870–1945*, ed. Emily Rosenberg (Princeton, NJ: Princeton University Press, 2012), 849, 861, 868.

74. Rosenberg, "Transnational Currents in a Shrinking World," 877; Swami Vivekananda, "Swami Vivekananda on Truth in All Religions in Welcoming Participants to the World Parliament of Religions," Berkley Center for Religion, Peace, and World Affairs, https://berkleycenter.georgetown.edu/quotes/swami-vivekananda-on-truth-in-all-religions-in-welcoming-participants-to-the-world-parliament-of-religions (accessed 22 August 2023).

75. Kristin L. Hoganson, *Consumers' Imperium: The Global Production of American Domesticity, 1865–1920* (Chapel Hill: University of North Carolina Press, 2007), 4, 11, 14, 30.

76. Emily S. Rosenberg, "Consuming the American Century," in *The Short American Century*, ed. Andrew J. Bacevich (Cambridge, MA: Harvard University Press, 2012), 38, 44.

77. Akira Iriye, "Toward Transnationalism," in Bacevich, *The Short American Century*, 122, 126; Rosenberg, "Consuming the American Century," 38; Petra Goedde, "US Mass Culture and Consumption in Global Context," in *The Cambridge History of America and the World*, vol. 4, ed. David C. Engerman, Max Paul Friedman, and Melani McAlister (New York: Cambridge University Press, 2021), 282.

78. Hoganson, *Consumers' Imperium*, 30.

79. Hoganson and Sexton, "Introduction," 10–11.

80. Zareena Grewal, "Christian and Muslim Transnational Networks," in Engerman et al., *The Cambridge History of America and the World*, 446.

81. Odd Arne Westad, *The Global Cold War: Third World Interventions and the Making of Our Times* (New York: Oxford University Press, 2005), chap. 1; Sara Lorenzini, *Global Development: A Cold War History* (Princeton, NJ: Princeton University Press, 2019), chap. 2.

82. Penny M. Von Eschen, "Globalizing Popular Culture in the 'American Century' and Beyond," *OAH Magazine of History* 20, no. 4 (July 2006): 58.

83. Christina Klein, *Cold War Orientalism: Asia in the Middlebrow Imagination* (Berkeley: University of California Press, 2003), 163–64.

84. Marc Levinson, *Outside the Box: How Globalization Changed from Moving Stuff to Spreading Ideas* (Princeton, NJ: Princeton University Press, 2020), 219–21, 226.

85. Von Eschen, "Globalizing Popular Culture," 57.

86. Stuart Hall, "'The Local and the Global,'" 27–28.

87. Lau, *New Age Capitalism*; Ronald E. Purser, *McMindfulness: How Mindfulness Became the New Capitalist Spirituality* (London: Repeater, 2019).

88. Rosenberg, "Transnational Currents," 849.

89. Wade Clark Roof, "Pluralism as a Culture: Religion and Civility in Southern California," *Annals of the American Academy of Political and Social Science* 612 (July 2007): 82, 84–85. See also Sandra Sizer Frankiel, *California's Spiritual Frontiers: Religious Alternatives in Anglo Protestantism, 1850–1910* (Berkeley: University of California Press, 1988). For a quantitative analysis of present-day religious diversity in California, see Bruce Phillips, "The Legacy of Religious Diversity in Los Angeles and Southern California," in *Religion in Los Angeles: Religious Activism, Innovation, and Diversity in the Global City*, ed. Richard Flory and Diane Winston (New York: Routledge, 2021), 229–61.

90. Ferenc Morton Szasz, *Religion in the Modern American West* (Tucson: University of Arizona Press, 2000), 25, as cited in Roof, "Pluralism as a Culture," 90.

91. See, for example, Josh Paddison, *American Heathens: Religion, Race, and Reconstruction in California* (Berkeley: University of California Press and Huntington Library, Art Collections, and Botanical Gardens, 2012); Mark Wild, *Street Meeting: Multiethnic Neighborhoods in Early Twentieth-Century Los*

Angeles (Berkeley: University of California Press, 2005), chap. 3; Deborah Dash Moore, *To the Golden Cities: Pursuing the American Jewish Dream in Miami and L.A.* (Cambridge, MA: Harvard University Press, 1994).

92. Fred J. Wilson, "Political Paragraphs," *San Pedro Daily News*, 7 September 1926, 4.

93. Lisa McGirr, *Suburban Warriors: The Origins of the New American Right* (Princeton, NJ: Princeton University Press, 2001); Eileen Luhr, *Witnessing Suburbia: Conservatives and Christian Youth Culture* (Berkeley: University of California Press, 2009); Darren Dochuk, *From Bible Belt to Sunbelt: Plain-Folk Religion, Grassroots Politics, and the Rise of Evangelical Conservatism* (New York: W.W. Norton, 2011).

94. Sean T. Dempsey, *City of Dignity: Christianity, Liberalism, and the Making of Global Los Angeles* (Chicago: University of Chicago Press, 2023); Eldon G. Ernst, "The Emergence of California in American Religious History," *Religion and American Culture: A Journal of Interpretation* 11, no. 1 (Winter 2001): 38–40; Flory and Winston, *Religion in Los Angeles*, Section II: Now.

95. Deverell, *Whitewashed Adobe*, 4.

96. Ernst, "The Emergence of California in American Religious History," 31-3, 35.

97. Charles A. Fraccia, "The Western Context: Its Impact on Our Religious Consciousness," *Lutheran Quarterly* 29 (1977): 14, as cited in Eldon G. Ernst, "Religion in California," *Pacific Theological Review* 19 (Winter 1986): 43. For an example of a "new religious movement" associated with California, see Jeffrey Kripal, *Esalen: America and the Religion of No Religion* (Chicago: University of Chicago Press, 2007).

98. Eldon G. Ernst, "Religion in California," 48.

99. Taylor, *Dark Green Religion*, 104, 110.

100. Dan Buettner, "New Wrinkles on Aging," *National Geographic* 208, no. 5 (November 2005): 2.

101. Carey McWilliams, *Southern California: An Island on the Land* (New York: Duell, Sloan, and Pearce, 1946), 257.

CHAPTER 1. "A PARADISE FOR THE HEALTHSEEKER
AND RETIRED CAPITALIST"

1. Katherine Tingley, *The Splendor of the Soul* (Pasadena, CA: Theosophical University Press, 1996, originally published 1927), https://www.theosociety.org/pasadena/splendor/spl-1a.htm; W. Michael Ashcraft, *The Dawn of the New Cycle: Point Loma Theosophists and American Culture* (Knoxville: University of Tennessee Press, 2002), 51.

2. See Robert Hine, *California's Utopian Colonies* (New Haven, CT: Yale University Press, 1953).

3. Mike Davis, *City of Quartz: Excavating the Future in Los Angeles* (New York: Verso, 1990), chap. 1.

4. Carey McWilliams, *Southern California Country: An Island on the Land* (New York: Duell, Sloan and Pearce, 1946), 252, 257.

5. J. Gordon Melton, "How New Is New?," in *The Future of New Religious Movements*, ed. David G. Bromley and Phillip E. Hammond (Macon, GA: Mercer University Press, 1987), 46–56, as cited in Philip Jenkins, *Mystics and Messiahs: Cults and New Religions in American History* (New York: Oxford University Press, 2000), 70.

6. The Universal Brotherhood was one thread of Theosophy's much larger international movement and intellectual tradition. There is an enormous literature on Theosophy. For a relatively recent overview, see Olav Hammer and Mikael Rothstein, eds., *Handbook of the Theosophical Current* (Chapel Hill: University of North Carolina Press, 2013). For an accessible history of the first generation of American Theosophy, see Michael Gomes, *The Dawning of the Theosophical Moment* (Wheaton, IL: The Theosophical Publishing House, 1987). For a history that includes that subsequent schism, including information about the Universal Brotherhood and the American Section of the Theosophical Society (ASTS), which founded Krotona, see Bruce F. Campbell, *Ancient Wisdom Revived: A History of the Theosophical Movement* (Berkeley: University of California Press, 1980). For a history of Point Loma, see Emmett A. Greenwalt *California Utopia: Point Loma, 1897–1942* (San Diego: Point Loma Publications, 1978) and, more recently, W. Michael Ashcraft, *The Dawn of the New Cycle*. For an intellectual history of occult and esoteric influences on Theosophy in the English-speaking world, see Joscelyn Godwin, *The Theosophical Enlightenment* (Albany: State University of New York Press, 1994). Finally, for a history of another Theosophist utopian community in California, see Paul Eli Ivey, *Radiance From Halcyon: A Utopian Experiment in Religion and Science* (Minneapolis: University of Minnesota Press, 2013).

7. Kenneth Pomeranz and J. R. McNeill, "Production, Destruction, and Connection, 1750–Present: Introduction," in *The Cambridge World History*, edited by J. R. McNeill and Kenneth Pomeranz (Cambridge: Cambridge University Press, 2015): 31; Emily Rosenberg, "Transnational Currents in a Shrinking World," in *A World Connecting 1870–1945*, ed. Emily Rosenberg (Cambridge, MA: Harvard Belknap, 2012), 868; C. A. Bayly, *The Birth of the Modern World, 1780–1914: Global Connections and Comparisons* (Malden, MA: Blackwell Publishing, 2004), 365, 479–80.

8. Jenkins, *Mystics and Messiahs*, 72–78.

9. T. J. Jackson Lears, *No Place of Grace: Antimodernism and the Transformation of American Culture, 1880–1920* (Chicago: University of Chicago Press, 1981), 5–6, 37, 54–58.

10. Lawrence Culver, *Frontier of Leisure: Southern California and the Shaping of Modern America* (New York: Oxford University Press, 2010), 10-1.

11. Phoebe Kropp, *California Vieja: Culture and Memory in a Modern American Place* (Berkeley: University of California Press, 2006), 105.

12. Iverson L. Harris, "Reminiscences of Lomaland: Madame Tingley and the Theosophical Institute in San Diego," *Journal of San Diego History* 20, no. 3 (Summer 1974).

13. Hine, *California's Utopian Colonies*, 44–45.

14. For an overview of the scholarly debate over the racial implications of Blavatsky's writing and its context, see Isaac Lubelsky, "Mythological and Real

Race Issues in Theosophy," in Hammer and Rothstein, *Handbook of the Theosophical Current*, 335–55; and James A. Santucci, "The Notion of Race in Theosophy," *Nova Religio: Journal of Alternative and Emergent Religions* 11, no. 3 (February 2008): 37–63.

15. Robert C. Fuller, "Esoteric Movements," in *Encyclopedia of Religion in America*, ed. Charles H. Lippy and Peter W. Williams (Washington, DC: CQ Press, 2010), 751–57.

16. Fuller, "Esoteric Movements," 757; Robert C. Fuller, "Occult and Metaphysical Religion," in Lippy and Williams, *Encyclopedia of Religion in America*, 1593–96.

17. Hine, *California's Utopian Colonies*, 38–39; J. Gordon Melton, "The Theosophical Communities and Their Ideal of Universal Brotherhood," in *America's Utopian Colonies*, ed. Donald E. Pitzer (Chapel Hill: University of North Carolina Press, 1997), 400.

18. Melton, "The Theosophical Communities and Their Ideal of Universal Brotherhood," 403–4.

19. Rosenberg, "Transnational Currents in a Shrinking World," 849.

20. Grace Knoche, "Theosophy, Katherine Tingley and Point Loma," *Oakland Tribune*, 9 September 1917, 15.

21. Anne McClintock, *Imperial Leather: Race, Gender, and Sexuality in Colonial Contest* (London: Taylor & Francis Group, 1995), 40.

22. Grace Converse, "Theosophy and the Realization of Southern California's Divine Destiny," in Flory and Winston, *Religion in Los Angeles: Religious Activism, Innovation, and Diversity in the Global City*, 127–29.

23. Ashcraft, *The Dawn of the New Cycle*, 1.

24. Bertha Damaris Knobe, "The Point Loma Community," *Munsey's Magazine* 29, no 3 (June 1903), 357.

25. Greenwalt, *California Utopia*, 78.

26. See Sarah Steinbeck-Pratt, *Educating the Empire: American Teachers and Contested Colonization in the Philippines* (New York: Cambridge University Press, 2021); Clif Stratton, *Education for Empire: American Schools, Race, and the Paths of Good Citizenship* (Oakland: University of California Press, 2016).

27. Knobe, "The Point Loma Community," 358.

28. Testimony during the libel case revealed that seventeen-year-old Matilda Kratzer had arrived for piano lessons but mostly worked as a servant. "Tune of Dishpans Point Loma Music," *Los Angeles Times*, 31 December 1902, 10.

29. Lears, *No Place of Grace*, xv, 57.

30. Ray Stannard Baker, "An Extraordinary Experiment in Brotherhood: The Theosophical Institution at Point Loma, California," *The American Magazine* 63, no. 3 (January 1907): 227, 232–33.

31. Jenkins, *Mystics and Messiahs*, 5, 13, 21–22.

32. Robert M. Fogelson, *The Fragmented Metropolis: Los Angeles, 1850–1930* (1967; reprint, Berkeley: University of California Press, 1993), 70, 72.

33. Fogelson, 126.

34. William Deverell, *Whitewashed Adobe: The Rise of Los Angeles and the Remaking of Its Mexican Past* (Berkeley: University of California Press, 2004), 5.

35. Mark Wild, *Street Meeting: Multiethnic Neighborhoods in Early Twentieth-Century Los Angeles* (Berkeley: University of California Press, 2005), 38.

36. Deverell, *Whitewashed Adobe*, 3.

37. Even as leaders may have wished otherwise, the number of non-white and foreign-born white migrants also expanded, so 360,000 of over 1.2 million residents in 1930 were non-white or foreign-born white. Wild, *Street Meeting*, 18–9.

38. Deverell, *Whitewashed Adobe*, 7-8.

39. Kelly Lytle Hernandez, *City of Inmates: Conquest, Rebellion, and the Rise of Human Caging in Los Angeles, 1771–1965* (Chapel Hill: University of North Carolina Press, 2017).

40. Culver, *The Frontier of Leisure*, 56.

41. Wild, *Street Meeting*, 42.

42. "Weird Babel of Tongues," *Los Angeles Times*, 18 April 1906, section 2, p. 1.

43. "The Adventists and Their Prophetess," *Los Angeles Times*, 18 September 1902, A2.

44. McWilliams, *Southern California Country*, 253.

45. "San Diego County: Point Loma Theosophists Denounced as Free-lovers," *Los Angeles Times*, 30 April 1897, 13; "At Spook Point: Search for Mysteries That Are Lost or Stolen," *Los Angeles Times*, 17 April 1899, 10; "Change in Theosophy: Autonomy Overthrown and an Autocracy Established," *Los Angeles Times*, 19 February 1898, 6; "A Female Autocrat," *Los Angeles Times*, 27 February 1898, B4; "San Diego County: Theosophists in Session at Spook Point," *Los Angeles Times*, 16 April 1899, A15; "The Apotheosis of the Purple Cow," *Los Angeles Times*, 23 April 1899, B6; "Mrs. Tingley Is a Mere Pretender," *Los Angeles Times*, 22 June 1901, 12.

46. "State Snapshots," *Los Angeles Times*, 19 December 1901, 10.

47. "Mrs. Tingley Under Fire: Artful Dodging and Juggling on Witness Stand," *Los Angeles Times*, 4 January 1903, 6; Anya Foxen, *Inhaling Spirit: Harmonialism, Orientalism, and the Western Roots of Modern Yoga* (New York: Oxford University Press, 2020), 194–95.

48. "Outrages at Point Loma. Exposed by an 'Escape' from Tingley," *Los Angeles Times*, 28 October 1901, 7.

49. "Curtain Held Over Past," *Los Angeles Times*, 20 December 1902, 10; "Sacred Dog 'Spot' Slips His Collar," *Los Angeles Times*, 21 December 1902, C1; "Morning Session: Shortridge Begins Speech. The Sacred Oath," *Los Angeles Times*, 11 January 1903, 6; "Tingley and 'Spot,'" *Los Angeles Times*, 22 January 1903, 6.

50. For an extended discussion of how mainstream churches received "mind-cure" religions, see Sandra Sizer Frankiel, *California's Spiritual Frontiers: Religious Alternatives in Anglo-Protestantism, 1850–1910* (Berkeley: University of California Press, 1988), chap. 6.

51. Jenkins, *Mystics and Messiahs*, 49–50.

52. "'Spooks' Roasted by San Diego Preacher," *Los Angeles Times*, 5 August 1901, 3; "Point Loma Spookery Under Hot Fire: San Diego Pastor Hits Right from the Shoulder," *Los Angeles Times*, 6 August 1901, 3; "War on Theosophists

at San Diego," *Los Angeles Times*, 19 August 1901, 5; "Church Controversy Stirring in San Diego," *Evening Sentinel* (Santa Cruz), 26 August 1901, 1; "Shot and Shell from Point Loma," *Los Angeles Herald*, 23 October 1901, 8; "Interest Continues in Debate on Christianity and Theosophy at Opera House," *San Diego Union and Daily Bee*, 2 October 1901, 3; Greenwalt, *California Utopia*, 52–53.

53. Willard Huntington Wright, "Los Angeles—The Chemically Pure," in *The Smart Set Anthology*, edited by Burton Rascoe and Groff Conklin (New York: Reynal and Hitchcock, 1934), 96, 99.

54. Sydney E. Ahlstrom, *A Religious History of the American People*, 2nd ed. (New Haven, CT: Yale University Press, 2004), 390–92, 432–34.

55. Upton Sinclair, *The Profits of Religion: An Essay in Economic Interpretation* (New York: AMS Press, 1918), 17.

56. Sinclair, 237, 256, 273.

57. Louis Adamic, "Katherine Tingley, Theosophical Boob-Baiter of San Diego," *Haldeman-Julius Monthly* 5 (February 1927), 60.

58. Louis Adamic, "The Morons of Los Angeles," *The Haldeman-Julius Monthly* 4, no. 6 (November 1926).

59. Adamic, "Katherine Tingley," 49, 51, 53, 57, 59, 60–62, 69.

60. Ashcraft, *The Dawn of the New Cycle*, 23, 40–41.

61. Melton, "The Theosophical Communities and Their Ideal of Universal Brotherhood," 405.

62. Board of Supervisors and Chamber of Commerce, "San Diego, California: The Harbor of the Sun," 1913, 1, 5, UC San Diego Special Collections & Archives, https://library.ucsd.edu/dc/object/bb6658062v.

63. Tim Rudbøg, "Point Loma, Theosophy, and Katherine Tingley," in Hammer and Rothstein, *Handbook of the Theosophical Current*, 58.

64. "San Diego County: San Diego Brevities," *Los Angeles Times*, 27 February 1897, 13.

65. See, for example, "Katherine Tingley's Work on Point Loma Reviewed," *San Diego Union and Daily Bee*, 17 June 1909, 10.

66. C. J. Ryan, "Mr. C. J. Ryan, the English Artist, Visits Loma Homestead," *San Diego Union*, 17 February 1901, 9.

67. See, for example, Ian Tyrrell, *Reforming the World: The Creation of America's Moral Empire* (Princeton, NJ: Princeton University Press, 2010).

68. Wright, "Los Angeles—The Chemically Pure," 95–96.

69. Penny B. Waterstone "Domesticating Universal Brotherhood: Feminine Values and the Construction of Utopia, Point Loma Homestead, 1897–1920" (PhD diss., University of Arizona, 1995), 215, 295, as cited in Evelyn A. Kirkley, "Starved and Treated Like Convicts," *Journal of San Diego History* 43, no. 1 (Winter 1997), n. 4. There is a deep literature about women's involvement in the Theosophical Movement in general and the Universal Brotherhood in particular. In addition to Waterstone, Kirkley, and Ashcraft, see Mary F. Bednarowski, "Outside the Mainstream: Women's Religion and Women Religious Leaders in Nineteenth Century America," *Journal of the American Academy of Religion* 48 (1980): 207–31; Robert Ellwood and Catherine Wessinger, "The Feminism of 'Universal Brotherhood': Women in the Theosophical Movement," in *Women's*

Leadership in Marginal Religions: Explorations Outside the Mainstream, ed. Catherine Wessinger (Urbana: University of Illinois, 1993), 68–87; and James Santucci, "Women in the Theosophical Movement," *Explorations: Journal for Adventurous Thought* 9 (Fall 1990): 71–94.

70. "Theosophical Leader Makes European Tour," *San Diego Union and Daily Bee*, 9 December 1912, 12.

71. Ashcraft, *The Dawn of a New Cycle*, 38–39, 76–77.

72. Wright, "Los Angeles—The Chemically Pure," 95–96.

73. Fogelson, *The Fragmented Metropolis*, 56, 62.

74. Kropp, *California Vieja*, Introduction.

75. Kevin Starr, *Americans and the California Dream, 1850–1915* (New York: Oxford University Press, 1973), 378; Kevin Starr, *Inventing the Dream: California Through the Progressive Era* (New York: Oxford University Press, 1986), 77; Charles Dudley Warner, *Our Italy* (New York: Harper & Brothers, 1891), https://www.gutenberg.org/files/28506/28506-h/28506-h.htm.

76. McWilliams, *Southern California Country*, 21–24, 70–83.

77. Paul A. Kramer, "Empires, Exceptions, and Anglo-Saxons: Race and Rule between the British and United States Empires, 1880–1910," *Journal of American History* 88, no. 4 (March 2002): 1319.

78. Kropp, *California Vieja*, 3, 8, 56–57.

79. Peter J. Holliday, *American Arcadia: California and the Classical Tradition* (New York: Oxford University Press, 2016).

80. Matthew Avery Sutton, *Aimee Semple McPherson and the Resurrection of Christian America* (Cambridge, MA: Harvard University Press, 2007), 82–84.

81. Ryan, "Mr. C. J. Ryan, the English Artist, Visits Loma Homestead."

82. Ralph Strong, "Universal Brotherhood's Home at 'Lomaland': Man's Betterment Is Here Sought For," *Los Angeles Herald Illustrated Magazine*, 10 November 1901, 8.

83. "Talks on Theosophy: Dr. Anderson Explains the Philosophy," *Los Angeles Herald*, no. 206, 24 April 1899, 3.

84. Theosophy Is Now Practical," *San Diego Union*, 28 January 1903, 3.

85. "The Purpose of the Universal Brotherhood and the Theosophical Society," *San Diego Union and Bee*, 7 October 1900, 22.

86. Dolores Hayden, *Seven American Utopias: The Architecture of Communitarian Socialism, 1790–1975* (Cambridge, MA: MIT Press, 1976), 43.

87. For the same reasons, American historians in the early twentieth century emphasized the importance of European—especially English—medieval history to the United States. Paul Freedman and Gabrielle M. Spiegel, "Medievalisms Old and New: The Rediscovery of Alterity in North American Medieval Studies," *American Historical Review* 103, no. 3 (June 1998): 682–83.

88. Holliday, *American Arcadia*, 158–59.

89. "The Great Amphitheatre," *Covina Argus*, 5 July 1902, 7; "Point Loma and Her Grecian Amphitheater," *Oxnard Courier*, 12 July 1902, 6.

90. For example, see "'Scientific Theosophy' Is Topic of Lecture at the Isis Theatre," *San Diego Union and Daily Bee*, 28 June 1909, 12; "Text of Lecture Delivered by J. H. Fussell at the Isis," *San Diego Union and Daily Bee*, 5 April

1916, 10; E. A. Neresheimer, "Katherine Tingley's Success and Its Secrets," *San Diego Union and Daily Bee*, 12 October 1902, 7.

91. Holliday, *American Arcadia*, 146–47; "Gorgeous Production 'Aroma of Athens' to Be Given at Greek Theater, Point Loma," *San Diego Union and Daily Bee*, 2 April 1911, 5.

92. Greenwalt, *California Utopia*, 101.

93. "Sacred Dog 'Spot' Slips His Collar," *Los Angeles Times*, 21 December 1902, C1. This was a topic throughout the libel trial. It also created rifts within the community, as members like Dr. Jerome Anderson listed the costumed pageantry as one of the grievances that led to his departure. See Greenwalt, *California Utopia*, 54.

94. "Talks on Theosophy," *Los Angeles Herald*.

95. "Gorgeous Production 'Aroma of Athens' to Be Given at Greek Theater, Point Loma."

96. Ashcraft, *Ancient Wisdom Revived*, 94, as cited in Rudbøg, "Point Loma, Theosophy, and Katherine Tingley," 63–64.

97. Charles Fletcher Lummis, "Those Terrible Mysteries," *Out West* 18, no. 1 (January 1903): 38, 39, 42, 44, 48.

98. "Lomaland: International Headquarters for Theosophy and Raja Yoga Throughout the World, Katherine Tingley Has Made It a Wonderland," *San Diego Union and Daily Bee*, 1 January 1909, 1, 4, 8.

99. Kropp, *California Vieja*, 105.

100. Ashcraft, *The Dawn of the New Cycle*, 147, 151–56.

101. Stratton, *Education for Empire*, 17–18.

102. Culver, *Frontier of Leisure*, 38.

103. Jennifer A. Watts, "Photography in the Land of Sunshine," *Southern California Quarterly* 87, no. 4 (2005–2006): 360.

104. Watts, "Photography in the Land of Sunshine," 356.

105. Ashcraft, *The Dawn of the New Cycle*, 70.

106. Watts, "Photography in the Land of Sunshine," 350–51, 356.

107. Paul A. Kramer, *Blood of Government: Race, Empire, the United States, and the Philippines* (Chapel Hill: University of North Carolina Press, 2006), 167.

108. Strong, "Universal Brotherhood's Home at 'Lomaland,'" 9. See also Charles Fletcher Lummis, "In the Lion's Den," *Out West* 17, no. 6 (December 1902), 735–38.

109. Stratton, *Education for Empire*, 3.

110. Lears, *No Place of Grace*, 57.

111. Stratton, *Education for Empire*, 24–26; Yorick, "On the Margin," *San Diego Union*, 10 January 1915, 1, as cited in Robert W. Rydell, *All the World's a Fair: Visions of Empire at American International Expositions, 1876–1916* (Chicago: University of Chicago Press, 1984), 209.

112. "San Diego, A Comprehensive Plan for Its Improvement" (Boston, 1908), 46, as cited in Starr, *America and the California Dream*, 402.

113. "At Spook Point: Search for Mysteries That Are Lost or Stolen," *Los Angeles Times*, 17 April 1899, 10.

114. Kropp, *California Vieja*, 105.

115. Ryan, "Mr. C. J. Ryan, the English Artist, Visits Loma Homestead."

116. "How a Ball Player Who Became a Millionaire Lives," *Los Angeles Herald Sunday Supplement*, 10 May 1903, 3.

117. "Point Loma, Home of Theosophy," *San Diego Union*, January 1, 1910, section 4, p. 1.

118. "Point Loma City," *San Diego Union*, 1 January 1910, section 9, 4–5.

119. See, for example, Dolores Hayden, *Seven American*; Christopher R. Clark, *The Communitarian Moment: The Radical Challenge of the Northampton Association* (Ithaca, NY: Cornell University Press, 1995).

120. Hine, *California's Utopian Colonies*, 51; Green, "California and Theosophy," 4.

121. "Scenic Trips to Grossmont and Point Loma Attract Many Out of Town Visitors," *San Diego Union and Daily Bee*, 9; Grace Knoche, "Theosophy, Katherine Tingley and Point Loma," *Oakland Tribune*, 9 September 1917, 15.

122. "International Theosophical Headquarters," *San Diego Union*, 1 January 1916, 5.

123. For reference to Tingley as the vice president of the association, see "California Editorial Association Sends Message to Peace Congress," *Oxnard Daily Courier*, 4 July 1913.

124. "The City of Bay'N'Climate," *Corona Independent*, 12 July 1907, 1.

125. See, for example, "Trips Over Bay and City Park," *San Diego Union and Daily Bee*, 20 February 1905, 3; "Educators Vote against Compulsion," *Hanford Weekly Sentinel*, 29 November 1906, 7; Baja California Very Interesting," *Healdsburg Tribune*, 5 April 1911, 1; "Nurses of State End Convention with Sightseeing," *San Diego Union and Daily Bee*, 9 July 1917, 12.

126. "Thousands Annually Visit The Point Loma Homestead," *San Diego Union*, 1 January 1908, 19; "San Diego and the County: What the Tourist Will Find—Brief History of the City," *San Diego Union and Daily Bee*, 1 January 1908, 39; "San Diego County Is Paradise for Motoring," *San Diego Union and Daily Bee*, 1 January 1910, section 12, p. 2.

127. "Lomaland: International Headquarters for Theosophy and Raja Yoga Throughout the World," 1, 4, 8.

128. John Steven McGroarty, "The Mission Play: Presented in the Mission Play House at Old San Gabriel Mission, California," San Gabriel, 1921. https://catalog.hathitrust.org/ Record/102340347 (accessed 14 June 2023).

129. The Federation of Women's Clubs documented by Phoebe Kropp took credit for the designation. See "Club Notes," *Sacramento Union*, 9 May 1915, 28. The notion of an "old Spanish lighthouse" proved irresistible despite vast evidence to the contrary. A 1926 history of the lighthouse documented the history of the lighthouse but pleaded that the materials and workers associated with the lighthouse justified maintaining the name. See Winifred Davidson, *A Brief History of the Old Spanish Lighthouse* (Point Loma, no publisher, 1926).

130. Ruth Kedzie Wood, *The Tourist's California* (New York: Dodd, Mead, and Company, 1914), 68, 350.

131. Effie Price Gadding, *Across the Continent by the Lincoln Highway* (New York: Rowland & Ives, 1915), 66; Porter, "Around San Diego Bay," 9.

132. Thos. D. Murphy, *On Sunset Highways* (Boston: L.C. Page and Company, 1915), 123–25; accessed via https://www.gutenberg.org/files/57580/57580 -h/57580-h.htm.

133. John S. McGroarty, "San Diego—The Harbor of the Sun" (Atchison, Topeka, and Santa Fe Railroad Company, 1915), n.p., Special Collections & Archives, UC San Diego, La Jolla, 92093-0175, https://library.ucsd.edu/dc /object/bb74431075.

134. Kropp, *California Vieja*, chap. 3.

135. "The San Diego Panama-California Exposition,' *Raja-Yoga Messenger* 10, no. 8 (October 1914), 17–20.

136. Jacob McKean resigned from Modern Times in May 2021 after allegations of sexual harassment. See Eric S. Page and Dana Griffin, "Modern Times Beer CEO Steps Down amid Craft Brewing's #MeTooMovement," NBC San Diego, 19 May 2021, https://www.nbcsandiego.com/ news/local/modern-times -ceo-steps-down-amid-craft-brewings-me-too-moment/2609078/; "A Statement from Jacob McKean," http://www.moderntimesbeer.com/blog/statement-jacob -mckean (accessed 5 June 2021).

137. Ronald G. Walters, *American Reformers 1815–1860* (New York: Hill and Wang, 1978, 1997), 61, 74. According to Waters, "Equitable commerce" in this instance meant "a system giving people the full value of their labor," although he also suggests this system of "absolute personal freedom" maximized the "freedom to quarrel."

138. "Lomaland," Modern Times Beer, http://www.moderntimesbeer.com /beer/lomaland (accessed 19 March 2020); Jacob McKean, "About," Modern Times Beer, http://www.moderntimesbeer.com/about (accessed 15 March 2020).

139. "Economic Impact of Craft Breweries in San Diego County," California State University, San Marcos, Office of Business Research and Analysis, 2019, https://www.csusm.edu/coba/obra/reports/sandiego_craftbeer_industry /adareports/2019adasandiego.pdf; Mariel Concepcion, "San Diego County's Craft Brewers Produce $1.2 Billion in 2018 Economic Impact," *San Diego Business Journal*, 13 August 2019, https://www.sdbj.com/news/2019/aug/13/san -diego-countys-craft-brewers-produce-12-billion/; Ian Anderson, "How's the San Diego Beer Industry Doing? It Depends Who You Ask," *San Diego Reader*, 23 August 2019, https://www.sandiegoreader.com/news/2019/aug/23/beer-hows -san-diego-beer-industry-doing-it-depends/.

140. Andrew Keatts, "Making the Case for 'San Diego Beer-First' Community," *Voices of San Diego*, 28 June 2013, https://www.voiceofsandiego.org /community/making-the-case-for-a-san-diego-beer-first-community/.

141. San Diego Economic Development Corporation, "San Diego's Craft Beer Industry," March 2018, https://www.sandiegobusiness.org/sites/default/files /Craft%20Beer_0.pdf; "The Craft Beer Boom," Visit California, 2020, https:// www.visitcalifornia.com/feature/craft-beer-boom.

CHAPTER 2. "EFFICIENT AMERICA," "SPIRITUAL INDIA,"
AND AMERICA'S TRANSNATIONAL RELIGIOUS IMAGINATION

1. *Autobiography of a Yogi* has sold over four million copies and entered its thirteenth edition in 2012. Paramahansa Yogananda, *Autobiography of a Yogi* (Los Angeles: Self-Realization Fellowship, 1946), 159, 480; Paramahansa Yogananda, "Last Speech Given by Yoganandaji," *Self-Realization Magazine*, May–June 1952, 70–71.

2. Joseph S. Alter, "Yoga, Bodybuilding, and Wrestling: Metaphysical Fitness," in Debra Diamond, *Yoga: The Art of Transformation* (Washington, DC: Arthur M. Sackler Gallery, Smithsonian Institution, 2013), 85.

3. Kimberly Lau, *New Age Capitalism: Making Money East of Eden* (Philadelphia: University of Pennsylvania Press, 2000), 11. See also Jeremy Carrette and Richard King, *Selling Spirituality: The Silent Takeover of Religion* (New York: Routledge and Francis, 2005).

4. Anya P. Foxen argues that Yogananda is overlooked in the history of modern yoga because his method resembled *hatha* yoga and mostly lacked *asanas*. See Anya P. Foxen, *Biography of a Yogi: Paramahansa Yogananda and the Origins of a Modern Yoga* (New York: Oxford University Press, 2017), 17.

5. Emily Rosenberg, "Transnational Currents in a Shrinking World," in *A World Connecting 1870–1945*, ed. Emily Rosenberg (Cambridge, MA: Harvard Belknap, 2012), 821.

6. Rosenberg, "Transnational Currents," 849, 868.

7. Stuart Hall, "'The Local and the Global': Culture, Globalization, and the World-System," in *Culture, Globalization, and the World-System*, ed. Anthony D. King (Minneapolis: University of Minnesota Press, 1997), 26–28.

8. Rosenberg, "Transnational Currents," 849, 868.

9. Andrea Jain: *Selling Yoga: From Counterculture to Pop Culture* (New York: Oxford University Press, 2015), 160–61.

10. Vijay Prashad, *The Karma of Brown Folk* (Minneapolis: University of Minnesota Press, 2000), x; Marie Louise Burke, *Swami Vivekananda in America: New Discoveries* (Calcutta: Advaita Ashrama, 1966), 135 as quoted in Prashad, *The Karma of Brown Folk*, 35; Rahul Sagar, "Hindu Nationalists and the Cold War," in *India and the Cold War*, ed. Manu Bhagavan (Chapel Hill: University of North Carolina Press, 2019), 232–37.

11. Wakoh Shannon Hickey, *Mind Cure: How Meditation Became Medicine* (New York: Oxford University Press, 2019), 79.

12. Srinivas Aravamudan, *Guru English: South Asian Religion in a Cosmopolitan Language* (Princeton, NJ: Princeton University Press, 2006), 7, 10.

13. Aravamudan, *Guru English*, 19, 220.

14. Prashad, *The Karma of Brown Folk*. For another work on the commoditization of Indian culture in the wake of the sixties, see Gita Mehta, *Karma Cola: Marketing the Mystic East* (New York: Simon & Schuster, 1979; reprint, New York: Vintage Books, 1994).

15. Akira Iriye, *Cultural Internationalism and World Order* (Baltimore: Johns Hopkins University Press, 1997), 29–30, 35; Rosenberg, "Transnational Currents," 861, 922–23.

16. Iriye, *Cultural Internationalism and World Order*, 3, 7–8, 61–62. See also Akira Iriye, *Global and Transnational History: The Past, Present, and Future* (New York: Palgrave Macmillan, 2013).

17. Foxen, *Biography of a Yogi*, 49–55.

18. Matthew Avery Sutton, "Religious World Views," in *The Cambridge History of America and the World*, vol. 3, 1900–1945, ed. Brooke L. Blower and Andrew Preston (New York: Cambridge University Press, 2021), 430–31, 437–38; Gary Gerstle, *American Crucible: Race and Nation in the Twentieth Century* (Princeton, NJ: Princeton University Press, 2001), 94.

19. Mrinalini Sinha, *Specters of Mother India: The Global Restructuring of an Empire* (Durham, NC: Duke University Press, 2006).

20. Eric Avila, *Popular Culture in the Age of White Flight: Fear and Fantasy in Suburban Los Angeles* (Berkeley: University of California Press, 2004), 20–24.

21. Paramahansa Yogananda, "Some Aims of *East-West*," *East-West World Wide*, November–December 1925, 16.

22. Partha Chatterjee, *The Nation and Its Fragments: Colonial and Postcolonial Histories* (Princeton: Princeton University Press, 1993), 5, as cited in Michael Goebel, *Anti-Imperial Metropolis: Interwar Paris and the Seeds of Third World Nationalism* (New York: Cambridge University Press, 2015), 255–61.

23. Iriye, *Cultural Internationalism and World Order*, 66.

24. Catherine L. Albanese, *A Republic of Mind and Spirit: A Cultural History of American Metaphysical Religion* (New Haven, CT: Yale University Press, 2007), 369.

25. Yogananda, *Autobiography of a Yogi*, 107.

26. Lola Williamson, *Transcendent in America: Hindu-Inspired Meditation Movements as New Religion* (New York: New York University Press, 2010), 14, 17.

27. Rosenberg, "Transnational Currents," 923; Zaheer Baber, *The Science of Empire: Scientific Knowledge, Civilization, and Colonial Rule in India* (New York: Oxford University Press, 1998), 221, 250. See also Kapil Raj, *Relocating Modern Science: Circulation and the Construction of Knowledge in South Asia and Europe, 1650–1900* (New York: Palgrave Macmillan, 2007).

28. Gyan Prakash, *Another Reason: Science and the Imagination of Modern India* (Princeton, NJ: Princeton University Press, 1999), 7, 35, 57, 88.

29. Williamson, *Transcendent in America*, 59.

30. Paramahansa Yogananda, "Yellow Journalism versus Truth: Are Eastern Teachings 'Dangerous'?" *East-West World Wide*, January–February 1928, 7.

31. Stefanie Syman, *The Subtle Body: The Story of Yoga in America* (New York: Farrar, Straus and Giroux, 2010), 170–72. Yogananda also endured a brief financial scandal in 1925.

32. For a fuller account of Yogananda's life-long role as an interfaith missionary in the United States, see David J. Neumann, *Finding God through Yoga: Paramahansa Yogananda and Modern America Religion in a Global Age* (Chapel Hill: University of North Carolina Press, 2019).

33. "Display Ad 20," *Los Angeles Times*, 7 November 1925, A2; "Display Ad 34," *Los Angeles Times*, 9 October 1925, A9; "Display Ad 40," *Los Angeles Times*, 20 January 1925, B11.

34. "Do Daily Dozen Easily in Mental Flip-Flops," *Charleston (WV) Daily Mail*, 23 December 1923, 4.

35. Robert Love, "Fear of Yoga," *Columbia Journalism Review* (November–December 2006): 85–86; "Hindu Cult Will Be Investigated," *Imperial Valley Press*, 10 January 1928, 2.

36. Neumann, *Finding God Through Yoga*, 97–101, 119. For more on the contours of the SRF's belief system—both as designed by Yogananda and currently practiced—see Williamson, *Transcendent in America*, chap. 3.

37. Williamson, *Transcendent in America*, 67.

38. Mark Singleton, "Globalized Modern Yoga," in Diamond, *Yoga: The Art of Transformation*, 95–96.

39. Jain, *Selling Yoga*, 27; Mark Singleton, *Yoga Body: The Origins of Modern Posture Practice* (New York: Oxford University Press, 2010), 131–32. For the possible sources of Yogananda's yogic practice, see Anya Foxen, "Yogi Calisthenics: What the 'Non-Yoga' Yogic Practice of Paramahansa Yogananda Can Tell Us about Religion," *Journal of the American Academy of Religion* 85, no. 2 (June 2017): 494–526 and Foxen, *Biography of a Yogi*, chap. 4.

40. "Paramahansa Yogananda Gives Concluding Talk," *Self-Realization Magazine*, November–December 1951, 35–36.

41. Singleton, "Globalized Modern Yoga," 97.

42. Susan Harding, *The Book of Jerry Falwell: Fundamentalist Language and Politics* (Princeton, NJ: Princeton University Press, 2000), 21, 62.

43. Luther Burbank, "Science and Civilization," *East-West World Wide*, November–December 1925, 16.

44. Philip Goldberg, *American Veda: From Emerson and the Beatles to Yoga and Meditation—How Indian Spirituality Changed the West* (New York: Harmony Books, 2010), 114–18.

45. "Guru's Exit," *Time*, 4 August 1952, 59.

46. Williamson, *Transcendent in America*, 56.

47. Lisa McGirr, *Suburban Warriors: The Origins of the New American Right* (Princeton, NJ: Princeton University Press, 2001); Darren Dochuk, *From Bible Belt to Sunbelt: Plain-Folk Religion, Grassroots Politics, and the Rise of Evangelical Conservatism* (New York: W.W. Norton, 2012); Eileen Luhr, *Witnessing Suburbia: Conservatives and Christian Youth Culture* (Berkeley: University of California Press, 2009); Elaine Tyler May, *Homeward Bound: American Families in the Cold War Era* (New York: Basic Books, 1988).

48. Christina Klein, *Cold War Orientalism: Asia in the Middlebrow Imagination* (Berkeley: University of California Press, 2003); Naoko Shibusawa, *America's Geisha Ally: Reimagining the Japanese Enemy* (Cambridge, MA: Harvard University Press, 2006), chaps. 1 and 2.

49. Klein, *Cold War Orientalism*, 9–13; Robert G. Lee, *Orientals: Asian Americans in Popular Culture* (Philadelphia: Temple University Press, 1999), 145–46 and 153–56; Jane Burbank and Frederick Cooper, *Empires in World History: Power and the Politics of Difference* (Princeton, NJ: Princeton University Press, 2011), 414–15.

50. Jain, *Selling Yoga*, 160.

51. Mark Singleton, *Yoga Body*; Mark Singleton and Ellen Goldberg, eds., *Gurus of Modern India* (New York: Oxford University Press, 2013); Jain, *Selling Yoga*; Syman, *The Subtle Body*.

52. Klein, *Cold War Orientalism*, 114.

53. Mary Louise Pratt, *Imperial Eyes: Travel Writing and Transculturation* (New York: Routledge, 1992), 7, 102; Mary Louse Pratt, "Arts of the Contact Zone," *Profession* (1991): 35.

54. Yogananda, *Autobiography of a Yogi*, 65–67, 107; "Follow the Self-Realization Highway to the Infinite," undated pamphlet (c. 1950–51), Theos Bernard Papers, Bancroft Library, University of California, Berkeley, folder 8, carton 6.

55. Yogananda, *Autobiography of a Yogi*, 322–23.

56. "International Fellowship," *Self-Realization Magazine*, September–October 1946, 34–35.

57. "Notes from the News," *Self-Realization Magazine*, January–February–March 1946, 20.

58. SRF "India Citizenship Bill Passes," *Self-Realization Magazine*, September–October–November 1946, 23; "Notes from the News," *Self-Realization Magazine*, November–December 1946, 29.

59. Barbara D. Metcalf and Thomas R. Metcalf, *A Concise History of Modern India*, 2nd ed. (New York: Cambridge University Press, 2006), 221–22.

60. For the importance of India to Cold War politics, see Manu Bhagavan, "Introduction," in Bhagavan, *India and the Cold War*, 1–15, and Pallavi Raghavan, "Journeys of Discovery," in Bhagavan, *India and the Cold War*, 19–35.

61. Anti-colonialism, anti-racism, and passive nonviolence represented another potential thread for cooperation. See Gerald C. Horne, *The End of Empires: African Americans and India* (Philadelphia: Temple University Press, 2009) and Nico Slate, *Colored Cosmopolitanism: The Shared Struggle for Freedom in the United States and India* (Cambridge, MA: Harvard University Press, 2012).

62. Vijaya Lakshmi Pandit, "India's Policy," *Self-Realization Magazine*, November–December 1951, 4.

63. Haridas Chaudhuri, "The Spirit of Indian Culture," *Self-Realization Magazine*, September–October 1951, 31–32.

64. "Follow the Self-Realization Highway to the Infinite."

65. Jane Iwamura, *Virtual Orientalism: Asian Religions and American Popular Culture* (New York: Oxford University Press, 2011), 20.

66. Mulk Raj Ahuja, "Paramahansa Yogananda: An Appreciation," *Self-Realization Magazine*, May–June 1952, 29.

67. "Tribute to PY by Ambassador Binay R. Sen," *Self-Realization Magazine*, May–June 1952, 68–69.

68. Shelly McKenzie, *Getting Physical: The Rise of Fitness Culture in America* (Lawrence: University of Kansas Press, 2013), 24–26.

69. See, for example, "Yoga Postures for Health," *Self-Realization Magazine*, November–December 1951, 13–14; "Yoga Postures for Health, *Self-Realization Magazine*, January–February 1952, 24–25; "Yoga Postures for

Health, *Self-Realization Magazine*, March–April 1952, 11–12; "Photos of SRF Convocation," *Self-Realization Magazine*, November–December 1951, 32.

70. Joseph Alter, *Yoga in Modern India: The Body Between Science and Philosophy* (New Delhi: New Age Books, 2009), 5 (originally printed by Princeton University Press, 2004).

71. Yogananda, *Autobiography of a Yogi*, 160.

72. "Yogananda Speaks Sunday in Phoenix," *Scottsdale Progress*, 30 September 1948, 9.

73. Yogananda, *Autobiography of a Yogi*, 235–36. Proponents of the benefits of yoga for health and fitness have continued to emphasize the scientific elements of the practice. See William J. Broad, *The Science of Yoga: The Risks and Rewards* (New York: Simon and Schuster, 2012).

74. See Paul E. Johnson, *A Shopkeeper's Millennium: Society and Revivals in Rochester, New York, 1815–1837* (New York: Hill and Wang, 1978); Diane Winston and John Michael Giggie, *Faith in the Market: Religion and the Rise of Urban Commercial Culture* (New Brunswick, NJ: Rutgers University Press, 2002); Bethany Moreton, *To Save God and Walmart: The Making of Christian Free Enterprise* (Cambridge, MA: Harvard University Press, 2010).

75. T. J. Jackson Lears, "From Salvation to Self-Realization: Advertising and the Therapeutic Roots of the Consumer Culture, 1880–1930," in *The Culture of Consumption: Critical Essays in American History, 1880–1980*, ed. T. J. Jackson Lears and Richard Wrightman Fox (New York: Pantheon Books, 1983).

76. Jain, *Selling Yoga*, 28; Elizabeth De Michelis, *A History of Modern Yoga: Patañjali and Western Esotericism* (New York: Continuum, 2004), 14, 186.

77. Singleton, *Yoga Body*, 129–32.

78. For other movements that focused on philosophical and meditative elements of yoga, see Jain, *Selling Yoga*, 28–36 and de Michelis, *A History of Modern Yoga*.

79. Eva Illouz, *Cold Intimacies: The Making of Emotional Capitalism* (Malden, MA: Polity Press, 2007), 43, 45.

80. Theodore Marvin Anderson, "Reimagining Religion: The Grounding of Spiritual Politics and Practice in Modern America, 1890–1940" (PhD diss., Yale University, 2008), 73, 87, 85.

81. "The Knowledge of India's Master Minds Belong to You," *Inner Culture* 6, no. 7 (May 1934), 29.

82. "The Summer Training School at Yogoda Sat-Sanga Headquarters," *East-West* 4, no. 8 (June 1932), 27–28.

83. "The Spread of Self-Realization Fellowship," *Inner Culture* 9, no. 5 (March 1937), 42.

84. Edmund Rucker, "Yoga Sect Holds Worldwide Lure," *San Diego Union*, 10 July 1949, 1

85. *Inner Culture* 12, no. 9 (July–August–September 1940), 50, 56, 58–59, 60.

86. Yogananda, *Autobiography of a Yogi*, 483.

87. "'Master' Yogananda Succumbs in L.A.," *San Diego Union*, 9 March 1952.

88. "Follow the Self-Realization Highway to the Infinite."

89. "Intuition," undated pamphlet, Theos Bernard Papers, Bancroft Library, University of California, Berkeley, carton 6, folder 18.

90. Nicole Aschoff, *The New Prophets of Capital* (Brooklyn, NY: Verso Books, 2015), 105–6.

91. "Kiwanis Invite Swami Yogananda," *Salt Lake Tribune*, 1 October 1931, 8; "'Self-Realization' Swami's Topic Before Ad Club," *San Diego Union*, 9 December, 1937, 9; Golden Lotus Temple advertisement, "Attracting True Abundance," *Coast Dispatch*, 10 November 1938, 3; Golden Lotus Temple advertisement, "The Divine Way of Increasing Your Earning Power," *Coast Dispatch*, 16 March 1939, 5.

92. William Davies, *The Happiness Industry: How the Government and Big Business Sold Us Well-Being* (Brooklyn, NY: Verso, 2015), 135.

93. See, for example, A. Lavagnini, "An International Language," *Self-Realization Magazine*, April–May–June 1945, 4.

94. In 1877, Sen gave a speech in Calcutta in which he noted, "While we learn in modern science from England, England learns ancient wisdom from India." See Metcalf and Metcalf, *A Concise History of Modern India*, 114–15 and chap. 5. For more on Tagore's use of the language of universalism, which recognized South Asia's complex and interconnected religious histories, as well as South Asians' participation in processes of modern economic globalization such as flows of money, laborers, and commodities, see Sugata Bose, *A Hundred Horizons: The Indian Ocean in the Age of Global Empire* (Cambridge, MA: Harvard University Press, 2009), chap. 7.

95. Iriye, *Cultural Internationalism and World Order*, 7–8.

96. Klein, *Cold War Orientalism*, 34–36, 41–43, 22–23; Michael E. Latham, *The Right Kind of Revolution: Modernization, Development, and U.S. Foreign Policy from the Cold War to the Present* (Ithaca, NY: Cornell University Press, 2011), 2, 4.

97. Shibusawa, *America's Geisha Ally*, 56–58.

98. Yogananda, *Autobiography of a Yogi*, 34, 72–73.

99. "India Specialized in Soul Culture," *Self-Realization Magazine*, April–May–June 1945, back cover.

100. Paramahansa Yogananda, "Last Speech Given by Yoganandaji," *Self-Realization Magazine*, May–June 1952, 70–71.

101. Melani McAlister, *Epic Encounters: Culture, Media, and U.S. Interests in the Middle East since 1945* (Berkeley: University of California Press, 2001), 43.

102. Hall, "The Local and the Global," 27, 33–34.

103. Vijay Prashad, *Everybody Was Kung Fu Fighting: Afro-Asian Connections and the Myth of Cultural Purity* (Boston: Beacon Press, 2001), 61.

104. "Villages of India," *Self-Realization Magazine*, September–October 1946, 27.

105. "A Night in India" program, June 1952, Theos Bernard Papers, Bancroft Library, University of California, Berkeley, Theos Bernard Papers, folder 18, carton 6.

106. "Lotus Festival Concert," *Self-Realization Magazine*, July–August 1951, 3–5.

107. "News of SRF," *Self-Realization Magazine*, September–October 1956, 34.

108. Kevin Kruse, *One Nation Under God: How Corporate America Invented Christian America* (New York: Basic Books, 2015), xiv.

109. Paramahansa Yogananda, "A Well-Balanced Life Means Happiness," *Self-Realization Magazine*, March–April 1953, 30.

110. "Highest Achievements through Self-Realization: Authentic Masters of India," Theos Bernard Papers, Bancroft Library, University of California, Berkeley, folder 18, carton 6.

111. Iwamura, *Virtual Orientalism*, 20.

112. Ronald Purser, *McMindfulness: How Mindfulness Became the New Capitalist Spirituality* (London: Repeater Books, 2019), 54.

113. Dick Fowler, "The Life of James J. Lynn," *Self-Realization Magazine*, March–June 1955, 4–16, reprinted from *Kansas City Star*, 13 May 1951.

114. Shibusawa, *America's Geisha Ally*.

115. "Highest Achievements through Self-Realization: Authentic Masters of India," 18.

116. Yogananda, *Autobiography of a Yogi*, 65.

117. "Words of Master about Mr. Lynn," *Self-Realization Magazine*, March–June 1955, 22.

118. *Self-Realization Magazine*, July–August 1955, inside cover.

119. "Mr. Lynn's Words about Master and SRF," *Self-Realization Magazine*, March–June 1955, 27–44.

120. *Self-Realization Magazine*, September–October 1955, inside back cover.

121. "Master and Mr. Lynn, Hand in Hand," *Self-Realization Magazine*, May–June 1957, inside cover.

122. Laurie Segall, "Steve Jobs' Last Gift," CNN, 10 September 2013, http://money.cnn.com/2013/09/10/ technology/steve-jobs-gift/.

123. Walter Isaacson, *Steve Jobs* (New York: Simon and Schuster, 2011), 48–49.

124. Aravamudan, *Guru English*, 7.

125. Iwamura, *Virtual Orientalism*, 21.

126. Hall, "'The Local and the Global,'" 28; Luc Boltanski and Eve Chiapello, *The New Spirit of Capitalism* (New York: Verso, 2005), 17, 438–41.

127. Aschoff, *The New Prophets of Capital*, 10–11.

128. Fred Turner, *From Counterculture to Cyberculture: Stewart Brand, the Whole Earth Network, and the Rise of Digital Utopianism* (Chicago: University of Chicago Press, 2006), 4; John Markoff, *What the Dormouse Said: How the Sixties Counterculture Shaped the Personal Computer Industry* (New York: Penguin, 2005), xiv.

129. "Ronald Reagan, "Remarks and Question-and-Answer Session with Students and Faculty at Moscow State University, 31 May 1988, as cited in Margaret O'Mara, *The Code: Silicon Valley and the Remaking of America* (New York: Penguin Press, 2019), 4 and Turner, *From Counterculture to Cyberculture*, 175.

130. Turner, *From Counterculture to Cyberculture*, 2, 12; Steven Lubar, "'Do Not Fold, Spindle, or Mutilate': A Cultural History of the Punch Card," *Journal of American Culture* 15, no. 4 (Winter 1992): 46–48.

131. Turner, *From Counterculture to Cyberculture*, 28–37.

132. Theodore Roszak, *The Making of a Counter Culture* (Garden City, NY: Anchor Books, 1969), 5–7.

133. Roszak, *The Making of a Counter Culture*, 205–8.

134. T. J. Jackson Lears, *No Place of Grace: Antimodernism and the Transformation of American Culture, 1880–1920* (Chicago: University of Chicago Press, 1981).

135. Turner, *From Counterculture to Cyberculture*, 38.

136. Angus Burgin, "Market Politics in an Age of Automation," in *Beyond the New Deal Order: U.S. Politics from the Great Depression to the Great Recession*, ed. Gary Gerstle, Nelson Lichtenstein, and Alice O'Connor (Philadelphia: University of Pennsylvania Press, 2019), 149; O'Mara, *The Code*, 118–19.

137. Michael Swaine and Paul Freiberger, *Fire in the Valley: The Making of the Personal Computer* (New York: McGraw Hill, 1984); Theodore Roszak, *The Cult of Information: The Folklore of Computers and the True Art of Thinking* (New York: Pantheon Books, 1986), 136, 141, 143, 206.

138. Katie Hafner and Matthew Lyon, *Where Wizards Stay Up Late: The Origins of the Internet* (New York: Simon & Schuster, 1996), 40.

139. Andy Crouch, "Steve Jobs, the Secular Prophet," *Wall Street Journal*, 8 October 2011.

140. "When We Invented the Personal Computer, We Created a New Kind of Bicycle," *Wall Street Journal*, 13 August 1980, 28.

141. "Apple Launches iPad," Apple, 27 January 2010, https://www.apple.com/newsroom/ 2010/ 01/27Apple-Launches-iPad/.

142. O'Mara, *The Code*, 214, 220.

143. Jean-Louis Gassee, "Business: The New Frontier," *Los Angeles Times*, 1 March 1987, M59.

144. Roszak, *The Making of a Counter Culture*, 208; Doug Rossinow, *The Politics of Authenticity: Liberalism, Christianity, and the New Left in America* (New York: Columbia University Press, 1998).

145. Markoff, *What the Dormouse Said*, xix, 58–68; Malcolm Harris, *Palo Alto: A History of California, Capitalism, and the World* (New York: Little, Brown and Company, 2023), 282–87.

146. Roszak, *The Cult of Information,* 19, 22–23, 40.

147. Michael S. Malone, *The Big Score: The Billion-Dollar Story of Silicon Valley* (Garden City, NY: Doubleday & Company, Inc., 1985), 374–75.

148. Harris, *Palo Alto*, 536–40; Levinson, *Outside the Box*, 136.

149. Davies, *The Happiness Industry*, 136; Wilson, *Neoliberalism*, 128–29; Levinson, *Outside the Box*, 132.

150. Elizabeth Currid-Halkett, *The Sum of Small Things: A Theory of the Aspirational Class* (Princeton, NJ: Princeton University Press, 2017), 18.

151. Harris, *Palo Alto*, 452–55.

152. Malone, *The Big Score*, 366.

153. Dennis Toruish and Ashly Pinnington, "Transformational Leadership, Corporate Cultism, and the Spirituality Paradigm: An Unholy Trinity in the Workplace?" *Human Relations* 55 (2002): 147, as cited in Ehrenreich, *Bright Sided: How Positive Thinking Is Undermining America* (New York:

Metropolitan Books, 2009), 111; Michelle Conlin, "Religion in the Workplace," *Business Week*, 1 November 1999, 150, and Frank Rose and Wilton Woods, "A New Age for Business?" *Fortune*, 8 October 990, 157, cited in Ehrenreich, *Bright Sided*, 111–12.

154. Crouch, "Steve Jobs, the Secular Prophet."

155. Harris, *Palo Alto*, 531; Currid-Halkett, *The Sum of Small Things*, 21, 54, 118, 127.

156. "Wandering in India, Steve Jobs Learned Intuition," *Hindustan Times*, 25 October 2011.

157. Isaacson, *Steve Jobs*, 49. For an account of Steve Jobs as a spiritual seeker, see James Dennis LoRusso, "Zen and the Art of Microprocessing: Liberating the Entrepreneurial Spirit in Silicon Valley," in *Spirituality, Corporate Culture, and American Business: The Neoliberal Ethic and the Spirit of Global Capital* (New York: Bloomsbury, 2017), 81–96.

158. Farah Godrej, *Freedom Inside? Yoga and Meditation in the Carceral State* (New York: Oxford University Press, 2022), 9.

159. Susannah Crockford, *Ripples of the Universe: Spirituality in Sedona, Arizona* (Chicago: University of Chicago Press, 2021), 18–19.

160. Byung-Chul Han, *Psycho-Politics: Neoliberalism and New Technologies of Power*, trans. Erik Butler (Brooklyn, NY: Verso Books), 2–3, 7, 18; Ehrenreich, *Bright Sided*, 8–9.

161. Ehrenreich, *Bright Sided*, 109–10.

162. Steve Jobs, *Make Something Wonderful: Steve Jobs in His Own Words* (Apple Books, 2023), 95, 194. While not a direct quotation, it might be a reference to chapter 15, where Yogananda paraphrases French scientist Charles Robert Richet describing future scientific discoveries and concluding, "The truths—those surprising, amazing, unforeseen truths—which our descendants will discover, are even now all around us, staring us in the eyes, so to speak, and yet we do not see them." The quotation appears one page after Yogananda suggests, "Intuition is soul guidance." Yogananda, *Autobiography*, 159–60.

163. See Ron Suskind, "Faith, Certainty and the Presidency of George W. Bush," *New York Times Magazine*, 17 October 2004.

164. Sarah Banet-Weiser, *Authentic™: The Politics of Ambivalence in a Brand Culture* (New York: New York University Press, 2012), 195.

165. Walter Isaacson, "The Genius of Jobs," *New York Times*, 29 October 2011.

166. See Michael Adas, *Machines as the Measure of Men: Science, Technology, and Ideologies of Western Dominance* (Ithaca, NY: Cornell University Press, 1989), chap. 5.

167. Malcom Gladwell, "The Tweaker: The Real Genius of Steve Jobs," *New Yorker*, 14 November 2011.

CHAPTER 3. MESSAGE ON A BOTTLE

1. Charles Leroux, "Soap Opera: Dr. Bronner's Eccentric Philosophy of Peace, Love and Cleanliness Finally Wins Over the Most Important Convert: His Son," *Chicago Tribune*, 7 December 1999, 1. Bronner referenced this period

in *The Moral ABC*, "After our father-mother-wife perished in concentration camps, we were tortured, blinded, forced to sleep on the roof of the YMCA, penniless with the pigeons!" Dr. E. H. Bronner, *The Moral ABC of Astronomy's Eternal All-One-God-Faith Unites the Human Race!* (Vista, CA: n.p., 2015), 24; James Simon Kunen, "Dr. Bronner's Magic," *Esquire*, December 1973, 314.

2. Ann Japenga, "A Philosopher and His Soap: Bronner Has a Mission, a Message and an Unusual Medium," *Los Angeles Times*, 28 July 1987, F1; Pat Sherman, "In the Spirit of Soap," *San Diego Magazine*, 31 January 2007, http://www.sandiegomagazine.com/San-Diego-Magazine/February-2007/In-the -Spirit-of-Soap/index.php?cparticle=1&siarticle=0#artanc.

3. *Dr. Bronner's All One! Report* (2016), https://www.drbronner.com/media -center/all-one-reports/, 5; Tom Foster, "The Undiluted Genius of Dr. Bron- ner's," *Inc. Magazine*, 3 April 2012, https://www.inc.com/magazine/201204 /tom-foster/the-undiluted-genius-of-dr-bronners.html; "150 Years and 5 Gen- erations of Soapmaking," https://www.drbronner.com/about/ourselves/the-dr -bronners-story/ (accessed 5 April 2018).

4. Authors who have addressed the connection between consumerism and religion in American history include Kevin Kruse, *One Nation Under God: How Corporate America Invented Christian America* (New York: Basic Books, 2015); Bethany Moreton, *To Save God and Walmart: The Making of Christian Free Enterprise* (Cambridge, MA: Harvard University Press, 2010); Eileen Luhr, *Witnessing Suburbia: Conservatives and Christian Youth Culture* (Berkeley and Los Angeles: UC Press, 2009); Sarah Banet-Weiser, *AuthenticTM: The Politics of Ambivalence in a Brand Culture* (NY: New York University Press, 2012), 166.

5. See Stuart Hall, "'The Local and the Global': Culture, Globalization, and the World-System," in *Culture, Globalization, and the World-System*, ed. Anthony D. King (Minneapolis: University of Minnesota Press, 1997) and Jane Iwamura, *Virtual Orientalism: Asian Religions and American Popular Culture* (New York: Oxford University Press, 2010).

6. Anna S. King, "Spirituality: Transformation and Metamorphosis," *Reli- gion* 26 (1996): 345.

7. Andrea Jain *Selling Yoga: From Counterculture to Pop Culture* (New York: Oxford University Press, 2015), 43–46.

8. Lizabeth Cohen, *A Consumers' Republic: The Politics of Mass Consump- tion in Postwar America* (New York: Knopf, 2003).

9. Luc Boltanski and Eve Chiapello, *The New Spirit of Capitalism* (New York: Verso, 2005), 17, 438–41; Jo Littler, "Green Products and Consumer Activism," in eds. Mukherjee and Banet-Weiser, *Commodity Activism*, 77.

10. Thomas Frank, *The Conquest of Cool: Business Culture, Counterculture, and the Rise of Hip Consumer* (Chicago: University of Chicago Press, 1998).

11. Sarah Schrank, *Free and Natural: Nudity and the American Cult of the Body* (Philadelphia: University of Pennsylvania Press, 2019).

12. Joshua Clark Davis, *From Head Shops to Whole Foods: The Rise and Fall of Activist Entrepreneurs* (New York: Columbia University Press, 2017), 2–5.

13. Nancy Tomes, *Remaking the American Patient: How Madison Avenue and Modern Medicine Turned Patients into Consumers* (Chapel Hill, NC: UNC

Press, 2016); Laura J. Miller, *Building Nature's Market* (Chicago: University of Chicago Press, 2017).

14. Sarah McFarland Taylor, *Ecopiety: Green Media and the Dilemma of Environmental Virtue* (New York: New York University Press, 2019), 3. See also Jo Littler, *Radical Consumption: Shopping for Change in Contemporary Culture* (New York: McGraw Hill, 2009); Roopali Mukherjee and Sarah Banet-Weiser, *Commodity Activism: Cultural Resistance in Neoliberal Times* (New York: New York University Press, 2012); Banet-Weiser, *AuthenticTM*.

15. Noel Castree, "The Future of Environmentalism," *Soundings* 34 (2006), 12, as cited in Jo Littler, "Green Products and Consumer Activism," in Mukherjee and Banet-Weiser, *Commodity Activism*, 80.

16. Tomes, *Remaking the American Patient*, 5.

17. Josee Johnston and Kate Cairns, "Eating for Change," in Mukherjee and Banet-Weiser, *Commodity Activism*, 225.

18. David Vogel, *The Market for Virtue: The Potential and Limits of Corporate Social Responsibility* (Washington, DC: Brookings Institution Press, 2005), 26, 25, as cited in Laurie Ouellette, "Citizen Brand: ABC and the Do Good Turn in US Television," in Mukherjee and Banet-Weiser, *Commodity Activism*, 62.

19. For example, in May 2015, the CEO of McDonald's, Steve Easterbrook, vowed to make the corporation into a "modern progressive burger company." Bill Chappell, "McDonald's CEO Promises 'Modern, Progressive Burger Company,'" NPR, *The Two Way*, 4 May 2015, https://www.npr.org/sections/thetwo-way/2015/05/04/404166605/mcdonald-s-ceo-promises-modern-progressive-burger-company.

20. Littler, "Green Products and Consumer Activism," 77.

21. "Tracing the History and Accomplishments of Dr. Bronner's," http://www.drbronner.hk/website/about-us-2/brand-history/ (accessed 22 May 2019). See also Christina Lubinski and Marvin Menniken, "Emanuel Bronner," in *Immigrant Entrepreneurship: German-American Business Biographies, 1720 to the Present*, vol. 5, ed. R. Daniel Wadhwani (German Historical Institute, 2013), http://www.immigrantentrepreneurship.org/entry.php?rec=134 (accessed 1 June 2019).

22. Bronner, *The Moral ABC*, 66.

23. Chuck Fager, "Who Is Dr. Bronner, Anyway?" *New Age*, September 1976, 46.

24. "Police Probe Motive for Bizarre Crucifixion of Tavern Porter," *Jefferson City Daily Capital News*, 10 March 1945, 2; "Rabbi has Soapy Crusade," *Press Democrat* (Santa Rosa), 24 October 1980, 30–31.

25. "Crucified Man Held Martyr to His Own Ideas," *Chicago Tribune*, 10 March 1945, 1. A follow-up story stated that Walcher "smiled with pleasure" when told his picture was in the newspaper, as he stated, "I had rather be crucified than suffer bloodshed in war." Bronner later lamented that no reporter highlighted information from the packets that Bronner distributed at the hospital. He met up with Walcher in northern California many years later. "Victim's Hands Offer Clue to His Crucifiers," *Chicago Tribune*, 11 March 1945, 25; Kunen, "Dr. Bronner's Magic," 221. Walcher was charged with disorderly conduct and fined $100 for staging the event.

26. Roger Chapman, "Dr. Bronner's 'Magic Soaps' Religion," *Journal of Religion and Popular Culture* 25, no. 2 (Summer 2013): 290–91; Ann Japenga, "A Philosopher and His Soap: Bronner Has a Mission, a Message and an Unusual Medium," *Los Angeles Times*, 28 July 1987, F1; Kunen, "Dr. Bronner's Magic," 314. I could find no mention of Bronner's arrest in the University of Chicago's student newspaper, *The Maroon*.

27. Leroux, "Soap Opera."

28. Sherman, "In the Spirit of Soap"; "BOY excellent typist, short hair," *Times-Advocate* (Escondido), 17 September 1971, 21.

29. Japenga, "A Philosopher and His Soap."

30. Peter Rowe, "Dr. Bonner Speaks! North County's late, eccentric soap maker returns on LP," *San Diego Union Tribune*, 27 January 2017, http://www.sandiegouniontribune.com/lifestyle/people/sd-me-bronner-abc-20170117-story.html; Dan Weisman, "Dr. Bronner Rises from the Grave to Say," *Escondido Grapevine*, 25 April 2021, https://www.escondidograpevine.com/2021/04/25/dr-bronner-rises-from-the-grave-to-say/.

31. Sherman, "In the Spirit of Soap."

32. "Stay Free," *Times-Advocate* (Escondido), 24 September 1966, 15; "All One God Faith in One—God's State," *Times-Advocate* (Escondido), 11 July 1969, 18.

33. Bronner, *The Moral ABC*, 21.

34. Bronner, *The Moral ABC*, 23.

35. Chapman, "Dr. Bronner's 'Magic Soaps' Religion," 287–88.

36. Chapman, "Dr. Bronner's 'Magic Soaps' Religion," 292–94.

37. Elliot N. Dorff, *The Jewish Approach to Repairing the World (Tikkun Olam): A Brief Introduction for Christians* (Woodstock, VT: Jewish Lights Publishing, 2008), 4, as quoted in Chapman, "Dr. Bronner's 'Magic Soaps' Religion," 295

38. Chapman, "Dr. Bronner's 'Magic Soaps' Religion," 295–96.

39. Bronner, *The Moral ABC*, 66.

40. Sam Binkley, *Getting Loose: Lifestyle Consumption in the 1970s* (Durham, NC: Duke University Press, 2007), 138–39. Given that Bronner constantly revised *The Moral ABC*, it's difficult to tell when he incorporated the concept of "spaceship earth," but the earliest newspaper reference I could find was from 1973, when the label bore a clear resemblance to its current form. See Bill Baker, "The Great Dr. Bronner Peppermint Oil Pure-Castile-Soap Adventure," *Florida Today*, 23 December 1973, 8–9.

41. Jennifer Thomson, *The Wild and the Toxic: American Environmentalism and the Politics of Health* (Chapel Hill: University of North Carolina Press, 2019), 77.

42. Brian Allen Drake, *Loving Nature, Fearing the State: Environmentalism and Antigovernment Politics before Reagan* (Seattle: University of Washington Press, 2013), 55.

43. Thomson, *The Wild and the Toxic*, 7.

44. Drake, *Loving Nature, Fearing the State*, 60–63.

45. Harvey Levenstein, *Paradox of Plenty: A Social History of Eating in Modern America* (New York: Oxford University Press, 1993), 161.

46. Drake, *Loving Nature, Fearing the State*, 54; Gretchen Ann Reilly, "'Not a So-Called Democracy': Anti-Fluoridationists and the Fight over Drinking Water," in *The Politics of Healing: Histories of Alternative Medicine in Twentieth-Century North America*, ed. Robert D. Johnson (New York: Routledge, 2004), 136.

47. Drake, *Loving Nature, Fearing the State*, 58.

48. Kunen, "Dr. Bronner's Magic," 314, 316.

49. "Fluoridation Plan Flayed by Chemist in Speech Here," *Press Telegram*, 2 May 1957, 12.

50. "Dr. Bronner to Move Research Laboratory Here by February," *Hereford Brand* (Texas), 18 September 1952, 1.

51. Stan Leppard, "Town Hall Hears Heated Debate on Fluoridation," *Press Telegram*, 11 December 1969, B1.

52. Everette Varner, "Fluoridation Probe," *Santa Ana Register*, 22 March 1966, A10.

53. "Speeches to Hit at Fluoridation," *Albuquerque Journal*, 6 July 1968, 29.

54. "Fluoridation of Drinking Water Is a Criminal Act!" *Kenosha Evening News* (WI), 19 March 1955, 5.

55. "The Case for Fluoridation: the MOH Answers Critics," *The Kilmarnock Standard*, 17 May 1952, 5.

56. James Ratliff, "Pandora was a Piker," *Cincinnati Enquirer*, 29 March 1953, 20. The local paper in Lawrence, Kansas, consulted local chemists for counter claims and researched Bronner after he lectured the City Commission. Les Sheppeard, "Fluoride's Use Hit as a Plot by Reds," *Lawrence Daily Journal World*, 12 October 1955, 1, 9.

57. "Fluoridation Plan Flayed by Chemist in Speech Here."

58. Kunen, "Dr. Bronner's Magic," 314, 316; "Health and 'One World Religion,'" *Los Angeles Mirror*, 8 July 1950, 6; "Free Health Class," *California Eagle*, 5 April 1951, 11.

59. Probers Cut Fluoride Foe Off," *Pasadena Star News*, 11 August 1966, 3.

60. Years later, the company's toothpaste did not include fluoride as an ingredient, which it explained in sales presentations. See "Dr. Bronner's All-One Sales Training Presentation," 9 October 2017, https://www.drbronner.com/rsmdocs/training_tools/sale_training_ppt_october_27_2017.pdf.

61. Ruth Clifford Engs, *Clean Living Movements: American Cycles of Health Reform* (Westport, CT: Praeger, 2000), 181.

62. Binkley, *Getting Loose*, 102–5.

63. Theodore Roszak, *The Making of a Counter Culture: Reflections on the Technocratic Society and Its Youthful Opposition* (Garden City, NY: Anchor Books, 1969), 206.

64. Richard L. and Claudia L. Bushman, "The Early History of Cleanliness in America," *Journal of American History* 74, no. 4 (March 1988): 1215, 1217, 1233.

65. Marilyn Thornton Williams, *Washing 'The Great Unwashed': Public Baths in Urban America, 1840–1920* (Columbus: Ohio State University Press, 1991), 10–12.

66. Anne McClintock, *Imperial Leather: Race, Gender, and Sexuality in Colonial Contest* (London: Taylor & Francis Group, 1995), 206.

67. Peter Ward, *The Clean Body: A Modern History* (Chicago: McGill-Queen's University Press, 2019), 5, 22.

68. Williams, *Washing 'The Great Unwashed.'*

69. Bushman and Bushman, "The Early History of Cleanliness in America," 1219.

70. Kathryn Lofton, *Consuming Religion* (Chicago: University of Chicago Press, 2017), 85–86, 92–94.

71. Geoffrey Jones, *Beauty Imagined: A History of the Global Beauty Industry* (New York: Oxford University Press, 2010), 81.

72. "Henry Ward Beecher's opinion of Pears' Soap," *Life*, 21 March 1889, 178.

73. Ward, *The Clean Body*, 109.

74. Jones, *Beauty Imagined*, 23, 58, 75.

75. Bushman and Bushman, "The Early History of Cleanliness in America," 1236.

76. Bushman and Bushman, 1234, 1236.

77. Ward, *The Clean Body*, 113–15, 122.

78. Ronald G. Walters, *American Reformers, 1815–1860*, revised edition (New York: Hill and Wang, 1978, 1997), 18, 148, 150–51.

79. Engs, *Clean Living Movements*, 54.

80. Michael Hau, *The Cult of Health and Beauty in Germany* (Chicago: University of Chicago Press, 2003), 2–3.

81. Hau, 11.

82. Miller, *Building Nature's Market*, 62; for more information about early advocates of alternative diets in the United States, see Ronald M. Deutsch, *The Nuts among the Berries* (New York: Ballantine Books, 1961).

83. The company's website offers an overview of the family's history of soapmaking. See "Tracing the History and Accomplishments of Dr. Bronner's," http://www.drbronner.hk/website/about-us-2/brand-history/ (accessed 22 May 2019).

84. Hau, *The Cult of Health and Beauty in Germany*, 19.

85. "Fluoride Opponent Will Speak," *Independent* (Pasadena), 19 April 1966, 9.

86. Miller, *Building Nature's Market*, 64, 91.

87. Bob Frost, "The Pope of Soap," *California* 15, no 11 (November 1990): 100.

88. See "Try Dr. Bronner's Substitute for Salt," *News Tribune* (Tacoma), 20 June 1951, 2; "Dr. Bronner—Salt & Broth," *Times–Advocate* (Escondido, CA), 19 October 1951, 7.

89. Gilman's Health Foods, *Mason City Globe Gazette*, 11 October 1962, 17. A year earlier, he had sent telegrams to government officials to protest the nuclear tests for Operation Gnome, which took place outside Carlsbad, New Mexico, near a unique form of salt deposit—one of four of its kind in the world—that he claimed to use for these organic mineral salts. See "Atom Tests in Salt Beds Protested," *Oakland Tribune*, 7 December 1961, 12.

90. Display Ad 49, *Los Angeles Times*, 23 March 1956, B3; Frost, "The Pope of Soap," 98.

91. Haseltine's Nutrition Center, *Long Beach Independent Press Telegram*, 15 February 1959, p. 88.

92. Display Ad 156, *Los Angeles Times*, 21 June 1959, GV_A12.

93. "Dr. Bronner," *Times Advocate* (Escondido, CA), 30 April 1964, 13.

94. Fager, *New Age*, 46–47; Frost, "The Pope of Soap," 100–101.

95. Display Ad 81, *Los Angeles Times*, 23 April 1973, G14; Display Ad 1524, *New York Times*, 16 October 1977, 435.

96. Binkley, *Getting Loose*, 135.

97. Levenstein, *Paradox of Plenty*, 183–84.

98. Jones, *Beauty Imagined*, 243.

99. Sarah Jaquette Ray, *The Ecological Other: Environmental Exclusion in American Culture* (Tucson: University of Arizona Press, 2013), 2–3, 6.

100. Jones, *Beauty Imagined*, 275–82; Davis, *From Head Shops to Whole Foods*, 3.

101. Jones, *Beauty Imagined*, 282–86.

102. Chrisann Brennan, *The Bite in the Apple: A Memoir of My Life with Steve Jobs* (New York: St. Martin's Press, 2013), chap. 10.

103. Jones, *Beauty Imagined*, 153.

104. Fager, *New Age*, 45; Kunen, "Dr. Bronner's Magic," 316. The 1976 article in *New Age* reiterated the one hundred fifty thousand gallon/year estimate that appeared in *Esquire*.

105. Fager, *New Age*, 45.

106. Fager, 45.

107. Sherman, "In the Spirit of Soap."

108. Wendy Bounds, "Suds and Philosophy Lather Up Business for Odd Dr. Bronner—Hippies' Soap Maker of Choice Finds New Agers Swooning Over Decades-Old Formula," *Wall Street Journal* (Eastern Edition), 26 November 1993, A1.

109. Binkley, *Getting Loose*, 106–7.

110. Kunen, "Dr. Bronner's Magic," 316.

111. *Bronner vs. Commissioner*, https://www.leagle.com/decision/1983783 45gutcm7381581 (accessed June 13, 2018).

112. Josh Harkinson, "The Audacity of Soap," *Mother Jones* (January–February 2014): 42.

113. Foster, "Radical Chic," *Inc. Magazine* (April 2012), 80.

114. "Created in California: Dr. Bronner's Soap for Any Subculture; His Vision and 'Magic' Products Live On at Progressive Family Firm," *Los Angeles Times*, 16 July 2023, A1.

115. Foster, "Racial Chic," 74,78; Harkinson, "The Audacity of Soap," 41.

116. Harkinson, "The Audacity of Soap," 41.

117. Binkley, *Getting Loose*, 4.

118. See "All-One: Read About Our Commitment to You and Spaceship Earth," https://www.allone.report/all-reports (accessed 16 November 2023).

119. Michael Bronner, "Introduction," in Dr. E. H. Bronner, *The Moral ABC*, xi.

120. Gail Grenier Sweet, "Next to Godliness," *The Sun*, January 2001, https://www.thesunmagazine.org/issues/301/next-to-godliness.

121. See Robert N. Bellah et al., *Habits of the Heart: Individualism and Commitment in American Life* (Berkeley: University of California Press, 1983).

122. Taylor, *Deep Green Religion: Nature Spirituality and the Planetary Future* (Berkeley: University of California Press, 2010), 13.

123. Taylor, 13.

124. Taylor, 195–97.

125. Taylor, 197.

126. Manfred B. Steger and Ravi K. Roy, *Neoliberalism: A Very Short Introduction* (New York: Oxford University Press, 2010), x.

127. Ken Pomeranz, "Neoliberalism: The History and Future of a Word," chair comments at annual meeting of the American Historical Association, 4 January 2019.

128. Miller, *Building Nature's Market*, 212.

129. Kevin Healey, "Searching for Integrity: The Politics of Mindfulness in the Digital Economy," *Nomos Journal*, 5 August 2013, https://nomosjournal.org /2013/ 08/searching-for-integrity/.

130. Geismer, *Left Behind: The Democrats' Failed Attempt to Solve Inequality* (New York: PublicAffairs, 2022), 268–69.

131. "Our Cosmic Principles," https://www.drbronner.com/about/ (accessed 30 May 2019).

132. "Dr. Bronner's Announces New "Old & Improved" Labels across All Product Lines," 2 March 2015, https://www.drbronner.com/media-center /press-release/dr-bronners-announces-new-old-improved-labels-across -product-lines/.

133. David Bronner, "One earth, one family, one love," Dr. Bronner's 2019 Annual Report, 7, https://info.drbronner.com/allone-reports/A1R-2019/all-one -report-2019.html#p=1 (accessed 24 May 2019).

134. Ralph Bronner, "Preface," in Bronner, *The Moral ABC*, v–vi.

135. Michael Bronner, "Introduction," in Dr. E. H. Bronner, *The Moral ABC*, xi.

136. David Bronner, "Afterword," in Bronner, *The Moral ABC*, 69–70

137. Davis, *From Head Shops to Whole Foods*, 17.

138. Miller, *Building Nature's Market*, 3–4. Miller writes specifically about the natural food movement.

139. Simon Usborne, "On His Soapbox," *Independent* (UK), 13 June 2014, 42.

140. Dana Brakman Reiser and Steven A. Dean, "The Social Enterprise Life Cycle," in *The Cambridge Handbook of Social Enterprise Law*, ed, Benjamin Means and Joseph W. Yockey (New York: Cambridge University Press, 2018), 223–40.

141. Elizabeth Currid-Halkett, *The Sum of Small Things: A Theory of Aspirational Class* (Princeton, NJ: Princeton University Press, 2017), chap. 5.

142. Sarah Banet-Weiser and Roopali Mukherjee, "Introduction: Commodity Activism in Neoliberal Times," in Banet-Weiser and Mukherjee, *Commodity Activism*, 9.

143. Rachel Slocum, "Whiteness, Space and Alternative Food Practice," *Geoforum* 38 (2007): 522, 526.

144. Lawrence Mishel and Julia Wolfe, "CEO Compensation Has Grown 940 percent since 1978," Economic Policy Institute, 14 August 2019, https://www.epi.org/publication/ceo-compensation-2018/.

145. Foster, "Radical Chic," 78; "Created in California."

146. Foster, "Radical Chic," 78.

147. Davis, *From Head Shops to Whole Foods*, 177.

148. James Dennis LoRusso, *Spirituality, Corporate Culture, and American Business: The Neoliberal Ethic and the Spirit of Global Capital* (New York: Bloomsbury, 2017), 97–118.

149. Paul Hawken, *The Ecology of Commerce: A Declaration of Sustainability* (New York: HarperCollins, 1993), xii–xiv.

150. Hawken, xiv–xv.

151. Hawken, 61.

152. Hawken, 139.

153. *Dr. Bronner's All One! Report* (2016), 2.

154. Harkinson, "The Audacity of Soap," 43.

155. Foster, "Radical Chic," 78.

156. Harkinson, "The Audacity of Soap," 43.

157. "Dr. Bronner's Launches Crowdfunding Campaign and New Educational Video on Fair Trade Palm Oil," *PR Newswire*, 12 November 2012.

158. Foster, "Radical Chic," 78.

159. Harkinson, "The Audacity of Soap," 43.

160. Foster, "Radical Chic," 80.

161. Davis, *From Head Shops to Whole Foods*, chap. 3. Miller, *Building Nature's Market*, 4.

162. Ray, *The Ecological Other*, 181.

163. Bruce Ramsey, "Initiative 522: A Test of What You Believe about Genetically Modified Foods," *Seattle Times*, 12 March 2013, http://old.seattletimes.com/html/opinion/2020542841_bruce13gmofoodsinitiative522xml.html?cmpid=2628.

164. "Dr. Bronner's Joins Leading Manufacturers, Retailers and Advocates to Launch Fair Pay Today Campaign to Support Raising Minimum Wage" (press release), 15 September 2016, https://www.drbronner.com/media-center/press-release/dr-bronners-joins-leading-manufacturers-retailers-advocates-launch-fair-pay-today-campaign-support-raising-minimum-wage/.

165. "Fair Pay Today: Good for Business—Good for Us All!" https://www.drbronner.com/about/our-community/fair-pay/ (accessed 20 June 2018).

166. "Dr. Bronner's Labels to Carry Political Message," *Beauty Packaging*, 18 May 2016, https://www.beautypackaging.com/contents/view_breaking-news/2016-05-18/dr-bronners-labels-to-carry-political-message.

167. Michael Bronner, "Standing with Immigrants and Refugees," *Dr. Bronner's All-One* (blog), 30 January 2017, https://www.drbronner.com/all-one-blog/2017/01/standing-immigrants-refugees/; "Dr. Bronner's Stands for Comprehensive Immigration Reform," *Dr. Bronner's All-One* (blog), 3 July 2018, https://www.drbronner.com/all-one-blog/2018/07/dr-bronners-stands-comprehensive-immigration-reform/.

168. Adrian Ivakhiv, "Toward a Geography of 'Religion': Mapping the Distribution of an Unstable Signifier," *Annals of the Association of American Geographers* 96, no. 1 (2006): 173.

169. David Harvey, *A Brief History of Neoliberalism* (New York: Oxford University Press, 2005), 41, 47.

CHAPTER 4. WELLNESS IN THE "BLUE ZONE"

1. "Health Lecture," *Woodland Daily Democrat*, 8 November 1911, 4.

2. Richard A. Schaefer, *The Glory of the Vision: An Unabridged History of Loma Linda University Health*, vol. 1 (Loma Linda, CA: Loma Linda University Health, 2016), 32.

3. Ellen G. White, *Loma Linda Messages Unabridged* (Tellico Plains, TN: Digital Inspiration, 2013), n.p.

4. Laura J. Miller, *Building Nature's Market* (Chicago: University of Chicago Press, 2017), 161–62; Harvey Levenstein, *Paradox of Plenty: A Social History of Eating in Modern America* (New York: Oxford University Press, 1993), 161–63.

5. Lucy M. Long, "Introduction," in *Culinary Tourism*, ed. Lucy M. Long (Lexington: University of Kentucky Press, 2003), 8.

6. Devon A. Mihesuah and Elizabeth Hoover, eds., *Indigenous Food Sovereignty in the United States: Restoring Cultural Knowledge, Protecting Environments, and Regaining Health* (Norman: University of Oklahoma Press, 2019).

7. David Bell and Gill Valentine, *Consuming Geographies: We Are Where We Eat* (New York: Routledge, 1997), 2–15; Etta M. Madden and Martha L. Finch, "Introduction," in ed. Madden and Finch, *Eating in Eden: Food and American Utopias* (Lincoln: University of Nebraska Press, 2006), 1–2.

8. Rachel Slocum, "Whiteness, Space, and Alternative Food Practice," *Geoforum* 38 (2007): 520, 526.

9. Deborah Lupton, *Food, the Body and the Self* (Thousand Oaks, CA: Sage Publications, 1996), 68.

10. Marion Nestle, *Food Politics: How the Food Industry Influences Nutrition and Health* (Berkeley: University of California Press, 2002), 27–28.

11. Nestle, *Food Politics*, 27-8.

12. Michel Foucault, *The History of Sexuality: An Introduction*, vol. 1, trans. Robert Hurley (New York: Random House, 1978), 137.

13. Lyra Kilston, *Sun Seekers: The Cure of California* (Los Angeles: Atelier Editions, 2019), 8.

14. M. Gatens and G. Lloyd, *Collective Imaginings: Spinoza, Past and Present* (London: Routledge, 1999), 143, as cited in Slocum "Whiteness, Space, and Alternative Food Practice," 528.

15. Gatens and Lloyd, 137–38.

16. For an explanation of evangelical Christian views of Seventh-day Adventism, see Philip Jenkins, *Mystics and Messiahs: Cults and New Religions in American History* (New York: Oxford University Press, 2000), 51.

17. "Nicole Spector, "What 'Blue Zone' City Loma Linda, California Can Teach Us about Living Longer," NBC News, 3 April 2019, https://www.nbcnews

.com/better/lifestyle/what-blue-zone-city-loma-linda-california-can-teach-us-ncna989661. Many Seventh-day Adventists are lacto-ovo vegetarians, which means they consume dairy and eggs but no flesh.

18. Malcolm Bull and Keith Lockhart, *Seeking a Sanctuary: Seventh-day Adventism and the American Dream*, 2nd ed. (Bloomington: Indiana University Press, 2007, originally published 1989), 7.

19. Michael Lipka, "A Closer Look at Seventh-day Adventists in America," *Pew Research Center*, 3 November 2015, https://www.pewresearch.org/fact-tank/2015/11/03/a-closer-look-at-seventh-day-adventists-in-america/. Much of the church's early proselytizing of African Americans took place in the South. All-Black congregations were common. The church elected its first Black president in 1979. See "Seventh-Day Adventists Elect a Black President," *Washington Post*, 13 January 1979.

20. R. Laurence Moore, *Religious Outsiders and the Making of America* (New York: Oxford University Press, 1986).

21. Bull and Lockhart, *Seeking a Sanctuary*, 9-10.

22. Peter Ward, *The Clean Body: A Modern History* (Montreal: McGill-Queen's University Press, 2019), 13-4.

23. Paul Starr, *The Social Transformation of American Medicine: The Rise of a Sovereign Profession and the Making of a Vast Industry* (New York: Basic Books, 1982), 33.

24. Bryan S. Turner, "The Government of the Body: Medical Regimens and the Rationalization of the Diet," *British Journal of Sociology* 33, no. 2 (June 1982): 259-66.

25. T. J. Jackson Lears, *No Place of Grace: Antimodernism and the Transformation of American Culture, 1880—1920* (Chicago: University of Chicago Press, 1981), 33-34.

26. Sylvester Graham, as cited in Kilston, *Sun Seekers*, 148.

27. E. Melanie DuPuis, *Dangerous Digestion: The Politics of American Dietary Advice* (Berkeley: University of California Press, 2015), 50-51.

28. Edward Jarvis, *Primary Physiology for Schools* (Philadelphia: Thomas Cowperthwait, 1850), 156, as cited in Michael Zakim, *Accounting for Capitalism: The World the Clerk Made* (Chicago: University of Chicago Press, 2018), 123.

29. Richard H. Shryock, "Sylvester Graham and the Popular Health Movement, 1830–1870," *Mississippi Valley Historical Review* 18, no. 2 (September 1931): 179-81.

30. Ronald G. Walters, *American Reformers 1815-1860* (New York: Hill and Wang, 1978, 1997), 151-52, 156.

31. Walters, *American Reformers*, 16-18, 147-48.

32. White denied that her visions were anything but original, but Adventist scholarship of the 1970s revealed at least twenty-three sources that she used. See Bull and Lockhart, *Seeking a Sanctuary*, 33.

33. Sydney Ahlstrom, *A Religious History of the American People*, 2nd ed. (New Haven, CT: Yale University Press, 2004), 478-81.

34. Bull and Lockhart, *Seeking a Sanctuary*, 7, 26, 29.

35. Ahlstrom, *A Religious History of the American People*, 478-81.

36. Ronald L. Numbers, *Prophetess of Health: Ellen G. White and the Origins of Seventh-day Adventist Health Reform*, revised and ·enlarged edition (Knoxville: University of Tennessee Press, 1992), 38–39.

37. Ellen G. White, MS dated February 12, 1854, as cited in Numbers, *Prophetess of Health*, 40.

38. George R. Knight, *A Brief History of Seventh-day Adventists* (Hagerstown, MD: Review and Herald, 2004), as cited in Adam D. Shprintzen, *The Vegetarian Crusade: The Rise of an American Reform Movement, 1817–1921* (Chapel Hill: University of North Carolina Press, 2013), 118.

39. William C. Andress, *Adventist Heritage of Health, Hope, and Healing* (Fort Oglethorpe, GA: Teach Services, Inc., 2014), 55–6.

40. Numbers, *Prophetess of Health*, 86.

41. Numbers, 173–74. Her rationale that meat consumption was cruel to animals did not arise until the 1890s.

42. James E. Vance, Jr., "California and the Search for the Ideal," *Annals of the Association of American Geographers* 62, no. 2 (June 1972): 188–89.

43. Shprintzen, *The Vegetarian Crusade*, 119; Numbers, *Prophetess of Health*, 87. See also James C. Whorton, *Crusaders for Fitness: The History of American Health Reformers* (Princeton, NJ: Princeton University Press, 1982), chap. 7.

44. Andress, *Adventist Heritage of Health, Hope, and Healing*, 57–59.

45. Andress, *Adventist Heritage of Health, Hope, and Healing*, 66–67.

46. Starr, *The Social Transformation of American Medicine*, 146–67.

47. Shprintzen, *The Vegetarian Crusade*, 121–22. According to Shprintzen, Kellogg began by changing the name of the institution from *sanitorium*, a term that referred to a "health resort" to treat British soldiers, to sanitarium, a term intended to connote both "recovery and learning." Shprintzen, *The Vegetarian Crusade*, 121. Gerald Carson, *Cornflake Crusade* (New York: Rinehart and Company, 1957), 98–99.

48. See Robert W. Rydell, *World of Fairs: The Century-of-Progress Expositions* (Chicago: University of Chicago Press, 1993), chap. 2.

49. DuPuis, *Dangerous Digestion*, 80.

50. Lupton, *Food, the Body and the Self*, 70; Levenstein, *Paradox of Plenty*, 9.

51. Turner, "The Government of the Body," 266.

52. Erika Rappaport, *A Thirst for Empire: How Tea Shaped the Modern World* (Princeton, NJ: Princeton University Press, 2019), chap. 4.

53. Nestle, *Food Politics*, 2.

54. Samuel Hopkins Adams, *The Great American Fraud: The Patent Medicine Evil* (Chicago: PF Collier & Son, 1905), 3; reprinted from *Collier's Weekly*, 7 October 1905.

55. Rappaport, *A Thirst for Empire*, 121, 125.

56. Miller, *Building Nature's Market*, 43–45.

57. Zakim, *Accounting for Capitalism*, 126.

58. "Program Pleases Loma Linda Folks," *San Bernardino Daily Sun*, 21 March 1916, 7.

59. Shprintzen, *The Vegetarian Crusade*, 122–23.

60. John E. Baur, *The Health Seekers of Southern California, 1870–1900* (San Marino, CA: The Huntington Library, 1959), 3–4; Douglas Cazaux Sackman, *Orange Empire: California and the Fruits of Eden* (Berkeley: University of California Press, 2005), 23–33.

61. Vance, "California and the Search for the Ideal," 191.

62. Shana Klein, *The Fruits of Empire: Art, Food, and the Politics of Race in the Age of American Expansion* (Berkeley: University of California Press, 2020), 4–5.

63. Lyra Kilston, *Sun Seekers*, 23, 23–43.

64. Kilston, 59.

65. Emily K. Abel, *Tuberculosis and the Politics of Exclusion: A History of Public Health and Migration to Los Angeles* (New Brunswick, NJ: Rutgers University Press, 2007), 6, 9, 33–35, 38.

66. William Deverell, *Whitewashed Adobe: The Rise of Los Angeles and the Remaking of Its Mexican Past* (Berkeley: University of California Press, 2004), chap. 5, 188.

67. Douglas Flamming, *Bound for Freedom: Black Los Angeles in Jim Crow America* (Berkeley: University of California Press, 2005), 17, 47, 56, 148; Lawrence B. De Graaf, "The City of Black Angels: Emergence of the Los Angeles Ghetto, 1890–1930, *Pacific Historical Review* 39, no. 3 (August 1970): 331.

68. Laura Kay Fleisch Hooton, "Co-Opting the Border: The Dream of African American Integration via Baja California" (PhD diss., University of California, Santa Barbara, 2018), 122–28; "$100,000 Negro Sanitarium to Be Established in Mexico," *Colorado Statesman*, 12 May 1923, 1. *California Eagle* published an article on the dubious fundraising efforts in 1927. See "War Declared on Lower California Land and Development Co.," *California Eagle*, 13 April 1927, 2.

69. "Health Ass'n Free Clinic Draws Crowd," *California Eagle*, 25 August 1938, 8; "Loma Linda Briefs," *San Bernardino Daily Sun*, 8 October 1926, 11; "Sanitarium in South L.A. Is Now Operating," *California Eagle*, 24 November 1933, 9; "South Los Angeles Sanitarium Re-Opens," *California Eagle*, 6 October 1933, 10; "Social Intelligence," *California Eagle*, 26 November 1926, 5; "South Los Angeles Sanitorium," *California Eagle*, 30 March 1934, 3; "Watch These Enemies," *California Eagle*, 16 May 1946, 7; "Business Personal Charlotte Brickhouse Kimbrough," *California Eagle*, 11 February 1922, 7; "Vernon Park Sanitarium," *California Eagle*, 10 February 1923, 5.

70. "Los Angeles Citywide Historic Context Statement/Context: African American History of Los Angeles," *SurveyLA: Los Angeles Historic Resources Survey*, February 2018, 154–55; "Outdoor Ass'n Dedicates 1st Rest Unit," *California Eagle*, 29 September 1938, 1; "OLHA to Open Duarte Home July 14," *California Eagle*, 20 June 1940, 20.

71. Baur, *The Health Seekers of Southern California*, 122.

72. "To Open Sanitarium," *Los Angeles Herald*, 1 October 1900, 5; Baur, *The Health Seekers of Southern California*, 86.

73. "Where Health and Pleasure Are Twins," *Los Angeles Herald*, 10 January 1903, 2.

74. Sackman, *Orange Empire*, 24.

75. R. S. Cantine, "Loma Linda Impressions, *Sunset*, June 1902, 141.

76. Miller, *Building Nature's Market*, 15; Bell and Valentine, *Consuming Geographies*, 15.

77. Miller, *Building Nature's Market*, 15–16.

78. Ellen Gould Harmon White, *Counsels on Health, and Instruction to Medical Missionary Workers* (Mountain View, CA: Pacific Press Publishing Association, 1923), 231.

79. Numbers, *Prophetess of Health*, 184–89.

80. White, *Counsels on Health, and Instruction to Medical Missionary Workers*, 232–33.

81. Andress, *Adventist Heritage of Health, Hope, and Healing*, 83.

82. "California," *California State Journal of Medicine* 13, no. 10 (October 1915): 413–14.

83. "To Establish a Medical School," *San Bernardino Daily Sun*, 3 March 1910, 3. The sanitarium's capacity was approximately seventy-five guests. See "Things Doing at Loma Linda," *San Bernardino Daily News*, 19 March 1910, 2.

84. "Loma Linda: 'The Hill Beautiful,'" *San Bernardino Daily Sun*, 11 December 1901, 46. The Loma Linda Bakery featured in the advertisement became The Sanitarium Food Company and then Loma Linda Foods, which was owned and operated by the Adventist Church from 1905 to 1990.

85. "Loma Linda Sanitarium," *Life and Health: The National Health Magazine* 28, no. 1 (January 2013): 46.

86. "Sanitaria," *Life and Health: The National Health Magazine* 28, no. 4 (April 1913): 145.

87. "Loma Linda Sanitarium," *Corona Courier*, 20 January 1910, 2.

88. "Local Adventist Elder Urges Less Ornamentation in Dress," *Sacramento Union*, 25 November 1915, 9.

89. No title, *San Bernardino Daily Sun*, 25 July 1912, 10.

90. Kilston, *Sun Seekers*, 146.

91. Harvey A. Levenstein, *Revolution at the Table: The Transformation of the American Diet* (New York: Oxford University Press, 1988), 7.

92. "Dinner, June 4, n.d.," Department of Archives and Special Collections, University Libraries, Loma Linda University, https://cdm.llu.edu/digital /collection/llshmc /id/18/rec/1 (accessed 11 February 2020); "Christmas Greetings; Loma Linda Sanitarium Loma Linda, Cal. Menu Christmas Day Nineteen Thirteen," Department of Archives and Special Collections, University Libraries, Loma Linda University, https://cdm.llu.edu/digital/collection/llshmc/id/83 /rec/36 (accessed 11 February 2020). Loma Linda University's archives do not have sanitarium menus with dates until 1918, which suggests that the June 4 menu derives from the earlier years of the institution.

93. Levenstein, *Revolution at the Table*, 7–8. Levenstein cites published reminiscences from the late nineteenth century.

94. "Hotel Alexandria (Mission Indian Grill)," Los Angeles Public Library, https://dbase1.lapl.org/images/menus/fullsize/a/13824-inside1.jpg (accessed 11 February 2020).

95. C.-E. A. Winslow, *The Evolution and Significance of the Modern Public Health Campaign* (New Haven, CT: Yale University Press, 1923), 57–58, as

cited in Paul Starr, *The Social Transformation of American Medicine*, 190–91; John C. Burnham, "American Physicians and Tobacco Use: Two Surgeons General 1929 and 1964," *Bulletin of the History of Medicine* 63, no. 1 (Spring 1989): 4.

96. Levenstein, *Revolution at the Table*, 75.

97. Ellen G. White, *The Ministry of Health and Healing* (Silver Springs, MD: Ellen G. White Estate, Inc., 2017), 61.

98. "About 'Colds,'" *San Bernardino Daily Sun*, 8 June 1910, 7.

99. "Practical Talk at Woman's Club," *San Bernardino Daily Sun*, 6 April 1910, 1.

100. "Social Notes," *San Bernardino Sun*, 25 March 1909, 6.

101. "Interesting Is Lecture," *San Bernardino News*, 27 February 1912, 8. These types of demonstrations continued for years and included tips on how to prepare meatless meals during a meatcutters strike in 1964. See Joel Baugh, "Beat the Strike, Eat without Meat," *San Bernardino Sun*, 11 December 1964, 21.

102. Burnham, "American Physicians and Tobacco Use," 6, 8.

103. White, *The Ministry of Health and Healing*, 222–23.

104. Burnham, "American Physicians and Tobacco Use," 2.

105. White, *The Ministry of Health and Healing*, 84.

106. Burnham, "American Physicians and Tobacco Use," 6.

107. "Interesting Is Lecture," 8; Burnham, "American Physicians and Tobacco Use," 11.

108. "Intermediate Boys Enjoy a Program," *San Bernardino Daily Sun*, 15 November 1913, 3.

109. Burnham, "American Physicians and Tobacco Use," 2.

110. Miller, *Building Nature's Market*, 3; Miller cites Wright 1972, Research Department of Prevention (1981, iii), and "Natural, Organic Food Sales Outpacing Conventional," *Whole Foods* 34, no. 8 (August 2011): 9. She notes that the 1979 figure is limited to health food stores, whereas the 2011 includes a variety of retailers as well as nonfood items (227n1).

111. Miller, *Building Nature's Market*, chap. 5.

112. Burnham, "American Physicians and Tobacco Use," 13–14.

113. Emily Esfahani Smith, "The Lovely Hill: Where People Live Longer and Happier," *Atlantic*, 4 February 2013, https://www.theatlantic.com/health/archive/2013/02/the-lovely-hill-where-people-live-longer-and-happier/272798/.

114. Ernest L. Wynder, Frank R. Lemon, and Irwin J. Bross, "Cancer and Coronary Disease among Seventh-day Adventists," *Cancer* 12, no. 5 (September–October 1959): 1028.

115. Allan M. Brandt, *The Cigarette Century: The Rise, Fall, and Deadly Persistence of the Product That Defined America* (New York: Basic Books, 2007), chap. 5.

116. Ernest L. Wynder, "Cancer, Coronary Disease, Artery Disease and Smoking: A Preliminary Report on Differences in Incidence between Seventh-day Adventists and Others," *California Medicine* 89, no. 4 (October 1958): 267–72.

117. "Smoking & Cancer (Contd.)," *Time* (5 May 1958), 62.

118. "Adventists Found to Resist Cancer," *New York Times*, 28 April 1958, 17.

119. Wynder et al, "Cancer and Coronary Disease Among Seventh-day Adventists."

120. Gary E. Fraser, "Adventist Health Studies: Past, Present, Future," *Adventist Review*, 24 June 2009, https://www.adventistreview.org/2009-1518 -16; https://adventisthealthstudy.org/studies (accessed 11 February 2020).

121. "Minority Community Data," Loma Linda University Health, https://adventisthealthstudy.org/studies/AHS-2/minority-community-data (accessed 14 February 2020). AHS-2 found that Black Adventists generally had better overall health than Black non-Adventists and pointed to structural factors that affected African Americans. See Susanne Montgomery et al., "Comparing Self-Reported Disease Outcomes, Diet, and Lifestyles in a National Cohort of Black and White Seventh-day Adventists," *Preventing Chronic Disease* 4, no. 3 (2007): A62.

122. Smith, "The Lovely Hill."

123. County of Los Angeles Public Health, *Health Atlas for the City of Los Angeles* (June 2013), 56 (https://web.archive.org/web/20130718055628if _/http://planning.lacity.org:80/cwd/framwk/healthwellness/text/HealthAtlas .pdf); City Overview for San Bernardino, "City Health Dashboard," https://www .cityhealthdashboard.com/CA/San%20Bernardino/city-overview?metricId=37 &dataPeriod=2015 (accessed 20 August 2023).

124. Jennifer Medina, "Fast-Food Outlet Stirs Concerns in a Mecca of Healthy Living," *New York Times*, 18 December 2011, https://www.nytimes .com/2011/12/19/us/loma-linda-calif-frets-about-first-mcdonalds-outlet.html.

125. Phil Willon, "McDonald's Proposal Divides Healthy Loma Linda," *Los Angeles Times*, 22 January 2012, http://articles.latimes.com/2012/jan/22/local /la-me-loma-linda-mcdonalds-20120122.

126. Medina, "Fast-Food Outlet Stirs Concerns in a Mecca of Healthy Living."

127. Numbers, *Prophetess of Health*, 188–89; Miller, *Building Nature's Market*, 11–16, 40, 66.

128. Bull and Lockhart, *Seeking Sanctuary*, 113–14.

129. Levenstein, *Paradox of Plenty*, 202–7.

130. Dan Buettner, "New Wrinkles on Aging," *National Geographic* 208, no. 5 (November 2005): 2.

131. Buettner, 2.

132. Dan Buettner, *The Blue Zone: Lessons for Living Longer from the People Who've Lived the Longest* (Washington, DC: National Geographic, 2008), 228.

133. Spector, "What 'Blue Zone' City Loma Linda, California Can Teach Us about Living Longer."

134. Meredith Minkler, "Personal Responsibility for Health?" A Review of the Arguments and the Evidence at Century's End," *Public Health & Behavior* 26, no. 1 (February 1999):124.

135. Pierre Bourdieu, *Distinction: A Social Critique of the Judgment of Taste* (Cambridge, MA: Harvard University Press, 1984); Wendy Brown, *Undoing the*

Demos: Neoliberalism's Stealth Revolution (Brooklyn, NY: Zone Books, 2015), 64–66.

136. T. Cole, "The Specter of Old Age: History, Politics and Culture in an Aging America," *Tikkun* 3, no 5 (1988), as cited in Minkler, "Personal Responsibility for Health?," 128.

137. John Howard Weeks, *The Healthiest People on Earth: Your Guide to Living 10 Years Longer with Adventist Family Secrets and Plant-Based Recipes* (Dallas, TX: Benbella Books, 2018), 2–3, 5–6.

138. Weeks, 24, 54.

139. John Howard Weeks, "Healthy Living: This Is Where Fast Food Nation Meets the Blue Zone," *Press Enterprise* (Redlands), 25 June 2019, https://www.pe.com/2019/06/25/healthy-living-this-is-where-fast-food-nation-meets-the-blue-zone/.

140. "Loma Linda: Inaugural Health Symposium Set," *Press-Enterprise* (Redlands), 5 September 2012, https://www.pe.com/2012/09/05/loma-linda-inaugural-health-symposium-set/.

141. "Global Conference on Health & Lifestyle," Adventist Health Ministries, March 2018, http://healthministries.com/events/2018/03/3rd-global-conference-health-and-lifestyle.

142. William Davies, *The Happiness Industry: How the Government and Big Business Sold Us Well-Being* (Brooklyn, NY: Verso, 2015), 191.

143. "City of Loma Linda General Plan," 1–4, https://www.lomalinda-ca.gov/our_city/general_plan (accessed 11 February 2020); San Bernardino Mayor and City Council, "Guiding Principles, 2020–2025 Key Strategic Targets and Goals," http://www.ci.san-bernardino.ca.us/about/city_vision_goals_n_more.asp (accessed 8 March 2020).

144. "The City of Loma Linda, California," https://web.archive.org/web/20170713013248/https://www.lomalinda-ca.gov/ (accessed 23 January 2020); cf. "Welcome," https://web.archive.org/web/20170501003036/https://www.lomalinda-ca.gov/ (accessed 23 January 2020).

145. Loma Linda Chamber of Commerce, "Building Healthy Businesses," 15 October 2017, https://web.archive.org/web/20171015123012/https://lomalindachamber.org/; Loma Linda Chamber of Commerce, "Promoting Healthy Business in the Zone," 29 January 2019, https://web.archive.org/web/201901 29023615/https://lomalindachamber.org/.

146. Loma Linda Chamber of Commerce, 8 February 2011, https://web.archive.org/web/20110208071345/http://lomalindachamber.org/ (accessed 23 January 2020).

147. Willon, "McDonald's Proposal Divides Healthy Loma Linda."

148. Nestle, *Food Politics*, 31.

149. "Life Expectancy at Birth, at 65 Years of Age, and at 75 Years of Age, by Race and Sex," Centers for Disease Control, https://www.cdc.gov/nchs/data/hus/2010/022.pdf (accessed 12 February 2020).

150. Nestle, *Food Politics*, 30.

151. Nestle, chap. 3.

152. Miller, *Building Nature's Market*, 220.

153. Gina Tenorio, "Keep McDonald's Out, Say Loma Linda Residents," *Redlands-Loma Linda Patch*, 15 June 2011, http://patch.com/california/redlands /keep-mcdonalds-out-say-loma-linda-residents.

154. Gina Tenorio, "Opponents of a McDonald's in Loma Linda Take Their Fight to City's Planning Commission," *Redlands-Loma Linda Patch*, 17 June 2011, https://patch.com/california/redlands/opponents-of-a-mcdonalds-in-loma -linda-take-their-figo514c64566.

155. Gina Tenorio, "'McDonald's Shopping Center Supported by Planning Commission," *Redlands-Loma Linda Patch*, 3 November 2011, https://patch .com/california/redlands/hede-here.

156. Neal Karlinksy and Melia Patria, "Food Fight: Loma Linda's Seventh-day Adventists Outraged over McDonald's," ABC News, 23 December 2011, https://abcnews.go.com/Health/loma-lindas-seventh-day-adventists-outraged -mcdonalds/story?id=15224296.

157. Willon, "McDonald's Proposal Divides Healthy Loma Linda."

158. Willon.

159. Sarah Milov, *The Cigarette: A Political History* (Cambridge, MA: Harvard University Press, 2019), 4–6, 164–65.

160. Bell and Valentine, *Consuming Geographies*, 10.

161. Medina, "Fast-Food Outlet Stirs Concerns in a Mecca of Healthy Living."

162. Medina.

163. Michael Nolan, "McDonald's Gets Down to Business in Loma Linda," *San Bernardino Sun*, 8 October 2013, http://www.sbsun.com/business/20131008 /mcdonalds-gets-down-to-business-in-loma-linda.

164. "Loma Linda Historian Honored by Chamber of Commerce," *Adventist Today.org*, March 2012, https://atoday.org/loma-linda-historian-honored-by -chamber-of-commerce/.

165. Nolan, "McDonald's Gets Down to Business in Loma Linda."

166. Jo Littler, "Green Products and Consumer Activism," in Mukherjee and Banet-Weiser, *Commodity Activism*, 77–82; Josee Johnston and Kate Cairns, "Eating for Change," in Mukherjee and Banet-Weiser, *Commodity Activism*, 221–22, 225.

167. Minkler, "Personal Responsibility for Health?, 124.

168. Even anti-smoking campaigns highlighted the impact of smoking on bystanders.

169. Bell and Valentine, *Consuming Geographies*, 11; Levenstein, *Paradox of Plenty*, 115–16.

170. Etta M. Madden and Martha L. Finch, "Introduction," *Eating in Eden: Food and America Utopias*, 1–2.

171. Eric Schlosser, *Fast Food Nation: The Dark Side of the All-American Meal* (Boston: Houghton Mifflin Harcourt, 2001).

172. Karlinksy and Patria, "Food Fight."

173. Laurie Ouellette, "Citizen Brand," in Mukherjee and Banet-Weiser, *Commodity Activism*, 62.

174. "City of Loma Linda City Council Agenda: City of Loma Linda Official Report," 10 September 2013, 3, www.lomalinda-ca.gov.

175. Nolan, "McDonald's Gets Down to Business.".

176. "City of Loma Linda City Council Agenda," 17.

177. "Loma Linda Ordinance 712," http://qcode.us/codes/lomalinda/revisions /712.pdf (accessed 26 March 2019).

178. Davies, *The Happiness Industry*, 112, 135.

179. Blue Zones, https://www.bluezones.com/#section-1 (accessed 18 February 2020).

180. United States Census Bureau, "Health Insurance Coverage in 2005," https://www.census.gov/population/pop-profile/dynamic/HealthInsurance.pdf (accessed 18 February 2020).

181. Samantha Artiga, "The Impact of the Coverage Gap for Adults in States Not Expanding Medicaid by Race and Ethnicity," *Kaiser Family Foundation*, 26 October 2015, https://www.kff.org/disparities-policy/issue-brief/the -impact-of-the-coverage-gap-in-states-not-expanding-medicaid-by-race-and -ethnicity/.

182. Brown, *Undoing the Demos*, 50, 207–8.

CHAPTER 5. SEEKER, SURFER, YOGI

1. Mike Anton, "Madonna Finds No Sanctuary," *Los Angeles Times*, 24 June 2011.

2. Sarah Schrank, *Art and the City: Civic Imagination and Cultural Authority in Los Angeles* (Philadelphia: University of Pennsylvania Press, 2009).

3. 3 I use the term *progressive* as a nomenclature for describing a range of liberal causes centering primarily on principles of social, economic, and cultural amelioration.

4. Adrian Ivakhiv, "Toward a Geography of 'Religion': Mapping the Distribution of an Unstable Signifier," *Annals of the Association of American Geographers* 96, no. 1 (2006): 171.

5. Juan Onesimo Sandoval, Hans P. Johnson, and Sonya M. Tafoya, "Whose Your Neighbor? Residential Segregation and Diversity in California," *California Counts* 4, no. 1 (August 2002): 1, 4, 13. The 2010 census showed that the city's demographics had not changed significantly: the white population went from 81 percent of the city's population to 79 percent.

6. Bryan Anderson and Madelin Ashmun, "Gavin Newsom's Housing Lawsuit Put 47 California Cities on Notice. Is Yours on the List?" *Sacramento Bee*, 19 February 2019, https://www.sacbee.com/news/politics-government /capitol-alert/article226293135.html; Barbara Henry, "Encinitas to Pursue Safe, Overnight Parking Area for Homeless People," *San Diego Union-Tribune*, 21 November 2019, https://www.sandiegouniontribune.com/communities/north -county/encinitas/story/2019-11-21/encinitas-to-pursue-safe-overnight-parking -area-for-homeless-people; Kayla Jimenez, "Encinitas Parking Lot for the Homeless Continues to Stir Fears and Anger," *Voice of San Diego*, 15 January 2020, https://www.voiceofsandiego.org/topics/news/encinitas-parking-lot-for-the -homeless-continues-to-stir-fears-and-anger.

7. Mike Davis, Kelly Mayhew, and Jim Miller, "Introduction," *Under the Perfect Sun: The San Diego Tourists Never See* (New York: The New Press, 2003), 3.

8. Mike Freeman, "Report: San Diego's Tech Sector Shows Signs of Improvement," *U-T San Diego*, 12 July 2011, http://www.utsandiego.com/news/2011/jul/12/report-san-diegos-tech-sector-makes-gains/; Bradley J. Fikes, "Life Science Industry Keeps Growing in San Diego County," *North County Times*, 2 February 2012; Ronald D. White, "California Reigns as a Green-Tech Innovator," *Los Angeles Times*, 20 March 2013, B3.

9. Lily Geismer, *Don't Blame Us: Suburban Liberals and the Transformation of the Democratic Party* (Princeton, NJ: Princeton University Press, 2014), 1–7; George Lipsitz, *The Possessive Investment in Whiteness: How White People Profit from Identity Politics* (Philadelphia: Temple University Press, 1998), xviii.

10. Sydney E. Ahlstrom, *A Religious History of the American People* (New Haven, CT: Yale University Press, 1972), 1115–17.

11. Eldon G. Ernst, "Religion in California," *Pacific Theological Review* 19 (Winter 1986): 44, 48.

12. Stuart Hall, "The Local and the Global': Culture, Globalization, and the World-System," in *Culture, Globalization, and the World-System*, ed. Anthony D. King (Minneapolis: University of Minnesota Press, 1997), 27, 33–34.

13. Kimberly Lau, *New Age Capitalism: Making Money East of Eden* (Philadelphia: University of Pennsylvania Press, 2000), 8–11.

14. Sarah Banet-Weiser and Charlotte Lapsansky, "RED Is the New Black: Brand Culture, Consumer Citizenship and Political Possibility," *International Journal of Communication* 2 (2008): 1248, 1251–54.

15. Lau, *New Age Capitalism*, 11.

16. See Jane Iwamura, *Virtual Orientalism: Asian Religions and American Popular Culture* (New York: Oxford University Press, 2010) and Jeremy Carrette and Richard King, *Selling Spirituality: The Silent Takeover of Religion* (New York: Routledge and Francis, 2005).

17. Paramahansa Yogananda, *Autobiography of a Yogi* (Los Angeles: Self-Realization Fellowship, 1946), 480.

18. Zenia Cleigh, "Self-Realization Fellowship's Land Offers Fertile Ground for the Spirit," *San Diego Tribune*, 30 August 1988, C-1; Pam Kragen, "After Nearly Two-Year Closure, Self-Realization Fellowship's Meditation Gardens Have Reopened," *San Diego Union-Tribune*, 5 January 2022, B-1.

19. Pat Stein, "Downtown Encinitas Renovation Captures Flavor, Appeal of City's Heritage," *San Diego Union-Tribune*, 17 February 2002, I1.

20. Robert C. Ritchie, *The Lure of the Beach: A Global History* (Oakland: University of California, 2021), 15, 18, 117, 169, 230; James E. Vance Jr., "California and the Search for the Ideal," *Annals of the Association of American Geographers* 62, no. 2 (June 1972): 187.

21. "Here's Contentment," *The San Diego Union*, 1 January 1896, 7; "San Diego Beaches are Ideal Spots to Spend Your Hot Weather Days," *Imperial Valley Press*, 9 August 1921, 4; "Come to San Diego," *Imperial Valley Press*, 25 April 1939, 2.

22. Peter Westwick and Peter Neushul, *The World in the Curl: An Unconventional History of Surfing* (New York: Crown, 2013), 74; Matt Warshaw, "San Diego, San Diego County," in *The Encyclopedia of Surfing* (New York: Harcourt, 2005), 519–20.

23. Helen Shaffer, "Sea Cliff Park Offers Something for Everybody," *San Diego Union*, 15 February 1984, AT EASE-4.

24. Kathie L. Taylor, "Park Name Changes Mapped for Encinitas, Solana Beach," *San Diego Evening Tribune*, 18 June 1987.

25. Westwick and Neushul, *The World in the Curl*, 2.

26. Bron Taylor, *Dark Green Religion: Nature Spirituality and the Planetary Future* (Berkeley: University of California Press, 2010),104, 110.

27. Matt Warshaw, *The History of Surfing* (San Francisco: Chronicle Books, 2010), 353.

28. Nadia Borowski Scott, "Swami's," *San Diego Union-Tribune*, 23 January 2005.

29. Quoted in Mike Lee, "Encinitas Beach Famed for Communal Charm, Smokin' Waves," *San Diego Union-Tribune*, 20 June 2009, A-1.

30. Quoted in Angela Lau, "Summoned to Swami's," *San Diego Union-Tribune*, 17 July 2005, N-1.

31. Warshaw, *History of Surfing*, 269.

32. Elle Hunt, "Blue Spaces: Why Time Spent Near Water Is the Secret of Happiness," *Guardian*, 3 November 2019, https://www.theguardian.com/lifeandstyle/2019/nov/03/blue-space-living-near-water-good-secret-of-happiness.

33. Ronald E. Purser, *McMindfulness: How Mindfulness Became the New Capitalist Spirituality* (London: Repeater Books, 2019), chap. 3.

34. Wallace J. Nichols, *Blue Mind: The Surprising Science That Shows How Being Near, in, on, or under Water Can Make You Happier, Healthier, More Connected, and Better at What You Do* (New York: Little, Brown and Company, 2014), 6.

35. Nichols, 161, 40.

36. Nichols, 114–19.

37. Nichols, 218, 183.

38. Nichols, 185, 250.

39. Purser, *McMindfulness*, 7–8.

40. Ritchie, *The Lure of the Beach*, 182, 230; Allison Rose Jefferson, *Living the California Dream: African American Leisure Sites during the Jim Crow Era* (Lincoln: University of Nebraska Press, 2020), chaps. 2–3; Lonnie G. Bunch, "'The Greatest State for the Negro': Jefferson L. Edmonds, Black Propagandist of the California Dream," in *Seeking El Dorado: African Americans in California*, eds Lawrence B. de Graaf, Kevin Mulroy, and Quintard Taylor (Seattle: University of Washington Press, 2001), 142; Lawrence B. de Graaf, "The City of Black Angels: Emergence of the Los Angeles Ghetto, 1890–1930," *Pacific Historical Review* 39, no. 3 (August 1970): 343–45, 348–49.

41. William Davies, *The Happiness Industry: How Government and Big Business Sold Us Well-Being* (Brooklyn, New York: Verso, 2015), 5.

42. Warshaw, *History of Surfing*, 263–73, 123.

43. Taylor, *Dark Green Religion*, 112.

44. Tony Perry, "'Swami's Will Never Be the Same," *Los Angeles Times*, 3 November 2015, https://www.latimes.com/local/lanow/la-me-ln-swamis-surfer-deaths-20151103-story.html.

45. Logan Jenkins, "For Everyone, a Lot Rides on Swami's Debate," *U-T San Diego*, March 14, 2010, NCT-3NIT-3.

46. "Stop Surfing Contests at Swamis," http://www.thepetitionsite.com/1 /stop-surfing-contests-at-swamis/ (accessed 9 August 2014).

47. Tanya Mannes, "Women's Event Facing Rough Waters," *U-T San Diego*, 8 November 2009, B-1.

48. "March 10, 2010, City Council Meeting," City of Encinitas Streaming Media Archive, http://webcasts.encinitasca.gov/.

49. "March 10, 2010, City Council Meeting."

50. Roger Showley, "SRF Offers Meditative Link to God," *San Diego Union*, 6 January 1976.

51. "March 10, 2010, City Council Meeting."

52. Bruce Lieberman, "The Neighboring Site's Serenity a Concern," *San Diego Union-Tribune*, 17 March 2010, B-1; Logan Jenkins, "Goddess of Surfing Makes a Sacrifice," *San Diego Union-Tribune*, 21 March 2010, NCT-3.

53. Taylor, *Dark Green Religion*, 104, 109.

54. Michael Gardner, "Surfing Madonna Loses Round in Sacramento," *U-T San Diego*, 25 April 2012, B-3.

55. Krista Comer, *Surfer Girls in the New World Order* (Durham, NC: Duke University Press, 2010), 165; Warshaw, *History of Surfing*, 264, 394–95.

56. Taylor, *Dark Green Religion*, 111, 116.

57. Jonathan Horn, "State Says No to Surfing Madonna," *U-T San Diego*, 16 March 2012, B-1.

58. Comer, *Surfer Girls*, 21.

59. Scott Laderman, *Empire in Waves: A Political History of Surfing* (Oakland: University of California Press, 2014).

60. Westwick and Neushul, *The World in the Curl*, chap. 2.

61. See Carey McWilliams, *Southern California Country: An Island on the Land* (New York: Duell, Sloan, and Pearce, 1946); Phoebe Kropp, *California Vieja: Culture and Memory in a Modern American Place* (Berkeley: University of California Press, 2006).

62. Ernesto C. Lopez, "Local Latinos, Catholics Split on 'Surfing Madonna,'" *North County Times*, 17 June 2011.

63. The organization gave $56,000 to Encinitas parks and recreation between 2013 and 2017, but donations ceased after 2017. In 2020, the charity threatened to remove the mosaic if its event permits were not approved. See Jeff McDonald, "Board Salaries Climb at Surfing Madonna Ocean Project as Revenue, Grants Dip," *San Diego Union Tribune*, 12 January 2020, https://www.sandiegouniontribune.com/news/watchdog/story/2020-01-12/board -salaries-climb-at-surfing-madonna-oceans-project-as-revenue-grants-dip; Jeff McDonald, "Chairman of Surfing Madonna Charity Calls for an End to Relationship with Encinitas," *San Diego Union-Tribune*, 11 February 2020, https://www.sandiegouniontribune.com/news/watchdog/story/2020-02-11 /chairman-of-surfing-madonna-charity-calls-for-an-end-to-relationship-with -encinitas.

64. "Best Surf Towns: No. 3 Encinitas, CA," *Surfer*, 5 April 2009, http://www.surfermag.com/features/best-surf-towns-no-3.

65. Debra Kamin, "Encinitas, Calif.: A Beach Town Where Prices Rise with the Tide," *New York Times*, 18 February 2020, https://www.nytimes.com/2020/02/18/realestate/encinitas-calif-a-beach-town-where-prices-rise-with-the-tide.html.

66. Jo Littler, "Good Housekeeping: Green Products and Consumer Activism," in *Commodity Activism: Cultural Resistance in Neoliberal Times*, ed. Roopali Mukherjee and Sarah Banet-Weiser (New York: New York University Press, 2012), 77.

67. Logan Jenkins, "Time to Get Serious and Approve a Home for the Surfing Madonna," *U-T San Diego*, 26 January 2012, NCT-4.

68. Barbara Henry, "Encinitas Mural Sparks Conversation," *San Diego Union-Tribune*, 26 February 2015, https://www.sandiegouniontribune.com/sdut-downtown-encinitas-mural-sparks-controversy-2015feb26-story.html (accessed 21 February 2020); Promise Yee, "'Harmony' Mural Continues to Stir Up Controversy," *San Diego Union-Tribune*, 10 May 2015, https://www.thecoastnews.com/harmony-mural-continues-to-stir-up-controversy/.

69. Catherine Cocks, *Doing the Town: The Rise of Urban Tourism in the United States, 1850–1915* (Berkeley: University of California Press, 2001), 176, 194.

70. "About Us," National Center for Law and Policy," https://web.archive.org/web/20121028042727/http://www.nclplaw.org/about-us/nclp/ (accessed 11 January 2015).

71. *Sedlock v. Timothy Baird*, 37-2013-00035910-CU-MC-CTL (1 July 2013), 36; "Yoga Is Being Shorn of Hindu Cultural Ties in the Land of the Free," *Economic Times*, 6 July 2013.

72. *Sedlock v. Timothy Baird*. In March 2015, a state appeals court heard arguments for an appeal.

73. Deborah Sullivan Brennan, "Parents Fuming over School Yoga Spending," *San Diego Union Tribune*, 3 June 2016, https://www.sandiegouniontribune.com/news/education/sdut-encinitas-school-district-yoga-2016jun03-story.html. In 2021, the state of Alabama lifted a ban that had been in place since 1993 allowing yoga instruction in public schools; the law required parental permission and stipulated the use of Sanskrit names for poses or chanting. Neil Vigdor, "Alabama Lifts Its Ban on Yoga in Schools," *New York Times*, 20 May 2021, https://www.nytimes.com/2021/05/20/us/alabama-yoga-ban-public-schools.html.

74. Barbara and John Ehrenreich, "The Professional-Managerial Class," in *Between Labor and Capitol: The Professional-Managerial Class*, ed. Pat Walker (Boston: South End Press, 1979): 5–45, quoted in Geismer, *Don't Blame Us*, 8.

75. US Census Bureau, "State and County Quick Facts: Encinitas," http://quickfacts.census.gov/qfd/states/06/0622678.html (accessed 28 July 2014); United States Census Bureau, "State and County Quick Facts: San Diego County," http://quickfacts.census.gov/qfd/states/06/06073.html (accessed 28 July 2014).

76. C. Richard Right, "The Spread of Self-Realization Fellowship," *Inner Culture*, March 1937, 45–46; Edmund Rucker, "Yoga Sect Holds Worldwide Lure," *San Diego Union*, July 10, 1949.

77. Stefanie Syman, *The Subtle Body: The Story of Yoga in America* (New York: Farrar, Straus and Giroux, 2010), 273–74.

78. Bethany McLean, "Whose Yoga Is It, Anyway?" *Vanity Fair*, April 2012, http://www.vanityfair.com/business/2012/04/krishna-pattanbhi-trophy-wife-ashtanga-yoga; Mimi Swartz, "Downward Dog," *Texas Monthly*, May 2012, 160.

79. Sarah Banet-Weiser, *Authentic™: The Politics of Ambivalence in a Brand Culture* (New York: New York University Press, 2012), 190.

80. See Mark Singleton and Ellen Goldberg, eds., *Gurus of Modern Yoga* (New York: Oxford University Press, 2014); William Broad, *The Science of Yoga: The Risks and Rewards* (New York: Simon and Schuster, 2012); Mark Singleton, *Yoga Body: The Origins of Modern Posture Practice* (New York: Oxford University Press, 2010); Robert J. Love, *The Great Oom: The Improbable Birth of Yoga in America* (New York: Viking, 2010); Anya Foxen, *Inhaling Spirit: Harmonialism, Orientalism, and the Western Roots of Modern Yoga* (New York: Oxford University Press, 2020).

81. Andrea R. Jain, "Who Is to Say Modern Yoga Practitioners Have It All Wrong? On Hindu Origins and Yogaphobia," *Journal of the American Academy of Religion* 82, no. 2 (June 2014): 429, 459. See also Anya Foxen, "Yogi Calisthenics: What the 'Non-yoga' Yogic Practice of Paramahansa Yogananda Can Tell Us about Religion," *Journal of the American Academy of Religion* 85, no. 2 (June 2017): 494–526.

82. See Mabel Potter Daggett, "The Heathen Invasion," *Hampton-Columbian Magazine* 27, no. 4 (October 1911): 399–411.

83. Sasha Lilley, "On Neoliberalism: An Interview with David Harvey," *MRZine*, http://mrzine.monthlyreview.org/2006/lilley190606.html (accessed July 17, 2014); "*Yoga Journal* Releases 2012 Yoga in America Market Study," *Yoga Journal*, 6 December 2012, http://www.yogajournal.com/article/press-releases/yoga-journal-releases-2012-yoga-in-america-market-study/.

84. Lau, *New Age Capitalism*, 95.

85. Robert Crawford quoted in "Health as a Meaningful Social Practice," *Health: An Interdisciplinary Journal for the Social Study of Health, Illness, and Medicine* 10, no. 4 (2006): 410, as cited in Samantha King, "Civic Fitness: The Body Politics of Commodity Activism," in Mukherjee and Banet-Weiser, *Commodity Activism*, 200–203.

86. Purser, *McMindfulness*, chap. 8.

87. Jorian Polis Schutz, "The State of Stretching: Yoga in America," *Baffler*, April 2013, http://www.thebaffler.com/salvos/the-state-of-stretching.

88. Syman, *The Subtle Body*, 284.

89. Schutz, "The State of Stretching."

90. California State Board of Education, *Physical Education Framework for California Public Schools* (Sacramento: California Department of Education, 2009), 8.

91. Christine Wood, "Letter of Support," Encinitas Unified School District, http://eusd.net/Parents/health%20and%20wellness/Letter%20of%20Support%20Dr%20Wood%20El%20Camino%20Pediatrics (accessed 16 January 2013).

92. Judd Handler, "EUSD and Jois Foundation Respond to Concerns," *Encinitas Patch*, 29 October 2012, http://encinitas.patch.com/articles/eusd-and-jois-foundation-respond-to-concerns-about-religious-yoga.

93. Farah Godrej, *Freedom Inside? Yoga and Meditation in the Carceral State* (New York: Oxford University Press, 2022), 9, 45, 50–56.

94. In keeping with the way that news accounts referred to yoga curriculum opponents, I refer to them as "Christians," although many proponents of the yoga curriculum also identified themselves as "Christians."

95. Vincent Crapanzano, *Serving the Word: Literalism in America from the Pulpit to the Bench* (New York: The New Press, 2001), 61–62.

96. *Sedlock v. Timothy Baird*, 25–27.

97. Will Carless, "Yoga Class Draws a Religious Protest," *New York Times*, 16 December 2012, A-35.

98. See Harvey Green, *Fit for America: Health, Fitness, Sport, and American Society* (New York: Pantheon Books, 1986) and Dominick Cavallo, *Muscles and Morals: Organized Playgrounds and Urban Reform, 1880–1920* (Philadelphia: University of Pennsylvania Press, 1981).

99. Handler, "EUSD and Jois Foundation Respond to Concerns about Religious Yoga."

100. Encinitas Union School District, "Yoga Program Frequently Asked Questions," http://www.eusd.net/Parents/health%20and%20wellness/FAQ (accessed 16 January 2013). Parents could opt out of the classes, and evidence during the trial suggested that about 2 percent of students did.

101. Carol Horton, "Yoga Is Not Dodgeball: Mind-Body Integration and Progressive Education," in *Yoga, the Body, and Embodied Social Change: An Intersectional Feminist Analysis*, ed. Beth Berila et al. (Lanham, MD: Lexington Books, 2016): 109–10.

102. When pretrial hearings began, the presiding judge admitted that he had been practicing Bikram for over a month and that he had no knowledge of spiritual connotations with the practice. Gary Worth, "Judge Adds New Twist to School Yoga Case," *U-T San Diego*, 29 March 2013, B-1.

103. Banet-Weiser, *Authentic*™, 196. In 2013–14, the district had about 20.6 percent Latinx and 68 percent white students. California Department of Education, "Encinitas Union Elementary Enrollment by Ethnicity for 2013–4," 24 March 2014, http://dq.cde.ca.gov/dataquest/Enrollment/EthnicGrade.aspx?cChoice=DstEnrAll&cYear=2013-14&cSelect=3768080--Encinitas%20Union%20Elementary&TheCounty=&cLevel=District&cTopic=Enrollment&myTimeFrame=S&cType=ALL&cGender=B/; Mukherjee and Banet-Weiser, "Introduction: Commodity Activism in Neoliberal Times," in *Commodity Activism*, 8–9.

104. Matthew T. Hall, "Public School Yoga: Relaxation or Religious Doctrine?" *U-T San Diego*, 22 October 2012.

105. Carless, "Yoga Class Draws a Religious Protest."

106. Logan Jenkins, "Encinitas Parents Bent out of Shape over Yoga on Campus," *U-T San Diego*, 17 October 2012.

107. Banet-Weiser, *Authentic*™, 196.

108. Crapanzano, *Serving the Word*, 2.

109. Banet-Weiser, *Authentic*™, 167.

110. Crapanzano, *Serving the Word*, 19, 21, 66.

111. Hall, "Public School Yoga."

112. Gary Worth, "Classroom Yoga Issue Packs Meeting," *North County Times* (Escondido), 6 December 2012, NC-1NI-1.

113. Christian Smith, *Christian America? What Evangelicals Really Want* (Berkeley: University of California Press, 2000), 67.

114. Smith, 147–50.

115. Ivakhiv, "Toward a Geography of 'Religion,'" 173.

116. David Harvey, *A Brief History of Neoliberalism* (New York: Oxford University Press, 2005), 41, 47.

117. Michael Denning, *Culture in the Age of Three Worlds* (New York: Verso, 2004), 23.

EPILOGUE

1. Elijah Wolfson, "Whooping Cough: A Comeback Story Nobody Loves," *Newsweek Global* 161, no. 36, 11 October 2013.

2. "Vaccinations, Not Scare Tactics," *Los Angeles Times*, 27 February 2014, A14; "Good News on Vaccinations," *Los Angeles Times*, 24 December 2014, A10.

3. Paloma Esquivel and Sandra Poindexter, "Immunity at Risk; More Parents Seeking Vaccination Exemptions," *Los Angeles Times*, 3 September 2014, A1.

4. Phil Willon and Melanie Mason, "State Bars Vaccine Belief Exemptions," *Los Angeles Times*, 1 July 2015, A1; Soumya Karlamangla, "Parents Turn to Doctors to Avoid Vaccines," *San Diego Union-Tribune*, 13 July 2018, 1; Salini Mohanty et al., "Experiences with Medical Exemptions after a Change in Vaccine Exemption Policy in California," *Pediatrics* 142, no. 5 (November 2018): 6.

5. Emily Foxhall, "Vaccine Opponents Hold Firm," *Los Angeles Times*, 26 January 2015, B1. In the wake of the vaccination law, rates inched up to 95 percent, but medical exemptions began to creep up in certain pockets of the state; in 2018, in 785 of the 6,500 elementary schools in the state, vaccination levels were at 90 percent or fewer of kindergarteners; there were twenty schools where more than a quarter of students were unvaccinated. Doctors estimated that, at most, about 3 percent of children might have legitimate medical reasons for remaining unvaccinated. Karlamangla, "Parents Turn to Doctors to Avoid Vaccines."

6. Richard A. Stein, "Vaccination: A Public Health Intervention That Changed History and Is Changing with History," *American Biology Teacher* 73, no. 9 (November–December 2011): 513.

7. Diederik F. Janssen, "A Familiar Species of Crank: Anti-Vaccinationists in Medical History," *Vaccine* 40 (2022): 4135.

8. "Anti-vaccination," *Los Angeles Herald*, 23 February 1899, 4.

9. Elena Conis, "The History of the Personal Belief Exemption," *Pediatrics* 145, no. 4 (April 2020): 1.

10. Cary Funk, Alec Tyson, Brian Kennedy, and Giancarlo Pasquini, "Americans' Largely Positive Views of Childhood Vaccines Hold Steady," *Pew Research Center*, 16 May 2023, https://www.pewresearch.org/science/2023/05/16/americans-largely-positive-views-of-childhood-vaccines-hold-steady.

11. Mike Stobbe, "US Kindergarten Vaccine Rate Dropped Again, Data Shows," Associated Press, 12 January 2023, https://apnews.com/article/health-immunizations-children-measles-acba3eb975fdfcd41732ed87511387f2.

12. Corina Knoll, "Shrinking California Still Dreams, but More Modestly," *New York Times*, 27 August 2023, https://www.nytimes.com/2023/08/27/us /california-population-decline-housing-crisis.html.

13. Andrea R. Jain, *Peace Love Yoga: The Politics of Global Spirituality* (New York: Oxford University Press, 2020), 4–5.

14. Derek Beres, Matthew Remski, and Julian Walker, *Conspirituality: How New Age Conspiracy Theories Became a Health Threat* (New York: Public Affairs, 2023), 101.

15. Joan B. Trauner, "The Chinese as Medical Scapegoats in San Francisco, 1870–1905," *California History* 57, no. 1 (Spring 1978); John E. Baur, *The Health Seekers of Southern California, 1870–1900* (San Marino, CA: The Huntington Library, 1959).

16. Janssen, "A Familiar Species of Crank," 4136.

17. Bernice L. Hausman, Mecal Ghebremichael, Philip Hayek, and Erin Mack, "'Poisonous, Filthy, Loathsome, Damnable Stuff': The Rhetorical Ecology of Vaccination Concern," *Yale Journal of Biology and Medicine* 87 (2014): 406.

18. James Colgrove, "'Science in a Democracy': The Contested Status of Vaccination in the Progressive Era and the 1920s," *Isis* 96, no. 2 (June 2005): 168, 182.

19. Nadav Davidovich, "Negotiating Dissent: Homeopathy and Anti-vaccinationism at the Turn of the Twentieth Century," in *The Politics of Healing: Histories of Alternative Medicine in Twentieth-Century North America*, ed. Robert D. Johnson (New York: Routledge, 2004), 15, 20.

20. Hausman et al., "'Poisonous, Filthy, Loathsome, Damnable Stuff,'" 403.

21. Colgrove, "'Science in a Democracy,'" 171–72, 177–79. See also Martin Kaufman, "The American Anti-vaccinationists and Their Arguments," *Bulletin of the History of Medicine* 41, no. 5 (September–October 1967): 463–78; Davidovich, "Negotiating Dissent," 20.

22. Kendall Hoyt, "Vaccine Innovation: Lessons from World War II," *Journal of Public Health Policy* 27, no. 1 (2006): 38.

23. Leslie J. Reagan, *Dangerous Pregnancies: Mothers, Disabilities, and Abortion in America* (Berkeley: University of California Press, 2010), 207, as cited in Elena Conis, *Vaccine Nation: America's Changing Relationship with Immunization* (Chicago: University of Chicago Press, 2015), 110.

24. In 2023, the family of Henrietta Lacks reached a settlement with the pharmaceutical company over the use of her cell line. See Max Matza, "Henrietta Lacks: Family of Black Woman Whose Cells Were Taken Settle Case," BBC, 1 August 2023, https://www.bbc.com/news/world-us-canada-66376758. In 2003, the nonprofit Institute of Medicine commissioned a panel of health care experts to document historic and ongoing racial disparities in medical treatment and to provide recommendations to address the issues. See Brian D. Smedley, Adrienne Y. Stith, Alan R. Nelson, eds., *Unequal Treatment: Confronting Racial and Ethnic Disparities in Health Care* (Washington, DC: National Academies Press, 2003).

25. Ivan Illich, *Medical Nemesis: The Expropriation of Health* (New York: Pantheon, 1976), as cited in Nancy Tomes, *Remaking the American Patient:*

How Madison Avenue and Modern Medicine Turned Patients into Consumers (Chapel Hill: University of North Carolina Press, 2016), 259.

26. Tomes, *Remaking the American Patient*, 258, 297–300; Jennifer A. Reich, *Calling the Shots: Why Parents Reject Vaccines* (New York: New York University Press, 2016), 11.

27. Meredith Minkler, "Personal Responsibility for Health? A Review of the Arguments and the Evidence at Century's End," *Health Education & Behavior* 26, no. 1 (February 1999): 123; Conis, *Vaccine Nation*, chap. 5; Elena Conis, "A Mother's Responsibility," *Bulletin of the History of Medicine* 87, no. 3 (Fall 2013): 414, 418.

28. Conis, "A Mother's Responsibility," 408.

29. Tish Davidson, *The Vaccine Debate* (Santa Barbara, CA: Greenwood, 2019), 134–35.

30. T. J. Jackson Lears and Richard Wrightman Fox, "Introduction," in Lears and Fox, *The Culture of Consumption*, xii.

31. Gary Gerstle, *The Rise and Fall of the Neoliberal Order: America and the World in the Free Market Era* (New York: Oxford University Press, 2022), 8–9, 12.

32. Susannah Crockford, *Ripples of the Universe: Spirituality in Sedona, Arizona* (Chicago: University of Chicago Press, 2021), 186.

33. Philip J. Smith, Susan Y. Chu, and Lawrence E. Barker, "Children Who Have Received No Vaccines: Who Are They and Where Do They Live?" *Pediatrics* 114, no. 1 (July 2004): 187, 189.

34. Jessica E. Atwell et al., "Nonmedical Vaccine Exemptions and Pertussis in California, 2010," *Pediatrics* 132, no. 4 (October 2013): 628.

35. Esquivel and Poindexter, "Immunity at Risk."

36. Chris Bobel, *The Paradox of Natural Mothering* (Philadelphia: Temple University Press, 2002), 26, as cited in Jennifer A. Reich, "Neoliberal Mothering and Vaccine Refusal: Imagined Gated Communities and the Privilege of Choice," *Gender and Society* 28, no. 5 (October 2014): 681–82.

37. Paul Sisson, "Private Schools See Fewer Vaccines," *San Diego Union-Tribune*, 8 February 2015, A-1.

38. Paloma Esquivel and Sandra Poindexter, "Immunity at Risk: More Parents Seeking Vaccination Exemptions," *Los Angeles Times*, 3 September 2014, A1.

39. Howard Blume, "As Mask Mandates Ease, Should California Schools Be Next?" *Los Angeles Times Communications LLC*, 8 February 2022.

40. Esquivel and Poindexter, "Immunity at Risk, A1.

41. Olav Hammer *Claiming Knowledge: Strategies of Epistemology from Theosophy to the New Age* (Leiden: Brill, 2004), as cited in Crockford, *Ripples of the Universe*, 171.

42. Crockford, *Ripples of the Universe*, 162.

43. Cindy Carcamo, "Moving the Needle; She's a Dancing Syringe Touting Shots in O.C.," *Los Angeles Times*, 2 April 2022, B1. Also see Paul Sisson and Lauren J. Mapp, "Distrust Hinders Vaccine Effort for Some Groups—Many Indigenous, Black, Residents Skeptical of Safety," *San Diego Union-Tribune*, 21 November 2021, A-1.

44. Robert Crawford, "Healthism and the Medicalization of Everyday Life," *International Journal of Health Services* 10, no. 3 (1980): 365–88.

45. Conis, *Vaccine Nation*, chapter 6.

46. Laura J. Nelson, "Wellness Devotees Embrace QAnon," *Los Angeles Times*, 25 June 2021, A1. See also Beres et al., *Conspirituality*.

47. Jennifer Thomson, *The Wild and the Toxic: American Environmentalism and the Politics of Health* (Chapel Hill: University of North Carolina Press, 2019), 5.

48. Reich, "Neoliberal Mothering," 688.

49. Esquivel and Poindexter, "Immunity at Risk," A1.

50. Sisson, "Private Schools See Fewer Vaccines," A-1.

51. Barbara Ehrenreich, *Bright Sided: How Positive Thinking Is Undermining America* (New York: Metropolitan Books, 2009).

52. Bron Taylor, *Dark Green Religion: Nature Spirituality and the Planetary Future* (Berkeley: University of California Press, 2010), 3.

53. Daniel T. Rodgers, *Age of Fracture* (Cambridge, MA: Belknap Press of Harvard University Press, 2011), 5–6.

54. Crockford, *Ripples of the Universe*, 182.

Bibliography

ARCHIVES

California Digital Newspaper Collection, Center for Bibliographic Studies and Research, University of California, Riverside

Department of Archives and Special Collections, University Libraries, Loma Linda University

Graduate Theological Union, Berkeley

Los Angeles Public Library

Theos Bernard Papers, Bancroft Library, University of California, Berkeley

UC San Diego Special Collections & Archives

NEWSPAPERS

Albuquerque Journal
California Eagle (Los Angeles)
Charleston (WV) Daily Mail
Chicago Tribune
Coast Dispatch (Encinitas, CA)
Colorado Statesman (Denver)
Corona Courier
Corona Independent
Coronado Strand
Economic Times
Encinitas Patch
Evening Sentinel (Santa Cruz)
Hanford Weekly Sentinel
Healdsburg Tribune
Hereford Brand (Texas)
Hindustan Times
Independent-Press-Telegram (Long Beach)
Independent (UK)
Jefferson City Daily Capital News
Kenosha Evening News (Wisconsin)
Kilmarnock Standard (Scotland)
Lawrence Daily Journal World
Los Angeles Herald
Los Angeles Herald Illustrated Magazine

Los Angeles Times
Marin Journal
Mason City Globe Gazette
Morning Echo (Bakersfield)
New York Times
North County Times
Oakland Tribune
Oxnard Courier
Pasadena Star News
Placerville Mountain Democrat
Press Democrat (Santa Rosa, CA)
Press Enterprise (Redlands, CA)
Press Telegram (Long Beach, CA)
PR Newswire
Redlands-Loma Linda Patch
Sacramento Bee

Sacramento Union
Salt Lake Tribune
San Bernardino Daily Sun
San Diego Business Journal
San Diego Evening Tribune
San Diego Reader
San Diego Union and Bee
San Diego Union
San Diego Union-Tribune
Santa Ana Daily Register
Seattle Times
Times-Advocate (Escondido)
Voices of San Diego
Wall Street Journal
Woodland (California) Daily
    Democrat

MAGAZINES

Adventist Review
Atlantic
California
California State Journal of Medicine
East-West World Wide
Esquire
Florida Today
Inc. Magazine
Inner Culture
Life
Life and Health: The National Health
    Magazine

Mother Jones
Munsey's Magazine
National Geographic
New Age
New Yorker
Self-Realization Magazine
Sun
Sunset
Texas Monthly
Time
Vanity Fair
Yoga Journal

ARTICLES, BOOKS, AND PUBLIC REPORTS/COURT CASES

Abel, Emily K. *Tuberculosis and the Politics of Exclusion: A History of Public Health and Migration to Los Angeles.* New Brunswick, NJ: Rutgers University Press, 2007.

Adamic, Louis. "Katherine Tingley, Theosophical Boob-Baiter of San Diego." *Haldeman-Julius Monthly* 5 (February 1927).

———. "The Morons of Los Angeles." *Haldeman-Julius Monthly* 4, no. 6 (November 1926).

Adams, Samuel Hopkins. *The Great American Fraud: The Patent Medicine Evil.* Chicago: P.F. Collier & Son, 1905.

Adas, Michael. *Machines as the Measure of Men: Science, Technology, and Ideologies of Western Dominance.* Ithaca, NY: Cornell University Press, 1989.

Ahlstrom, Sydney E. *A Religious History of the American People*. 2nd ed. New Haven, CT: Yale University Press, 2004.

Albanese, Catherine L. *America: Religions and Religion*. 3rd ed. Belmont, CA: Wadsworth Publishing Company, 1999.

———. *A Republic of Mind and Spirit: A Cultural History of American Metaphysical Religion*. New Haven, CT: Yale University Press, 2007.

Alexander, Michael Scott. *Making Peace with the Universe: Personal Crisis and Spiritual Healing*. New York: Columbia University Press, 2020.

Alter, Joseph. *Yoga in Modern India: The Body Between Science and Philosophy*. New Delhi: New Age Books, 2009. Originally printed by Princeton University Press, 2004.

Altglas, Véronique. *From Yoga to Kabbalah: Religious Exoticism and the Logics of Bricolage*. New York: Oxford University Press, 2014.

Anderson, Theodore Marvin. "Reimagining Religion: The Grounding of Spiritual Politics and Practice in Modern America, 1890–1940." PhD diss., Yale University, 2008.

Andress, William C. *Adventist Heritage of Health, Hope, and Healing*. Fort Oglethorpe, GA: Teach Services, Inc., 2014.

Aravamudan, Srinivas. *Guru English (Translation/Transnation)*. Princeton, NJ: Princeton University Press, 2005.

Artiga, Samantha. "The Impact of the Coverage Gap for Adults in States Not Expanding Medicaid by Race and Ethnicity." *Kaiser Family Foundation* (October 26, 2015).

Aschoff, Nicole. *The New Prophets of Capital*. Brooklyn, NY: Verso Books, 2015.

Ashcraft, W. Michael. *The Dawn of the New Cycle: Point Loma Theosophists and American Culture*. Knoxville: University of Tennessee Press, 2002.

Atwell, Jessica E. et al. "Nonmedical Vaccine Exemptions and Pertussis in California, 2010." *Pediatrics* 132, no. 4 (October 2013): 624–30.

Avila, Eric. *Popular Culture in the Age of White Flight: Fear and Fantasy in Suburban Los Angeles*. Berkeley: University of California Press, 2004.

Baber, Zaheer. *The Science of Empire: Scientific Knowledge, Civilization, and Colonial Rule in India*. New York: Oxford University Press, 1998.

Bacevich, Andrew J., ed. *The Short American Century*. Cambridge, MA: Harvard University Press, 2012.

Bhagavan, Manu, ed. *India and the Cold War*. Chapel Hill: University of North Carolina Press, 2019.

Baker, Ray Stannard. "An Extraordinary Experiment in Brotherhood: The Theosophical Institution at Point Loma, California." *The American Magazine* 63, no. 3 (January 1907).

Banet-Weiser, Sarah. *Authentic™: The Politics of Ambivalence in a Brand Culture*. New York: New York University Press, 2012.

Banet-Weiser, Sarah, and Charlotte Lapsansky. "RED Is the New Black: Brand Culture, Consumer Citizenship and Political Possibility." *International Journal of Communication* 2 (2008): 1248-1268.

Baur, John E. *The Health Seekers of Southern California, 1870–1900*. San Marino, CA: The Huntington Library, 1959.

Bayly, C. A. *The Birth of the Modern World, 1780–1914: Global Connections and Comparisons*. Malden, MA: Blackwell Publishing, 2004.

Bell, David, and Gill Valentine. *Consuming Geographies: We Are Where We Eat*. New York: Routledge, 1997.

Bednarowski, Mary F. "Outside the Mainstream: Women's Religion and Women Religious Leaders in Nineteenth Century America." *Journal of the American Academy of Religion* 48 (1980): 207–31.

Bellah, Robert N., et al. *Habits of the Heart: Individualism and Commitment in American Life*. Berkeley: University of California Press, 1985.

Beres, Derek, Matthew Remski, and Julian Walker. *Conspirituality: How New Age Conspiracy Theories Became a Health Threat*. New York: Public Affairs, 2023.

Best, Joel. *Flavor of the Month: Why Smart People Fall for Fads*. Berkeley: University of California Press, 2006.

Binkley, Sam. *Getting Loose: American Lifestyle Consumption in the 1970s*. Durham, NC: Duke University Press, 2007.

Blower, Brooke L., and Andrew Preston, eds. *The Cambridge History of America and the World*, volume III, 1900–1945. New York: Cambridge University Press, 2021.

Boltanski, Luc, and Eve Chiapello. *The New Spirit of Capitalism*. Translated by Gregory Elliott. New York: Verso, 2005.

Bose, Sugata. *A Hundred Horizons: The Indian Ocean in the Age of Global Empire*. Cambridge, MA: Harvard University Press, 2009.

Bourdieu, Pierre. *Distinction: A Social Critique of the Judgment of Taste*. Cambridge, MA: Harvard University Press, 1984.

Brandt, Allan M. *The Cigarette Century: The Rise, Fall, and Deadly Persistence of the Product that Defined America*. New York: Basic Books, 2007.

Brennan, Chrisann. *The Bite in the Apple: A Memoir of My Life with Steve Jobs*. New York: St. Martin's Press, 2013.

Broad, William. *The Science of Yoga: The Risks and Rewards*. New York: Simon and Schuster, 2012.

Bronner, E. H. *The Moral ABC of Astronomy's Eternal All-One-God-Faith Unites the Human Race!* Vista, CA: n.p., 2015.

Brown, Wendy. *Undoing the Demos: Neoliberalism's Stealth Revolution*. Brooklyn, New York: Zone Books, 2015.

Buettner, Dan. *The Blue Zone: Lessons for Living Longer from the People Who've Lived the Longest*. Washington, DC: National Geographic, 2008.

———. "New Wrinkles on Aging." *National Geographic* 208, no. 5, November 2005.

Bull, Malcolm, and Keith Lockhart. *Seeking a Sanctuary: Seventh-day Adventism and the American Dream*, 2nd ed. Bloomington: Indiana University Press, 2007. Originally published 1989.

Bunch, Lonnie G. "'The Greatest State for the Negro': Jefferson L. Edmonds, Black Propagandist of the California Dream." In *Seeking El Dorado: African Americans in California*, edited by Lawrence B. de Graaf, Kevin Mulroy, and Quintard Taylor, 129–48. Seattle: University of Washington Press, 2001.

Bunyan, John. *The Pilgrim's Progress: From this World to That Which Is to Come*. 1678. https://www.gutenberg.org/files/131/131-h/131-h.htm.

Burbank, Jane, and Frederick Cooper. *Empires in World History: Power and the Politics of Difference*. Princeton, NJ: Princeton University Press, 2011.

Burgin, Angus. "Market Politics in an Age of Automation." In *Beyond the New Deal Order: U.S. Politics from the Great Depression to the Great Recession*, edited by Gary Gerstle, Nelson Lichtenstein, and Alice O'Connor, 143–67. Philadelphia: University of Pennsylvania Press, 2019.

Burnham, John C. "American Physicians and Tobacco Use: Two Surgeons General 1929 and 1964." *Bulletin of the History of Medicine* 63, no. 1 (Spring 1989): 1–31.

Bushman, Richard L., and Claudia L. Bushman. "The Early History of Cleanliness in America." *Journal of American History* 74, no. 4 (March 1988): 1213–38.

California State Board of Education. *Physical Education Framework for California Public Schools*. Sacramento: California Department of Education, 2009.

Campbell, Bruce F. *Ancient Wisdom Revived: A History of the Theosophical Movement*. Berkeley: University of California Press, 1980.

Carrette, Jeremy, and Richard King. *Selling Spirituality: The Silent Takeover of Religion*. New York: Routledge and Francis, 2005.

Carson, Gerald. *Cornflake Crusade*. New York: Rinehart and Company, 1957.

Cavallo, Dominick. *Muscles and Morals: Organized Playgrounds and Urban Reform, 1880–1920*. Philadelphia: University of Pennsylvania Press, 1981.

Chapman, Roger. "Dr. Bronner's 'Magic Soaps' Religion." *Journal of Religion and Popular Culture* 25, no. 2 (Summer 2013): 287–301.

Clark, Christopher R. *The Communitarian Moment: The Radical Challenge of the Northampton Association*. Ithaca, NY: Cornell University Press, 1995.

Cocks, Catherine. *Doing the Town: The Rise of Urban Tourism in the United States, 1850–1915*. Berkeley: University of California Press, 2001.

Cohen, Lizabeth. *A Consumers' Republic: The Politics of Mass Consumption in Postwar America*. New York: Knopf, 2003.

Colgrove, James. "'Science in a Democracy': The Contested Status of Vaccination in the Progressive Era and the 1920s." *Isis* 96, no. 2 (June 2005): 167–91.

Comer, Krista. *Surfer Girls in the New World Order*. Durham, NC: Duke University Press, 2010.

Conis, Elena. "The History of the Personal Belief Exemption." *Pediatrics* 145, no. 4 (April 2020): 1–3.

———. "A Mother's Responsibility." *Bulletin of the History of Medicine* 87, no. 3 (Fall 2013): 407–35.

———. *Vaccine Nation: America's Changing Relationship with Immunization*. Chicago: University of Chicago Press, 2015.

Converse, Grace. "Theosophy and the Realization of Southern California's Divine Destiny." In Flory and Winston, *Religion in Los Angeles: Religious Activism, Innovation, and Diversity in the Global City*, 122–36.

Crapanzano, Vincent. *Serving the Word: Literalism in America from the Pulpit to the Bench*. New York: The New Press, 2001.

Crawford, Robert. "Healthism and the Medicalization of Everyday Life." *International Journal of Health Services* 10, no. 3 (1980): 365–88.

Crockford, Susannah. *Ripples of the Universe: Spirituality in Sedona, Arizona.* Chicago: University of Chicago Press, 2021.

Cross, Whitney. *The Burned-Over District: The Social and Intellectual History of Enthusiastic Religion in Western New York, 1800–1850.* New York: Harper & Row, 1950.

Culver, Lawrence. *The Frontier of Leisure: Southern California and the Shaping of Modern America.* New York: Oxford University Press, 2010.

Currid-Halkett, Elizabeth. *The Sum of Small Things: A Theory of the Aspirational Class.* Princeton, NJ: Princeton University Press, 2017.

Daggett, Mabel Potter. "The Heathen Invasion." *Hampton-Columbian Magazine* 27, no. 4 (October 1911).

Davidovich, Nadav. "Negotiating Dissent: Homeopathy and Anti-Vaccinationism at the Turn of the Twentieth Century." In *The Politics of Healing: Histories of Alternative Medicine in Twentieth-Century North America*, edited by Robert D. Johnson, 11–28. New York: Routledge, 2004.

Davidson, Tish. *The Vaccine Debate.* Santa Barbara, CA: Greenwood, 2019.

Davidson, Winifred. *A Brief History of the Old Spanish Lighthouse.* Point Loma, California: n.p., 1926.

Davies, William. *The Happiness Industry: How the Government and Big Business Sold Us Well-Being.* Brooklyn: Verso Books, 2015.

Davis, Joshua Clark. *From Head Shops to Whole Foods: The Rise and Fall of Activist Entrepreneurs.* New York: Columbia University Press, 2017.

Davis, Mike. *City of Quartz: Excavating the Future in Los Angeles.* New York: Verso, 1990.

Davis, Mike, Kelly Mayhew, and Jim Miller. *Under the Perfect Sun: The San Diego Tourists Never See.* New York: The New Press, 2003.

de Graaf, Lawrence B. "The City of Black Angels: Emergence of the Los Angeles Ghetto, 1890–1930." *Pacific Historical Review* 39, no. 3 (August 1970): 323–52.

de Graaf, Lawrence B., and Quintard Taylor. "Introduction: African Americans in California History, California in African American History." In *Seeking El Dorado: African Americans in California*, edited by Lawrence B. de Graaf, Kevin Mulroy, and Quintard Taylor. Seattle: University of Washington Press, 2001.

De Michelis, Elizabeth. *A History of Modern Yoga: Patañjali and Western Esotericism.* New York: Continuum, 2004.

Dempsey, Sean T. *City of Dignity: Christianity, Liberalism, and the Making of Global Los Angeles.* Chicago: University of Chicago Press, 2023.

Denning, Michael. *Culture in the Age of Three Worlds.* New York: Verso, 2004.

Deutsch, Ronald M. *The Nuts among the Berries.* New York: Ballantine Books, 1961.

Deverell, William. "Privileging the Mission over the Mexican." In *Many Wests: Place, Culture, and Regional Identity*, edited by David W. Wrobel and Michael C. Steiner, 235–58. Lawrence: University Press of Kansas, 1997.

———. *Whitewashed Adobe: The Rise of Los Angeles and the Remaking of Its Mexican Past.* Berkeley: University of California Press, 2004.

Diamond, Debra. *Yoga: The Art of Transformation.* Washington, DC: Arthur M. Sackler Gallery, Smithsonian Institution, 2013.

Dochuk, Darren. *From Bible Belt to Sunbelt: Plain-Folk Religion, Grassroots Politics, and the Rise of Evangelical Conservatism.* New York: W.W. Norton, 2011.

Drake, Brian Allen. *Loving Nature, Fearing the State: Environmentalism and Antigovernment Politics before Reagan.* Seattle: University of Washington Press, 2013.

DuPuis, E. Melanie. *Dangerous Digestion: The Politics of American Dietary Advice.* Berkeley: University of California Press, 2015.

Duckworth, Angela. *Grit: The Power of Passion and Perseverance.* New York: Simon and Schuster, 2016.

Dweck, Carol S. *Mindset: The New Psychology of Success.* New York: Ballantine Books, 2007.

Ehrenreich, Barbara. *Bright Sided: How Positive Thinking Is Undermining America.* New York: Metropolitan Books, 2009.

Ellwood, Robert, and Catherine Wessinger. "The Feminism of 'Universal Brotherhood': Women in the Theosophical Movement." In *Women's Leadership in Marginal Religions: Explorations Outside the Mainstream,* edited by Catherine Wessinger, 68–87. Urbana: University of Illinois, 1993.

Engerman, David C., Max Paul Friedman, and Melani McAlister, eds. *The Cambridge History of America and the World.* New York: Cambridge University Press, 2021.

Engs, Ruth Clifford. *Clean Living Movements: American Cycles of Health Reform.* Westport, Conn.: Praeger, 2000.

Ernst, Eldon G. "The Emergence of California in American Religious History." *Religion and American Culture: A Journal of Interpretation* 11, no. 1 (Winter 2001): 31–52.

———. "Religion in California." *Pacific Theological Review* 19 (Winter 1986): 43–51.

Fager, Chuck. "Who Is Dr. Bronner, Anyway?" *New Age,* September 1976.

Finke, Roger, and Rodney Stark. *The Churching of America, 1776–1990: Winners and Losers in Our Religious Economy.* New Brunswick, NJ: Rutgers University Press, 1992.

Flamming, Douglas. *Bound for Freedom: Black Los Angeles in Jim Crow America.* Berkeley: University of California Press, 2005.

Flory, Richard, and Diane Winston, eds. *Religion in Los Angeles: Religious Activism, Innovation, and Diversity in the Global City.* New York: Routledge, 2021.

Fogelson, Robert M. *The Fragmented Metropolis: Los Angeles, 1850–1930.* Cambridge, MA: Harvard University Press, 1967. Reprint, Berkeley: University of California Press, 1993.

Foster, Tom. "Radical Chic." *Inc. Magazine,* 3 April 2012. https://www.inc.com /magazine/201204/tom-foster/the-undiluted-genius-of-dr-bronners.html.

Foucault, Michel. *The History of Sexuality: An Introduction,* vol. 1. Translated by Robert Hurley. New York: Random House, 1978.

Foxen, Anya P. *Biography of a Yogi: Paramahansa Yogananda and the Origins of a Modern Yoga*. New York: Oxford University Press, 2017.

———. *Inhaling Spirit: Harmonialism, Orientalism, and the Western Roots of Modern Yoga*. New York: Oxford University Press, 2020.

———. "Yogi Calisthenics: What the 'Non-Yoga' Yogic Practice of Paramahansa Yogananda Can Tell Us about Religion." *Journal of the American Academy of Religion* 85, no. 2 (June 2017): 494–526.

Frank, Thomas. *The Conquest of Cool: Business Culture, Counterculture, and the Rise of Hip Consumer*. Chicago: University of Chicago Press, 1998.

Frankiel, Sandra Sizer. *California's Spiritual Frontiers: Religious Alternatives in Anglo Protestantism, 1850–1910*. Berkeley: University of California Press, 1988.

Freedman, Paul, and Gabrielle M. Spiegel. "Medievalisms Old and New: The Rediscovery of Alterity in North American Medieval Studies." *American Historical Review* 103, no. 3 (June 1998): 677–704.

Frost, Bob. "The Pope of Soap." *California* 15, no. 11, November 1990.

Fuller, Robert C. "Esoteric Movements." In Lippy and Williams *Encyclopedia of Religion in America*, 751–57.

———. "Occult and Metaphysical Religion, in Lippy and Williams, *Encyclopedia of Religion in America*, 1593–96.

Funk, Cary, Alec Tyson, Brian Kennedy, and Giancarlo Pasquini. "Americans' Largely Positive Views of Childhood Vaccines Hold Steady." *Pew Research Center*, 16 May 2023. https://www.pewresearch.org/science/2023/05/16/americans-largely-positive-views-of-childhood-vaccines-hold-steady/.

Gadding, Effie Price. *Across the Continent by the Lincoln Highway*. New York: Rowland & Ives, 1915.

Geismer, Lily. *Don't Blame Us: Suburban Liberals and the Transformation of the Democratic Party*. Princeton, NJ: Princeton University Press, 2014.

———. *Left Behind: The Democrats' Failed Attempt to Solve Inequality*. New York: PublicAffairs, 2022.

Gerstle, Gary. *American Crucible: Race and Nation in the Twentieth Century*. Princeton, NJ: Princeton University Press, 2001.

———. *The Rise and Fall of the Neoliberal Order: America and the World in the Free Market Era*. New York: Oxford University Press, 2022.

Godrej, Farah. *Freedom Inside? Yoga and Meditation in the Carceral State*. New York: Oxford University Press, 2022.

Godwin, Joscelyn. *The Theosophical Enlightenment*. Albany: State University of New York Press, 1994.

Goebel, Michael. *Anti-Imperial Metropolis: Interwar Paris and the Seeds of Third World Nationalism*. New York: Cambridge University Press, 2015.

Goedde, Petra. "US Mass Culture and Consumption in Global Context." In *The Cambridge History of America and the World*, vol. 4, edited by David C. Engerman, Max Paul Friedman, and Melani McAlister, 281–303. New York: Cambridge University Press, 2021.

Goldberg, Philip. *American Veda: From Emerson and the Beatles to Yoga and Meditation—How Indian Spirituality Changed the West*. New York: Harmony Books, 2010.

Gomes, Michael. *The Dawning of the Theosophical Moment*. Wheaton, IL: The Theosophical Publishing House, 1987.

Green, Harvey. *Fit for America: Health, Fitness, Sport, and American Society*. New York: Pantheon Books, 1986.

Greenwalt, Emmett A. *California Utopia: Point Loma, 1897–1942*. San Diego: Point Loma Publications, 1955.

Grewal, Zareena. "Christian and Muslim Transnational Networks." In *The Cambridge History of America and the World*, vol. 4, edited by David C. Engerman, Max Paul Friedman, and Melani McAlister, 440–64. New York: Cambridge University Press, 2021.

Hafner, Katie, and Matthew Lyon. *Where Wizards Stay Up Late: The Origins of the Internet*. New York: Simon & Schuster, 1996.

Hall, David. D., ed. *Lived Religion in America: Toward a History of Practice*. Princeton, NJ: Princeton University Press, 1997.

Hall, Stuart. "'The Local and the Global': Culture, Globalization, and the World-System." In *Culture, Globalization, and the World-System*, edited by Anthony D. King, 19–40. Minneapolis: University of Minnesota Press, 1997.

Hammer, Olav, and Mikael Rothstein, eds. *Handbook of the Theosophical Current*. Chapel Hill: University of North Carolina Press, 2013.

Han, Byung-Chul. *Psycho-Politics: Neoliberalism and New Technologies of Power*. Translated by Erik Butler. Brooklyn, New York: Verso Books, 2017.

Harding, Susan. *The Book of Jerry Falwell: Fundamentalist Language and Politics*. Princeton, NJ: Princeton University Press, 2000.

Harkinson, Josh. "The Audacity of Soap." *Mother Jones*, January–February 2014.

Harris, Iverson L. "Reminiscences of Lomaland: Madame Tingley and the Theosophical Institute in San Diego." *Journal of San Diego History* 20, no. 3 (Summer 1974).

Harris, Malcom. *Palo Alto: A History of California, Capitalism, and the World*. New York: Little, Brown and Company, 2023.

Harvey, David. *A Brief History of Neoliberalism*. New York: Oxford University Press, 2005.

Hau, Michael. *The Cult of Health and Beauty in Germany*. Chicago: University of Chicago Press, 2003.

Hausman, Bernice L., Mecal Ghebremichael, Philip Hayek, and Erin Mack. "'Poisonous, Filthy, Loathsome, Damnable Stuff': The Rhetorical Ecology of Vaccination Concern." *Yale Journal of Biology and Medicine* 87 (2014): 403–16.

Hawken, Paul. *The Ecology of Commerce: A Declaration of Sustainability*. New York: HarperCollins, 1993.

Hayden, Dolores. *Seven American Utopias: The Architecture of Communitarian Socialism, 1790–1975*. Cambridge, MA: MIT Press, 1976.

Healey, Kevin. "Searching for Integrity: The Politics of Mindfulness in the Digital Economy." *Nomos Journal*, 5 August 2013. https://nomosjournal.org /2013/08/searching-for-integrity/.

Hernandez, Kelly Lytle. *Bad Mexicans: Race, Empire, and Revolution in the Borderlands*. New York: W.W. Norton, 2022.

———. *City of Inmates: Conquest, Rebellion, and the Rise of Human Caging in Los Angeles, 1771–1965.* Chapel Hill: University of North Carolina Press, 2017.

Hickey, Wakoh Shannon. *Mind Cure: How Meditation Became Medicine.* New York: Oxford University Press, 2019.

Hine, Robert. *California's Utopian Colonies.* New Haven, CT: Yale University Press, 1953.

Hoganson, Kristin L. *Consumers' Imperium: The Global Production of American Domesticity, 1865–1920.* Chapel Hill: University of North Carolina Press, 2007.

Hoganson, Kristin, and Jay Sexton. *Crossing Empires: Taking U.S. History into Transimperial Terrain.* Durham, NC: Duke University Press, 2020.

Holliday, Peter J. *American Arcadia: California and the Classical Tradition.* New York: Oxford University Press, 2016.

Hooton, Laura Kay Fleisch. "Co-Opting the Border: The Dream of African American Integration via Baja California." PhD diss., University of California, Santa Barbara, 2018.

Horne, Gerald C. *The End of Empires: African Americans and India.* Philadelphia: Temple University Press, 2009.

Horton, Carol. "Yoga Is Not Dodgeball: Mind-Body Integration and Progressive Education." In *Yoga, the Body, and Embodied Social Change: An Intersectional Feminist Analysis,* edited by Beth Berila, Melanie Klein, and Chelsea Jackson Roberts, 109–23. Lanham, MD: Lexington Books, 2016.

Hoyt, Kendall. "Vaccine Innovation: Lessons from World War II." *Journal of Public Health Policy* 27, no. 1 (2006): 38–57.

Illouz, Eva. *Cold Intimacies: The Making of Emotional Capitalism.* Malden, MA: Polity Press, 2007.

Iriye, Akira. *Cultural Internationalism and World Order.* Baltimore: Johns Hopkins University Press, 1997.

———. *Global and Transnational History: The Past, Present, and Future.* New York: Palgrave Macmillan, 2013.

———. Toward Transnationalism." In Bacevich, *The Short American Century,* 121–41.

Isaacson, Walter. *Steve Jobs.* New York: Simon and Schuster, 2011.

Ivakhiv, Adrian. "Toward a Geography of 'Religion': Mapping the Distribution of an Unstable Signifier." *Annals of the Association of American Geographers* 96, no. 1 (2006): 169–75.

Ivey, Paul Eli. *Radiance From Halcyon: A Utopian Experiment in Religion and Science.* Minneapolis: University of Minnesota Press, 2013.

Iwamura, Jane. *Virtual Orientalism: Asian Religions and American Popular Culture.* New York: Oxford University Press, 2010.

Jain, Andrea R. *Peace Love Yoga: The Politics of Global Spirituality.* New York: Oxford University Press, 2020.

———. *Selling Yoga: From Counterculture to Pop Culture.* New York: Oxford University Press, 2015.

———. "Who Is to Say Modern Yoga Practitioners Have It All Wrong? On Hindu Origins and Yogaphobia." *Journal of the American Academy of Religion* 82, no. 2 (June 2014): 427–71.

James, William. *The Varieties of Religious Experience: A Study in Human Nature*. Auckland: The Floating Press, 1994. Originally published 1902.

Janssen, Diederik F. "A Familiar Species of Crank: Anti-Vaccinationists in Medical History." *Vaccine* 40 (2022): 4135–41.

Jefferson, Allison Rose. *Living the California Dream: African American Leisure Sites during the Jim Crow Era*. Lincoln: University of Nebraska Press, 2020.

Jenkins, Philip. *Mystics and Messiahs: Cults and New Religions in American History*. New York: Oxford University Press, 2000.

Jobs, Steve. *Make Something Wonderful: Steve Jobs in His Own Words*. Cupertino, CA: Apple Books, 2023.

Johnson, Paul E. *A Shopkeeper's Millennium: Society and Revivals in Rochester, New York 1815–1837*. New York: Hill and Wang, 1978.

Johnston, Josee, and Kate Cairns. "Eating for Change." In Mukherjee and Banet-Weiser, *Commodity Activism*, 219–39.

Jones, Geoffrey. *Beauty Imagined: A History of the Global Beauty Industry*. New York: Oxford University Press, 2010.

Karlinksy, Neal, and Melia Patria. "Food Fight: Loma Linda's Seventh-day Adventists Outraged over McDonald's." ABC News, 23 December 2011. https://abcnews.go.com/Health/loma-lindas-seventh-day-adventists-outraged-mcdonalds/story?id=15224296.

Kaufman, Martin. "The American Anti-Vaccinationists and Their Arguments." *Bulletin of the History of Medicine* 41, no. 5 (September–October 1967): 463–78.

Kessler, Sarah. *Gigged: The End of the Job and the Future of Work*. New York: St. Martin's Press, 2018.

Kilston, Lyra. *Sun Seekers: The Cure of California*. Los Angeles: Atelier Editions, 2019.

King, Anna S. "Spirituality: Transformation and Metamorphosis." *Religion* 26, no. 4 (1996): 343–51.

Kirkley, Evelyn A. "Starved and Treated Like Convicts." *Journal of San Diego History* 43, no. 1 (Winter 1997): 272–88. https://sandiegohistory.org/journal/1997/january/theosophical/.

Klein, Christina. *Cold War Orientalism: Asia in the Middlebrow Imagination*. Berkeley: University of California Press, 2003.

Klein, Shana. *The Fruits of Empire: Art, Food, and the Politics of Race in the Age of American Expansion*. Oakland: University of California Press, 2020.

Knibbe, Kim, and Helena Kupari. "Theorizing Lived Religion: Introduction." *Journal of Contemporary Religion* 35, no. 2 (2020): 157–76.

Kramer, Paul A. *Blood of Government: Race, Empire, the United States, and the Philippines*. Chapel Hill: University of North Carolina Press, 2006.

———. "Empires, Exceptions, and Anglo-Saxons: Race and Rule between the British and United States Empires, 1880–1910." *Journal of American History* 88, no. 4 (March 2002): 1315–53.

Kripal, Jeffrey J. *Esalen: America and the Religion of No Religion*. Chicago: University of Chicago Press, 2007.

Kropp, Phoebe. *California Vieja: Culture and Memory in a Modern American Place*. Berkeley: University of California Press, 2006.

Kruse, Kevin. *One Nation Under God: How Corporate America Invented Christian America*. New York: Basic Books, 2015. '

Kunen, James Simon "Dr. Bronner's Magic." *Esquire*, December 1973.

Laderman, Scott. *Empire in Waves: A Political History of Surfing*. Oakland: University of California Press, 2014.

Lambert, Frank. *The Founding Fathers and the Place of Religion in America*. Princeton, NJ: Princeton University Press, 2006.

Latham, Michael E. *The Right Kind of Revolution: Modernization, Development, and U.S. Foreign Policy from the Cold War to the Present*. Ithaca, NY: Cornell University Press, 2011.

Lau, Kimberly. *New Age Capitalism: Making Money East of Eden*. Philadelphia: University of Pennsylvania Press, 2000.

Leach, William. *Land of Desire: Merchants, Power, and the Rise of a New American Culture*. New York: Vintage Books, 1993.

Lears, T. J. Jackson. *No Place of Grace: Antimodernism and the Transformation of American Culture, 1880–1920*. Chicago: University of Chicago Press, 1981.

Lears, T. J. Jackson, and Richard Wrightman Fox, eds. *The Culture of Consumption: Critical Essays in American History, 1880–1980*. New York: Pantheon Books, 1983.

———. "From Salvation to Self-Realization: Advertising and the Therapeutic Roots of the Consumer Culture, 1880–1930." In Lears and Fox, *The Culture of Consumption*, 1–38.

———. "Introduction." In Lears and Fox, *The Culture of Consumption*, vii–xii.

Lee, Robert G. *Orientals: Asian Americans in Popular Culture*. Philadelphia: Temple University Press, 1999.

Levenstein, Harvey A. *Paradox of Plenty: A Social History of Eating in Modern America*. New York: Oxford University Press, 1993.

———. *Revolution at the Table: The Transformation of the American Diet*. New York: Oxford University Press, 1988.

Levinson, Marc. *Outside the Box: How Globalization Changed from Moving Stuff to Spreading Ideas*. Princeton, NJ: Princeton University Press, 2020.

Lilley, Sasha. "On Neoliberalism: An Interview with David Harvey." *MRZine*, 19 June 2006. http://mrzine.monthlyreview.org/2006/lilley190606.html.

Lipka, Michael. "A Closer Look at Seventh-day Adventists in America." *Pew Research Center*, 3 November 2015. https://www.pewresearch.org/fact-tank/2015/11/03/a-closer-look-at-seventh-day-adventists-in-america/.

Lippy, Charles H., and Peter W. Williams, eds. *Encyclopedia of Religion in America*. Washington, DC: CQ Press, 2010.

Lipsitz, George. *The Possessive Investment in Whiteness: How White People Profit from Identity Politics*. Philadelphia: Temple University Press, 1998.

Littler, Jo. "Green Products and Consumer Activism." In Mukherjee and Banet-Weiser, *Commodity Activism*.

———. *Radical Consumption: Shopping for Change in Contemporary Culture*. New York: McGraw Hill, 2009.

Lofton, Kathryn. *Consuming Religion*. Chicago: University of Chicago Press, 2017.

Loma Linda Chamber of Commerce. "Building Healthy Businesses." October 2017. https://web.archive.org/web/20171015123012/https://lomalinda chamber.org/.

———. "Promoting Healthy Business in the Zone." January 2019. https://web .archive.org/web/20190129023615/https://lomalindachamber.org/.

Long, Lucy M., "Introduction." In *Culinary Tourism*, edited by Lucy M. Long. Lexington, KY: The University Press of Kentucky, 2004.

Lorenzini, Sara. *Global Development: A Cold War History*. Princeton, NJ: Princeton University Press, 2019.

LoRusso, James Dennis. *Spirituality, Corporate Culture, and American Business: The Neoliberal Ethic and the Spirit of Global Capital*. New York: Bloomsbury, 2017.

"Los Angeles Citywide Historic Context Statement/Context: African American History of Los Angeles." *SurveyLA: Los Angeles Historic Resources Survey*, February 2018.

Love, Robert J. "Fear of Yoga." *Columbia Journalism Review*, November–December 2006.

———. *The Great Oom: The Improbable Birth of Yoga in America*. New York: Viking, 2010.

Lubar, Steven. "'Do Not Fold, Spindle, or Mutilate': A Cultural History of the Punch Card." *Journal of American Culture* 15, no. 4 (Winter 1992): 43–55.

Lubelsky, Isaac. "Mythological and Real Race Issues in Theosophy." In Hammer and Rothstein, *Handbook of the Theosophical Current*, 335–55.

Lubinski, Christina, and Marvin Menniken. "Emanuel Bronner." In *Immigrant Entrepreneurship: German-American Business Biographies, 1720 to the Present*, vol. 5, edited by R. Daniel Wadhwani. Washington, DC: German Historical Institute, 2013. https://www.immigrantentrepreneurship.org /entries/emanuel-bronner/.

Lucia, Amanda J. *White Utopias: The Religious Exoticism of Transformational Festivals*. Oakland: University of California Press, 2020.

Luhr, Eileen. *Witnessing Suburbia: Conservatives and Christian Youth Culture*. Berkeley: University of California Press, 2009.

Lummis, Charles Fletcher. "In the Lion's Den" *Out West* 17, no. 6, December 1902, 735–38.

———. "Those Terrible Mysteries." *Out West* 18, no. 1, January 1903, 35–48.

Lupton, Deborah. *Food, the Body and the Self*. Thousand Oaks, CA: Sage Publications, 1996.

Madden, Etta M., and Martha L. Finch, eds. *Eating in Eden: Food and American Utopias*. Lincoln: University of Nebraska Press, 2006.

Malone, Michael S. *The Big Score: The Billion-Dollar Story of Silicon Valley*. Garden City, NY: Doubleday & Company, Inc., 1985.

Markoff, John. *What the Dormouse Said: How the Sixties Counterculture Shaped the Personal Computer Industry*. New York: Penguin, 2005.

May, Elaine Tyler. *Homeward Bound: American Families in the Cold War Era*. New York: Basic Books, 1988.

McAlister, Melani. *Epic Encounters: Culture, Media, and U.S. Interests in the Middle East since 1945*. Berkeley: University of California Press, 2001.

McClintock, Anne. *Imperial Leather: Race, Gender, and Sexuality in Colonial Contest*. London: Taylor & Francis Group, 1995.

McGirr, Lisa. *Suburban Warriors: The Origins of the New American Right*. Princeton, NJ: Princeton University Press, 2001.

McGroarty, John S. "San Diego—The Harbor of the Sun." Atchison, Topeka, and Santa Fe Railroad Company, 1915.

McKenzie, Shelly. *Getting Physical: The Rise of Fitness Culture in America*. Lawrence: University of Kansas Press, 2013.

McWilliams, Carey. *Southern California: An Island on the Land*. New York: Duell, Sloan, and Pearce, 1946.

Mehta, Gita. *Karma Cola: Marketing the Mystic East*. New York: Simon & Schuster, 1979; New York: Vintage Books, 1994.

Melton, J. Gordon. "The Theosophical Communities and Their Ideal of Universal Brotherhood." In Pitzer, *America's Utopian Colonies*, 396–418.

Metcalf, Barbara D., and Thomas R. Metcalf. *A Concise History of Modern India*, 2nd ed. New York: Cambridge University Press, 2006.

Mihesuah, Devon A., and Elizabeth Hoover, eds. *Indigenous Food Sovereignty in the United States: Restoring Cultural Knowledge, Protecting Environments, and Regaining Health*. Norman: University of Oklahoma Press, 2019.

Miller, Laura J. *Building Nature's Market*. Chicago: University of Chicago Press, 2017.

Milov, Sarah. *The Cigarette: A Political History*. Cambridge, MA: Harvard University Press, 2019.

Minkler, Meredith. "Personal Responsibility for Health? A Review of the Arguments and the Evidence at Century's End." *Health Education & Behavior* 26, no. 1 (February 1999): 121–41.

Mohanty, Salini et al. "Experiences with Medical Exemptions after a Change in Vaccine Exemption Policy in California." *Pediatrics* 42, no. 5 (November 2018): 1–10.

Montgomery, Susanne et al. "Comparing Self-Reported Disease Outcomes, Diet, and Lifestyles in a National Cohort of Black and White Seventh-day Adventists." *Preventing Chronic Disease* 4, no. 3 (2007): A62.

Moore, Deborah Dash. *To the Golden Cities: Pursuing the American Jewish Dream in Miami and L.A.* Cambridge, MA: Harvard University Press, 1994.

Moore, R. Laurence. *Religious Outsiders and the Making of America*. New York: Oxford University Press, 1986.

———. *Selling God: American Religion in the Marketplace of Culture*. New York: Oxford University Press, 1995.

Moreton, Bethany. *To Save God and Walmart: The Making of Christian Free Enterprise*. Cambridge, MA: Harvard University Press, 2010.

Morgan, Edmund. *Visible Saints: The History of a Puritan Idea*. Ithaca, NY: Cornell University Press, 1965.

Mukherjee, Roopali, and Sarah Banet-Weiser. *Commodity Activism: Cultural Resistance in Neoliberal Times*. New York: New York University Press, 2012.

Murphy, Thomas D. *On Sunset Highways*. Boston: L.C. Page and Company, 1915.

Nestle, Marion. *Food Politics: How the Food Industry Influences Nutrition and Health*. Berkeley: University of California Press, 2002.

Neumann, David J. *Finding God through Yoga: Paramahansa Yogananda and Modern American Religion in a Global Age*. Chapel Hill: University of North Carolina Press, 2019.

Nichols, Wallace J. *Blue Mind: The Surprising Science That Shows How Being Near, in, on, or under Water Can Make You Happier, Healthier, More Connected, and Better at What You Do*. New York: Little, Brown and Company, 2014.

Numbers, Ronald L. *Prophetess of Health: Ellen G. White and the Origins of Seventh-day Adventist Health Reform*. Revised and enlarged edition, Knoxville: University of Tennessee Press, 1992.

O'Mara, Margaret. *The Code: Silicon Valley and the Remaking of America*. New York: Penguin Press, 2019.

Orsi, Robert. "Everyday Miracles: The Study of Lived Religion." In Hall, *Lived Religion in America*, 3–21.

Paddison, Josh. *American Heathens: Religion, Race, and Reconstruction in California*. Berkeley: University of California Press and Huntington Library, Art Collections, and Botanical Gardens, 2012.

Phillips, Bruce. "The Legacy of Religious Diversity in Los Angeles and Southern California." In Flory and Winston, *Religion in Los Angeles*, 229–61.

Phillips-Fein, Kim. "The History of Neoliberalism." In *Shaped by the State: Toward a New Political History of the Twentieth Century*, edited by Brent Cebul, Lily Geismer, and Mason B. Williams, 347–62. Chicago: University of Chicago Press, 2018.

Pitzer, Donald E., ed. *America's Communal Utopias*. Chapel Hill: University of North Carolina Press, 1997.

Pomeranz, Ken. "Neoliberalism: The History and Future of a Word." Chair panel comments at Annual Meeting of the American Historical Association, 4 January 2019.

Pomeranz Kenneth, and J. R. McNeill. "Production, Destruction, and Connection, 1750–Present: Introduction." In *The Cambridge World History*, edited by J. R. McNeill and Kenneth Pomeranz, 1–48. Cambridge: Cambridge University Press, 2015.

Prakash, Gyan. *Another Reason: Science and the Imagination of Modern India*. Princeton, NJ: Princeton University Press, 1999.

Prashad, Vijay. *Everybody Was Kung Fu Fighting: Afro-Asian Connections and the Myth of Cultural Purity*. Boston: Beacon Press, 2001.

———. *The Karma of Brown Folk*. Minneapolis: University of Minnesota Press, 2000.

Pratt, Mary Louse. "Arts of the Contact Zone." *Profession* (1991): 33–40.

———. *Imperial Eyes: Travel Writing and Transculturation*. New York: Routledge 1992.

Proctor, James. "Religion as Trust in Authority: Theocracy and Ecology in the United States." *Annals of the Association of American Geographers* 96, no. 1 (2006): 188–96.

Purser, Ronald E. *McMindfulness: How Mindfulness Became the New Capitalist Spirituality.* London: Repeater, 2019.

Raghavan, Pallavi. "Journeys of Discovery." In Bhagavan, *India and the Cold War*, 19–35.

Raj, Kapil. *Relocating Modern Science: Circulation and the Construction of Knowledge in South Asia and Europe, 1650–1900.* New York: Palgrave Macmillan, 2007.

Rappaport, Erika. *A Thirst for Empire: How Tea Shaped the Modern World.* Princeton, NJ: Princeton University Press, 2019.

Ray, Sarah Jaquette. *The Ecological Other: Environmental Exclusion in American Culture.* Tucson: University of Arizona Press, 2013.

Reich, Jennifer A. *Calling the Shots: Why Parents Reject Vaccines.* New York: New York University Press, 2016.

———. "Neoliberal Mothering and Vaccine Refusal: Imagined Gated Communities and the Privilege of Choice." *Gender and Society* 28, no. 5 (October 2014): 679–704.

Reilly, Gretchen Ann. "'Not a So-Called Democracy': Anti-Fluoridationists and the Fight over Drinking Water." In *The Politics of Healing: Histories of Alternative Medicine in Twentieth-Century North America*, edited by Robert D. Johnson, 131–49. New York: Routledge, 2004.

Reiser, Dana Brakman, and Steven A. Dean. "The Social Enterprise Life Cycle." In *The Cambridge Handbook of Social Enterprise Law*, edited by Benjamin Means and Joseph W. Yockey, 223–40. New York: Cambridge University Press, 2018.

Ritchie, Robert C. *The Lure of the Beach: A Global History.* Oakland: University of California Press, 2021.

Rodgers, Daniel T. *Age of Fracture.* Cambridge, MA: Belknap Press of Harvard University Press, 2011.

Roof, Wade Clark. "Pluralism as a Culture: Religion and Civility in Southern California." *Annals of the American Academy of Political and Social Science* 612 (July 2007): 82–99.

———. *Spiritual Marketplace: Baby Boomers and the Remaking of American Religion.* Princeton, NJ: Princeton University Press, 1999.

Rosenberg, Emily S. "Consuming the American Century." In Bacevich, *The Short American Century*, 38–58.

———, ed. *A World Connecting, 1870–1945.* Princeton, NJ: Princeton University Press, 2012.

Rossinow, Doug. *The Politics of Authenticity: Liberalism, Christianity, and the New Left in America.* New York: Columbia University Press, 1998.

Roszak, Theodore. *The Cult of Information: The Folklore of Computers and the True Art of Thinking* New York: Pantheon Books, 1986.

———. *The Making of a Counter Culture.* Garden City, NY: Anchor Books, 1969.

Rudbøg, Tim. "Point Loma, Theosophy, and Katherine Tingley." In Hammer and Rothstein, *Handbook of the Theosophical*, 51–72.

Rydell, Robert W. *All the World's a Fair: Visions of Empire at American International Expositions, 1876–1916.* Chicago: University of Chicago Press, 1984.

———. *World of Fairs: The Century-of-Progress Expositions*. Chicago: University of Chicago Press, 1993.

Sackman, Douglas Cazaux. *Orange Empire: California and the Fruits of Eden*. Berkeley: University of California Press, 2005.

Sagar, Rahul. "Hindu Nationalists and the Cold War." In Bhagavan, *India and the Cold War*, 229–53.

Sanchez, George. *Becoming Mexican American: Ethnicity, Culture and Identity in Chicano Los Angeles, 1900–1945*. New York: Oxford University Press, 1993.

Sandoval, Juan Onesimo, Hans P. Johnson, and Sonya M. Tafoya. "Whose Your Neighbor? Residential Segregation and Diversity in California." *California Counts* 4, no. 1 (August 2002): 1–18.

Santucci, James A. "The Notion of Race in Theosophy." *Nova Religio: Journal of Alternative and Emergent Religions* 11, no. 3 (February 2008): 37–63.

———. "Women in the Theosophical Movement." *Explorations: Journal for Adventurous Thought* 9 (Fall 1990): 71–94.

Schaefer, Richard A. *The Glory of the Vision: An Unabridged History of Loma Linda University Health*, vol. 1. Loma Linda, CA: Loma Linda University Health, 2016.

Schiller, Reuel. "Regulation and the Collapse of the New Deal Order, or How I Learned to Stop Worrying and Love the Market." In *Beyond the New Deal Order: U.S. Politics from the Great Depression to the Great Recession*, edited by Gary Gerstle, Nelson Lichtenstein, and Alice O'Connor, 168–85. Philadelphia: University of Pennsylvania Press, 2019.

Schlosser, Eric. *Fast Food Nation: The Dark Side of the All-American Meal*. Boston: Houghton Mifflin Harcourt, 2001.

Schmidt, Leigh Eric. *Restless Souls: The Making of American Spirituality*. New York: HarperCollins, 2005.

Schrank, Sarah. *Art and the City: Civic Imagination and Cultural Authority in Los Angeles*. Philadelphia: University of Pennsylvania Press, 2009.

———. *Free and Natural: Nudity and the Cult of the American Body*. Philadelphia: University of Pennsylvania Press, 2019.

Schutz, Jorian Polis. "The State of Stretching: Yoga in America." *Baffler*, April 2013. http://www.thebaffler.com/salvos/the-state-of-stretching.

Sherman, Pat. "In the Spirit of Soap." *San Diego Magazine*, January 31, 2007.

Shibusawa, Naoko. *America's Geisha Ally: Reimagining the Japanese Enemy*. Cambridge, MA: Harvard University Press, 2006.

Shprintzen, Adam D. *The Vegetarian Crusade: The Rise of an American Reform Movement, 1817–1921*. Chapel Hill: University of North Carolina Press, 2013.

Shryock, Richard H. "Sylvester Graham and the Popular Health Movement, 1830–1870." *Mississippi Valley Historical Review* 18, no. 2 (September 1931): 172–83.

Sinclair, Upton. *The Profits of Religion: An Essay in Economic Interpretation*. New York: AMS Press, 1918.

Singleton, Mark. *Yoga Body: The Origins of Modern Posture Practice*. New York: Oxford University Press, 2010.

Singleton, Mark, and Ellen Goldberg, eds. *Gurus of Modern Yoga*. New York: Oxford University Press, 2014.

Sinha, Mrinalini. *Specters of Mother India: The Global Restructuring of an Empire*. Durham, NC: Duke University Press, 2006.

Slate, Nico. *Colored Cosmopolitanism: The Shared Struggle for Freedom in the United States and India*. Cambridge, MA: Harvard University Press, 2012.

Slocum, Rachel. "Whiteness, Space and Alternative Food Practice." *Geoforum* 38 (2007): 520–33.

Smedley, Brian D., Adrienne Y. Stith, and Alan R. Nelson, eds., *Unequal Treatment: Confronting Racial and Ethnic Disparities in Health Care*. Washington, DC: National Academies Press, 2003.

Smith, Christian. *Christian America? What Evangelicals Really Want*. Berkeley: University of California Press, 2000.

Smith, Emily Esfahani. "The Lovely Hill: Where People Live Longer and Happier." *Atlantic*, 4 February 2013. https://www.theatlantic.com/health/archive/2013/02/the-lovely-hill-where-people-live-longer-and-happier/272798/.

Smith, Philip J., Susan Y. Chu, and Lawrence E. Barker. "Children Who Have Received No Vaccines: Who Are They and Where Do They Live?" *Pediatrics* 114, no. 1 (July 2004): 187–95.

Starr, Kevin. *Americans and the California Dream, 1850–1915*. New York: Oxford University Press, 1973.

———. *Inventing the Dream: California through the Progressive Era*. New York: Oxford University Press, 1986.

Starr, Paul. *The Social Transformation of American Medicine: The Rise of a Sovereign Profession and the Making of a Vast Industry*. New York: Basic Books, 1982.

Steger, Manfred B., and Ravi K. Roy. *Neoliberalism: A Very Short Introduction*. New York: Oxford University Press, 2010.

Stein, Richard A. "Vaccination: A Public Health Intervention That Changed History and Is Changing with History." *American Biology Teacher* 73, no. 9 (November–December 2011): 513–19.

Steinbeck-Pratt, Sarah. *Educating the Empire: American Teachers and Contested Colonization in the Philippines*. New York: Cambridge University Press, 2021.

Stratton, Clif. *Education for Empire: American Schools, Race, and the Paths of Good Citizenship*. Oakland: University of California Press, 2016.

Sutton, Matthew Avery. *Aimee Semple McPherson and the Resurrection of Christian America*. Cambridge, MA: Harvard University Press, 2007.

———. "Religious World Views." In Blower and Preston, *The Cambridge History of America and the World: Volume 3, 1900–1945*, 429–51.

Swaine, Michael, and Paul Freiberger. *Fire in the Valley: The Making of the Personal Computer*. New York: McGraw Hill, 1984.

Sweet, Gail Grenier. "Next to Godliness." *The Sun Magazine*, January 2001. https://www.thesunmagazine.org/issues/301/next-to-godliness.

Syman, Stefanie. *The Subtle Body: The Story of Yoga in America*. New York: Farrar, Straus and Giroux, 2010.

Taylor, Bron. *Dark Green Religion: Nature Spirituality and the Planetary Future*. Berkeley: University of California Press, 2010.

Taylor, Sarah McFarland. *Ecopiety: Green Media and the Dilemma of Environmental Virtue*. New York: New York University Press, 2019.

Thomson, Jennifer. *The Wild and the Toxic: American Environmentalism and the Politics of Health*. Chapel Hill: University of North Carolina Press, 2019.

Tingley, Katherine. *The Splendor of the Soul*. Pasadena, CA: Theosophical University Press, 1996. Originally published 1927. https://www.theosociety.org/pasadena/splendor/spl-1a.htm.

Tomes, Nancy. *Remaking the American Patient: How Madison Avenue and Modern Medicine Turned Patients into Consumers*. Chapel Hill: University of North Carolina Press, 2016.

Trachtenberg, Alan. *The Incorporation of America*. New York: Hill and Wang, 1982.

Trauner, Joan B. "The Chinese as Medical Scapegoats in San Francisco, 1870–1905." *California History* 57, no. 1 (Spring 1978): 70–87.

Turner, Bryan S. "The Government of the Body: Medical Regimens and the Rationalization of the Diet." *British Journal of Sociology* 33, no. 2 (June 1982): 254–69.

Turner, Fred. *From Counterculture to Cyberculture: Stewart Brand, the Whole Earth Network, and the Rise of Digital Utopianism*. Chicago: University of Chicago Press, 2006.

Tyrrell, Ian. *Reforming the World: The Creation of America's Moral Empire*. Princeton, NJ: Princeton University Press, 2010.

Vance, James E. Jr. "California and the Search for the Ideal." *Annals of the Association of American Geographers* 62, no. 2 (June 1972): 185–210.

Von Eschen, Penny M. "Globalizing Popular Culture in the 'American Century' and Beyond." *OAH Magazine of History* 20, no. 4 (July 2006): 56–63.

Walters, Ronald G. *American Reformers 1815–1860*. New York: Hill and Wang, 1978, 1997.

Ward, Peter. *The Clean Body: A Modern History*. Montreal: McGill-Queen's University Press, 2019.

Warner, Charles Dudley. *Our Italy*. New York: Harper & Brothers, 1891. https://www.gutenberg.org/files/28506/28506-h/28506-h.htm.

Warshaw, Matt. *The Encyclopedia of Surfing*. New York: Harcourt, 2005.

———. *The History of Surfing*. San Francisco: Chronicle Books, 2010.

Watts, Jennifer A. "Photography in the Land of Sunshine." *Southern California Quarterly* 87, no. 4 (2005–2006): 339–76.

Weber, Max. *The Protestant Ethic and the Spirit of Capitalism*. Translated by Talcott Parsons. New York: Charles Scribner's Sons, 1958.

Weeks, John Howard. *The Healthiest People on Earth: Your Guide to Living 10 Years Longer with Adventist Family Secrets and Plant-Based Recipes*. Dallas, Texas: Benbella Books, 2018.

Westad, Odd Arne. *The Global Cold War: Third World Interventions and the Making of Our Times*. New York: Oxford University Press, 2005.

Westwick, Peter, and Peter Neushul. *The World in the Curl: An Unconventional History of Surfing.* New York: Crown, 2013.

White, Ellen Gould Harmon. *Counsels on Health, and Instruction to Medical Missionary Workers.* Mountain View, CA: Pacific Press Publishing Association, 1923.

———. *The Ministry of Health and Healing.* Silver Springs, MD: Ellen G. White Estate, Inc., 2017.

Whorton, James C. *Crusaders for Fitness: The History of American Health Reformers.* Princeton, NJ: Princeton University Press, 1982.

Wild, Mark. *Street Meeting: Multiethnic Neighborhoods in Early Twentieth-Century Los Angeles.* Berkeley: University of California Press, 2005.

Williams, Marilyn Thornton. *Washing 'The Great Unwashed': Public Baths in Urban America, 1840–1920.* Columbus: Ohio State University Press, 1991.

Williamson, Lola. *Transcendent in America: Hindu-Inspired Meditation Movements as New Religion.* New York: New York University Press, 2010.

Winston, Diane, and John Michael Giggie. *Faith in the Market: Religion and the Rise of Urban Commercial Culture.* New Brunswick, NJ: Rutgers University Press, 2002.

Wolfson, Elijah. "Whooping Cough: A Comeback Story Nobody Loves." *Newsweek Global* 161, no. 36, 11 October 2013.

Wood, Ruth Kedzie. *The Tourist's California.* New York: Dodd, Mead, and Company, 1914.

Wright, Willard Huntington. "Los Angeles—The Chemically Pure." In *The Smart Set Anthology,* edited by Burton Rascoe and Groff Conklin. New York: Reynal and Hitchcock, 1934.

Wynder, Ernest L. "Cancer, Coronary Disease, Artery Disease and Smoking: A Preliminary Report on Differences in Incidence between Seventh-day Adventists and Others." *California Medicine* 89, no. 4 (October 1958): 267–72.

Wynder, Ernest L., Frank R. Lemon, and Irwin J. Bross. "Cancer and Coronary Disease among Seventh-day Adventists." *Cancer* 12, no. 5 (September–October 1959): 1016–28.

Yogananda, Paramahansa. *Autobiography of a Yogi.* Los Angeles: Self-Realization Fellowship, 1946.

Zakim, Michael. *Accounting for Capitalism: The World the Clerk Made.* Chicago: University of Chicago Press, 2018.

Index

Founded in 1893,
UNIVERSITY OF CALIFORNIA PRESS
publishes bold, progressive books and journals
on topics in the arts, humanities, social sciences,
and natural sciences—with a focus on social
justice issues—that inspire thought and action
among readers worldwide.

The UC PRESS FOUNDATION
raises funds to uphold the press's vital role
as an independent, nonprofit publisher, and
receives philanthropic support from a wide
range of individuals and institutions—and from
committed readers like you. To learn more, visit
ucpress.edu/supportus.